Waste Matters: New Perspectives of Food and Society

For many thought-provoking and supportive discussions of food and food-waste, Anne would like to thank Virginia Olesen (University of California, San Francisco), the late Tony Coxon (University of Cardiff), Lindy Sharpe (City University, London), Peter Jackson (Sheffield University), Anne Pyburn (Indiana University), Rick Wilk (Indiana University) and Harry West (SOAS, University of London) as well as colleagues at the now defunct Institute for Science and Society (University of Nottingham) and in the Food Writers' Group (SOAS, University of London). She particularly appreciates Hugh's and David's tremendous colleagueship and friendship that made putting this collection together so especially interesting and congenial.

Series editor's introduction

Chris Shilling

General issues of waste, and the debates and controversies associated specifically with food waste, feature rarely in overviews of the subject matter of sociology and hardly ever in accounts of the sociological tradition. In recent decades, however, sociology and the social sciences have highlighted, through analyses of such matters as globalization, embodiment and environmentalism, the importance of attending to issues that address social relationships and cultural processes in the context of our existence within a single planetary eco-system (eg Flynn *et al.*, 2010; McLachlan, 2010; Urry, 2010; Shilling, 2012). It is against this background, amidst the continuing global crisis of capital realization and deep international inequalities in levels of production and consumption, that David Evans's, Hugh Campbell's and Anne Murcott's *Waste Matters: New Perspectives of Food and Society* constitutes a powerful collection of articles that not only demonstrate the importance of food waste to individuals and societies, but also make significant contributions to ongoing debates in sociological research and theory.

In terms of its implications for individuals and societies, *Waste Matters* appears at an important historical juncture involving a rising demand for foodstuffs amidst an increasing global population, food shortages in particular countries and regions, and levels of waste in the production, circulation and consumption of food that can be described justifiably as staggering. International and national reports on food waste have garnered increasing attention and media coverage over the last few years, and the latest Institute of Mechanical Engineers (IMG) report from the UK has claimed recently that as much as 50 per cent of all food produced in the world is never eaten; a figure which should be viewed alongside the labour, water, fertilizer and land involved in this unconsumed production (IMG, 2013). Food waste and losses occur throughout the supply chain, from post-harvesting to consumer practices, and this is not just a problem confined to the Global North (IMG, 2013).

Reports such as these, valuable though they are, overlook, or only touch upon, a range of sociological questions that are crucial to our understanding of who gets to define what is and what is not food and waste, and how the organization and production of waste is important to a number of issues regarding cultural identities, the creation of space, differences in diet, and the fluctuating webs of interdependence that characterize relations between groups and

The Sociological Review, 60:S2, pp. 1–4 (2013), DOI: 10.1111/1467-954X.12048
© 2013 The Author. Editorial organisation © 2013 The Editorial Board of the Sociological Review. Published by John Wiley & Sons Ltd, 9600 Garsington Road, Oxford OX4 2DQ, UK and 350 Main Street, Malden, MA 02148, USA

nations (Mennell, 1985; Quilley, 2011). It is in this context that David Evans, Hugh Campbell and Anne Murcott do an excellent job in their editorial introduction of providing a framework in which can be appreciated the specific sociological contributions made by the analyses in this collection. Without replicating their discussion, I want to highlight here two general features of *Waste Matters* that I think are of particular importance to the discipline.

First, the contributors to *Waste Matters* conduct a sustained interrogation of those *residual categories* that help define sociology and related disciplines. As Parsons (1968 [1937]: 17–18) notes, every theoretical system involves 'the positive definition of certain empirically identifiable variables or other general categories' while tending to marginalize others; turning those disregarded into pale shadows of normative concerns. In this context, while sociology may have placed such issues as the Hobbesian 'problem of order' at the centre of its systemic focus, Munro's contribution makes particularly clear that this involved unexamined assumptions about what societies categorized as waste and what they disposed of in order to maintain governance. As he goes on to argue, this waste can be seen as residual in the discipline – even though such classics as Anderson's (1923) *The Hobo*, Whyte's (1943) *Street Corner Society* and Bittner's (1967) *The Police on Skid Row* can be interpreted as analyses of the 'detritus of social order' – and remains so despite being challenged by those contemporary studies of health and the social services which reveal how those who fail to conform to the normative expectations and embodied trajectories sanctioned by these organizations are treated as (waste) 'matter out of place' (Munro, p. 224; see also Douglas, 1966).

In identifying residual categories surrounding its subject matter, and turning them into positively defined features of their explanations, the contributors to *Waste Matters* reveal the significance of phenomena previously hidden or marginalized. Within this context, Hawkins analyses how food packaging can be seen not simply as waste but as a 'market device' that helps turn consumers into recyclers, while Milne identifies food labelling as playing an active role in governmental conceptions of 'responsible citizens'. The contributions by Cappellini and Parsons, Watson and Meah, and Coles and Hallet IV, in contrast, explore the material practices that turn food into waste and waste into food. The final contribution to this collection returns us to Munro's insightful uncovering of how waste is organized in modernity as a central albeit increasingly hidden feature of the extensions, connections and networks that are always already involved in people's relationships and actions.

The second general sociological contribution I want to highlight here concerns the manner in which the articles that follow on food waste provide us with an excellent example of how the recent turn to what has been referred to as 'the new materialism', in and beyond sociology and cultural studies, can inform research on issues of substantive importance (Coole and Frost, 2010). This turn to material grew out of a dissatisfaction with textual and discursive approaches that tended to reduce questions of ontology to issues of knowledge, alongside a related objection to Cartesian conceptions that treated matter as inert, discreet and consequential merely in terms of its acting as a 'standing reserve' for human designs (Heidegger, 1977). In their place, this contemporary and much broader approach identifies inorganic as well as organic matter as active, dynamic and possessed of an efficacy or 'agency' that can shape and obstruct human designs (Bennett, 2001; Coole and Frost, 2010). Instead of viewing social actors as separate from their environments, moreover, it conceptualizes embodied subjects as permeated thoroughly by and 'entangled' within the multiple forms of materiality that surround them (Barad, 2007).

Within this context, the articles in *Waste Matters* provide fascinating explorations of the various modalities through which food waste constitutes an integral, embedded and active part of the economy, as well as of people's actions, identities and relationships, and a compelling case for why these issues should be taken seriously sociologically. The four contributions by Krzywoszynska, Gille, O'Brien, and Edwards and Mercer, for example, each, in very different ways and with reference to very different dimensions of its materiality, explore how food waste is central to the production of value, and contributes to the reproduction of international, national and local patterns of inequality, while Metcalfe *et al.*, reveal the household dimension of local food disposal systems to be a potentially polluting and infecting agent that enters into and actively shapes familial interrelationships. Taken together, these articles complement and extend further the reach of this, the first collection on food waste to be published, and are an important reminder of sociology's power to illuminate what C. Wright Mills referred to as the 'personal troubles of milieu' and the 'public issues' enmeshed within the social and material environments that we depend upon for our existence and our future (Mills, 1959: 8).

The *Sociological Review* Monograph series publishes special supplements of the journal in collections of original refereed papers and could not continue without the goodwill, advice and guidance of members of the Board of *The Sociological Review*, and of those anonymous referees who assess and report on each of the papers submitted for consideration for these collections. I would like to thank all of those involved in this process, especially Harry West for his very considerable input into the collection as a whole, all of the referees, Gordon Fyfe, Carolyn Baggaley, and also the editors of *Waste Matters* for having produced such a stimulating and timely volume.

References

Anderson, N., (1923), *The Hobo. The Sociology of the Homeless Man*. Chicago, IL: University of Chicago Press.
Barad, K., (2007), *Meeting the Universe Halfway*, Durham, NC: Duke University Press.
Bennett, J., (2001), *The Enchantment of Modern Life*, Princeton, NJ: Princeton University Press.
Bittner, E., (1967), 'The police on skid row: a study of peace keeping', *American Sociological Review*, 32 (5): 699–717.
Coole, D. and Frost, S., (2010), 'Introducing the new materialisms', in D. Coole and S. Frost (eds), *New Materialisms*, Durham, NC: Duke University Press.

Douglas, M., (1966), *Purity and Danger: An Analysis of the Concepts of Pollution and Taboo*, London: Ark.

Flynn, R., Bellaby, R. and Ricci, M., (2010), 'The "value-action gap" in public attitudes towards sustainable energy: the case of hydrogen energy', in B. Carter and N. Charles (eds), *The Sociological Review, Special Supplement: Nature, Society and Environmental Crisis*, Oxford: Wiley Blackwell.

Heidegger, M., (1977), *The Question Concerning Technology and Other Essays*, London: Harper Perennial.

Institute of Mechanical Engineers, (2013), *Global Food. Waste Not, Want Not*, London: IMG.

McLachlan, C., (2010), 'Technologies in place: symbolic interpretations of renewable energy', in B. Carter and N. Charles (eds), *The Sociological Review, Special Supplement: Nature, Society and Environmental Crisis*, Oxford: Wiley Blackwell.

Mennell, S. J., (1985), *All Manners of Food: Eating and Taste in England and France from the Middle Ages to the Present*, Oxford: Blackwell.

Mills, C. W., (1959), *The Sociological Imagination*, Oxford: Oxford University Press.

Parsons, T., (1968 [1937]), *The Structure of Social Action*, Vol. 1, New York, NY: The Free Press.

Quilley, S., (2011), 'Entropy, the anthroposphere and the ecology of civilization', in N. Gabriel and S. Mennell (eds), *The Sociological Review, Special Supplement. Norbert Elias and Figurational Research: Processual Thinking in Sociology*, Oxford: Wiley Blackwell.

Shilling, C., (2012), *The Body and Social Theory*, 3rd edn, London: Sage.

Urry, J., (2010), 'Sociology and climate change', in B. Carter and N. Charles (eds), *The Sociological Review, Special Supplement: Nature, Society and Environmental Crisis*, Oxford: Wiley Blackwell.

Whyte, W. F., (1943), *Street Corner Society. The Social Structure of an Italian Slum*, Chicago, IL: University of Chicago Press.

The Sociological Review, 60:S2, pp. 1–4 (2013), DOI: 10.1111/1467-954X.12048

A brief pre-history of food waste and the social sciences

David Evans, Hugh Campbell and Anne Murcott

Abstract: Food waste is a compelling and yet hugely under-researched area of interest for social scientists. In order to account for this neglect and to situate the fledgling body of social science scholarship that is starting to engage with food waste, the analysis here does a number of things. It explores the theoretical tendencies that have underpinned the invisibility of waste to the sociological gaze alongside the historical transitions in global food relations that led to the disappearance of concerns about food scarcity – and with them, concerns about food waste – from cultural and political life. It also sketches out some of the processes through which waste has recently (re-)emerged as a priority in the realms of food policy and regulation, cultural politics and environmental debate. Particular attention is paid to the intellectual trajectories that have complemented food waste's rising profile in popular and policy imaginations to call forth sociological engagement with the issue. With this in place, the stage is set for the individual contributions to this *Sociological Review Monograph* – papers that engage with food waste in a number of contexts, at a variety of scales and from a range of disciplinary perspectives. Together they represent the first attempt collectively to frame potential sociological approaches to understanding food waste.

Keywords: food, waste, environmental policy, garbage, cultural politics of food

Food waste is a compelling and yet hugely under-researched area of interest for social scientists. In this collection, we have brought together the small, emergent group of scholars who have begun to engage with the issue as a means of laying the ground for sociological approaches to understanding food waste. The impetus for doing so stems from several interrelated observations. The first is that, despite a number of interesting developments in 'waste scholarship', these have yet to be extended to analyses of food. Concomitantly, although sociological engagement with food is now extensive, it has barely begun to attend to waste. Third, and more broadly, the issue of waste – and food waste in particular – is one that is rapidly gaining traction in the realms of policy and regulation, cultural politics and environmental debate. Accordingly, we take the view that sociology is uniquely placed to engage with an issue of growing popular and political significance (as we were finalizing this chapter yet another example of media coverage declaring '[T]oo much food gets thrown away' appeared in *The Economist*, 2012.) Finally,

The Sociological Review, 60:S2, pp. 5–26 (2013), DOI: 10.1111/1467-954X.12035

it can be noted that although 'waste' has for a long time been invisible to the sociological gaze; once rendered visible, it opens up a number of interesting avenues for thinking sociologically (O'Brien, 2007). To that, we would add that a focus on *food* waste offers a useful lens through which to tend to a number of live debates and contemporary issues in sociology and social theory.

Of course, the major incentive for this *Sociological Review Monograph* is that food waste – like waste in general – has hitherto been neglected by sociology. Such neglect is, perhaps, not surprising given the glacial speed with which sociologists began to engage with 'taken for granted' matters like food. It took the emergence of a named 'sociology of everyday life' in the 1970s to direct the attention of those in the wider sociological community – yet to discover Goffman (1959) and the Chicago School – to the minutiae of daily encounters (primarily through the work of scholars such as Jack Douglas, 1970, and, later, Michel de Certau, 1984 [1980]). This opening up of the familiar-as-new terrain of enquiry was highly influential in the belated appearance of a 'sociology of food' (eg Murcott, 1983). Even in the world of taken-for-granted objects in everyday life, much of the early work cited focused on the new cultures, ideologies and discourses of daily life, thus failing to account for a phenomenon that is already overlooked in everyday life in all kinds of social settings in both the global 'North' and the 'South'. The classification of items as 'waste', and thereby dealt with by some sort of disposal, leads to their becoming 'out of sight, out of mind' – culturally invisible – and thus without an explicit scholarly effort of reflexivity they risk remaining inaccessible to the gaze of the social sciences.

In this opening chapter, we explore the cultural and intellectual invisibility of food waste before tracing the various contours that have led to food waste emerging as an issue inviting attention from the social sciences. In so doing, we introduce and set the stage for the individual contributions that together represent a first statement from the new social scientific scholarship on food waste.

Waste scholarship

At one level, the papers collected here are testimony to the increasing visibility of 'waste' in social scientific scholarship and the exciting directions in which these researches are currently heading. Traditionally, waste has been a marginal and somewhat niche concern for social scientists and, to the extent that it has featured, it has been approached in very particular ways. Typically it has been imagined as something – most likely a practical problem – that needs to be managed, and, accordingly, engagement has occurred under the auspices of environmental policy and planning. The emphasis here has been on questions of governing, of evaluating waste policies and their consequences and, typically, of assessing the potential for 'recovering' waste materials through recycling. Whilst this is no doubt interesting, it rests on a particular set of (tacit and interrelated) assumptions about how to conceptualize waste. The first is that waste is uncomplicatedly the rejected and worthless stuff that needs to be

The Sociological Review, 60:S2, pp. 5–26 (2013), DOI: 10.1111/1467-954X.12035

distanced from the societies that produced it or otherwise converted it into value via technological and organizational innovation. The second is that waste is a fixed and self-evident category – an innate property or characteristic of certain things. The third assumption is that this unproblematic designation of certain things as 'waste' is given by the imperatives of waste management. As Gregson and Crang (2010: 1027) point out: 'that which is managed as waste is waste, and that which is waste is what is managed'. Finally, that waste is located at the 'end of pipe' – the final by-products and outputs in linear processes of production, consumption and disposal. In sum, waste is imagined as that which is left over – the redundant afterwards of social life that only register when the need to do something about them has been identified. We take it that these assumptions are ripe for problematizing and inspecting, sociologically, and that they indicate at some level, a conflation of the characterization of the topic as a practical and policy problem and its characterization as a social scientific topic for investigation.

These understandings and representations of waste can be situated in relation to its rather awkward positioning between key scholarly boundaries. Existing somewhere across traditional divisions between the social and environmental sciences, between production and consumption, between spaces and non-spaces, waste has become an absent presence that is orphaned from any single disciplinary home. Moreover, it has not been immediately clear that sociology might indeed have some purchase on the issue; and certainly, the tendencies outlined above have served to position waste as a void that lies beyond the boundaries of cultural and economic organization. As such, it has remained the 'shadow' of processes and relations that are sociologically interesting rather than appearing as an object of enquiry in its own right – or light. At best, it has been seen as tangential to processes of social ordering, and thus engagement has been limited to those branches of the social sciences dedicated to issues associated with the practical management of this 'void', issues that are scarcely of concern or interest to mainstream sociology.

To the extent that waste gets imagined as anything more than a void, it has conventionally been conceptualized as a metaphor or a hazard. With regard to the former, the negative connotations that have long been associated with the term 'waste' readily allow it to stand for something else in the course of moral condemnation that masquerades as critique. These allegories range from the unproductive expenditure of time and money, through the alleged excesses of global consumer capitalism and their environmental impacts, to the fall-out and consequences of modernity. As something hazardous or contaminating, the emphasis has been on the risks associated with wastes of various sorts, and existing research within this paradigm has been dominated by environmental discourse and alarmist or moralist rhetoric (Hawkins, 2006). Similarly, work in the tradition of environmental justice has explored the ways in which social inequalities are marked and mirrored by exposure or proximity to waste. More generally, various social histories (Laporte, 1999; Melosi, 2004) have equated social order with processes of expelling, distancing and hiding wastes from those societies that produced them – or at least from the respectable and decent members of these societies. So, even when imagined as more than a void, waste retains its location beyond the boundaries of the social, where it is taken as a fixed category that can only ever gesture back to the societies that produced it.

However, this is starting to change. An emerging body of work now recognizes waste as a dynamic category that needs to be understood in relation to the contexts (social, economic, historical) through which it has been put to work, the relationships in which it is embedded, and the complexity of meanings attributed to it. The precursors to this work are well known: first, Mary Douglas's *Purity and Danger* (1966) drew attention to the cultural categorization of dirt and the analytic importance of investigating the classifications that 'produce' and reject this so-called 'matter out of place'. Second, in the early 1970s William Rathje began his work on what he called 'garbology' (collaborating later with Murphy in 1992), research in which archaeological methods are applied to the study of garbage, with the suggestion that explorations of trash yield important insights regarding the cultures that produce it. Finally, Michael Thompson's *Rubbish Theory* (1979) suggests that a focus on waste is central to understanding how value is socially controlled. Recent approaches to waste, however, do not locate it beyond the boundaries of the social as do these earlier studies, stressing instead that quite aside from revealing who we are, waste is also *constitutive* of who we are.

Whilst very little of this work is sociological in origin; much of it is sociological in orientation – see, for example, Susan Strasser's historical account (1999) of the complex processes through which disposal became separated from production, consumption and use. Equally important is Gay Hawkins' theoretical work *The Ethics of Waste* (2006)[1] in which she takes note of our various relationships with waste. In doing so, she makes visible the ways in which we live with, value, classify and manage 'things'. Sticking in the realms of cultural theory, John Scanlan's *On Garbage*[2] (2005: 8) looks beyond 'mere' waste materials to explore the connections between 'the variety of hidden, forgotten, thrown away and residual phenomena that attend life at all times'. Here, he eloquently demonstrates that metaphorical garbage – the detached leftover of separating the valuable from the worthless – is at once omnipresent and central to (Western) ways of thinking about the world. Of particular note is the work of geographer Nicky Gregson who has – across a number of projects and with a range of collaborators – explored human relationships with waste on a variety of scales, whilst also tending to a number of theoretical and substantive concerns. See, for example: Gregson and Crewe (2003) on second-hand consumption; Gregson (2007) and Gregson et al. (2007) on the ways in which households live with and get rid of things; Gregson et al. (2010b) on the agency of materials in transformative states and their appearance in processes of demolition; and Gregson et al. (2010a) on the global flows of materials as things fall apart or are purposely disassembled.

The key unequivocally sociological contributions to this emerging body of waste scholarship are Martin O'Brien's *A Crisis of Waste* (2007) and Zsuzsa

The Sociological Review, 60:S2, pp. 5–26 (2013), DOI: 10.1111/1467-954X.12035

Gille's *From the Cult of Waste to the Trash Heap of History* (2007). Gille's work views waste neither as a given nor as the simple outcome of policy that defines things as such. Rather she develops the concept of 'waste regimes' to account for the institutions and conventions that determine what wastes are considered valuable and the ways in which their production and distribution is managed, represented and politicized. She highlights how these regimes vary across space and time, thus highlighting the contingent and relational character of 'waste' at the same time as paying serious attention to the physical reality of these materials. Crucially, in addition to acknowledging that differing definitions of waste are expressive of different regimes; she emphasizes that they are also constitutive and sustaining of them. O'Brien's work suggests that the invisibility of waste in sociological thought is a reflection of its invisibility in popular and political imaginations – and thus sets out to rescue it, to give it the sociological attention it deserves, and to develop a 'rubbish imagination' that interrogates the generative role of waste in social life. He urges that contemporary Western societies should be understood as 'rubbish societies' and, as such, he suggests that sociology might focus on the practices, institutions, innovations and relations that have emerged to govern waste and its transformation into value. Despite these significant developments in waste scholarship, they have yet to be extended systematically to offer a dedicated analysis of food waste. Thankfully, both Gille and O'Brien have contributed chapters to this volume in response to an invitation that they extend their path-breaking analyses to the specific issue of food waste.

Perhaps more astonishing is the fact that waste has yet to register in the research – sociological or otherwise – on food. This is particularly surprising not only given the emerging politics of food waste (discussed below) but also because, after all, waste is a logical and unavoidable consequence of eating. Beyond the peelings and cores of food preparation, beyond what the catering trades describe as plate waste, there are wastes in lavatories and sewers as well as nappies (diapers) and incontinence pads. Widespread etiquette deems these 'wastes' as unmentionable in the same breath as food (unless concerned with infant care, see Murcott, 1993) – a proscription brilliantly illuminated in Luis Buñuel's 1974 film *The Phantom of Liberty*. That said, there are a number of notable exceptions. For instance, Jack Goody (1982) pays passing attention to waste in his anthropological work on cuisines and their relation to societal stratification (see Klein and Murcott, forthcoming). So does Gary Alan Fine (1996) in his ethnography of restaurant kitchens, where discarding food that has been paid for before it gets to diners' plates represents a measurable economic loss. In none of these, however, is the topic really pursued. David Marshall's broad-ranging edited collection, *Food Choice* (1995), includes a final chapter by Rolland Munro in which attention is drawn to the ways in which 'the meal' may – or may not – be disposed of by passing, and acting back, through multiple conduits in material and symbolic registers. These themes have also been picked up in Benedetta Cappellini's empirical analysis (2009) of consuming leftovers. More generally, David Evans' ethnographic research (2011, 2012a, 2012b) has (following Hetherington, 2004, and Gregson *et al.*, 2007) extended work on material culture and consumption as disposal to analyses of household food waste.

Another notable exception to the neglect of waste in social scientific approaches to food is the useful introduction and overview offered by Catherine Alexander and colleagues in *The Handbook of Food Research* (2013). In sketching a number of potential avenues for food waste research, they locate food waste within three key traditions that have (arguably) dominated much food research and social scientific scholarship more generally: first, political economy; second, the 'cultural turn'; and thirdly, post-humanism. Many of the contributions offered here can be readily located within or across these pillars and so can be viewed as fleshing out the sketch offered by Alexander *et al.* (2013). Thus, the contributions offered by Gille, O'Brien and Krzywoszynska emerge from (and to varying extents, react against) political economy approaches insofar as they deal with waste across the food supply chain whilst also engaging with questions of value, governance and power. In doing so, they exemplify the importance of recognizing the links between the various economic and cultural processes that give rise to waste, reminding us that it is essential to research food waste as it appears within different national, institutional and regulatory contexts.

Several contributors to the present volume write out of the so-called 'cultural turn' insofar as they are dealing with the cultures, ideologies and politics of food and consumption. For example, Watson and Meah, Parsons and Cappellini, and Metcalfe *et al.* develop a number of perspectives on the processes and practices that lie behind the generation (and possible prevention) of food waste in UK households. Travelling to more marginal practices (and Australia), Edwards and Mercer explore counter-institutional responses to the cultures that give rise to food waste. From a slightly different angle, Coles and Hallet's contribution invites important questions about the ways in which waste problematizes cultural understandings of food and edible matter. More generally, Munro's contribution builds on his earlier work to rescue disposal from its connotations of waste and to consider its primacy in processes of production, consumption and the circulation of relations.

Finally, before turning to outline what we think of as the pre-history to the current modest growth of scholarship in the field, we must observe that it is not surprising that social scientific scholarship on food waste connects rather readily to the various strands of sociological thinking (ranging from Actor-Network Theory (ANT) to ethnographies of material culture) that take seriously the role of the non-human in processes of 'social' (inverted commas fully intended) organization. On the one hand, the apposite developments in waste scholarship (see the articles in *Environment and Planning A*, 42 (5), 2010; Alexander and Reno, 2012) have stressed the importance of attending to the *stuff* of waste via a fuller engagement with materiality (Gregson and Crang, 2010). On the other, more general social scientific engagement with materiality is increasingly turning to the vitality and vibrancy of matter by stressing that objects exist in constant flux and do not have fixed properties or qualities (Bennett, 2010; Edensor, 2005;

The Sociological Review, 60:S2, pp. 5–26 (2013), DOI: 10.1111/1467-954X.12035
© 2013 The Authors. Editorial organisation © 2013 The Editorial Board of the Sociological Review

Ingold, 2007). Accepting that food is susceptible to spoilage, decay and rapid transformation, positions it as a specific genre of material culture that is well placed to become part of these debates. In recognizing food as lively and sentient 'stuff' (Bennett, 2007), it follows that practices of food waste are caught up with a range of non-human actors: microbial life, packaging, preservation technologies, containers and domestic appliances alongside scientific methods of treatment, disposal and management. Several contributions here deal directly with post-humanism and food waste – Hawkins' encounter with food packaging, and Milne's discussion of use-by dates and food labelling (possibly a response to the threat of microbial life). Beyond this, however, many of the contributions emerging from political economy or the cultural turn appear – quite independently of one another – to have departed from their origins to arrive at a post-humanist reading. Given the current vogue for such perspectives in sociology and social theory, it is hoped that readers who may not necessarily be interested in the substantive topics of food and waste will also find these accounts of food waste relevant to their interests.

Historically contextualizing the 'new' politics of waste

Scholarly interest has been emerging in close connection with a wider surge of interest in waste in the realms of policy and regulation, cultural politics and environmental debate. One frequently repeated theme of recent non-academic commentaries is that the current visibility of waste is something new. Moreover, so the thinking goes, in recognizing the 'problem' of waste in multiple realms we are coming to a political and cultural moment of transition that reveals one, or some combination, of the consequences of a long trajectory of economic expansion, unsustainable resource use and/or 'out of control' consumerism. In the process, it is suggested that this new visibility in formal and cultural politics marks something of an epiphany that holds the promise of a 'game-changing' reorientation of our practices, institutions and policies of resource management. Before considering in more detail the multiple and complex processes that appear to be constituting a new contemporary politics of food waste, one key issue of food waste history needs to be addressed. This is the implicit assumption in much of the contemporary (particularly non-academic) work that we are in transition from a historical relationship characterized by the invisibility of waste to one that is characterized by greater (and thus more challengeable) visibility. We have, however, one particular concern with such a framing of this historical transition: how and why has the presumption of invisibility arisen in the first place?

Historical transitions in food waste 1: from visibility to invisibility?

Tracing a more nuanced and considered history of twentieth-century transitions in the cultural positioning of food waste may be quite difficult, for it both presupposes and requires that counting 'how much is wasted' can be done with confidence. First impressions suggest that sufficient variation exists in sample sizes and degrees of cooperation by respondents – let alone what is and is not to be included in counts of food waste over the last century – to make firm comparison between the measurements available a perilous enterprise (see discussion in O'Brien, 2007, and compare for instance, Jones *et al.*, 2008; Singer and Smart, 1977; Waste and Resources Action Programme (WRAP), 2009; Wenlock *et al.*, 1980). While there is likely to be a great deal of information on waste embedded in other food histories, the scholarly work that will disinter this material and reassemble it into a coherent history of food waste in modernity looks as if it has yet to be done. With this caveat in mind, and in the hope of prompting just such scholarly endeavour, the following sketch outlines – albeit speculatively and tentatively, a small contribution to the historiography that has yet to be written – a series of transitions in food waste.

The relative visibility of food waste in the mid-nineteenth to mid-twentieth century

Food waste is especially visible when its prevention is being counselled. This section narrows the focus briefly to consider evidence of such counsel found in English-language cookery books and household manuals of the mid-nineteenth and early twentieth century. In such sources, closely associated notions of thrift and advice for the avoidance of waste are readily identifiable. To start with, what is claimed to be 'the most famous English cookery book ever published' (Humble, 2000: vii), Isabella Beeton's 1861 *Book of Household Management* makes stern reference to the need for careful conservation and storage of food once it has been brought into the house: 'More waste is often occasioned by the want of judgment, or of necessary care in this particular, than by any other cause' (Humble, 2000 [1861]: 55). Mrs Beeton died in 1865, but manuals and cookery books that continued to appear in her name perpetuated her notions of frugality. The much smaller *Mrs Beeton's Cookery Book* therefore provides a list of 'kitchen maxims' including the injunction: 'The liquor in which a joint of meat has been boiled should never be thrown away' (Beeton, 1899: 16) and, in a section addressed 'To cooks and kitchen maids', we find the severe instruction: 'Never waste or throw away anything that can be turned to account' (1899: 26). A later edition of the same book published at the very end of World War I (when the shortage of domestic servants was an emerging 'problem' for the better off) changes the section title to 'Advice for the kitchen' but retains the admonition (Beeton, c. 1918: 19). Rather later, an even shorter edition called *Mrs Beeton's Family Cookery* (clearly aimed at smaller families/households) carries a new section on 'The art of "using up" cold remains': 'great care' is to be taken so that nothing that could be used 'is thrown away or suffered to be wasted in the kitchen' (Beeton, c. 1925: 293).

Themes of thrift and prudent kitchen management can just as readily be found in other cookery books of the period. The chapter on fish and shellfish in

The Sociological Review, 60:S2, pp. 5–26 (2013), DOI: 10.1111/1467-954X.12035

the cookery book published by the now well-established *Good Housekeeping Magazine* carries a subsection comprising eight recipes for 'fish left-overs', prefaced with the comment that 'The remains of almost any kind of cooked fish can be re-dressed and made up in some dainty way' (Jack, 1925: 32). Elizabeth Craig, a widely published cookery book author of the 1930s, provides a section early in her *New Standard Cookery (Illustrated)* on 'Keeping Down the Household Bills' including a subdivision on 'Making the most of leftovers' (from hard boiled eggs, various vegetables, fish, puddings and more) and the modern-sounding 'dodges to prevent waste' (1932: 53). The exact phrase 'Making the most of leftovers' also appears in *Economical Cookery* (Anon., c. 1937).

Similar themes and exhortations can be found in US cookery books across the same decades. They range from Miss Beecher's 1873 *Housekeeper and Healthkeeper*'s recurrent references to thrift, saving labour, time and fuel to the use for soup of '[R]emnants of cooked meats' (1873: 30) and 'remnants of bread . . . potatoes, hominy, rice, grits' and more to make '[T]he most economical Breakfast Dish' (1873: 71). And not only does Rombauer list the attractive ways in which 'eggs and left-overs' may be served (1931: 33), she too devotes a whole section in her famous *The Joy of Cooking* to '[R]ecipes and suggestions for left-over food' (1931: 380).

The theme of thrift recurs too in the manuals and texts prepared for the newly emerging schools designed to train young women as school teachers for the variously named 'domestic [later consumer] science' and 'home economics'. Such schools and training colleges opened through the nineteenth century across the industrializing world. Brembeck's discussion of their history illustrates the way such innovations were geared to what is needed for running a well-managed household in both Sweden and Scotland and which, centrally, included advice on the prudence necessary to its accomplishment (Brembeck, 2013).

While extrapolation from advice in cookery books and training manuals to actual kitchen practices can never be straightforward, *ideas* about the virtue of preventing the waste of food are undeniably extant in print. It is likely, then, that the exhortations to use food carefully and avoid throwing away what could be (re)used to conserve supplies in wartime would already be familiar to at least some segments of the population at large. In the US, the campaign against wasting food had culminated in 1918 with a poster carrying the memorably pointed slogan 'Food *is* Ammunition. Don't waste it'. By World War II, British propaganda posters similarly urged saving kitchen scraps for hens instead of throwing them away ('pig bins' were still placed at the end of suburban streets in London in 1953, the year before all food rationing finally ended). Reminders from the Ministry of Food that '[T]oday's scraps are tomorrow's savouries' (quoted in Fearnley-Whittingstall, 2010) echoed the 1890 'dainty little rissoles' of *Mrs Beeton's Every Day Cookery New Edition*.

While a far more systematic content analysis is needed to confirm the proposal, it is likely that the need to make the most of leftovers largely disappeared from cookery books in the post-World War II era of rising incomes, full employment and the spread of refrigerator ownership. In part, cookery book styles, at least in the UK, altered, giving way to the rise of greater specialization in the genre. That trend itself, however, provided a niche for Marika Hanbury Tenison's (1971) *Leftover for Tomorrow* – a whole book devoted to using up what might otherwise be wasted. By and large, however, the refrain seems to fade as the children and grandchildren of those growing up in World War II became increasingly used to feeling better off than their forbears.

The pivotal decade: 1950s

In contrast to the visible cultural practices specifically designed to avoid wasting food that was characteristic of advice on household waste practices among many classes and situations in the first half of the twentieth century, the 1950s signalled a decade of significant transition. Various scholars have attempted to describe the extent and outcomes of this transition for the wider global food system. While the arguments vary, all are in agreement that something highly significant happened in the way in which international, national and (many) local food relationships were configured in the period after the end of post-World War II rationing.

The most prominent contributors to this discussion are Friedmann and McMichael (1989), who situate the 1950s as the key pivot around which a new global 'food regime' took shape. The food regime narrative (briefly reviewed in Gille's chapter in this volume in order to set the scene for her analysis of 'waste regimes') is built around a broad historical transition from a global-scale set of food relationships within empires; that is, one based on the creation of farming colonies to feed the burgeoning population of the Industrial Revolution (The Imperial Food Regime) (see also Crosby, 1986; Davis, 2001; Wolf, 1982). This regime collapsed into crisis in the period between World War I, the Great Depression and World War II, and this collapse eventually provided a significant threat to the food security of Western Europe (something that Campbell, 2012, argues had been absent since the 1840s). The late-1940s/1950s response took the form of a set of relationships between policy, technology and economics that combined new production practices, farming approaches, production technologies and food commodities at the heart of a new regime of global food relations (the Cold War Food Regime) (Friedmann and McMichael, 1989). This new regime not only shifted the main emphasis on agricultural production away from the colonies and back into the farming regions of the Developed World, but also instituted policy frameworks (subsidies in Europe, food aid policies in the USA) that directed farmers towards producing the maximum possible amount of food without regard for the potential market for the resulting foodstuffs.

The result was a regime of excess food. During the Marshall Plan, surplus US grain was disposed of in the cause of restoring European food markets. From 1954, US farming was so productive that PL480 (later named the 'Food for Peace' law) was instituted to dispose of surplus production in the form of food aid abroad – eventually dispersing 25 per cent of US grain production

The Sociological Review, 60:S2, pp. 5–26 (2013), DOI: 10.1111/1467-954X.12035

(Campbell, 2012). In Europe, policies aimed at subsidizing the regeneration of the productive capacity of farmers were equally successful, with Europe moving from post-war scarcity to massive food surpluses in only a couple of decades. On the other side of the Cold War divide, Soviet industrial agriculture was promoted throughout the Communist bloc, with trade relations between countries like the USSR and Cuba solidified around the trade in large quantities of basic commodities such as sugar.

The food regimes narrative characterizes the 1950s as the period when: global food relations moved from scarcity to surplus; food security was formally constituted as a policy concern that justified state investment into agricultural productivity; and food rapidly became cheap and abundant. The Cold War regime was characterized by large-scale corporate investment in agriculture, but also increasing pressure on food processors and retailers to find ways of remaining profitable in a period where the world food economy was increasingly awash with cheap food commodities. This resulted in techniques of extensive food processing (Levenstein, 1993); fast food franchises; elaboration of branding; and what Nestle (2003) characterizes as the 'supersizing' of food. It was, we would add, a period in which food waste becomes increasingly invisible and culturally less relevant. In a world of excessive and cheap food, it is not difficult to imagine frugality and careful household management offering a poor fit with the 'zeitgeist' of the Cold War food regime.

While the food regime approach that frames the preceding paragraphs centres the argument on a set of political, economic and technological transitions in the post-World War II period, it is not the only way to try and account for a move from visibility to invisibility of food waste during this period. An alternative way of describing the dramatic transformation of science, technology and social relations that characterized food relations in the post-war decades can be found in the idea of a prevailing ideology of 'technological optimism' (Krier and Gillette, 1985) – an ideology that became hegemonic in a period where governments were investing heavily in science, science education and technological R&D during the Cold War period (see Goodman *et al.*, 1987; Goodman and Redclift, 1991). In this narrative, food production/processing is aligned with many other new technologies at the centre of a cultural order that privileged science-induced productivity. The end result is remarkably similar to that of the food regime narrative – the developed world becomes increasingly characterized by techno-industrial production that, as one of its exemplar achievements, underwrites spectacular increases in food production with the resulting decrease of food prices and increase in availability in the developed North (Levenstein, 1993). Food is culturally positioned within the 'technological optimism' frame as the product of science expertise and as such demonstrates the success of the techno-centric society (Krier and Gillette, 1985). Again, food waste has no place in such relationships, primarily founded as they are on productivity, efficiency and excess. The idea of being scientifically clever about how to deal with food waste seems out of touch in an era of celebration of massively excessive food production.

Whether we privilege the kinds of political/economic relations that characterize the food regime narrative or the cultural/technological promises at the heart of the narrative of technological optimism, there is clear common ground in both accounts. Food relations experience a rapid transition from scarcity to abundance. In other words, a pre-existing cultural concern with food waste (among many other things) that characterized the first half of the twentieth century is superseded by a pervasive invisibility of food waste in the post-World War II period. Twenty-first century accounts of a newly heightened visibility of food waste, never mind reports of continued increase in its volume, therefore need to be considered in the light of a far longer historical background. These recent accounts proclaim something completely novel and, if set against a (probably short-lived) period of historical invisibility, the designation of novelty appears warranted. But considered in longer historical perspectives, such a designation seems misplaced: issues of food waste might better be thought of as something older resurfacing. Far from invisibility being a long-standing precursor to early twenty-first century visibility, therefore, it can probably be better understood as a brief, albeit dramatic, period which temporarily inverted the historical norm. And so, with that caveat to the contemporary account, we now give more careful consideration to how and why food waste has very recently become such a visible issue.

Historical transitions 2: from invisibility to visibility – the contemporary politics of food waste

Our argument is that no single factor has been dominant in rendering food waste more visible in political and cultural life. Rather, a complex congruence of seemingly quite different and recently aligned dynamics have brought about the 'new' interest in food waste. These dynamics can be roughly grouped into four: first, sudden events and crises that have altered hitherto taken-for-granted certainties; secondly, national and international governance and policy shifts; thirdly, activist and cultural politics; and fourthly, longer-term technological and environmental trends.

Sudden events and crises

The global food crisis of 2008 (and two subsequent spikes in global commodity prices) can be seen as a singularly disruptive event. Rosin *et al.* (2012), together with Almas and Campbell (2012), argue that the 2008 crisis signalled a break with numerous modernist certainties, including the assumption that food prices would, in perpetuity, continue to get cheaper. Since 2008, food prices have actually begun to increase cyclically, and have created an environment where the relative cost of food has become a matter of consumer and public concern. This sudden relative rise in food prices has, arguably, not been experienced to any great degree since the consumer price inflation crisis of the late-1970s (a shock

The Sociological Review, 60:S2, pp. 5–26 (2013), DOI: 10.1111/1467-954X.12035

that also partly legitimized the neoliberal revolution in various developed world economies in the 1980s). Via a linked set of relationships, Rosin *et al.* (2012) suggest that the global financial crisis of 2008 was also implicated in the sudden rise in food prices when financial trading in food commodity futures became relatively more attractive compared to now-risky new financial instruments. The global financial crisis, we suggest, also brought an end to nearly fifteen years of consumer spending underpinned by cheap credit. The combination of both crises meant that certainties around the cost of food, the availability of cheap credit, and the ever-rising security of middle-class households could no longer be taken for granted. The linkage of recent global crises and the place of food in our lives is also exacerbated by debates over various responses to those 2008 crises – particularly around the phenomenon of corporate 'land-grabbing', investments in biofuels, and calls to pull back from more environmentally friendly approaches to food production (see Almas and Campbell, 2012). This provides one important context in which the new concern for food waste has emerged: namely that the increasing cost of food creates an environment where it is both less desirable, and harder to afford, to waste food. Seen in this light, the new visibility of food waste is both a pragmatic/economic necessity as well as demonstrating a wider shift in previously taken-for-granted cultural certainties about the cheapness and abundance of food.

National and international governance and policy shifts

In the European Union (EU), the single biggest transition in waste and waste policy is the 1999 Landfill Directive (1999/3/EC); a policy that set out to reduce the negative effects of sending waste to landfill in relation to the environment and human health. This document set legally binding targets to which member states are to adhere. At its core is the ambition to manage wastes in a manner that diverts them from landfill, with the emphasis on resource (and value) recovery via reuse, recycling and transformation into energy (a process otherwise known as moving up the 'waste hierarchy'). The targets are exceptionally ambitious – not least the obligation to reduce biodegradable waste (the category to which food waste belongs) to 35 per cent of 1995 levels by 2016, or by 2020 for some countries (including the UK). In addition to putting waste firmly on the political agenda, these targets put immense pressure on national governments to respond. In the UK, these requirements passed into legislation through the landfill (England and Wales) Regulations 2002. However, the crucial response in the UK (at least in terms of the story of the visibility of food waste) was the government's decision to set up the Waste and Resources Action Programme (WRAP).

Established as a not-for-profit company in 2000, WRAP is supported by funding from the four national governments of the UK (as well as the EU) and appears to have been highly effective not only in creating an agenda that highlights the issues associated with wastes of all kinds, but also in advocating practical solutions premised on resource efficiency. In addition to collating and publicizing records and data from government departments and beyond, it also contributes to the generation of new data; monitors and publicizes problems; creates partnerships; brokers voluntary agreements; and develops initiatives to minimize and prevent waste across all sectors. Undoubtedly, WRAP has been instrumental in putting food waste on the public and policy agenda in the UK. Their work on household food waste (WRAP, 2009; see also Quested *et al.*, 2011) quantified the extent of the problem and the results were certainly alarming: these data suggested that UK households throw away 8.3 million tonnes of uneaten food each year – enough to fill Wembley Stadium ten times over[3] – and that at least 5.3 million of these tonnes are avoidable. The annual financial cost of this avoidable waste is estimated at £12 billion (£480 per household), while the environmental impact is equivalent to 20 million tonnes of carbon dioxide emissions (the same impact as the emissions generated by a quarter of the cars on UK roads). These figures gave rise to the headline-grabbing observation that UK households waste roughly one-third of the food they buy for consumption.

WRAP have also been involved in practical, government-funded efforts to reduce household food waste since 2006, notably through their 2007 *Love Food Hate Waste*[4] campaign that aimed to raise awareness and engage the public on this issue. Of particular note is the campaign's website, which includes a 'recipes' section intended to help households use more of the food they buy through providing suggestions on what to cook with leftover ingredients.[5] This marks a rather neat parallel to the pre-1950s cookery books discussed above. It is also instructive – if unsurprising – to note it is WRAP's work on *household* food waste that gained traction in popular and policy imaginations. Overwhelmingly, waste policy has focused on municipal waste streams (as opposed, say, to the by-products of industrial food production processes) and the resulting measures have been restricted to a focus on households and the municipal authorities charged with the management of post-consumer discards (Bulkeley and Gregson, 2009). One might argue (see Alexander *et al.*, 2013) that this mirrors the invisibility of (food) waste discussed above insofar as such waste has been positioned as a problem to be managed at the 'end of pipe'. That said, WRAP themselves do not confine their attention to the household: they unarguably recognize the importance of tackling food waste across the supply chain and pay particular attention to retail, food service and hospitality.

Beyond the UK and more recently, the reduction of food waste has emerged as a specific policy goal for the European Union. On 19 January 2012, the European Parliament passed a resolution to tackle food waste and called on the European Commission (EC) to halve current volumes of food waste by 2025 (EC estimates suggest 90 million tonnes are produced annually in the EU). Significantly, in the discussions surrounding these movements the emphasis is on the perversity of wasting food when more than 70 million people in the EU live below the poverty line and 16 million depend on food aid to stave off malnutrition. Here, therefore, we see food waste tied intimately to food poverty. It is also worth noting that the resolution recognizes that food waste occurs across the supply chain and so calls for a coordinated strategy 'from farm to fork'. That

The Sociological Review, 60:S2, pp. 5–26 (2013), DOI: 10.1111/1467-954X.12035

said, the specific measures they identify tend to focus on education, packaging and labelling – again mirroring the more general tendency to position food waste as a consumer issue although, along with WRAP, they do acknowledge the role of retail, hospitality and even public procurement. Finally, it is important to note that the European Parliament make explicit mention that meeting these ambitious targets would go a long way towards meeting the targets set by the 1999 Landfill Directive. There is even talk of designating 2014 as the 'European year against food waste'.

Food waste has also gained recognition as a global issue and priority. In 2011, the Food and Agriculture Organization of the United Nations (FAO) published the results of their initial study into the extent and causes of global food waste. Again, the results of this study are alarming: they estimate that one-third of the food produced for human consumption is lost or wasted globally – equivalent to 1.3 billion tonnes annually. In contrast to specific UK and EU discourses on food waste, the FAO acknowledges more thoroughly the waste that occurs in processes of food production and so manages to shift further away from the idea that it is a problem to be managed at the level of households and consumers. Accordingly, it calls for further research and coordination in order to better understand and tackle food waste across the supply chain. It is also worth noting that given its focus on the global South, the FAO links the issue of food waste to questions of food security, food safety and economic development. Taken together, food waste can be viewed as an issue that is firmly on the agenda at a variety of geographic scales and is intimately tied to a number of economic, social, ethical and environmental priorities.

Activist and cultural politics

Since the derailing of the World Trade Organization (WTO) trade negotiations in Seattle in 1999 and the subsequent disruption of the WTO 'Doha Round' in Cancun in 2003, the possibility has begun to arise that we are entering a period in which non-state actors are starting to play an increasingly important role in prompting political change. While this idea remains rather speculative, the 'new' politics of food waste indeed seems to bear out the proposition that a wide range of non-governmental political actors are becoming more influential.

First, there has been the rise of authors writing with an overt agenda of waste activism. Notably, Tristram Stuart's (2009) *Waste: Uncovering the Global Food Scandal* provides a landmark *tour de force* signifying an important moment in the popularizing of a particular political agenda around food waste. This publication was quickly followed by Jonathan Bloom's (2011) equally impressive *American Wasteland: Why America Throws Away Nearly Half Its Food (and What We Can Do About It)*. These two books have compiled statistics and highlighted the extent of the problem in a popular and accessible way. Both books have also been hugely successful in terms of sales, awards and publicity (including media appearances and active web presence), which has served to make food waste much more visible to the wider public. Further, they have given the authors a platform for their own food waste activism. Stuart, for example, has staged a number of 'feeding the five-thousand' events in which the public are given a meal fashioned (with suitable food safety advice) entirely out of produce that would have otherwise gone to waste.[6]

Second, these books can linked to the wider – if more amorphous – phenomenon of freeganism. Freeganism is a loosely connected set of practices targeting food waste as both a political act and as a form of alternative (and for some, entertaining) self-provisioning. Most notably, the act of 'dumpster diving' (or 'skip dipping' in some countries) involves freegans exploiting the seemingly arbitrary nature of 'use-by' labels. Edwards and Mercer (this volume) describe how 'dumpster divers' have developed a sophisticated critique of use-by labels and are mobilizing alternative, embodied approaches to whether food is fit to eat (thus returning to techniques used by humans throughout history) (see also Ferrell, 2006). Stuart (2009) similarly documents how dumpster diving has become part of the repertoire of certain forms of youth activism as well as an important self-provisioning source for the urban poor. Accordingly, this site of action is contested by the supermarkets, who find their dumpsters are being raided (and in O'Brien's account in this volume, also find themselves increasingly contested in the legal framing of ownership of waste).

More generally, increasing murmurings of 'grass roots' responses to the issue of food waste can be heard. The examples are too numerous to mention, but, to give one illustration, at the time of writing the village of Pince in the north-west of France has proposed giving two chickens to each household in an attempt to better manage the disposal of surplus food and prevent it from being wasted.[7] It should be noted, however, that stringent EU regulations governing what can be fed to animals are liable to render this illegal. It has also been claimed that consumers have mobilized in response to an issue related to food waste: the waste of food packaging. Market research suggests that in addition to thinking that products are over-packaged, consumers are uncomfortable with the waste that this generates and have consequently put pressure on retailers to reduce it. What is interesting here, however, is that food waste and packaging waste are very different waste issues – and yet until very recently, the issue of packaging had been much more visible (this is not to say that packaging is tangential to analyses of food waste: see Hawkins, this volume).

That said, ethnographic research suggests that households are indeed troubled by the act of wasting food (Evans, 2011, 2012a). There is something about food waste that is bound to trouble people; its status as necessity of life itself, or perhaps simply as a lingering reminder of childhood invocations to finish our supper given that people are starving elsewhere in the world. We might speculate here that it has the potential to capture people's imaginations in ways that other issues connecting food and (environmental) politics do not, or even cannot. However, we also note that the most common reaction is to imagine food waste as a consequence of food labelling (discussed by Milne, this volume) or people being unable to resist the allure of offers to Buy One Get One Free (BOGOF) (see Evans, 2011 for a critique).

These kinds of new political challenges to the consumption and disposal of food are also clearly connected to a wider set of political concerns about the industrialization of food. In particular, one of the qualities of ongoing industrialization of food production and processing has been the conversion of potentially wasted by-products into processed foods to enable greater extraction of profit from a narrow set of basic commodity production platforms like soy, corn and beef (Morgan, 1979). One example that has been relatively uncontentious is the development of margarine as an outlet for some by-products of oilseed production (particularly in combination with soy cake as an industrial stock food). Much more contentious is the development of both ethanol and High Fructose Corn Syrup (HFCS) as highly industrialized means of 'disposing' of vastly excessive production of corn in the USA (Goodman and Redclift, 1991). Both are now the subject of vigorous resistance from food activist groups. A more recent addition has been the exotically named 'pink slime' which is generated specifically to utilize otherwise wasted components of beef carcasses and which became a widely circulated activist meme in 2012 (see, eg, http://stoppinkslime.org/ or http://www.pinkslime.biz/).

A further important contributor to an emerging cultural politics of food waste is the more formal involvement of charities and other NGOs. Most notable are the organizations who work to redistribute discarded food to the (primarily) urban poor. Organizations like Second Harvest in the US, and FoodCycle or FareShare in the UK, have negotiated arrangements with major food retailers to divert surplus food from the waste stream and into community kitchens with the aim of reducing 'food poverty' as well as reducing waste. It is worth noting that against a backdrop of rising relative food prices (discussed above), the number of people relying on these channels of redistribution has increased significantly. Beyond these activities, it is also important to acknowledge the role of organizations such as the Sustainable Restaurant Association (SRA) – a not-for-profit membership organization that focuses on sustainability in food service and hospitality (mirroring to some extent the locus of policy attention outside of the household). A significant element of their activities has been their 'too good to waste' campaign, launched in London in 2011 and geared to persuading diners of the virtues of a 'doggy box' (their variant on the 'doggy bag') as a means of taking leftover food home for reuse – so, it is hoped, saving it from wastage. Crucially, this campaign attracted a huge amount of attention with over 40 pieces of trade, national and online coverage giving 120 million opportunities to see it – approximately £1 million of media value.

A final group who are becoming increasingly prominent in wider food politics – particularly in the UK – have been celebrity chefs. Although their commitment and advocacy is far more notable in other political issues (for example, animal welfare or local foods) this group is, arguably, also beginning to mobilize around food waste. For example, in 2011, UK celebrity chef Hugh Fearnley-Whittingstall filmed a series of TV programmes that investigated current practices in the fishing industry. This eventually led to 'Hugh's Fish Fight': a campaign aimed at changing the EU laws and arrangements that currently lead to the discarding – and wasting – of half the fish caught in the North Sea. The campaign garnered much support from NGOs, the fishing industry, and local and national policy-makers as well as the general public. To date there are over 813,000 signatories on his petition to the EC for a discard ban and a new common fisheries policy. This lends support to our conjecture that there is something about wasted food that has the potential to capture people's imaginations and mobilize certain forms of political action.

Longer-term technological and environmental trends

At first glance, all the above three strands involve relatively recent interventions into the politics and regulation of food. It is important to balance these with due acknowledgement of some of the longer-term trends that have clearly influenced these more recent dynamics. The first such trend is the ever-rising profile of environmental problems – particularly those that are starting to alarm the fretful citizen at the heart of Beck's risk society thesis (1992). Global climate change and 'peak oil' are both threshold crises in the global environment that have direct and dangerous implications for the citizenry of developed countries. Given the regulatory responses (or potential future responses) and political energy being devoted to contesting or shaping reactions to these two crises, it is hard for even the most affluent and well-resourced developed world citizen to ignore the wider politics of our engagement with environmental questions. In this context, the post-World War II era of cultural acceptance of technology, progress and (implicitly) massive food surplus is increasingly becoming less stable.

The second long-term trend that influences this arena of food politics is the proliferation of increasingly sophisticated information and communications technology (ICT). From increasingly coordinated attacks on the WTO by NGOs, through the broadening of knowledge exchange by the various actors identified above, to the ability to disseminate statistical information and claims about waste, new ICT has arguably facilitated the shift of food waste politics from being part of the background noise of rising environmental concern to being a more central issue that poses a threat to the citizenry of the risk society.

Finally, it is important to note the changing role of technologies for the treatment and management of food waste. Against the demands of reducing the amount of food (and other materials) being sent to landfill, technological solutions are becoming an attractive option to policy-makers. The possibility of composting of food or converting it to energy through anaerobic digestion signals the hope of transforming 'waste' into 'value' and so making an economic virtue out of ecological challenges.

Waste matters: new perspectives on food and society

The account above is necessarily truncated and something of a 'potted history'. The four strands identified nevertheless indicate that – in combination – the factors giving rise to the new politics of food waste are gratifyingly (if alarmingly) complex, and go far beyond accusing householders of fecklessness. In all this recent activity, a subtle and ongoing relationship between food waste scholarship and food waste politics has developed and strengthened. Both WRAP and Stuart (2009) draw strongly upon sources of information and expertise that reside in the world of formal scholarship and research (either in the academy or in government). However, much of this research has been of a style and content that has provided a rather limited and narrow account of food waste. Our intention in the rest of this monograph is to provide an opportunity for the parallel work of social scientists working on food waste to be considered.

In sum, this *Sociological Review Monograph* aims to begin remedying several lacunae: not only the notable gulf between the new politics of food waste and the (lack of) attention it has received in sociological researches generally, but also the absence of food in the sociology of waste and the absence of waste in the sociology of food. And so having summarized the 'new' politics of food waste and introduced the key themes, theories and approaches that seem to characterize the new social scientific scholarship on food waste, we now hand over to the individual contributors. In reading these, we trust that it will become apparent that sociology can engage usefully with the issue. Additionally – and following in the wake of Martin O'Brien's plea (2007) for a sociology of the 'rubbish society' – it should become apparent that a substantive focus on food waste helps to think through a number of concerns in contemporary sociological thinking and theorizing.

Notes

1 See also Hawkins and Muecke (2004).
2 See also Clark and Scanlan (2010).
3 More recent estimates (WRAP, 2011; see also Quested *et al.*, forthcoming) suggest the total volume of household food waste has reduced to 7.2 million tonnes. This is still enough to fill Wembley Stadium nine times over.
4 http://www.lovefoodhatewaste.com (accessed 21 August 2012).
5 http://www.lovefoodhatewaste.com/recipes (accessed 21 August 2012).
6 http://www.feeding5k.org/ (accessed 21 August 2012).
7 http://www.bbc.co.uk/news/world-europe-17540287.

References

Alexander, C. and Reno, J. (eds), (2012), *Economies of Recycling: The Global Transformation of Materials, Values and Social Relations*, London and New York: Zed Books.
Alexander, C., Gregson, N. and Gille, Z., (2013), 'Food waste', in A. Murcott, W. Belasco and P. Jackson (eds), *The Handbook of Food Research*, London: Bloomsbury.
Almas, R. and Campbell, H. (eds), (2012), *Rethinking Agricultural Policy Regimes: Food Security, Climate Change and the Future Resilience of Global Agriculture*, Bingley: Emerald.
Anon., (c. 1937), *Economical Cookery: and Menus for Every Day of the Year*, London: A Daily Express Publication.

Beck, U., (1992), *Risk Society: Towards a New Modernity*, London: Sage.

Beecher, C. E., (1873), *Housekeeper and Healthkeeper*, New York: Harper & Bros.

Beeton, I. M., (1899), *Mrs Beeton's Cookery Book: New and Enlarged Edition*, London: Warde Lock & Co.

Beeton, I. M., (c. 1918), *Mrs Beeton's Cookery Book: All about Cookery, Household Work, Marketing, Trussing, Carving, etc*, London: Warde Lock & Co.

Beeton, I. M., (c. 1925), *Mrs Beeton's Family Cookery*, London: Warde Lock & Co.

Bennett, J., (2007), 'Edible matter', *New Left Review*, 45: 133–145.

Bennett, J., (2010), *Vibrant Matter: A Political Ecology of Things*, London: Duke University Press.

Bloom, J., (2011), *American Wasteland: How America Throws Away Nearly Half of Its Food (and What We Can Do About It)*, Cambridge, MA: De Capo Press.

Brembeck, H., (2013), 'The twenty-first century "food consumer": the emergence of consumer science', in A. Murcott, W. Belasco and P. Jackson (eds), *The Handbook of Food Research*, London: Bloomsbury.

Bulkeley, H. and Gregson, N., (2009), 'Crossing the threshold: municipal waste policy and household waste generation', *Environment and Planning A*, 41: 929–945.

Campbell, H., (2012), 'Let us eat cake? Historically reframing the problem of world hunger and its purported solutions', in C. Rosin, P. Stock and H. Campbell (eds), *Food Systems Failure: The Global Food Crisis and the Future of Agriculture*, London: Earthscan.

Cappellini, B., (2009), 'The sacrifice of re-use: the travels of leftovers and family relations', *Journal of Consumer Behaviour*, 8: 365–375.

Clark, J. and Scanlan, J. (eds), (2010), *The World Turned Inside Out: Waste in History and Culture*, Newcastle upon Tyne: Cambridge Scholars Publishing.

Craig, E. (ed.), (1932), *New Standard Cookery (Illustrated)*, London: Odhams Press.

Crosby, A., (1986), *Ecological Imperialism: The Biological Expansion of Europe, 900–1900*, Cambridge: Cambridge University Press.

Davis, M., (2001), *Late Victorian Holocausts: El Nino Famines and the Making of the Third World*, London and New York: Verso.

De Certau, M., (1984 [1980]), *The Practice of Everyday Life*, Berkeley: University of California Press.

Douglas, J., (1970), *Understanding Everyday Life*, Chicago: Aldine.

Douglas, M., (1966), *Purity and Danger*, London: Routledge.

Edensor, T., (2005), 'Waste matter: the debris of industrial ruins and the disordering of the material world', *Journal of Material Culture*, 10: 311–332.

Evans, D., (2011), 'Blaming the consumer – once again: the social and material contexts of everyday food waste practices in some English households', *Critical Public Health*, 21 (4): 429–440.

Evans, D., (2012a), 'Beyond the throwaway society: ordinary domestic practice and a sociological approach to household food waste', *Sociology*, 46 (1): 43–58.

Evans, D., (2012b), 'Binning, gifting and recovery: the conduits of disposal in household food consumption', *Environment and Planning D: Society and Space*, 30 (6): 1123–1137.

Fearnley-Whittingstall, J., (2010), *The Ministry of Food*, London: Hodder and Stoughton.

Ferrell, J., (2006), *Empire of Scrounge: Inside the Urban Underground of Dumpster Diving, Trash Picking and Street Scavenging*, New York: New York University Press.

Fine, G. A., (1996), *Kitchens: The Culture of Restaurant Work*, Berkeley and Los Angeles: University of California Press.

Friedmann, H. and McMichael, P., (1989), 'Agriculture and the state system', *Sociologia Ruralis*, 29 (2): 93–117.

Gille, Z., (2007), *From the Cult of Waste to the Trash Heap of History: The Politics of Waste in Socialist and Postsocialist Hungary*, Bloomington: University of Indiana Press.

Goffman, E., (1959), *The Presentation of Self in Everyday Life*, Harmondsworth: Penguin.

Goodman, D. and Redclift, M., (1991), *Refashioning Nature: Food, Ecology and Culture*, London: Routledge.

Goodman, D., Sorj, B. and Wilkinson, J., (1987), *From Farming to Biotechnology: A Theory of Agro-Industrial Development*, Oxford: Basil Blackwell.

The Sociological Review, 60:S2, pp. 5–26 (2013), DOI: 10.1111/1467-954X.12035
© 2013 The Authors. Editorial organisation © 2013 The Editorial Board of the Sociological Review

Goody, J., (1982), *Cooking, Cuisine and Class: A Study in Comparative Sociology*, Cambridge: Cambridge University Press.

Gregson, N., (2007), *Living with Things: Ridding, Accommodation, Dwelling*, Oxford: Sean Kingston.

Gregson, N. and Crang, M., (2010), Guest Editorial, 'Materiality and waste: inorganic vitality in a networked world', *Environment and Planning A*, 42 (5): 1026–1032.

Gregson, N., Crang, M., Ahamed, F., Akter, N. and Ferdous, R., (2010a), 'Following things of rubbish value: end-of-life ships, "chock-chocky" furniture and the Bangladeshi middle class consumer', *Geoforum*, 41: 846–854.

Gregson, N. and Crewe, L., (2003), *Second Hand Cultures*, Oxford: Berg.

Gregson, N., Metcalfe, A. and Crewe, L., (2007), 'Identity, mobility, and the throwaway society', *Environment and Planning D: Society and Space*, 25: 682–700.

Gregson, N., Watkins, H. and Calestani, M., (2010b), 'Inextinguishable fibres: demolition and the vital materialisms of asbestos', *Environment and Planning A*, 42: 1065–1083.

Hanbury Tenison, M., (1971), *Leftover for Tomorrow*, London: Penguin.

Hawkins, G., (2006), *The Ethics of Waste: How We Relate to Rubbish*, Lanham, MD: Rowman and Littlefield.

Hawkins, G. and Muecke, S. (eds), (2004), *Waste and Culture: The Creation and Destruction of Value*, Lanham, MD: Rowman and Littlefield.

Hetherington, K., (2004), 'Secondhandedness: consumption, disposal and absent presence', *Environment and Planning D: Society and Space*, 22: 157–173.

Humble, N., (2000), 'Introduction', in *Mrs Beeton's Book of Household Management* (abridged edn), Oxford: Oxford University Press Oxford World's Classics.

Ingold, T., (2007), 'Materials against materiality', *Archaeological Dialogues*, 14 (1): 1–16.

Jack, F. B., (1925), *Good Housekeeping Cookery Book*, London: Good Housekeeping Magazine.

Jones, A., Nesaratnam, S. and Porteous, A., (2008), *The Open University Household Waste Study: Key findings from 2008*, Milton Keynes: Open University for DEFRA, http://www.defra.gov.uk/evidence/statistics/environment/waste/research/download/ou-rpt-20081008.pdf (accessed 23 February 2010).

Klein, J. A. and Murcott, A. (eds), (forthcoming), *Food Consumption in Global Perspective: Essays in the Anthropology of Food in Honour of Jack Goody*, London: Palgrave.

Krier, J. E. and Gillette, C. P., (1985), 'The un-easy case for technological optimism', *Michigan Law Review*, 84 (3): 405–429.

Laporte, D., (1999), *A History of Shit*, Cambridge, MA: MIT Press.

Levenstein, H., (1993), *Paradox of Plenty: A Social History of Eating in Modern America*, New York: Oxford University Press.

Marshall, D. (ed.), (1995), *Food Choice and the Consumer*, London: Blackie.

Melosi, A., (2004), *Garbage in the Cities: Refuse, Reform, and the Environment* (rev. edn), Pittsburgh: University of Pittsburgh Press.

Morgan, D., (1979), *Merchants of Grain*, New York: Viking Press.

Murcott, A. (ed.), (1983), *The Sociology of Food and Eating*, Aldershot: Gower.

Murcott, A., (1993), 'Purity and pollution: body management and the social place of infancy', in D. Morgan and S. Scott (eds), *Body Matters: Essays on the Sociology of the Body*, London: Falmer Press/Taylor Francis.

Munro, R., (1995), 'The disposal of the meal', in D. Marshall (ed.), *Food Choice and the Consumer*, London: Blackie.

Nestle, M., (2003), *Food Politics: How the Food Industry Influences Nutrition and Health*, Berkeley: University of California Press.

O'Brien, M., (2007), *A Crisis of Waste? Understanding the Rubbish Society*, London and New York: Routledge.

Quested, T., Parry, A., Easteal, S. and Swannell, R., (2011), 'Food and drink waste from households in the UK', *Nutrition Bulletin*, 26: 460–467.

Quested, T., Marsh, E., Stunell, D. and Parry, A., (forthcoming), 'Spaghetti soup: the complex world of food waste behaviours', *Journal of Resources, Conservation and Recycling*.

Rathje, W. and Murphy, C., (1992), *Rubbish: the Archaeology of Garbage*, New York: HarperCollins.

Rombauer, I. S., (1931), *The Joy of Cooking*, New York: Simon and Schuster.

Rosin, C., Stock, P. and Campbell, H. (eds), (2012), *Food Systems Failure: The Global Food Crisis and the Future of Agriculture*, London: Earthscan.

Scanlan, J., (2005), *On Garbage*, London: Reaktion Books.

Singer, D. and Smart, G., (1977), 'Food waste survey unit', *Nutrition and Food Science*, 77 (4): 6–7.

Strasser, S., (1999), *Waste and Want: The Social History of Trash*. London: Metropolitan Books.

Stuart, T., (2009), *Waste: Uncovering the Global Food Scandal*, New York: W.W. Norton.

Economist, The, (2012), 'Clean plates', *The Economist*, 1–17 September, 404 (8800): 49.

Thompson, M., (1979), *Rubbish Theory: The Creation and Destruction of Value*, Oxford: Oxford University Press.

Wenlock, R. W., Buss, D. H., Derry, B. J. and Dixon, E., (1980), 'Household food wastage in Britain', *British Journal of Nutrition*, 43 (1): 53–70.

Wolf, E., (1982), *Europe and the People without History*, Berkeley: University of California Press.

WRAP (Waste and Resources Action Programme), (2009), *Household Food and Drink Waste in the UK*, http://www.wrap.org.uk/retail/case_studies_research/report_household.html.

WRAP, (2011), *New Estimates for Household Food and Drink Waste in the UK*, http://www.wrap.org.uk/sites/files/wrap/New%20estimates%20for%20household%20food%20and%20drink%20waste%20in%20the%20UK%20FINAL%20v2%20(updated%207thAugust2012).pdf.

The Sociological Review, 60:S2, pp. 5–26 (2013), DOI: 10.1111/1467-954X.12035

From risk to waste: global food waste regimes

Zsuzsa Gille

Abstract: This article utilizes the concept of waste regimes in order to understand the global connections involved in generating food waste. This concept treats waste as a social relationship and assumes that in any economy there is a waste circulation in addition to a value circulation, and that the two are interdependent. For this reason, the author critiques metaphors, such as value chains or supply chains, that have dominated the scholarship on food and agriculture. Creatively utilizing secondary empirical data on the Global North and South from that scholarship, the findings indicate that the unequal organization of uncertainty is a key structural determinant of food waste production in both. The relationship between risk and waste stretches across not only geographical but also scalar boundaries, revealing that solutions to the 'food waste problem' limited to technological innovation and a few sites or even countries will prove insufficient and will likely exacerbate existing inequalities.

Keywords: food waste, organization of uncertainty, waste regimes, risk, scales

Introduction: value versus waste chains

Social scientists studying the worlds of food (Morgan *et al.*, 2006) talk about food as either a final product or as resulting from material, aesthetic and social transformations of value creation. In the historical and social science literature on specific food commodities and culinary traditions, together with the various brands and industries that produce them, issues of taste, price, production and consumption trends tend to take centre stage. Even the more analytical studies frame such stories with the metaphors of commodity chains, supply chains or value chains. Furthermore, studies of famine – that talk about food from the perspective of its absence – also implicitly locate food in the register of worth, value and a host of other positive categories. What would happen to this comforting view of food – presented through the positive concepts of tastes, values, and supply – if we recognized that the economy is not simply a place where value begets value, but where value also begets waste, waste also begets value and, even more importantly, waste begets waste? What would it mean to view the world of food from the perspective of

The Sociological Review, 60:S2, pp. 27–46 (2013), DOI: 10.1111/1467-954X.12036

waste rather than of goods; from the perspective of disuse rather than use; and from the perspective of loss rather than gain? How would we think about nutrition and cuisine if we stopped lying to ourselves about food's ontology: if we stopped both assuming that value outweighs waste, and acting as if waste was derivative and thus inconsequential?

In this article I want to start from the opposite position: that without disuse there is no use, and without waste there is no value. Thanks to a number of scholars, this is no longer simply a presumption. Georges Bataille (1988), chronologically the first, argued that nature is always profligate and as a result, a key task for any society is to solve the problem of surplus: a problem solved, as he documents, through a variety of rituals and institutions. More recently, Kevin Hetherington (2004) and Nicky Gregson (2007) have shown that new consumption necessitates disposal and other wasting practices, and thus it is misguided for scholars of consumption to focus exclusively on tastes and acts of purchases. Martin O'Brien (2008), another British waste scholar, has argued that the relative absence and/or failure of waste regulations makes possible a particular social life – and, as such, is constitutive of society. Finally Hetherington (2004) and I (Gille, 2007) have revealed the way in which waste materials 'bite back' and keep haunting society even after their disposal. This thesis about the necessity, the inevitability, or – if you will – the 'naturalness' of waste, however, does not mean that there is 'nothing wrong' with the amount and kind of wastes generated. To demonstrate both the inevitability and the socialness of waste we need to conceptualize waste as exhibiting social systemicity both at the macro and micro levels.[1] To this end, I not only advance a view of the economy as a waste chain, but also demonstrate how waste chains themselves participate in maintaining value chains.

First, I argue for a new conceptual framework to capture the systemicity of food waste: the concept of waste regimes. My argument here is primarily dedicated to analysing the production of waste in order to balance the unevenness of the literature mentioned above. Secondly, I conceptualize this aspect of the food waste regime as the dynamic interrelatedness of value chains and waste chains, with risk avoidance strategies comprising the most important transmission belt between the two. In the third section of the article I analyse currently dominant representations of food waste and demonstrate how they affect waste generation. Finally, in the fourth section, I reflect on the politics of food waste, particularly the non-waste-related causes served by food waste solutions.

Food waste regimes

The concept of waste regimes is one I proposed in my book, *From the Cult of Waste to the Trash Heap of History: The Politics of Waste in Socialist and Postsocialist Hungary* (Gille, 2007). While the term 'food waste regime' may inevitably create an association with the concept of food regimes coined by Friedmann and McMichael (1987), my conceptualization originates in Oran

The Sociological Review, 60:S2, pp. 27–46 (2013), DOI: 10.1111/1467-954X.12036

Young's (1982) formulation of resource regime.[2] But similarities exist to Friedmann and McMichael's model. Just as McMichael (2009) argues that food regimes conceptualize food as a social relation rather than as a commodity, I suggest that waste constitutes a social relationship, and as such should be studied as something produced materially and conceptually by profoundly social relations. Finally, parallel to McMichael's genealogy of food regimes, I use the concept of food waste regimes for historical or epochal analysis. Here the goal is to provide cross-temporal comparisons among different food waste regimes, as well as for a more 'bottom-up' analysis of different regions and actors' roles in any particular food waste regime. Waste regimes, as I have argued elsewhere (Gille, 2010), are quintessentially macro-entities; however, as I explain below, they also make possible a cross-scalar analysis.

Waste regimes consist of social institutions and conventions that not only determine what wastes are considered valuable but also regulate their production and distribution. Waste regimes, therefore, differ from each other according to the production, representation and politics of waste. In studying the production of waste, we are exploring which social relations determine waste production and what the material composition of wastes may be. When we inquire into the representation of waste, we are asking which side of key dichotomies waste is seen to lie (efficiency/inefficiency; usefulness/uselessness; order/disorder; gain/loss; clean/dirty; alive/dead; fertile/sterile), alongside how and why waste's materiality has been misunderstood and with what consequences. Here I also investigate the key bodies of knowledge and expertise mobilized in dealing with wastes. In researching the politics of waste, we ask: whether – or to what extent – waste issues are a subject of public discourse; what is taboo; what are the tools of policy; who is mobilized to deal with waste issues; and what non-waste goals such political instruments serve. Finally, no waste regime is static, we must study them dynamically, as they unfold, and as they develop unintended consequences and crises.

I have previously elaborated this concept as a tool to understand the historical changes of how primarily industrial wastes were seen and treated in one country, Hungary, over half a century. There, the concept functioned as a device to illuminate continuities and discontinuities in the realm of a wide range of by-products within one country. Here I want to use this concept to focus on one set of wastes in the present, rather than all wastes historically. Faced with that task, the concept of waste regime must be modified in one important aspect, it must shed its national constraints; that is, it must incorporate cross-national and even cross-scalar linkages that affect the production, the representation and the politics of waste. In my investigation of food waste, I have found that risk constitutes one key link among those geographical units and scales – or, more precisely, the types of social arrangements aimed at lessening or avoiding risks. Here I use Michael Power's (2007) term 'the organization of uncertainty' to discuss these social arrangements, and also to demonstrate how the organization of uncertainty constructs waste and value chains in food production and consumption.

The organization of uncertainty and the production of farm waste

Farming is an inherently risky economic activity. The vagaries of weather, pest outbreaks, and market fluctuation make for an uncertain environment for producing food. Different societies have developed different ways to mitigate such agricultural risks. Farmers in pre-capitalist societies (where most production is for subsistence), together with the poorest peasants – even in capitalist societies – have tended to strive for what James Scott (1976) calls subsistence security. Rather than maximizing income or minimizing the rate of expropriation by the state, the church or landlords, for these farmers the primary goal is to achieve stability and security. While this may be seen as a backward, risk-averse or non-entrepreneurial attitude, it is actually a rational mentality in conditions that pose perpetual threats to survival. Anthropologists, historians and sociologists have described many methods of risk pooling, such as various patron-client relations, religious obligations, various cultural traditions, family and kin arrangements, as well as more modern state interventions, such as price and tax policies or government-run agricultural infrastructures and institutions, all of which aim to keep peasants above the subsistence crisis zone.

Market societies, in which farmers produce primarily for the market, typically had little protection built into the social and economic fabric of society (Davis, 2001; Polanyi, 1944) until futures trading and insurance were institutionalized (Cronon, 1991). As Rebecca Gresh (2011) argues, however, the development of more complex financial instruments on Wall Street in the last 15–20 years – in part due to the deregulation of the banking and investment sectors – has now introduced more uncertainty than risk mitigation for farmers and for consumers. In addition, globalization and the increasing interconnectedness of the world have produced new risk relations. The vast body of scholarship in rural sociology and anthropology, alongside peasant or agrarian studies, the voluminous literature in political economy, Marxism and world-system theory, has provided ample documentation and analysis of the historically changing inequalities, subsistence risks (including famine) and social organizations of uncertainty in rural communities. While some of this literature has incorporated the environmental effects and causes of these social developments – most prominently political ecology – what has been missing from this literature is a more systematic focus on farm and food waste. Here I aim to remedy this by bringing in risk and waste studies in order to put findings of more traditional agrarian literature to a new use, namely, the analysis of the currently dominant global food waste regime.

What makes it important to highlight risk is not simply the transition to a new stage of modernity in which risks increasingly determine inequality, as Ulrich Beck (1992) argues. More importantly, food today raises feelings of anxiety that speak to a new constellation of risks, uncertainties and threats to health and subsistence. Paying attention to risk and uncertainty not only recognizes billions of people's relationship to food (Jackson and Everts, 2010; Jackson, 2010), but also forces us to recognize how risks themselves are a key

The Sociological Review, 60:S2, pp. 27–46 (2013), DOI: 10.1111/1467-954X.12036

aspect of power. In this article, therefore, I go beyond cultural approaches to food anxiety and the study of famines by arguing that the ability to shield oneself from risks and to increase another's exposure to them is a key source and result of power.

In fact, what counts as risk is itself a power-laden issue. There are many definitions of risk in the social sciences: most recently, there has been a tendency to affiliate it with practices of analysis, governance and management. Unlike Mary Douglas and Aaron Wildavsky (1983), who see risks as omnipresent and argue that talk of risks is always informed by cultural and political concerns with order, Ulrich Beck (1992) and Michael Power (2007) see something qualitatively new happening in the last quarter of the twentieth century. Beck, focusing on environmental and health risks, does not claim a quantitative change – that is, that living is riskier today – but rather argues that new risks are qualitatively different from old risks in that they tend to be more global than personal; they are faced without people's knowledge and consent; they escape laypeople's perception and ability to calculate them; and they tend to originate from the oversupply rather than the undersupply of hygienic technologies.

For Power risk is a broader category than for Beck – it includes economic and legal, in addition to technological, risks – and he claims that from the 1990s developed countries have seen a sudden increase in the organization of uncertainty. Again, Power (2007) argues that it is not so much that we face increased uncertainties, but rather that we have enrolled uncertainties in management techniques to an unprecedented degree. For him, an uncertainty is not a risk until it becomes an object to be managed, hence his concept of the organization of uncertainty.[3]

A further rationale for using the broader term 'uncertainty' is that we have tended to apply double standards to uncertainties faced by poor farmers as opposed to those faced by rich farmers and food processors in the developed countries. The uncertainties peasants face in the developing world primarily threaten their subsistence, while the latter's uncertainties are further removed economic ones related to profit margins, market share, liability or image. Typically, we have mostly applied the concept of risk to the latter group. 'Risk talk' in the context of food producers in the Global North, therefore, has focused on biological, technological and legal factors that pose economic threats, such as food safety, quality and environmental impact – risks to which the food industry's and governments' response has been the implementation of standards and certificate systems to reduce producer liability. The key difference between the two 'worlds', as Power would point out, is that poor farmers have not been able to organize their uncertainties into risk institutions, while food producers and processors in the developed world have.

However, a handful of scholars now want to reclaim the concept of risk to address threats to subsistence – in effect going back to Scott's use of the term, namely to illuminate the role risk-pooling and risk-spreading strategies such as the ones mentioned above play in the moral economy of the peasant. Most of these scholars position themselves in the postsocialist context. Yanitsky (2000) and Rinkevicius (2000), for example, talk about postsocialist Russia and Lithuania as 'double risk' societies because they face both the more traditional economic uncertainties associated with first-stage modernity and the new environmental and health risks Beck associated with reflexive modernity. In a recent article, Mincyte (2011) – also a student of post-socialist Lithuania – has pointed out that Western actors, whether supermarket chains or the organs of the European Union, pay exclusive attention to technological and biological risks in food production. The small dairy farmers she studies, meanwhile, struggle with profound economic uncertainties in part due exactly to the implementation of standards that aim to avoid precisely these technological and biological risks. In her study of fresh fruit and vegetable producers in Africa, Freidberg (2004) also mentions this contrast, while Clapp (1994) demonstrates an even more direct connection between the two types of uncertainties, finding that in Honduran banana cultivation the contracting company's quality standards are tightened during overproduction. In fact, the volume in which his chapter appeared (Little and Watts, 1994) argues that contract farming is itself a risk avoidance strategy. Contract farming effectively avoids the risk of large fixed investments in corporate plantations (in which the corporation owns the land and the farm workers are employees) especially in the case of produce that is more routinely threatened by devastating pests, as is the case with bananas. Furthermore, not having an employment relationship with farm workers (which would be the case if the food processor or retailer owned the land) also avoids the risk of strikes. As the authors demonstrate, however, economic uncertainty is not correspondingly reduced for the farmers in these contract relations. Instead of reserving the concept of risk for managed uncertainties, as Power does, I follow these later scholars who aim to broaden the concept of risk to include threats to subsistence even when such threats have not been subjected to legal or technical control, that is, they have not been formally organized. I do so because the concept of risk carries more power as a conceptual tool and commands more attention than that of uncertainty, and it is this power I wish to harness for designating and calling attention to those risks of the most fundamental kind faced by the poor.

In what follows I describe the production component of the currently dominant global food waste regime by demonstrating the relationship between farm waste and risks. I delineate economic, technological and legal risks separately for the sake of analytic clarity, with the proviso that in reality they feed into each other and are often mutually convertible. In fact, the ability to render risk fungible increases one's capacity to ward off uncertainties, and thus constitutes an aspect of the risk-power nexus outlined above.

The production of food waste

Economic risks: one man's surplus, another man's loss?

Economic risks are a key aspect of the production of waste. In this section I illustrate – with selected examples from existing literature on food aid and US

The Sociological Review, 60:S2, pp. 27–46 (2013), DOI: 10.1111/1467-954X.12036

agricultural policies – how efforts to shield oneself from economic uncertainties generate food waste in different stages of production and consumption. In particular, I explore the key link between hunger and food waste, and in this I rely heavily on Roger Thurow and Scott Kilman's investigative reporting on Ethiopia. I do so to demonstrate the importance of a broader understanding of food waste as not simply 'wasted produce' but also as 'wasted resources' that could have been used for meeting human nutrition needs.

The idea that there can be food waste in a country such as Ethiopia, which has been one of the most food insecure nations in the world, may come as a shock. Yet that is exactly what Thurow and Kilman (2009) found. While Ethiopia may not produce enough to provide for its own population, it could certainly use some of its produce to satisfy hunger. Many farmers, however, cannot sell their produce – such as their sizeable surpluses of wheat, corn, beans and peas – because US food aid, which arrives in the form of US-grown produce, makes local produce superfluous. This makes local farming unprofitable and thus creates disincentives to grow food locally.[4]

While there have been many calls for food aid to include some cash payments (Barrett *et al.*, 2011; Sen, 1995), which then could be used to buy food locally, the agricultural lobby has so far successfully resisted that change. US farmers would suffer from chronic overproduction were it not for the government buying their surpluses and distributing them as aid in the Global South. The government therefore steps in to protect farmers from the risk of insufficient demand. At the same time, in developing countries, neoliberal reforms have forced governments to get out of the economy, leaving their farmers with no corresponding risk-absorbing institutions. While in developed countries wealthier private actors – such as merchants, processors, banks and insurance agencies – can absorb such risks, in former colonies the private sector is simply not robust enough to hedge against uncertainties. In developing countries, before the implementation of structural adjustment reforms, only the government commanded sufficient resources to build roads and warehouses, or to buy from farmers at fixed prices. It was also the state, exclusively, that could shoulder a proportion of the economic burden of modernizing agriculture, and thus make it possible for farmers to invest in seeds and agricultural technologies, and ultimately to achieve food security. Today, that role has been eliminated, and the common policy wisdom is that it makes more sense for these farmers to rely on food aid cheaply produced in the US than to become self-reliant. US food aid, however, has followed political objectives (Gottlieb, 2001) and itself is dependent on the size of surpluses – in sum, it carries another set of uncertainties for recipients.

The same dynamic is facilitated by the domestic farm subsidies provided by the US and the EU, which render their produce cheaper vis-à-vis produce in the Global South, where the World Bank and IMF long ago intervened to eliminate any such support. The WTO, whose role is to eliminate tariff and non-tariff trade barriers in its member countries, has so far proven helpless in forcing the most powerful countries to observe the same free trade principles they advocate as a panacea for developing countries, though some changes have indeed been made in the size and conditionalities of these subsidies. In the context of this unequal distribution of economic risks, Ethiopian farmers' produce remains unharvested in the fields or rotting in merchants' warehouses.[5]

Thurow and Kilman (2009) report the lament of some Ethiopian farmers and merchants that, under these conditions, farmers simply do not want to go back to farming: they no longer want to take the risks and are content with feeding their families on food aid. Clearly, as the uneven playing field increased the risk level of their farming – eventually contributing significantly to the famine of 2003 – many now err on the side of caution, which means idle fields and idle labour power, creating a downward spiral in economic and civic vitality.

However, economic risk avoidance also creates farm waste in the most developed countries. Bloom (2011: 109) describes the phenomenon of 'walk-by' in the US, in which farmers commonly grow too much to hedge against natural eventualities, and then do not bother harvesting a sizeable portion of the produce if the market outlook is unfavourable. Farmers told Bloom that selling only half of what they produce is the normal state of affairs. The cumulative outcome is that the better the harvest is, the more farm waste there will be. That is, we live in a food waste regime in which there is not only a mechanism for bad weather and pests to result in food waste, but also a mechanism in which good natural conditions lead to waste as well.

Technological risks

Stuart (2009) and Bloom (2011) have done much research to demonstrate the relationship between the proliferation of quality and safety standards and the amount of farm waste in the Global North.[6] Geographer Susanne Freidberg (2004) has also demonstrated the effect of these standards on the livelihood of French bean growers in Africa. She shows how aesthetic standards – many of which are rooted in national imagined culinary traditions[7] – have been imposed on contract farmers alongside safety standards, but with all the associated costs borne by the growers rather than the retailers. From a different context, Clapp (1994) argues that the enforcement of quality standards is stricter when supply exceeds demand, effectively cutting the risks of observing contractual obligations for the exporter at the expense of the grower, who then does not get paid. Food left on the farm unharvested, or food abandoned in warehouses due to having failed such aesthetic tests has not only caused economic losses but has also wasted the energy, water,[8] soil and human labour that could have been harnessed to produce food for subsistence. That is, waste circulates throughout the economy and, in material terms, what economists call 'opportunity costs'[9] mean that farm waste will reduce the amount of food available for subsistence.

Many of these standards are cosmetic, such as the European Union's rules concerning the length and curvature of bananas and other shape and blemish-free requirements for fruits and vegetables. Regulation No. 2257/95, for example, stipulates that bananas sold in the EU must be 'free of abnormal curvature' and at least 14 cm long. As a result of the loosening of these regulations for 26 products in 2008, formerly 'abnormal' bananas, carrots with 'limbs and noses' as well as 'knobbly' bell peppers (capsicums) are now legal, and substandard produce can now be more easily sold for processing or in raw form in grocery stores on the condition that it is labelled as such. However, cosmetic standards for table fruits, such as apples, citrus fruits, kiwi fruit, lettuces, peaches, nectarines, pears, strawberries, grapes and tomatoes, remain on the books.[10]

While at least one of these standards was introduced to maintain favourable export conditions for former colonies of current EU member states, the vast majority of them – whether demanded by the EU or by corporations – aim to protect retailers (rather than primary producers of the former colonies) from risks associated with perishability and hygiene. According to an increasing number of reports (Brown, 2005; Brown and Sander, 2007; Pimbert *et al.*, 2001; Government Office for Science, 2011; Agriculture and Natural Resources Team of the UK Department for International Development 2004), small farmers cannot participate in designing these standards. Typically, they have few resources with which to get certified and afford monitoring, let alone afford equipment needed for compliance. This exacerbates already existing tendencies towards land concentration, because it is easier for bigger farms to get into – and stay within – supply chains operated by large Northern retailers in the Global North. Land concentration has two effects: first, it jeopardizes poor peasants' subsistence, and second, it may lengthen commodity chains, which in turn tends to increase food waste. This once again demonstrates the relationship between waste and value chains as mediated by the uneven distribution of risks.

The current structure, in which all risks from outgrades and demand fluctuations are borne by the producer rather than shared by the retailer, introduces a further mechanism for increasing food waste. As Bloom (2011) and Stuart (2009) explain, retailers currently have no incentive to plan their orders, because any produce remaining on their shelves will be returned unpaid to the producer. However, should a supplier fail to deliver the amount expected, they will face expulsion from the pool of suppliers (Stuart, 2009).[11] In such circumstances, producers will produce the maximum amount, and would rather remain unpaid and deal with the waste than reduce their output. That is, these producers also choose the option Scott (1976) describes in *The Moral Economy of the Peasant*, namely the one that provides greater long-term security rather than the one that brings higher returns in the shorter run.

Legal and political risks

Legal risks primarily have to do with liabilities resulting from biological and technological hazards. As mentioned above, therefore, different types of risks should be seen as related to – or even convertible into – each other. Stuart (2009) and Bloom (2011), for example, have each analysed how the consumer discards food when he or she is unsure of its expiry date. Such information is conveyed on packaging with different wordings, such as 'best by', 'use by', 'best before', or 'sell by', while some products have only dates (Bloom, 2011: 162). Scholars studying food risks have found that shopkeepers and consumers tend to err on the side of caution, especially in the wake of a series of food safety scandals (Jackson, 2010). The amount of still edible food discarded for such reasons is now such that a sizeable population of poor people and, freegans, can cover their nutritional needs by 'dumpster diving' – though, of course, they still risk getting sick from eating something genuinely out of date (Coyne, 2009; Schantz, 2005). Scholars of food safety and food waste have all called for clearer labelling, but such a move will not come easily, since this cacophony of dates (Bloom, 2011, calls them 'confuse-by dates') is also a potent tool to protect food processors and retailers from possible liability.

In closing this section, I want to mention one example of political risks. The economic and technological risks discussed previously also have strong implications for political uncertainties. One is farm subsidies by the EU and the US. To be sure, the reason mentioned for the implementation of these subsidies in the first place – namely, to ensure a secure economic environment for an otherwise risky sector – is the most immediate cause, but it does not explain the current reluctance to reduce or to eliminate such support. Once the subsidies are in place for a long period of time, as they have been in the EU and in the US, a set of political interests in maintaining them develops. Though the segment of the population that one can call farmers is exceedingly small in both places (5 per cent and 2 per cent, respectively), the political leverage of the agricultural lobbies is enormous. Once we also take into consideration that the price of land is strongly determined by the income one can expect to make from it – whether that income is from government subsidies or from the sale of produce grown on it – one can start appreciating what the economic consequences for real estate values of and mortgages on farmland would be should these subsidies be eliminated. No wonder that no politician is willing to take that risk.

Avoiding political risks by maintaining the policy status quo also motivates other actors, such as food aid NGOs. NGOs' survival and legitimacy depend to a great extent on their ability to bring resources to the areas they serve. As Thurow and Kilman (2009) describe, US-based food aid organizations in particular have a greater interest in delivering and distributing US-grown grain than in collecting cash with which to buy up local food surpluses first. This is because aid in cash will always be substantially less than the value of in-kind food aid whose disbursement is beneficial for the overproducing US growers, as I explained above.[12]

In sum, therefore, we can detect causes of food waste at multiple scales, in a similar fashion to Blaikie's (1985) 'Chinese boxes' explanation of soil erosion. His model looks at social interests in soil erosion as well as in soil conservation on a hierarchical spatial level. The individual, the household, the village or local community, the local bureaucracy, the government and international agencies all have particular stakes in soil erosion, all of which have to be explored both for analysis and policy design. I diverge from his analysis in that, for him, the local, national and global are still arranged in a nesting hierarchy – which may indeed have been an apt representation of social relations through the 1980s. In contrast, my analysis of the production of food waste sheds light on how these scales are jumbled up (Brenner, 1999; Sassen, 2000), and how there is tremendous strategic effort involved in pushing issues to one scale or another – projects that Tsing has called 'scale-making' (2000). We can therefore no longer assume that a particular cause of food waste naturally arises at a particular scale, nor that causes cascade down from the global to the local level via the national. Rather, the national (for example, the Ethiopian national scale) can drop out of the picture altogether, and the local concerns of a US bean grower will directly affect the nature of the global context that determines whether the surplus of a grain merchant in Nazareth, Ethiopia, will be sold or will go to waste. The unequal ability of actors to scale up and thereby organize their risks cannot be captured with either the Chinese boxes model or the linear supply, value or commodity chain models (see below). The organization of uncertainty by up- or downscaling is a key aspect of the transnational nature of our current food waste regime.

Another key difference between my waste regime concept and Blaikie's model is that my approach creates analytical room for demonstrating how the construction of the food waste problem contributes to the production of the problem itself. To demonstrate, I now turn to the representation of food waste, the second element of food waste regimes.

The representation of food waste

Most articles on a social problem will, rightly, start with a description of its current constructions in policy and scholarship. My goal in this article, however, is to demonstrate the merits of the concept of food waste regimes, and for that reason it is imperative to see the most accepted constructions of food waste as part and parcel of the dominant global food waste regime. For this reason, I am tackling such constructions not through the medium of a literature review but as part of my description of the global food waste regime itself. Currently, dominant representations of food waste primarily reflect the interest in avoiding the various types of risks described in the previous section. I am not advancing a Marxian base-superstructure model, however, in which the economic interests 'cause' certain ideologies or views of a social problem. Rather, I want to demonstrate how current thinking on food waste does not merely reflect risk avoidance strategies, but also how that thinking affects how we actually produce food waste.

But before we begin to explore these approaches it is important to admit that, just as with all wastes, food waste statistics are unreliable. Rather than seeing this lack of data as evidence of simple ignorance, we must question which of the above-described strategies to avoid risks leads to such an inability to calculate food waste. While the space of this article prevents a detailed explanation, suffice it to say that in a policy-making environment that needs hard scientific evidence and straightforward cause-effect relationships, leaving data unreliable or raising doubts about calculations is a key tool in delaying regulation, as we have seen in the example of debates on global climate change in the US. Indicative of both this state of affairs and the importance of managing scientific uncertainty – in addition to the other uncertainties detailed above – is the effort of a group of DEFRA-affiliated researchers mobilizing uncertainty analysis for estimating food waste (Langley *et al.*, 2009).[13]

In policies as well as in common Western parlance, waste is usually identified with one or the other side of the key dichotomies listed above (efficient/inefficient; useful/useless; order/disorder; clean/dirty; alive/dead; fertile/sterile).[14] The dominant view – that is, the policy-makers' and industry representatives' perspective – understands food waste in developing countries as arising out of the inefficiency of agricultural, storage and transportation technologies (Gustavsson *et al.*, 2011; Nellemann *et al.*, 2009; Hodges *et al.*, 2011; World Resources Institute 1998–1999). In contrast, in the Global North, food waste is primarily talked about in terms of uselessness and dirtiness or contamination – to be more precise, as resulting from consumers letting food go bad, their anxiety about eating 'old' food or their lack of knowledge in reusing leftovers.[15] Once the problem is defined as such, these actors call for more 'green revolution', including GMOs, in the case of developing countries, and for nanotechnology in packaging, clearer expiry date labelling or teaching consumers how to use leftovers in the Global North.[16] In both cases, exclusively technological expertise seems to provide the most important foundation for policy-making. While technological innovations are certainly not superfluous (as decades of research in environmental sociology and political ecology shows), they must be complemented by social analysis, and should not be implemented at the expense of social equalities and fairness. If we approach waste as arising from social relations, including those that traverse multiple scales, then other, more sociological definitions of waste will become possible – definitions which are more likely to foment justice-oriented policies.

Approaching waste as a function of social relations allows us to ask questions such as: what if the reason behind so much pre-consumption loss in the Global South is primarily because there is too much post-consumer waste in developed countries? What if the two are connected or have the same cause – a particular set of social relations leading to particular practices in both? Certainly, some recently published frameworks for the analysis of food waste already hint at the relational and multi-scalar nature of the problem. It has become increasingly common, for example, to represent the generation of food waste with models analogous to value or supply chains. These models delineate a series of stages – usually of production, distribution and consumption – and attribute different causes of food waste to each stage.[17]

For example, the UK Government Office for Science report (2011: 5) proposes a simple and relatively short chain distinguishing stages identified as: 'growers; storage and distribution; manufacturing and retail; and post-consumer', and attributes the following causes of food waste: 'in-field or harvesting losses, spillage, spoilage, out-grades; post-harvest losses, in-storage spillage, spoilage, losses in distribution; loss in process, spillage, spoilage, contamination, off-spec production; by-products, losses in retail/market; and losses at consumer stage; household, hospitality sector, institutional canteens'. For their part, policy experts Julian Parfitt, Mark Barthel and Sarah MacNaughton (2010) advance a longer spectrum they call the food supply chain (FCS). Their causes are more diversified and detailed than the previous report, which tends to emphasize spillage and spoilage:

1. Harvesting
2. Threshing
3. Drying
4. Storage
5. Primary processing[18]
6. Secondary processing[19]
7. Product evaluation
8. Packaging
9. Marketing and distribution
10. Post-consumer
11. End of life.

Linear models such as these nuance the picture common in agro-industry's representations of food waste: a picture which tends to reduce all food waste to a problem of inefficiency and technological inadequacy. Linear models can take into consideration food waste arising from outgrades or from market uncertainties, and even point to structural causes of food waste such as the length of FSCs themselves (Parfitt *et al.*, 2010). As such they can be helpful tools for policy. However, they suffer from two shortcomings. First, the danger of linear models is their tendency to assume that the causes of food waste reside within the stages in which they appear. While Parfitt *et al.* (2010), for example, correctly point to food waste arising on the farm due to standards set at another stage of the FSC, in some stages (such as their post-consumption stage), all the causes cited are related to consumers ignoring labelling or packaging size – factors that of course originate well outside the household. A second problem is that linear models are too rigid to represent the dynamics of waste circulation throughout the chain due to their assumption that the waste chain is identical to, and a derivative of, the value chain. Where in this linear model, for example, would one place the Keralan peasant's crops that died on the vine due to Coca-Cola's depletion of ground water? What about edible fish and birds decimated by pesticides or fertilizers? How about leftovers composted rather than fed to pigs due to the new hygienic regulation of animal feed (Law and Mol, 2009; Stuart, 2009;

Alexander *et al.*, 2013)? Is it even acceptable in our current food waste regime to see the use of arable lands for growing animal feed or fuel rather than edible plants and crops itself as food waste?

Questions such as these reveal the blind spots inherent in the current global food waste regime and compel us to see the definition of the food waste problem as part of the problem itself. To get out of this vicious cycle we need to do two things in our analysis: first, stop conflating the location with the cause of waste; and, secondly, make visible how resource waste and food waste are interconnected. If we want to find places for intervention, those relations that cross not only geographical and political boundaries but also scales must be analysed. The problem for policy-making, however, is that it is exactly these types of complex and multi-scalar forms of food waste that are the hardest to quantify and therefore the hardest to eliminate.

There has been, as a result, a tendency to concentrate on accidental farm waste, for instance crop loss due to weather and pests (Gustavsson *et al.*, 2011; Nellemann *et al.*, 2009; Hodges *et al.*, 2011; World Resources Institute, 1998–1999). This corresponds to what Jesse Ribot (2010) calls the hazard model of vulnerability, which sees losses as coming from hazards, rather than from – as the social constructionist paradigm holds – the structural context that makes one vulnerable to hazards in the first place. The differential policy implications are significant. If food loss is caused by non-human factors – weather or pests – the solution is greater mastery over nature: that is, technological innovation. However, if food loss is caused by social arrangements, the solution resides in new institutions and the reorganising of structures leading to systemic loss. My general view is that both accidental/natural and systemic/social causes of food waste must be attended to.[20] In this article, however, I have tended to concentrate on the latter primarily because this has received far less attention in the scholarship and in policy circles. Furthermore, a focus on systemicity also sheds light on how social inequalities are embedded in the generation of food waste, a perspective that may prevent us from wanting to solve food and farm waste issues at the expense of social inequalities. Reversing Freidberg's beautiful argument that 'the question of where food should come from [supplied locally or globally] is also a question about whose food provisioning livelihoods we should care about' (2004: 31), we could say that the question of which aspect of food waste we should focus on also has implications for whose ability to avoid risks we prioritize.

The literature on food waste has tended to view such inequalities in terms of a seemingly natural difference between developed and developing countries, arguing that food waste in the former arises primarily at the post-consumer stage, while in the latter it happens between the harvest and consumer phases of the value chain.[21] In fact, so distinct and isolated do authors and policy makers want the two instances to seem that they even invoke different names: post-consumer waste is called 'food waste', while post-harvest but pre-consumption waste is called 'food loss'.[22] The use of the term 'loss' for pre-consumption food waste suggests accidental causes, thus reaffirming the hazard paradigm mentioned above.

The politics of waste: a conclusion

In conclusion, let me focus on the last component of food waste regimes, asking how and which aspects of food waste issues are politicized, what is taboo, and what non-waste goals the resulting political instruments serve. Without aiming at a comprehensive analysis of the currently dominant global food waste regime from the perspective of the politics of waste, I simply want to indicate a few characteristics of the regime, building on the examples I have used above.

As I have shown, public discourse on food waste in the developed countries concentrates on consumer responsibility and individual attitudes and values. Structural causes or causes that are outside the household's control – such as portion size, marketing campaigns (such as two-for-one deals), labelling, the length of supply chains, the politics of food prices, all of which have led to a 'race to the bottom' and ever harsher competition among food producers – have not received much attention until lately (Bloom, 2011; Stuart, 2009; Prendergast *et al.*, 2005). Current efforts towards technological solutions, such as those that focus on extending the life of food or clarifying how fresh a product is, promised by the application of nanotechnology in packaging materials, reflect this view. Needless to say, such a technology will also reduce producers' and retailers' technological and biological risks and thus legal liabilities. Other solutions include consumer education, now part and parcel of the overall European agenda of developing consumer citizens. The objective of consumer citizenship is not to extend individual rights or the classical political influence of citizens through voting or social activism to demand greater control over production technologies or over pricing mechanisms, but rather to enhance consumers' ability to choose among different products. While some are optimistic about the ability of consumer choice to eventually eliminate politically or environmentally harmful products, structural constraints – such as purchasing power and access to, and legibility of information on, products – make such an outcome more the exception than the rule. Such solutions, therefore, are more likely to serve other purposes than the reduction or elimination of food waste.

As outlined above, in the developing world, public discourse focuses on accidental losses due to natural causes, and policy makers therefore tend to emphasize technological improvements in production, storage and distribution. Such proposals serve the interest of suppliers of agricultural technologies, machinery, pesticides and hybrid or genetically modified seeds, most of which are located in the Global North. At the same time, structural explanations have remained a taboo – for example, the roles retail power and food aid play in generating food waste have been ignored. Overall, we have seen that political mobilization occurs around those constructions of the food waste problem that preserve the ability of the most powerful actors to protect themselves from economic, technological, legal and political risks.

If we want to reduce food waste substantially we must also mitigate the risks associated with farming for the poor. We must therefore devise new institutions that can pool risks rather than distribute them unequally. Obviously, better technology alone cannot remedy this situation. The approach I have advanced here, the view of food waste through the lens of the waste regime concept, has demonstrated the need for a more nuanced and more sociological analysis. First, I have shown how food waste results not merely from technological shortfalls and inefficiencies, but rather from risk avoidance strategies that, in turn, impact the production, representation and the politics of waste – the three elements of waste regimes. Second, the global food waste regime concept discloses the ways in which action (economic, technological, cultural-ideological) at one scale affects waste at another scale and the ways in which waste at one scale may lead to a particular waste outcome at another scale. Together this analysis has suggested that policies aimed at reducing food waste should attend to all of these realms – production, representation and politics – at the local, national and global scales.

Acknowledgements

I thank Rachel Schurman, Susanne Freidberg, the editors of this volume and anonymous reviewers for their constructive suggestions. I am grateful to Rebecca Gresh for assisting me with research on this project, which ESRC-SSRC and the University of Illinois have supported financially.

Notes

1 While not a pretty term, by social systemacity sociologists mean that the phenomenon under study is the result of identifiable patterns of social relationships, rather than, let us say, the result of nature or accidents. In this case, while nature and accidental factors can play a role in the production and treatment of food waste, their effects are mediated by society. This is not to deny actor network theory or environmental history approaches, however, which argue that society itself is vulnerable to nature and the seemingly chance confluence of objects. In fact, generally I take the position of hybridity and co-production (Cronon, 1991; Latour, 1993, 2005; Mitchell, 2002; Pickering, 1995) and see my discussion of this in the section on the representation of food waste.

2 In his terminology, resource regimes are social institutions that determine what natural resources are considered valuable by society, lay down the principles of valuation, and resolve the resulting value-conflicts. Their core is a structure of rights and rules which imply a certain distribution of advantages and disadvantages. These regimes are, consequently, always subject to pressures for reinterpretation and change. Therefore, according to Young, they possess the general qualities of social institutions, such as deviance, formal and informal channels and decisions, and unintended consequences of operation.

3 US environmental sociologist Michael Bell (1998) also defines risk this way.

4 For another critical view of aid and post-harvest losses in the developing world, see Reusse (2002).

5 The relationship between agricultural protectionism and free trade is more historically complex than I am able to articulate in the space of this article: interested scholars should look at Nützenadel's (2008) concept of the Green Internationale.

6 While not scholars, their stories and data are useful in constructing an analytical framework that discloses the relationship between risk and waste: many academics and policy-makers refer to their work.

7 She focuses on the thinness and the cut of French beans for UK versus French markets.

8 On the relationship between wasted water and wasted food see Lundqvist *et al.* (2008).

9 Opportunity costs are the costs from not taking an alternative path of investment or of forgoing an alternative use of available resources.

10 The US is not free from such standards either (Bloom, 2011).

11 While retailers may have different arrangements, due to the cut-throat competition in the industry only a state-enforced regulation can prevent the unequal distribution of economic risks. I only know of one country where such product take-back clauses are currently outlawed: the Czech Republic (Government Office for Science 2011).

12 Recently, some of this aid has been converted into cash payments which have delivered the benefits I outline above. Barrett *et al.* (2011) and Sen (1995) describe similar, earlier UNICEF experiments in Ethiopian relief camps.

13 Uncertainty analysis includes different statistical tools to estimate the impact of certain unknown factors, and was pioneered in computer simulation in the aerospace industry.

14 There is now also a robust debate about whether over-nutrition should also be included in our definitions of food waste (Blair and Sobal, 2006; Stuart, 2009; Parfitt *et al.*, 2010; Government Office for Science, 2011). Unfortunately, including these definitional struggles in this article is not possible for reasons of space.

15 In the UK the government now sponsors workshops that teach people how to cook with leftovers as part of its 'Love food, hate waste' campaign: http://england.lovefoodhatewaste.com/content/uk-media-resources

16 A paradigmatic example is recent efforts on the part of the European Union Parliament to implement an anti-food-waste policy, as part of which it declared 2014 the 'European year against food waste': http://www.europarl.europa.eu/news/en/pressroom/content/20120118IPR 35648/html/Parliament-calls-for-urgent-measures-to-halve-food-wastage-in-the-EU

17 Studies applying commodity chain models include Mena *et al.* (2011). For a critical analysis of the use of commodity chains see Jackson *et al.* (2006) and Faße *et al.* (2009).

18 Eg cleaning, de-hulling, pounding, grinding, soaking, winnowing, milling.

19 Eg mixing, cooking, frying, moulding, cutting, extrusion.

20 Mike Davis (2001) provides a valuable model for demonstrating the dynamic between climatological or natural and social causes of famine in his book on nineteenth-century waves of famine.

21 This developed-developing country dichotomy is certainly simplistic, and some studies now advance a more nuanced classification of nation states (Parfitt *et al.*, 2010; Government Office for Science, 2011).

22 See Gustavsson *et al.* (2011) and Nellemann *et al.* (2009). As should be clear by now, in this article I have not only followed Parfitt *et al.* (2010) in calling both products 'food waste', but also demonstrated that the two are interconnected.

References

Agriculture and Natural Resources Team of the UK Department for International Development, (2004), *Concentration in Food Supply and Retail Chains*, available at: http://dfid-agriculture-consultation.nri.org/summaries/wp13.pdf (accessed 14 December 2011).

Alexander, C., Gregson, N. and Gille, Z., (2013), 'Food, leftovers and waste', in A. Murcott, W. Belasco and P. (eds), *The Handbook of Food Research*, London: Bloomsbury.

Barrett, C. B., Lentz, E. C., Mathys, C., Upton, J. B. and Villa, K. M., (2011), 'Misconceptions about food assistance', Cornell University Policy Brief No. 2, June 2011, Global Public Policy Institute.

Bataille, G., (1988), *The Accursed Share: An Essay on General Economy*, New York: Zone Books.

Beck, U., (1992), *Risk Society: Towards a New Modernity*, London: Sage.

Bell, M., (1998), *An Invitation to Environmental Sociology*, Thousand Oaks, CA: Pine Forge Press.

Blaikie, P., (1985), *The Political Economy of Soil Erosion in Developing Countries*, London and New York: Longman.

Blair, D. and Sobal, J., (2006), 'Luxus consumption: wasting food resources through overeating', *Agriculture and Human Values*, 23 (1): 63–74.

Bloom, J., (2011), *American Wasteland: How America Throws Away Nearly Half of Its Food (and What We Can Do About It)*, Cambridge, MA: De Capo Press.

Brenner, N., (1999), 'Beyond state-centrism? Space, territoriality, and geographical scale in globalization studies', *Theory and Society*, 28 (1): 39–78.

Brown, O., (2005), *Supermarket Buying Power, Global Commodity Chains and Smallholder Farmers in the Developing World*, Human Development Report Office Occasional Paper 2005/4, New York: UN Development Programme, available at: http://hdr.undp.org/en/reports/global/hdr2005/papers/HDR2005_Brown_Oli_41.pdf (accessed 14 December 2011).

Brown, O. and Sander, C., (2007), *Supermarket Buying Power: Global Supply Chains and Smallholder Farmers*, Winnipeg, Canada: International Institute for Sustainable Development, available at: http://www.iisd.org/publications/pub.aspx?pno=851 (accessed 14 December 2011).

Clapp, R., (1994), 'The moral economy of the contract', in P. Little and M. Watts (1994), *Living under Contract: Contract Farming and Agrarian Transformation in Sub-Saharan Africa*, 78–97, Madison: University of Wisconsin Press.

Coyne, M., (2009), 'From production to destruction to recovery: freeganism's redefinition of food value and circulation', *Iowa Journal of Cultural Studies*, 10/11, available at: http://www.uiowa.edu/~ijcs/waste/coyne.htm (accessed 1 August 2011).

Cronon, W., (1991), *Nature's Metropolis: Chicago and the Great West*, New York: W. W. Norton.

Davis, M., (2001), *Late Victorian Holocausts: El Niño Famines and the Making of the Third World*, New York: Norton.

Douglas, M. and Wildavsky, A., (1983), *Risk and Culture: An Essay on the Selection of Technological and Environmental Dangers*, Berkeley: University of California Press.

Faße A., Grote, U. and Winter, E., (2009), 'Value chain analysis: methodologies in the context of environment and trade research', Discussion Paper No. 429, Wirtschaftswissenschaftliche Fakultät, Hannover, Germany, available at: http://www.wiwi.uni-hannover.de/Forschung/Diskussionspapiere/dp-429.pdf (accessed 14 December 2011).

Freidberg, S., (2004), *French Beans and Food Scares: Culture and Commerce in an Anxious Age*, New York: Oxford University Press.

Friedmann, H. and McMichael, P., (1987). 'Agriculture and the state system: the rise and fall of national agricultures, 1870 to the present', *Sociologia Ruralis*, 29 (2): 93–117.

Gille, Z., (2007), *From the Cult of Waste to the Trash Heap of History: The Politics of Waste in Socialist and Postsocialist Hungary*, Bloomington: Indiana University Press.

Gille, Z., (2010), 'Reassembling the macrosocial: modes of production, actor networks and waste regimes', *Environment and Planning A*, 42: 1049–1064.

Gottlieb, R., (2001), *Environmentalism Unbound: Exploring New Pathways for Change*, Cambridge, MA: MIT Press.

Government Office for Science, (2011), *Expert Forum on the Reduction of Food Waste: 'How Can Waste Reduction Help to Healthily and Sustainably Feed a Future Global Population of Nine Billion People?'* Workshop Report, organized by the UK Science and Innovation Network in collaboration with Foresight, 23–24 February 2010, The Rubens Hotel, London, available at: http://www.bis.gov.uk/assets/bispartners/foresight/docs/food-and-farming/workshops/11-608-w4-expert-forum-reduction-of-food-waste (accessed 14 December 2011).

Gregson, N., (2007), *Living with Things: Ridding, Accommodation, Dwelling*. Wantage: Sean Kingston Publishing.

Gresh, R., (2011), 'Speculative practices and the value of food', paper presented at the Annual Transnational Sociology Workshop 'Credits, Mortgages, and Derivatives: Understanding the Global Financial Crisis', Urbana-Champaign, 11–12 November 2011.

Gustavsson, J., Cederberg, C., Sonesson, U., van Otterdijk, R. and Meybeck, A., (2011), *Global Food Losses and Food Waste: Extent, Causes, and Prevention*, Rome: United Nations Food and Agriculture Organization.

Hetherington, K., (2004), 'Secondhandedness: consumption, disposal, and absent presence', *Environment and Planning D: Society and Space*, 22 (1): 157–173.

Hodges, R. J., Buzby, J. C. and Bennett, B., (2011), 'Foresight project on global food and farming futures: postharvest losses and waste in developed and less developed countries: opportunities to improve resource use', *Journal of Agricultural Science*, 149: 37–45.

Jackson, P., (2010), 'Food stories: consumption in an age of anxiety', *Cultural Geographies*, 17 (2): 147–165.

Jackson, P. and Everts, J., (2010), 'Anxiety as social practice', *Environment and Planning A*, 42: 2791–2806.

Jackson, P., Ward, N. and Russell, P., (2006), 'Mobilising the commodity chain concept in the politics of food and farming', *Journal of Rural Studies*, 22 (2): 129–141.

Langley, J., Yoxall, A., Manson, G., Lewis, W., Waterhouse, A., Thelwall, D., Thelwall, S., Parry, A. and Leech, B., (2009), 'The use of uncertainty analysis as a food waste estimation tool', *Waste Management and Research*, 27 (3): 199.

Latour, B., (1993), *The Pasteurization of France*, Cambridge, MA: Harvard University Press.

Latour, B., (2005), *Reassembling the Social: An Introduction to Actor-Network-Theory*, Oxford: Oxford University Press.

Law, J. and Mol, A., (2009), 'Globalisation in practice: on the politics of boiling pigswill', version of 9th April 2009, available at: http://www.heterogeneities.net/publications/LawMol2006 GlobalisationinPractice.pdf, (accessed 13 October 2011).

Little, P. and Watts, M., (1994), *Living under Contract: Contract Farming and Agrarian Transformation in Sub-Saharan Africa*, Madison: University of Wisconsin Press.

Lundqvist, J., de Fraiture, C. and Molden, D., (2008), 'Saving water: from field to fork – curbing losses and wastage in the food chain', SIWI Policy Brief, available at: http://www.siwi.org/documents/Resources/Policy_Briefs/PB_From_Filed_to_Fork_2008.pdf (accessed 25 March 2013).

McMichael, P., (2009). 'A food regime genealogy', *Journal of Peasant Studies*, 36 (1): 139–169.

Mena, C., Adenso-Diaz, B. and Yurt, O., (2011), 'The causes of food waste in the supplier–retailer interface: evidences from the UK and Spain', *Resources, Conservation and Recycling*, 55 (6): 648–658.

Mincyte, D., (2011), 'The politics of subsistence and sustainability in the New Europe', *Sociologia Ruralis*, 51 (2): 101–118.

Mitchell, T., (2002), *Rule of Experts: Egypt, Techno-Politics, Modernity*, Berkeley: University of California Press.

Morgan, K., Marsden, T. and Murdoch, J., (2006), *Worlds of Food: Place, Power, and Provenance in the Food Chain*, Oxford and New York: Oxford University Press.

Nellemann, C., MacDevette, M., Manders, T., Eickhout, B., Svihus, B., Prins, A. G., Kaltenborn, B. P. (eds), (2009), 'The environmental food crisis – the environment's role in averting future food crises', *a UNEP rapid response assessment*, United Nations Environment Programme, GRID-Arendal, www.grida.no. Printed by Birkeland Trykkeri AS, Norway.

Nützenadel, A., (2008), 'A Green International? Food markets and transnational politics *c.* 1850–1914', in A. Nützenadel and F. Trentmann (eds), *Food and Globalization: Consumption, Markets and Politics in the Modern World*, 153–172, Oxford: Berg.

O'Brien, M., (2008), *A Crisis of Waste? Understanding the Rubbish Society*, New York: Routledge.

Parfitt, J., Barthel, M. and MacNaughton S., (2010), 'Food waste within food supply chains: quantification and potential for change to 2050', *Philosophical Transactions of the Royal Society B: Biological Sciences*, 365 (1554): 3065–3081.

45

Pickering, A., (1995), *The Mangle of Practice: Time, Agency, and Science*, Chicago: University of Chicago Press.

Pimbert, M., Thompson, J. and Vorley, W., with Fox, T., Kanji, N. and Tacoli, C., (2001), *Global Restructuring, Agri-Food Systems and Livelihood*, Gatekeeper Series No. 100, London: International Institute for Environment and Development.

Polanyi, K., (1944), *The Great Transformation: The Political Economy and the Origins of Our Time*, Beacon Hill, MA: Beacon Hill Press.

Power, M., (2007), *Organized Uncertainty: Designing a World of Risk Management*, Oxford: Oxford University Press.

Prendergast, G., Shi, Y. and Cheung, K., (2005), 'Behavioural response to sales promotion tools', *International Journal of Advertising*, 24 (4): 467–486.

Reusse, E., (2002), *The Ills of Aid: An Analysis of Third World Development Policies*, Chicago: University of Chicago Press.

Ribot, J., (2010), 'Vulnerability does not just fall from the sky: toward multi-scale pro-poor climate policy', in R. Mearns and A. Norton (eds), *Social Dimensions of Climate Change: Equity and Vulnerability in a Warming World*, Washington, DC: The World Bank.

Rinkevicius, L., (2000), 'Public risk perceptions in a "double-risk" society: the case of the Ignalina Nuclear Power Plant in Lithuania', *Innovation: The European Journal of Social Sciences*, 13 (3): 279–289.

Sassen, S., (2000), 'Spatialities and temporalities of the global: elements for a theorization', *Public Culture*, 12 (1): 215–232.

Schantz, J., (2005), 'One person's garbage . . . another person's treasure: dumpster diving, freeganism, and anarchy', *Verb*, 3 (1): 9–19, available at: http://verb.lib.lehigh.edu/index.php/verb/article/viewArticle/19/18 (accessed 14 December 2011).

Scott, J., (1976), *The Moral Economy of the Peasant*, New Haven: Yale University Press.

Sen, A., (1995), 'Food, economics, and entitlements', in J. Dreze, A. Sen and A. Hussein (eds), *The Political Economy of Hunger*, 50–68, Oxford: Clarendon Press.

Stuart, T., (2009), *Waste: Uncovering the Global Food Scandal*, New York: W. W. Norton.

Thurow, R. and Kilman, S., (2009), *Enough: Why the World's Poorest Starve in an Age of Plenty*, New York: Public Affairs.

Tsing, A., (2000), 'The Global Situation', *Cultural Anthropology*, 15 (3): 327–360.

World Resources Institute, (1998–1999), 'Disappearing food: how big are post harvest losses?' available at: http://www.wri.org/publication/content/8386 (accessed 20 July 2012).

Yanitsky, O., (2000), 'Sustainability and risk: the case of Russia', *Innovation: The European Journal of Social Sciences*, 13 (3): 265–277.

Young, O., (1982), *Resource Regimes: Natural Resources and Social Institutions*, Berkeley: University of California Press.

The Sociological Review, 60:S2, pp. 27–46 (2013), DOI: 10.1111/1467-954X.12036

'Waste? You mean by-products!' From bio-waste management to agro-ecology in Italian winemaking and beyond

Anna Krzywoszynska

Abstract: This paper engages in a critique of Italian and EU agricultural bio-waste policy, taking a relational approach to understanding the role of these materials in socio-material networks of production. Specifically, I consider how the challenges posed by excess materials of agricultural production fit into larger concerns about rural sustainability, both social and environmental. Drawing on a number of case studies from the Italian winemaking industry, I demonstrate the legislative creation of waste from the by-products of winemaking such as grape marc and vine wood. By physically removing bio-wastes from the socio-material context of their production, the current legislation privileges capital and technologically intensive methods for the management of bio-wastes. This process results in environmental contradictions and an unequal distribution of economic and societal benefits from the utilization of these materials. What is needed, I argue, is the incorporation of excess materials into thinking about local agro-ecologies as environmentally, economically and culturally sustainable.

Keywords: food waste, bio-waste, winemaking, agro-ecology, risk

Relational materiality of bio-wastes

In recent years, the social sciences have started making important inroads into the issues posed by food waste. However, attention has been mainly directed to post-consumption food wastes (Evans, 2011, 2012; Quested *et al.*, 2011). Macro food wastes, and especially bio-wastes – resulting from the production rather than the consumption of food-stuffs – remain under-explored.[1,2] In this article I demonstrate that the political, regulatory and economic pathways of those excess materials are important when thinking about risk, and ecological and economic sustainability in the context of agro-food production.

In this article I examine the socio-material pathways of bio-wastes in the Italian winemaking industry, demonstrating the importance of social and material relations to the valuation of these materials. The pathways of the excess materials of winemaking are strongly informed by legislation on the one

The Sociological Review, 60:S2, pp. 47–65 (2013), DOI: 10.1111/1467-954X.12037

hand, and by the increasingly institutionalized preference of capital markets for financially profitable methods of bio-waste revalorization on the other. In accordance with Gille (2010), I suggest that the labelling of materials as wastes is not necessarily linked with the politics of value, or indeed with environmental concerns. What waste legislation affords is a uniquely powerful regulatory intervention into the spaces of agro-food production as sites of risk, be it environmental or economic. This kind of waste legislation works by severing the socio-material connections linking excess materials with their local context, often by physically lifting these materials from the hands of their producers. With regard to winemaking bio-wastes in Italy, the current legislation privileges techno-scientific and capital-intensive methods of waste revalorization to the detriment of local and potentially less environmentally and socially harmful solutions. The legislation results in environmental contradictions and in an unequal distribution of economic and societal benefits from the utilization of bio-wastes. Different, and potentially nourishing and productive uses for winemaking's excess materials, the local knowledge which relates to these uses, and the metabolic relations between society and nature on which agro-food activities such as winemaking depend, are thus devalued in favour of distant capital markets (FitzSimmons and Goodman, 1998).

In undertaking this analysis, I consider how the challenges posed by waste materials fit into larger concerns about rural sustainability, both economic and environmental. Mechanisms of waste regulation in the Italian winemaking sector are typical of wider trends in rural governance, particularly the hygienic-bureaucratic mode of governance that imagines rural spaces as spaces of risk (see Lee and Marsden, 2009; Marsden, 2003; and Morgan *et al.*, 2006). An important consequence of this arm's-length governance is an institutionalized blindness both to questions of scale (Haila, 2002), and to the local specificity of materials in social and ecological relations. I argue that to integrate winemaking's excess materials into sustainable rural landscapes we must be sensitive to the materiality, temporality and spatiality of these bio-waste materials. Local actors, such as wine producers, can show great inventiveness when it comes to reincorporating bio-waste materials into economically and socially significant flows of transforming matter. Appropriately aided by waste management regimes, these actors can contribute to the realization of bio-waste materials as crucial elements in the achievement of local alternatives to the agro-industrial model of food production, as called for by many authors (for a discussion, see Horlings and Marsden, 2011).

In the following sections I draw on my ethnographic research to get close to the processes of material transformation of excess matter into waste in Italian winemaking. The category 'waste', I argue, acts as a powerful legislative tool, often preventing local revaluation of excess materials while enabling less ecologically sound techno-scientific solutions. By showcasing innovation around local revaluation of winemaking bio-wastes, I highlight the role relational materiality of bio-wastes has to play in the achievement of 'real' ecological modernization of agriculture (Horlings and Marsden, 2011).

Research context

The data informing this chapter comes from a year-long ethnographic study of wine production in northern Italy, conducted between 2008 and 2009. The research included interviews with producers, oenologists and viticultural workers at twenty wineries in northern and central Italy (Piemonte, Veneto, Abruzzo, Marche and Toscana), accompanied by prolonged periods of participant observation at four of these sites. For the purposes of this article, additional phone interviews were conducted with six of the original participants.

The majority of producers interviewed for this research produced wines from organically or biodynamically grown grapes. At the root of both these approaches lies the ideal of farms as metabolically closed units of nutrient and energy circulation in which, in the words of the EU organic agriculture regulation, 'wastes and by-products of plant and animal origin should be recycled to return nutrients to the land' (EC No. 834/2007 of 28 June 2007). Both the organic, biodynamic and conventional producers showed a considerable awareness of, and interest in, bio-waste regulation.[3] Most producers were likely to question the existing bio-waste management solutions on ecological grounds, and to seek out alternative pathways for the utilization of these materials. As will become clear in the following sections, these producers showed real ingenuity and inventiveness in making value from winemaking waste materials.

Reutilizing waste materials is currently seen as a sign of environmental consciousness, as well as good business practice. Indeed, for the organic and biodynamic companies in my research, waste reutilization was seen to add further 'green credentials' to their company image. A particularly interesting example of how waste materials were revalued was the recovery and reuse of wooden barrels at the La Carina winery.[4] At La Carina, red wines were matured in oak barrels. Each barrel was used for a maximum of four years, after which time its capacity to impact on the wines' taste diminished. The cost of replacing the barrels was considerable, and, as the market for used barrels is rather small, resulted in large amounts of wasted wood. The owner of La Carina found a way of recovering both a significant amount of the capital invested in the barrels, and of using the materiality of oak wood to add environmental value to his company. Specifically, in collaboration with a Swiss barrel-maker, a share of the traditional barrels was gradually replaced with highly unusual square ones (Figure 1). The unorthodox shape made it possible to recover wooden planks once the barrels had served their original purpose. Coloured and hardened by the tannins that passed through their pores during the wine maturation process, the planks could then be used for flooring, panels or furniture. This spectacular reutilization of waste could be admired in La Carina's tasting room, floored with these unique rusty planks.

This innovative reincarnation of wood waste is the kind of story which is likely to make the headlines. The appealing materiality of wood is immediately graspable, the value recovery process easily understandable. Such stories of

Figure 1: *Square barrels at La Carina.*

win-win waste revalorization fit comfortably into the vision of the world as a manageable system of production: a vision put forward by ecological moderni- zation approaches, as I explain further below. However, very few excess mate- rials of agro-food production offer such straightforward ways of revalorization. On the contrary, when dealing with (a)mass(ed) agro-food bio-wastes, we often deal with materials whose characteristics are not immediately graspable. In contrast to trash (Reno, 2009), these materials challenge our capacity to ascribe use-value. In the context of production, the knowledge of local actors can contribute to finding less environmentally harmful or even potentially beneficial ways of managing such bio-materials. However, as I will show in the following sections, in Italian winemaking this local connection is hampered by regulation which physically removes bio-wastes from the socio-material context of their production. Detached and abstracted, these materials become valued in relation to their money-making potential on the 'waste materials' market. Research laboratories break up these materials into chemical components, and devise methods for extracting the (currently) most valuable elements (such as anti- oxidants from grape skins). Thus capital- and resource-intensive ways of man- aging bio-materials become preferred over local, low-impact solutions. This is not to say that the disposal of bio-wastes of winemaking on site is without problems. Pollution to air from vine shoot burning, and to soils due to acidifi- cation from the spreading of raw grape marc are examples of legitimate concerns over the environmental impact of vine cultivation. However, I argue that local and low-cost methods for managing the risks inherent to winemaking bio-wastes need to be considered alongside capital-intensive methods. Otherwise, the leg- islation risks further negative impacts on small and medium companies, which

The Sociological Review, 60:S2, pp. 47–65 (2013), DOI: 10.1111/1467-954X.12037

compose the majority of Italian wineries, and the socio-material networks in which they operate.

From matter to waste in wine production

Before we proceed, the concept of waste in agriculture needs to be addressed. The counter-intuitiveness of imagining waste in the context of agro-food production was a frequent stumbling block in my conversations about waste with the participants of this research. 'Waste? Well there are the bottles, the paper . . . Ah, you mean by-products', they would exclaim. The idea that agro-food production such as winemaking creates waste is not immediately obvious, and has a particular historical trajectory. As Allen (2007) notes, 'nature itself knows no waste'. In order to become waste something has to be no longer needed – it has to have been 'used up', like the oak barrels in the previous example. In nature, however, nothing 'is ever used up because nothing is, strictly speaking, used . . . Nothing in nature has an end, purpose, or design' (Allen, 2007: 203). The other dimension which designates matter as waste, that of risk, pollution or toxicity (Douglas, 1966; Van Loon, 2002), is also not automatically satisfied; agricultural by-products achieve toxicity only when highly concentrated. As a result, pre-agro-industrial agricultural activity was not seen to be linked with waste. The rural landscape was portrayed as a space devoid of waste, and contrasted with the pollution of the cities (Macnaghten and Urry, 1998).

The idea of agro-food waste is linked with the intensification of agro-food production, which became the paramount aim of post-World War II rural policy in Europe (Lowe *et al.*, 1997). This in turn resulted in agricultural pollution, soil degradation and increased concerns about the quality of agricultural produce amongst farmers and consumers alike (Atkins, 2010). The public and policy reaction was not to question the premise of the agro-industrial system, but instead to recast agriculture itself as a 'dirty business' and a threat to the unspoiled nature of the countryside. From a site of nature, agriculture became a site of risk. The risk posed by agro-food materialities to both rural environments and the bodies of consumers was to be contained through an increase in state intervention into all aspects of agro-food production. In this bureaucratic-hygienic mode of agro-food production (Marsden, 2003), the spaces and material flows of agricultural production came under scrutiny by a plethora of quality, health and environmental protection bodies. The multiplication of regulations, top-down certifications, and penalty systems is still a feature of the (European) agro-food landscape today. Importantly, in the light of my argument, the regulatory maze has been found to prevent rather than encourage the emergence of more ecologically sensitive approaches to agro-food production (Marsden, 2003).

Navigating the regulatory maze

The bureaucratic and financial strain of conforming to an ever-increasing number of quality and environmental protection regulations was an issue raised compose the majority of Italian wineries, and the socio-material networks in which they operate.

From matter to waste in wine production

Before we proceed, the concept of waste in agriculture needs to be addressed. The counter-intuitiveness of imagining waste in the context of agro-food production was a frequent stumbling block in my conversations about waste with the participants of this research. 'Waste? Well there are the bottles, the paper . . . Ah, you mean by-products', they would exclaim. The idea that agro-food production such as winemaking creates waste is not immediately obvious, and has a particular historical trajectory. As Allen (2007) notes, 'nature itself knows no waste'. In order to become waste something has to be no longer needed – it has to have been 'used up', like the oak barrels in the previous example. In nature, however, nothing 'is ever used up because nothing is, strictly speaking, used . . . Nothing in nature has an end, purpose, or design' (Allen, 2007: 203). The other dimension which designates matter as waste, that of risk, pollution or toxicity (Douglas, 1966; Van Loon, 2002), is also not automatically satisfied; agricultural by-products achieve toxicity only when highly concentrated. As a result, pre-agro-industrial agricultural activity was not seen to be linked with waste. The rural landscape was portrayed as a space devoid of waste, and contrasted with the pollution of the cities (Macnaghten and Urry, 1998).

The idea of agro-food waste is linked with the intensification of agro-food production, which became the paramount aim of post-World War II rural policy in Europe (Lowe *et al.*, 1997). This in turn resulted in agricultural pollution, soil degradation and increased concerns about the quality of agricultural produce amongst farmers and consumers alike (Atkins, 2010). The public and policy reaction was not to question the premise of the agro-industrial system, but instead to recast agriculture itself as a 'dirty business' and a threat to the unspoiled nature of the countryside. From a site of nature, agriculture became a site of risk. The risk posed by agro-food materialities to both rural environments and the bodies of consumers was to be contained through an increase in state intervention into all aspects of agro-food production. In this bureaucratic-hygienic mode of agro-food production (Marsden, 2003), the spaces and material flows of agricultural production came under scrutiny by a plethora of quality, health and environmental protection bodies. The multiplication of regulations, top-down certifications, and penalty systems is still a feature of the (European) agro-food landscape today. Importantly, in the light of my argument, the regulatory maze has been found to prevent rather than encourage the emergence of more ecologically sensitive approaches to agro-food production (Marsden, 2003).

Navigating the regulatory maze

The bureaucratic and financial strain of conforming to an ever-increasing number of quality and environmental protection regulations was an issue raised frequently during the course of my research. In contrast to Gille's waste regimes – that is, social institutions that determine the 'production, circulation, and transformation of waste as a concrete material' (2010: 1056) – waste regulations at work in the Italian winemaking sector do not express a singular logic. The waste regulations that impact on the flows of matter in wineries and vineyards derive from various levels of governance (regional, national or European), and are not necessarily wine-industry specific. Typically, they express a reaction of governance bodies to particular concerns about agro-food materials as sources of risk. These risks can be posed to the environment, as in the following examples of grape stalks and vine wood, but also to markets, as I explain further with regards to the grape marc regulation.

A diversity and multiplicity of waste-related regulations, combined with low levels of law enforcement, poses problems of compliance, and Italian wine producers frequently find themselves working in ignorance of the law. An example will illustrate this point. One of the companies in my research, Podere San Cristoforo, were faced with significant changes to the management of their bio-wastes when they applied for the ISO 14000 environmental quality certification. In the course of the audit it transpired that the company had been acting outside the law. They had been disposing of grape stems, which are separated at early stages of wine making, as green compost in their own vineyards. However, in their region of Abruzzo, grape stems were legally categorized as non-hazardous wastes. This discovery triggered a set of by-laws which required the company to involve an external contractor for their controlled removal and disposal. Understandably, the company sought to avoid the additional cost that such controlled disposal methods would introduce. Podere San Cristoforo was in a relatively privileged situation in that its financial standing allowed it to involve an external legal consultancy firm, which identified a convenient loophole. By applying for the status of a green waste disposal company, and jumping through a number of (costly) legal hoops, Podere San Cristoforo was allowed to continue the same practice they had been employing for decades, albeit under a different guise.

The fragmentary and reactive character of excess material regulation in Italian winemaking can be further seen in the case of vine wood. This excess material, which is produced every year during vine pruning, has recently been subjected to increasing levels of regulation as a result of fire safety and air pollution laws. The debate culminated in December 2010 with a national regulation in which vine wood was designated as 'waste'. As a result, producers of vine wood are forbidden from processing it in any way excepting for electricity production through incineration (DL n. 205 of 03/12/2010).

The impact of this law on excess materials is considerable. Every winter vineyards in Italy generate between two and two and a half tons of vine prunings per hectare (Corona and Nicoletti, 2010). Traditionally the branches were burnt in the vineyards, and the ashes spread on the ground. The ashes provided a readily available fertilizer, and prevented the spread of vine disease carriers, such as fungi and bacteria, which winter in the wood. More recently, fearing hefty fines, many producers began to till the branches into the soil of the vineyards. As a consequence some areas have seen a significant increase in vine diseases. This has led some to conclude that vine shoots should be removed for disease prevention, presenting producers with a problem of disposal – two and a half tonnes per hectare is a lot of wood! Fortunately for the producers yet another loophole was found: while the burning of vine shoots directly in the vineyards is prohibited, the same shoots can be burned in domestic stoves as a source of heating. The idea of collecting vine prunings and using them as bio-mass for the production of heat, or even electricity, took root in the Italian winemaking community.

This idea was taken up by organic and biodynamic producers in particular. Utilizing vine wood for heating was in line with their general interest in environmental sustainability issues, and a number of producers I spoke with had attempted to make use of this energy resource. However, while the legislation pointed to a route from waste to energy, the material, temporal and spatial conditions of vine wood production were ignored by the regulatory framework. Collection of the wood is difficult. Many vineyards are planted on steep slopes accessible only by machines of appropriate size, and even so with difficulty during the pruning season when the ground is wet and tractors can easily slip, damaging the vines, the machinery and the workers. Additionally, vine wood burns quickly, and needs to be compressed into bales or briquettes to be an efficient source of energy.

Using vine wood locally and legally requires a large investment of both capital and time. Nonetheless, a number of organic producers in my research sought to make use of this material. One producer began collaboration with a company that utilized vine shoots and other woody discards to make briquettes. The producer took on a significant time and financial cost associated with the collection of shoots (estimated by Corona and Nicoletti, 2010, to exceed €100 per hectare). However, this collaboration only lasted one season. The producer was struck with the paradox of the situation: his vine shoots travelled a large distance to be processed, and then another distance to be distributed to clients. When the briquettes burn, the producer hypothesized, they must surely release polluting chemicals, 'the glues they use to keep it together'. The environmental impact of producing and burning briquettes must therefore be significant. The irony of polluting legally where illegal burning would result in less pollution was not lost on this producer. Disenchanted, he decided to continue tilling the vine shoots into the ground, as he had done before.

Another producer, the owner of La Luna, became passionate about biomass energy generation. The idea of heating both his house and his winery with bales made of vine wood from his vineyards was appealing both as a financial saving, and as a step towards the material self-sufficiency that organic agriculture strives towards. The producer made calculations into the possibility of heating his house and winery with bales made from vine prunings collected in his and his neighbours' vineyards. He also borrowed a bailing machine, and created some experimental vine wood bales. He found, however, that to make a good use of

Figure 2: *Bales made from pruned vine wood at La Luna.*

the quick burning vine wood he would require an advanced stove with regulated air-flow, and a mechanized feeder to top up the stove automatically. The capital investment required was too large and no funding streams were available. When I visited La Luna in 2009, grass was growing on the experimental bales (Figure 2).

Regulatory abstraction of excess materials

The examples discussed above illustrate the ingenuity of wine producers in making value around excess materials produced in their vineyards and wineries. The regulatory creation of waste poses many problems to these producers, but it can also act as a spur to seek new ways of utilizing excess materials. However, finding ways of utilizing bio-wastes that are both legal and locally relevant are difficult due to the ways in which these materials are conceptualized in the regulatory framework.

The regulation that both creates and controls bio-wastes in Italian winemaking operates by rupturing the local material, spatial and temporal relations of their production. In the regulation, excess materials of wine production are labelled as either 'special' (hazardous), or 'normal' (non-hazardous) wastes. These labels define the spatial pathways of these materials, either lifting them from the context of their production, or enabling local solutions. When excess materials are labelled 'special waste', the control of their pathways is

The Sociological Review, 60:S2, pp. 47–65 (2013), DOI: 10.1111/1467-954X.12037

taken out of the hands of producers, and placed in the open market (unless otherwise specified). The movement and transformation of these materials becomes the purview of companies that physically remove them from their local contexts. As a result, the social and material relations that could give those materials value locally (as sources of fertilizer, compost or warmth) are severed. Instead, the value of these materials becomes linked to the sphere of the capital market. This, as I discuss further below, results in a privileging of capital-intensive socio-technical methods for utilizing bio-wastes, with the consequent unequal distribution of costs and benefits, both ecologically and socially.

As could be seen in the example of vine wood regulation, the same legislation which inhibits local methods for the utilization of bio-materials promotes valorization methods more in line with the ecological modernization (EM) agenda. EM is seen by many scholars as the primary method for Western countries to address their environmental problems (Blühdorn, 2001, cited in Baker, 2007: 297). Many commentators agree that, implicitly or explicitly, EM has been the dominant conceptual framework for European environmental regulation over the last two to three decades (Baker, 2007; Korhonen, 2008). In the EM approach, all ecological problems are seen as solvable through a combination of regulation and free market competition. With regards to waste management, EM has been critiqued as an approach founded on a techno-scientific 'alchemist's dream' (O'Brien, 2008), which proposes a conflict-less marrying of economic prosperity and environmental sustainability through waste revalorization. In an ideal world of EM production, waste and resource become one and the same thing, as companies – connected through mutually beneficial networks – constantly utilize one another's wastes instead of virgin resources (Pellow et al., 2000). This vision of economies mimicking ecosystems has an important twist. While the vision is inflected by the idea of cyclical time and an eternal return of the same material in different guises, it also includes the linear time of techno-scientific progress, and a progressive expansion of the economy (Van Loon and Sabelis, 1997).

In both the context of production, and in the context of waste management, the EM approach can be seen to annihilate both time and space, and to conceptualize the materiality of wastes as inherently malleable, transformable and available. However, the excess 'stuff' of vitiviniculture presents serious challenges to this approach to materiality.

As we can see in the vine wood example, whilst wine producers face increasingly strict regulations of the flows of materials, they are also being encouraged to imagine themselves as ecological entrepreneurs (Marsden and Smith, 2005; Reno, 2011). They are expected to pursue state and European-level environmental scheme payments, and to diversify their production and marketing activities to incorporate a range of 'environmental' outputs. Converting vine prunings wood into energy and heat was, for the producers in my research, just such a possibility. However, the practical challenges of participating in this mode of revalorization – issues which relate to the specific material qualities of vine shoots, the topographies and soils of vineyards, the temporalities of vine wood production, as well as to issues of capital access for small and medium producers – make the application of these methods on such a small scale difficult, if not impossible.

The legislation that seemingly encourages more ecologically sensitive ways of managing excess materials such as vine wood is, in effect, blind to the materiality, temporality and scale of such bio-wastes. As a result, it forecloses local, non-market linked sources of bio-waste valuation. These challenges are easier to manage for larger producers, who can benefit from economies of scale. In the case of vine shoots, Corona and Nicoletti (2010) calculated that if a large cooperative winery in Sicily organized a collection of vine shoots from an area of 2,350 ha, and constructed and staffed an electricity generation site, the cooperative would be able cover the current cost of electricity consumption (with the help of the Italian feed-in tariff), or substantially reduce their spending (without it). The ecological cost of transporting the vine shoots, the ecological problems associated with their concentrated incineration, and the lack of advantage for the medium and small producers supplying the necessary material would outweigh any benefits.

In the previous sections, I focused on instances of regulation based on the branding of winemaking's excess materials as environmentally hazardous. In the following, I discuss how the category 'waste' has been employed as a market protection mechanism. This example highlights the independence of waste regulation from the modes of production, as noted by Gille (2010). In European wine regulations, the category 'waste' is used independently from notions of environmental risk and pollution, and serves as a powerful tool for regulating unwelcome productive activity at the wineries.

Protecting wine markets from grape marc 'waste'

All of the producers in my research were affected by the grape marc disposal obligation, one waste regulation that was thoroughly enforced.[5] Marc became a 'risky' material in the eyes of legislation not due to its polluting characteristics, which are not significant, but due to the threat it was seen to pose to high quality wine markets. After the first pressing, water can be added to the grape skins, a second pressing can be undertaken, and the weaker juices fermented to make a low-grade, low-quality and cheap alcoholic drink known in France as the *piquette* (Unwin, 1991). The over-production crises in the 1970s and 80s, and the resulting increase in regulation of wine production in Europe cast the presence of marc at the wineries as a threat to the profitability of the wine industry. Designating grape marc a non-hazardous organic waste in the EU Common Organisation for Markets (COM) in Wine (EC n. 1493/19991) was a quick way of removing the danger. The legislation introduced compulsory distillation of wine by-products, including marc. Distilleries were paid a subsidy to distil the alcohol, which was then earmarked for industrial and energy uses. By being branded as 'waste', marc became locked into what Gregson and Crang term the

The Sociological Review, 60:S2, pp. 47–65 (2013), DOI: 10.1111/1467-954X.12037
© 2013 The Author. Editorial organisation © 2013 The Editorial Board of the Sociological Review

'teleological fix' of waste management where 'that which is managed as waste is waste, and that which is waste is what is managed' (2010: 1027), blocking alternative pathways of utilization.

During the period of my research in Italy (2008–2009), disposal of marc via distillation was becoming a considerable financial and bureaucratic burden for small and medium wine producers. Although the distilleries paid a small amount for the marc, it was the producers' obligation to pay for the cost of transport. As a result, and especially in more remote areas, producers were not only being constrained to dispose of a potentially useful by-product, but were in fact subsidizing the distilleries, with the marc transportation costs exceeding the price paid for it at the distillery. The market-protective legislation frustrated attempts at alternative uses of grape marc in the wineries. The arm's-length management of marc lifted it from the local ecosystem of grape production into the materially and spatially abstract category 'waste'. The result was a devaluation of local knowledge of ecosystems and material cycles in favour of market protection. Importantly for the organic producers in my research, the marc distillation law also struck at the heart of the organic principles of closed material circuits, the recycling of nutrients and farm self-sufficiency.

As a result, the distillation law did not go uncontested. In one case, a producer freely admitted to me that he had an understanding with a distillery, which provided him with false receipts for the transport of marc so that he could compost it and use it as a vegetal fertilizer in his vineyards. A small distillery owner similarly confirmed that his company provided some of the producers with 'adjusted' receipts, exaggerating the amount of marc actually received. Other companies in my research were also involved in a revalorization of marc on a local scale through small-scale in-house distillation, making local speciality foods such as a sweet preserve called *cunia*, and for cheese affinage. All these activities were undertaken illegally due to the obligation of marc distillation.

In the new European common organization for the market in wine, introduced in 2008 (EC No 479/2008), nation states were granted more autonomy in deciding the exact mechanisms of marc management. In Italy it was decided (Disposizioni Nazionali DM 27/11/081) that marc could either be distilled, or utilized by producers in other ways under supervision of national industry and environmental control bodies. The alternative uses allowed included energy production via anaerobic digestion or incineration, spreading on agricultural land (raw or composted), and use as a raw material for a production of other goods such as cosmetics and pharmaceuticals.

This change had the potential to encourage both local and perhaps less environmentally damaging solutions to the marc 'problem' through (legal) on-farm utilization. However, in practice the new legislation continued to enact a strong preference for techno-scientific rather than agro-ecological solutions to bio-waste management. The most cost effective method of marc disposal for producers is composting for use on their own land. The benefits of using composted marc in vineyards have been the topic of some research in recent years, and the data supports the already existing agricultural practices of raw and composted spreading on the fields (Ruggieri *et al.*, 2009). The post-2008 change in marc regulation in theory made it possible for producers to close the nutrient cycle and return marc to the vineyards as fertilizer. However, in practice the administrative burden of disposal under supervision from industry and environmental control bodies meant that distillation was still the easiest – if not the least costly – method for small and medium producers. One of my research participants described the situation to me:

> . . . the bureaucracy is terrible . . . One has to declare the intention five days before the disposal describing how much marc was produced, if the grapes were your own or someone else's, declare where and when they will be spread in the fields, or given to someone who produces energy or whatever . . . In theory it's all simple, but in practice . . . !

To ensure the marc is disposed of in an environmentally sound manner, the process is closely controlled by the Guardia Forestale (a specialized police force under the jurisdiction of the Ministry of Agriculture), which appears twenty days after the operation is disclosed to take soil samples, photograph the area and control winery documentation. Any omissions or mistakes in the procedure are penalized.

Value of bio-wastes and economies of scale

The recent marc regulation enacts a preference for techno-scientific and capital-intensive methods of bio-waste utilization, in effect penalizing small and medium producers. Distillation subsidies play an important role here. Distilleries, which are frequently part of large winemaking cooperatives, are subsidized by the European states for the distillation of grape marc. In Italy in 2010 alone €23.6 million were spent from the EU agricultural support budget on wine by-product distillation support payments in Italy (MIPAAF, 2011). Furthermore, the regulation of marc as excess material works to tie its value potential to the value of its particular chemical components (such as anti-oxidants). This in practice means encouraging private investment into techno-scientific methods for value recovery, an operation practically subsidized by small and medium producers who lose control over their excess materials.

The 2008 marc regulation opened new money-making potential for large processors, as wine by-products became available for the production of energy through bio-gas generation or incineration, or by-product extraction for cosmetic and pharmaceutical use. One recipient of masses of wine bio-wastes was the wine cooperative Caviro, the single biggest wine producer in Italy, employing 20,000 grape growers (Caviro, 2011). In national and international media, Caviro presented itself as a forerunner of sustainable winemaking. Its main claim to 'green fame' was the operations of its Faenza winery, where grape marc was reprocessed on a massive scale (Figure 3).[6] After recovery of alcohol through distillation, the used marc was pressed and underwent a process of

Figure 3: *Mountains of grape marc at Caviro (source: Caviro.it).*

mechanical and chemical separation. The grape skins were dried and used for composting, fed into the on-site incinerator, or sold to be used as animal feed. Stalks were similarly incinerated. Grape pips were sold to oil-makers to be used in the production of grape-seed oil. The watery distillation residue was further processed to obtain crystals of calcium citrate, which was also sold.

The intense processing of marc allowed Caviro to valorize grape marc through a creation of by-products utilizable by other industries, acquiring the resulting financial and market benefits. Apart from recovering by-products from grape marc, Caviro has also been producing bio-gas, and generating electricity through incineration. The vineyard and winery bio-wastes, however, are only available seasonally (another characteristic of the material overlooked by the legislation). To secure a continuous supply of matter for its incinerator, in 2010 Caviro entered into collaboration with Hera, an urban waste management company, which would provide material for the incinerator from urban food wastes (Gruppohera, 2011). This development raised a wave of public protest (Faenzanotizie, 2009, 2011a, 2011b). It was feared that the Caviro winery incinerator, based well within the town boundaries, would be used not only for the burning of bio-mass, but also of mixed urban waste. Members of the public voiced fears over noxious smells from the incinerator, and the discharge of dioxins and other harmful particles into the air in what is already the most heavily polluted region in Italy.

In spite of these public worries, Caviro continued to be portrayed as an emblematic example of the principles of ecological modernization at work. Its public relations and financial success in winery bio-waste utilization is illustrative of the institutionalized preference for large scale, techno-scientific methods for bio-waste management in the Italian wine industry. The ecological costs of the transport of marc from individual wineries to the distilleries, the energy and materials cost of the distillation, the ecological costs associated with the distribution and consumption of by-products which are not necessarily substitutes for raw materials, and the public and social costs of these centralized operations are all silenced in this tale of successful ecological modernization.

Bio-wastes and local agro-ecology

The above exploration of the role of bio-waste materials in the Italian winemaking industry has highlighted some serious shortcomings in existing bio-waste related regulation. It has shown that the spaces of wine production are regulated by waste legislation which works by physically disconnecting materials such as grape stalks, vine wood and grape marc from the local socio-natures of their production. By creating 'free-floating' materials through legislation, waste policies actually work to draw ever more practices and processes into the fold of liberalized markets (Mincyte, 2011). This situation places financial burdens on small and medium producers, restricts their access to the value of materials they produce, and results in a further disconnection of farmers from local nature. EU and Italian bio-waste policy can thus be seen to work against agro-ecological solutions to bio-waste management, and to contribute to the devaluation of local knowledge as valid ways of knowing agriculture (see also Clark and Murdoch, 1997; Kaljonen, 2006). What the policy expresses is a techno-scientific denial of the materiality (and temporality) of the agro-food world. As a result, the policy continues to prioritize economies and political economies of scale and concentration, while negating the importance of what Bunker and Ciccantell (2005) call the diseconomies of the local, decentralized and ecological spaces.

It would be tempting to see this drive towards scientification and capitalization of bio-wastes in the wine industry as an unfortunate side effect of a fragmented and reactive policy approach. However, there is some evidence to suggest that capital market valuation of excess materials of winemaking is becoming not only a norm, but is being encouraged as an industry standard. In California, which has been a forerunner of ecological wine production, the California Sustainable Winegrowing Alliance self-evaluation programme values technological solutions for bio-waste management over agro-ecological ones (California Sustainable Winegrowing Alliance, 2012). For instance, to obtain the highest (most sustainable) category for pomace and lees management, winemakers are required to remove marketable by-products from these materials by technological means. Composting these bio-wastes, feeding them to animals, or disposing of them off site, are seen as less valuable in this assessment.

In Europe, the question of winemaking bio-wastes is at the time of writing being tackled by the research project SUSTAVINO, funded under the EU

Seventh Framework Programme (SUSTAVINO, 2009). The aim of the programme is to establish an EU sustainable winemaking seal in order to enhance the competitiveness of the EU wine sector. While it is premature to judge the outcomes of this programme, I am worried by the preference for technological means for value recovery from winery waste materials expressed in the present publications of SUSTAVINO. While techno-scientific methods for waste revalorization can indeed create marketable products, the wider costs of lifting bio-wastes from the localities of their production need to be given more consideration. The negative agro-ecological consequences of removing plant residues from productive soils have been highlighted in various EU soil research programmes (eg Gobin *et al.*, 2011; Van-Camp *et al.*, 2004). Despite these findings, there has to date been no progress on directive level to encourage the re-incorporation of agro-food residues into productive soils. The current concerns with climate change, and the growing EU support for bio-mass incineration as an 'ecological' energy source, makes a future focus on plant residues as elements of agro-ecology even less likely. In light of this, it is probable that European winemaking's excess materials will continue to be constructed as more valuable as fuel or as raw materials for other industries, rather than elements of healthy agro-ecologies.

Towards relocalizing bio-wastes

In this paper I have suggested that the regulatory mechanisms concerning excess materials of agro-food production need to move away from a focus on the market value of materials, and recognize, utilize and capitalize on local agro-ecologies and local skills. I have argued that the relational materiality of bio-wastes must be seen as a key element of rural sustainability. The examples above describe how wine producers can show creativity and determination in creating (local) value around waste materials. Without romanticizing local knowledge, I argue that these kinds of valuations are only possible when the perspective of situated actors on the materials' utility is taken into account. What this article is calling for, then, is a legislation that recognizes and nurtures the local and contextual relationality of bio-waste materials.

As the 2008 change to wine bio-waste management demonstrates, the EU excess material legislation is not insensitive to questions of sustainability. However, the current legislation promotes a particular version of sustainability, one that has more to do with the patterns of ecological modernization than of agro-ecology. In spite of a seeming recognition of bio-wastes as materials that can be utilized locally, in practice the bio-waste legislation in the wine sector continues to be insensitive to the materiality and temporality of the 'stuff' it regulates. Like much environmental regulation (Meadowcroft, 2002), it is underlain by the ingrained assumption that the world is ruled by fundamental laws of physics, not the phenomenological laws of lived experience (Adam, 1998; Stengers, 1997). By privileging investment into techno-scientific bio-waste management, the legislation fails to recognize farmers both as knowledgeable actors and initiators of change. As a result the regulation does not serve the ecology of agro-food, but contributes to the technological modernization of agro-food spaces. Opening up previously non-marketable materials to market exchange, it facilitates (further) accumulation of capital, and the intensification and deeper penetration of existing markets. The result of the legislation is not a disappearance of waste, but an increase in both waste and pollution.

While it is beyond the scope of this article to propose definite solutions to the challenges of temporality (Adam, 1998) and scale (Haila, 2002; Meadowcroft, 2002) that bio-waste governance poses, it is possible to draw some lessons from both literature and existing practice. Latour (1998) notes that in every conflict in which the interests of 'nature' clash with those of the economies and/or national or local politics, it is very particular issues that are at stake: this river, that frog, this bio-material. For Latour, a focus on the socio-natural imbroglios of living in landscapes, and a multiplication of controversies surrounding these practices of living, is a possible answer. He calls for an intensification of attention towards specific materials and locales, and an empowerment of the people whose lives are implicated in these particular socio-natural networks. Latour's position is echoed in Marsden's (2003) call to re-embed physical and social natures into rural development processes, and to re-incorporate local knowledge into decision-making. Following the pathway of controversy and local empowerment implies an attention to the materialities and temporalities of particular materials, and to the multiple roles they play in the human and non-human entanglements in which they are implicated. In this vision of a world of networks, 'ecology has nothing to do with taking account of nature, its own interest or goals, but that it is rather another way of considering everything' (Latour, 1998: 235), be it 'human' or 'natural'.

A change in focus from centralized to localized governance expressed by Latour, Marsden and many others, is beginning to materialize. There has been a significant move towards multi-scalar and participatory environmental governance in Europe in the last two decades, although the success of these regulatory mechanisms has been difficult to evaluate (Newig and Fritsch, 2009). Similarly the interdependence of human and 'natural' activity is slowly being recognized, as the EU begins to support environmental management that puts stress on 'action through landscape', rather than 'action for landscape' (Matthews and Selman, 2006: 200). However, Matthews and Selman (2006) note that these more sophisticated regulatory frameworks continue to be dominated by economic imperatives. Conversely, the case studies presented in this paper show that we need to think about enabling ecological entrepreneurship (Marsden and Smith, 2005) beyond the level of production.

What is needed is an incorporation of excess materials into ways of thinking about local agro-ecologies as environmentally, economically and culturally sustainable. As the case studies in this paper have shown, there is no shortage of interest from local actors in creating locally relevant solutions to bio-waste management. I am reminded of the positive energy behind the drive towards the

The Sociological Review, 60:S2, pp. 47–65 (2013), DOI: 10.1111/1467-954X.12037

relocalization of agro-food production, and its prolific (and successful) establishment of innovative, local chains of provisioning. This relocalization of food production has now become stabilized, although not uncontested, in many rural areas in Europe (see eg Goodman, 2004). Learning from the production landscape, we could similarly imagine managing excess materials at local and regional scales in more socially and environmentally sensitive ways. The difficult and silenced bio-wastes of agriculture must not be allowed to slip through the cracks of rural and environmental governance; they must become inherent elements of sustainability policies. By challenging the interests at the heart of current winemaking bio-waste legislation, I hope this article contributes to these important and urgent challenges.

Acknowledgements

The research behind this paper was made possible by the ESRC-funded project 'The Waste of the World' (RES-060-23-0007). I would like to thank Hugh Campbell, Catherine Alexander and two external referees for their insightful and constructive comments on an earlier draft of this paper. Special thanks go to David Evans for his continuous support and encouragement. The usual disclaimers apply.

Notes

1 Although see Stuart (2009) on some insights on food waste in production and distribution.
2 By 'bio-wastes' I mean bio-degradable wastes of animal or plant origin. These materials need to be seen as being distinct from non-biodegradable trash also produced in making and consuming foods.
3 The waste-related regulations I discuss in this paper apply to all producers alike, whether conventional, organic or biodynamic.
4 With the exception of Caviro, all companies and persons in this text have been given pseudonyms.
5 Grape marc are the grape skins, pulp, pips, seeds, stems, yeast and juice which are leftover from wine pressing and fermentation. From 100 kg of grapes, one can expect to produce between 20 and 30 kg of marc.
6 Source: Provincia di Ravenna (2008) Provvedimento n. 703 del 23/12/2008.

References

Adam, B., (1998), *Timescapes of Modernity*, London: Routledge.
Allen, B., (2007), 'The ethical artifact: on trash', in J. Knechtel (ed.), *Trash*, 196–213, Cambridge, MA: MIT Press.
Atkins, P., (2010), *Liquid Materialities: A History of Milk, Science and the Law*, London: Ashgate.
Baker, S., (2007), 'Sustainable development as symbolic commitment: declaratory politics and the seductive appeal of ecological modernisation in the European Union', *Environmental Politics*, 16 (2): 297–317.

Bunker, S. G. and Ciccantell, P., (2005), 'Matter, space, time and technology: how local process drives global systems', in P. Ciccantell (ed.), *Nature, Raw Materials and Political Economy*, 23–44, London: Elsevier.

California Sustainable Winegrowing Alliance, (2012), http://www.sustainablewinegrowing.org (accessed 2 August 2012).

Caviro, (2011), *Caviro ed I suoi valori*, http://www.caviro.it/caviro.asp (accessed 29 November 2011).

Clark, J. and Murdoch, J., (1997), 'Local knowledge and the precarious extension of scientific networks: a reflection on three case studies', *Sociologia Ruralis*, 37 (1): 38–60.

Corona, G. and Nicoletti, G., (2010), 'Renewable energy from the production residues of vineyards and wine: evaluation of a business case', *New Medit*, 9 (4): 41–47.

Douglas, M., (1966), *Purity and Danger: An Analysis of the Concepts of Pollution and Taboo*, London: Routledge and Kegan Paul.

Evans, D., (2011), 'Blaming the consumer – once again: the social and material contexts of everyday food waste practices in some English households', *Critical Public Health*, 21 (4): 429–440.

Evans, D., (2012), 'Beyond the throwaway society: ordinary domestic practice and a sociological approach to household food waste', *Sociology*, 46 (1): 43–58.

Faenzanotizie, (2009), *Faenza, nel 2010 nuova centrale a biomasse per Caviro*, http://faenzanotizie.it/main/index.php?id_pag=23&id_blog_post=964 (accessed 29 November 2011).

Faenzanotizie, (2011a), *Fantinelli (Lega): 'Alla Caviro si nasconde un inceneritore di rifiuti?'*, http://faenzanotizie.it/main/index.php?id_pag=23&id_blog_post=6163 (accessed 29 November 2011).

Faenzanotizie, (2011b), *Fatti Sentire sull'accordo Caviro-Hera: 'L'energia da biomasse non è verde'*, http://faenzanotizie.it/main/index.php?id_pag=23&id_blog_post=6173 (accessed 29 November 2011).

FitzSimmons, M. and Goodman, D., (1998), 'Incorporating nature: environmental narratives and the reproduction of food', in B. Braun and N. Castree (eds), *Remaking Reality: Nature at the Millennium*, 194–220, London: Routledge.

Gille, Z., (2010), 'Actor network, modes of production, and waste regimes: reassembling the macro-social', *Environment and Planning A*, 42: 1049–1064.

Gobin, A., Campling, P., Janssen, L., Desmet, N., van Delden, H., Hurkens, J., Lavelle, P. and Berman, S., (2011), 'Soil organic matter management across the EU – best practices, constraints and trade-offs', Final Report for the European Commission's DG Environment, September.

Goodman, D., (2004), 'Rural Europe redux? Reflections on alternative agro-food networks and paradigm change', *Sociologia Ruralis*, 44: 3–16.

Gregson, N. and Crang, M., (2010), 'Materiality and waste: inorganic vitality in a networked world', *Environment and Planning A*, 42 (5): 1026–1032.

Gruppohera, (2011), *Herambiente e Caviro: partnership per produrre energia rinnovabile da biomasse*, http://www.gruppohera.it/gruppo/comunicazione/news/pagina294.html (accessed 29 November 2011).

Haila, Y., (2002), 'Scaling environmental issues: problems and paradoxes', *Landscape and Urban Planning*, 61 (2–4): 59–69.

Horlings, L. G. and Marsden, T. K., (2011), 'Towards the real green revolution? Exploring the conceptual dimensions of a new ecological modernisation of agriculture that could "feed the world" ', *Global Environmental Change*, 21: 441–452.

Kaljonen, M., (2006), 'Co-construction of agency and environmental management: the case of agro-environmental policy implementation at Finnish Farms', *Journal of Rural Studies*, 22: 205–216.

Korhonen, J., (2008), 'Reconsidering the economics logic of ecological modernization', *Environment and Planning A*, 40: 1331–1346.

Latour, B., (1998), 'To modernise or ecologise? That is the question', in B. Braun and N. Castree (eds), *Remaking Reality: Nature at the Millennium*, 220–241, London: Routledge.

Lee, R. and Marsden, T. K., (2009), 'The globalization and re-localization of material flows: four phases of food regulation', *Journal of Law and Society*, 36 (1): 129–144.

The Sociological Review, 60:S2, pp. 47–65 (2013), DOI: 10.1111/1467-954X.12037
© 2013 The Author. Editorial organisation © 2013 The Editorial Board of the Sociological Review

Lowe, P., Clark, J., Seymour, S. and Ward, N., (1997), *Moralizing the Environment: Countryside Change, Farming and Pollution*, London: Routledge.

Macnaghten, P. and Urry, J., (1998), *Contested Natures*, London: Sage.

Marsden, T. K., (2003), *The Condition of Rural Sustainability*, The Netherlands: Van Gorcum.

Marsden, T. K. and Smith, E., (2005), 'Ecological entrepreneurship: sustainable development in local communities through quality food production and local branding', *Geoforum*, 36 (4): 440–451.

Matthews, R. and Selman, P., (2006), 'Landscape as a focus for integrating human and environmental processes', *Journal of Agricultural Economics*, 57 (2): 199–212.

Meadowcroft, J., (2002), 'Politics and scale: some implications for environmental governance', *Landscape and Urban Planning*, 61: 169–179.

Mincyte, D., (2011), 'Subsistence and sustainability in post-industrial Europe: the politics of small-scale farming in Europeanising Lithuania', *Sociologia Ruralis*, 51 (2): 101–118.

MIPAAF, (2011), *Communicato stampa: Ministro Romano: soddisfazione per il pieno utilizzo dei fondi destinati al comparto* vitivinicolo, http://www.politicheagrocole.it/flex/cm/pages/Serve BLOB.php/L/IT/IDPagina/4299 (accessed 29 November 2011).

Morgan, K., Marsden, T. and Murdoch, J., (2006), *Worlds of Food: Place, Power and Provenance in the Food Chain*, Oxford: Oxford University Press.

Newig, J. and Fritsch, O., (2009), 'Environmental governance: participatory, multi-level – and effective?', *Environmental Policy and Governance*, 19: 197–214.

O'Brien, M., (2008), *A Crisis of Waste? Understanding the Rubbish Society*, London: Routledge.

Pellow, D. N., Schnaiberg, A. and Weinberg, A. S., (2000), 'Putting the ecological modernisation thesis to the test: the promises and performances of urban recycling', *Environmental Politics*, 9 (1): 109–137.

Quested, T. E., Parry, A. D., Easteal, S. and Swannell, R., (2011), 'Food and drink waste from households in the UK', *Nutrition Bulletin*, 36 (4): 460–467.

Reno, J., (2009), 'Your trash is someone's treasure. the politics of value at a Michigan landfill', *Journal of Material Culture*, 14 (1): 29–46.

Reno, J., (2011), 'Motivated markets: instruments and ideologies of clean energy in the United Kingdom', *Cultural Anthropology*, 26 (3): 389–413.

Ruggieri, L., Cadena, E., Martínez-Blanco, J., Gasol, C. M., Rieradevall, J., Gabarrell, X., Gea, T., Sort, X. and Sánchez, A., (2009), 'Recovery of organic wastes in the Spanish Wine industry: technical, economic and environmental analyses of the composting process', *Journal of Cleaner Production*, 17 (9): 830–838.

Stengers, I., (1997), *Power and Invention: Situating Science*, Minneapolis, MN: University of Minnesota Press.

Stuart, T., (2009), *Waste: Uncovering the Global Food Scandal*, London: Penguin.

SUSTAVINO, (2009), www.sustavino.eu (accessed 2 August 2012).

Unwin, T., (1991), *Wine and the Vine: An Historical Geography of Viticulture and the Wine Trade*, London: Routledge.

Van-Camp, L., Bujarrabal, B., Gentile, A.-R., Jones, R. J. A., Montanarella, L., Olazabal, C. and Selvaradjou, S-K., (2004), *Reports of the Technical Working Groups Established under the Thematic Strategy for Soil Protection EUR 21319 EN/3*, Luxembourg: Office for Official Publications of the European Communities.

Van Loon, J., (2002), *Risk and Technological Culture: Towards a Sociology of Virulence*, London: Routledge.

Van Loon, J. and Sabelis, I., (1997), 'Recycling time: temporal complexity of waste management', *Time and Society*, 6: 287–306.

The performativity of food packaging: market devices, waste crisis and recycling

Gay Hawkins

Abstract: Packaging is central to the economic and cultural organization of food. This mundane material has become fundamental to extending shelf life, brand strategies, the qualities of food and more. From the early twentieth century, packaging has unarguably functioned as a market device, helping to assemble and extend food markets and transforming consumer practices. Over that century, packaging also became a major source of solid waste: filling up landfills, littering streets and clogging waterways around the world. The rise of the waste crisis in urban governance from the mid-1960s has been directly connected to the proliferation of food packaging. This paper takes the stuff of food packaging seriously. Here, I seek to understand its activity as both a market device and major waste problem, and aim to develop an analysis attentive to packaging's performative agency. Rather than see packaging as a passive instrument of economic processes or as an environmental problem, my focus is on how it is enrolled and performs in different arrangements, and also how it acquires the capacity to affect those arrangements in specific ways. A performative analysis focuses on how packaging becomes implicated in producing ontological effects: that is, how it brings new realities and practices into being that have socially binding effects.

Keywords: packaging, market device, performativity, political materials, waste

Introduction

It is impossible to talk about food and waste without confronting the brute materiality of packaging. Consider the simple act of eating an apple. How often does this involve breaking a layer of cling film, lifting the apple out of its polystyrene tray, peeling off the sticky label featuring the brand – all before you even take the first bite? Getting to the apple involves a series of encounters with an assortment of mundane materials that no longer simply contain the food but also qualify it in a variety of ways: as hygienic, as branded, as convenient, and so on. At the end of the snack a range of synthetic stuff confronts you as waste: now, not simply the core must be disposed of but a significant pile of different types of plastic packaging.

The Sociological Review, 69:S2, pp. 66–83 (2013), DOI: 10.1111/1467-954X.12038
© 2013 The Author. Editorial organisation © 2013 The Editorial Board of the Sociological Review. Published by John Wiley & Sons Ltd, 9600 Garsington Road, Oxford OX4 2DQ, UK and 350 Main Street, Malden, MA 02148, USA

In observing this everyday encounter my intention is not to bemoan the wastefulness and excess of food packaging – to yearn for an unpackaged world. I do not want to rush to prescriptive environmental critique. Rather, my aim is to pay close attention to packaging, to notice the various ways in which it mediates food and makes specific demands on consumers. While packaging is often the material 'we see but don't see' (Cochoy and Grandclément-Chaffy, 2005: 646), taking serious note of it opens up a range of questions about its role in the transformation of food production, consumption and disposal. How has packaging altered the way food is manufactured and everyday practices of eating? How has it been problematized? And what sorts of governance systems have been established to manage its afterlife; its conversion into solid waste, litter, recyclables or whatever?

In this essay I take up these questions. I want to investigate how packaging has emerged as a crucial element in the reorganization and expansion of food markets. My main focus, however, is the afterlife of packaging itself. How have growing amounts of discarded food packaging contributed to changes in regimes of urban waste management? In what ways has the rise of food packaging in household garbage bins prompted new domestic habits and new perceptions of the relationship between waste and 'the environment'? My key examples will be disposability and recycling. In seeking to understand the relationship between food packaging and waste I investigate how packaging has emerged as a political problem and how it can be thought of as 'political matter' (Braun and Whatmore, 2010). By this I not only mean how packaging waste has become the object of political deliberations and new systems of urban administration, but also how it has prompted new forms of participation and helped constitute new subjectivities – specifically, the recycler. My central claim is that packaging has agency in both food markets *and* political processes; that aspects of its materiality participate in assembling consumers and recyclers in both productive and problematic ways. This agency, however, has to be enacted; it is not inherent in the material but rather emerges in the force field of relations in which packaging acquires the capacity to effect actions or prompt changed practices. The question is: how?

Drawing on approaches from science and technology studies, political theory and economic sociology, my argument will proceed in three steps. First I consider the rise of food packaging as a 'market device'. This term refers to the various objects, discourses and technical apparatuses that help articulate economic action in markets, invariably in relation to other devices (Muniesa *et al.*, 2007). While plenty of information exists about the history of food and how the development of specific processing methods and packaging materials impacted on preservation, this literature is predominantly technocratic. In contrast, my focus is on the performativity of packaging or the ways in which packages have been enrolled in food production and have become capable of prompting new market forms. Using a case study of the rise of the polyethylene terephthalate (PET) bottle of water, I investigate how packaging is implicated in the emergence of branding, product differentiation and shifting calculations about the qualities of water. In what ways has the package invited new consumer practices from disposability to mobile eating? And how did all these discarded packages lead to debates about littering and the problem of significant increases in amounts of urban waste?

I then investigate the rise of recycling from the 1960s onwards. Unlike earlier forms of recycling – based on scarcity and creative reuse – contemporary recycling has emerged in direct relation to the rapid accumulation of new consumer wastes, particularly discarded food packaging (Strasser, 1999). This significant growth in new waste materials has prompted a range of debates about the moral and environmental effects of consumption. Often represented as 'the waste crisis' it has increasingly led to the emergence of new regimes of urban governance which have reverberated all the way down to household garbage bins (Gandy, 1994; MacBride, 2012).

Finally, I explore food packaging as a crucial participant in constituting new forms of environmental citizenship. If 'doing the right thing' and sorting waste at home made a virtuous recycling citizen, what role did empty food containers play in this particular process of subjectification? How can we think about discarded packaging as a 'political device' – something that prompts the formation of new practices, new environmental awareness, and the articulation of various interests from saving the planet to serving the local authority?

Packaging as a market device

While much has been written about the development of industrialized systems of food production and the creation of untrammelled food choice in the global north, the role of packaging in these transformations remains seriously under-researched (Lang, 2003; Lang *et al.*, 2009; Montanari, 1996). A number of studies document the rapid and unprecedented changes in food systems in capitalist economies that began after the Second World War. These included, amongst others, changes in agriculture, the shift to regional and global supply chains, the rise of supermarkets, the blurring of seasons, and the development of fast foods (Shiva, 2000; Bailey *et al.*, 2010; Cook and Chaddad, 2000). In the same period, production of plastics, glass and cardboard grew spectacularly (Borgstrom, 1967; Imhoff, 2005). Much of this material was used in food packaging. Little analysis, however, has been done of the precise ways in which packaging was enrolled in the industrialization of food. Within food studies, insufficient attention has been paid to how the development of retail packaging served as a material vehicle for the reorganization and transformation of food markets and consumption.

One field that has investigated packaging closely is food technology and nutritional sciences. The focus here is on the history of preservation techniques and the increasing role of packaging as a key innovation central to transforming food processing (Risch, 2009; Robertson, 2010; Shephard, 2000; Thorne, 1986). This field shows that food preservation and packaging have a long history.

Various devices – from sacks to jars to barrels – have always been essential for storage, transportation and preservation. Initially, these forms of packaging were primarily instrumental. While they were unarguably used to extend the biological life of food, to manage scarcity or to facilitate exchange, until the early nineteenth century they were not used on a commercial scale. Throughout the nineteenth century, developments in canning and bottling developed rapidly in the major industrial nations of Europe, especially in response to the demands of population growth, urbanization and the expansion of navies and sea travel. For many of the urban poor, however, malnutrition remained a permanent reality and it was not until the turn of the century that improvements in food supply and preservation became both technically feasible and widely applied (Thorne, 1986). Even so, at the end of the nineteenth century canned foods continued to be considered a luxury item and most food products purchased from groceries in cities were still unpacked and sold in bulk. These products were weighed in front of the customer, wrapped in paper or put in the buyer's container. Home delivery of milk, for example, took place via a milkman going door to door with a dipper and a can (Borgstrom, 1967).

As urbanization and industrialization escalated in the early twentieth century, food production and distribution grew more complex. More people moving to cities needed more food and thus the flow of products from rural regions intensified. The food industry as a whole expanded, with grocery wholesalers not only taking on more raw products but also a growing volume of manufactured food to meet demand. A key element in this ongoing development of mass food production was the growth of packaging and extended distribution networks. As Borgstrom (1967: 386) argues 'these changes in processing were intimately connected with changes in packaging and distribution which, taken together, profoundly affected what people ate and the way in which they prepared it'.

Beyond these historical accounts, food technology studies have also documented the impacts of materials and design innovations in packaging on food production, consumer convenience and marketing. The focus here is on technological breakthroughs and the ways in which they have addressed various issues in food preservation and security. Packaging is generally hailed as one of the key developments affording protection against harmful bacteria, light, oxygen and contamination. It is also celebrated as an innovation that has significantly *reduced* food waste by extending the biological life of food and delivering the edible components without all the excess elements. Testin and Vergano (1991) capture this sentiment well:

> Food packaging can reduce waste. For example, a pod of fresh peas is 62 per cent inedible. In order to get a pound of fresh peas, about 2.6 pounds of peas and pods would have to be purchased, resulting in 1.6 pounds of discarded pods. However, buying 1 pound of frozen peas leaves the customer with only a 1 ounce plastic pouch to dispose of. (Testin and Vergano, 1991: 31)

The paradox with food technology studies is that in celebrating the technical benefits of packaging in reducing food wastage, the afterlife of the actual package has often been overlooked. This blindness to the waste impacts of packaging has been redressed in recent years with the rise of research into sustainable design, biomaterials and lifecycle management (Geiser, 2001; Fisher and Shipton, 2010). However, the overall emphasis on instrumentality and technocratic solutions persists. While a technocratic approach recognizes the role of the package in the transformation of food production and consumption, together with the ways in which design and materials matter, this framework ultimately renders packaging as passive. It is something that is recruited to solve technical problems or to facilitate economic expansion – but it is not acknowledged as a participant in these processes. It is an instrument that is applied to a problem in a pragmatic sense but it is not an 'actant' as Latour (1996) would say. It is not, therefore, something that can become a source of action; that might make things happen.

In response to the limitations of mainstream food studies and food technology I want to develop an alternative approach that investigates packaging as a 'market device'. This term neatly captures innovative thinking on economic processes. First, the focus on 'devices' reflects the emphasis in science and technology studies on the role of artefacts, objects and techniques in enabling social action. Secondly, the focus on 'markets' reflects an approach to economic activity that pays close attention to the dynamics of organization and the diverse forms that market arrangements can take. 'Market devices', therefore, refer to the various material, technical and discursive assemblages that are involved in the construction of markets. As Muniesa *et al.* (2007: 2) ask, 'can a market exist without a set of market devices?' The other key value of this approach is that a focus on devices understands them as both pragmatic *and* performative; as things that do not simply address problems in reality but also come to shape reality itself in particular ways.

This emphasis on performativity is heavily indebted to the work of Michel Callon (1998) and his insistence that economics does not analyse an external economy but rather helps create the phenomena it purports to describe. In this way, then, 'economics performs the economy' (Mackenzie and Millo, 2003: 108): it is actively involved in shaping economic realities. While performativity has been a central concept in new cultural theory, philosophy and linguistics, Callon is significant in bringing this concept to bear on economic processes. His approach to markets foregrounds the ways in which various devices and technical processes acquire the capacity to shape outcomes and actions.[1]

Economic sociology's focus on performativity also foregrounds the *distributed* nature of agency within market assemblages: the ways in which all actors in a market – human, non-human, technical and so on – can come to effect actions. Deleuze's notion of 'agencement', loosely translated as assemblage or arrangement, is crucial to this approach. For Deleuze, action is always dispersed, it is neither the exclusive preserve of humans nor of devices; rather, it emerges in specific arrangements and relations and is dependent on various forms of materiality. As Muniesa *et al.* (2007: 2) argue: 'Instead of considering distributed agency as the encounter of (already "agenced") persons and devices, it is

The Sociological Review, 69:S2, pp. 66–83 (2013), DOI: 10.1111/1467-954X.12038
© 2013 The Author. Editorial organisation © 2013 The Editorial Board of the Sociological Review

always possible to consider it as the very result of these compound *agencements* (and this applies to economic action in particular).'

This account of market devices and performativity is fundamental to an analysis of the growing centrality of packaging in food markets and its various effects. It foregrounds the ways in which packaging acquires agency: specifically, the capacity to articulate new economic actions and cultural practices around food. It also addresses how the socio-technicality of packages participates in the enactment of new modes of production, distribution and consumption, and the generation of new forms of value around food. The point here is not that the package was recruited to express some sort of inexorable or pre-given economic logic, that it was a passive instrument of new manufacturing processes or capital accumulation. Instead, as packaging became a key 'fixture or furnishing' in food markets, it made a difference to how they operated, it intervened and shaped them in a multitude of ways. As Cochoy (2007: 120) says 'packaging changes the product, the consumer and the producer all at once'. In other words, packaging's enrolment in food markets generated a range of performative effects, some of which were economic and many others which were not.

The issue is how has the performative agency or effect of packaging been realized? What alliances did packages form with – amongst others – the matter of food, production processes, retailing spaces and consumers to transform markets, shopping and eating? Cochoy and Grandclément-Chaffy (2005) offer one of the most incisive accounts of packaging's performative effects within economic sociology, arguing that packaging has been central to reordering the relations between products and consumers throughout the twentieth century. Packaged goods have inaugurated a more mediated relationship to products in which consumers rely on indirect, written or visual information to access knowledge of what they are buying (2005: 648). Direct physical encounters with the product have thus been replaced by apprehension of a *package*, which contains information about the physical, scientific or cultural dimensions of what is being purchased, information previously completely unknown or inaccessible. The growth of packaging has also made it possible (and, in fact, necessary) to invent and highlight product differences: this necessity has fuelled the expansion of branding and brand strategies, with the package providing a crucial surface for establishing the symbolic qualities of the product. Cochoy and Grandclément-Chaffy (2005) also argue that as packaging has become normalized in market assemblages, consumption becomes impossible without it – not simply for pragmatic reasons but because shoppers have come to *expect* packages as an integral part of the cultural meanings and practices of shopping and the qualification of food as hygienic, safe, convenient and so on. As they argue: '"Naked" products would trouble us now: there would be no images to stimulate our fancy and, more seriously, no product guarantee or traceability' (2005: 649).

These are some of the performative effects of packaging: namely, the ways in which the package participates in the reorganization of food production, marketing and consumption, always in relation to a variety of other market devices. In other words, packaging's impacts on food markets are ontological, they help bring new realities and practices into being that have socially binding effects (Butler, 2010). As mentioned, many of these effects are economic in the sense that they help expand and diversify food markets. Many others, however, are not, and are instead varied and unexpected. One of the most crucial of these unexpected effects, or 'shadow realities' as Law and Lien (2010) call them, has been increased waste generation. While Cochoy and Grandclément-Chaffy (2005) note the effects of the normalization of packaging throughout the twentieth century and the fact that 'naked products' trouble consumers, they do not investigate the complexities of this reality. Specifically, they do not examine the way in which consumers expect packages, the transitional role of such packaging in delivering the product, and the simultaneous blindness to packaging's afterlife. While the market enactment of the package is to frame and facilitate delivery of the product, its imminent afterlife as waste has to be vigorously suppressed. This is most powerfully expressed in the paradox of disposability and the single use item. Consider, for example, what it means to consume one of the most ubiquitous beverages around, the PET bottle of water: a beverage often hailed as 'the triumph of packaging'.

Packaging water: disposability and the PET bottle

In moving now to a case study of one specific package, and how it has been enrolled as a market device, I aim to show how the PET bottle is both pragmatic *and* performative. In the process of containerizing water and organizing new beverage markets this container has also helped reconfigure the meanings and value of water, drinking practices and waste management. In this way, then, the bottle has to be considered an actant, something that has become a material vehicle for the reorganization and transformation of water consumption – something that made new things happen.

In his analysis of the rise of bottled water, Wilk (2006) describes how bottled water markets took off in developed economies from the late 1980s. The key reasons for this included diversification in beverage markets, new discourses about nature and purity, and the intensification of branding. Wilk pays little attention to the bottle itself, although there is no question that the invention of the PET container was an important element in the formation of this market. While there is also no doubt that strategies of expansion within beverage companies were crucial, as were new consumer concerns and practices, the bottle was a key participant. The bottle played a significant role in assembling and shaping this market[2] not simply because of its material affordances and design qualities, but also because of the dynamics of relationality: that is, the ways in which the bottle became caught up in new networks and alliances with water, consumers and other elements that extended its capacity to produce effects.

The Sociological Review, 69:S2, pp. 66–83 (2013), DOI: 10.1111/1467-954X.12038

By the early 1960s, plastic bottles had successfully replaced glass and metals in most household containers, but application to the beverages industry proved difficult. The polyethylene used for bottling detergents and other non-drinkable fluids was considered unsuitable for carbonated drinks or fruit juice because the carbonation or acid tended to attack the plastic, leading to deterioration and fears of chemical contamination. Beverages, however, represented a vast field of possibility for the expansion of plastic packaging given that this was an area where glass bottles and (since the early 1960s) aluminium cans dominated. While the development of the single-use aluminium can had had a major effect on the growth of markets, particularly following Coca-Cola and Pepsi's decision to diversify into them in 1967 (Pinkham, 2002), there was still an interest in finding a stable plastic that could be used in the beverages industry.

In the early 1970s, a new form of polyethylene terephthalate was teased out of the lab at DuPont. While this plastic had been around since the 1940s, it was used almost exclusively as a synthetic fibre under the trade name 'polyester'. The 1970s, however, saw a shift that involved turning this plastic fibre into bottle form. Engineers in DuPont had long been focused on finding a plastic to replace glass bottles: an object pathway was in place but a material innovation was needed to pursue it – which came with an innovative new type of plastic mould-ing process. While bottle production had always involved blow moulding, the DuPont laboratory *stretched* the plastic material as the bottle was being blow moulded, which conferred remarkable new properties on the material. This bottle was very light and virtually unbreakable: stretching conferred astonishing strength on the plastic and also gave it remarkable optical qualities, rivalling glass (Brooks and Giles, 2002).

This account of the origins of PET foregrounds the instrumentality of indus-trial research and development processes. While there is no doubt that this new form of packaging was developed in order to address specific problems in beverage markets, its pragmatic functions were dramatically extended – and in many senses overshadowed – once the bottle was taken up in beverage markets; that is, once it became enrolled as a market device. In other words, the PET bottle was not so much applied to the beverages industry as a technocratic solution but *translated* via processes of interaction, refinement and co-evolution with markets, packaging designers, and consumers (Shove *et al.*, 2007). By the mid-1990s, PET packaging had become the dominant material used in the beverages industry, rapidly displacing glass and cans as the preferred material. Unsurprisingly, it was regarded as a global packaging success story (Brooks and Giles, 2002). Within this process of industry take-up and transformation, moreover, the PET bottle did not simply replace other forms of packaging and increase profits: it also generated new consumer practices, and made the devel-opment of a distinct economy of qualities for water possible. It began to have effects and create new realities that became socially binding, and in these effects we can see the performative agency of the bottle at work.

While these effects are diverse and also highly situated, two in parti-cular were both critical and generic: the requalification of water and the normalization of disposability. In terms of creating a new economy of qualities for water, bottles enabled the development of complex branding and valuing strategies. Apart from their translucency and 'flowing' design that mimicked the liquid contents and made them easy to hold, the package provided a surface on which brands and other information could be located. Stamped on the transparent plane of the PET bottle, an image or logo did not simply frame the water but also situated it in a complex network of new relations. Information surrounding the logo might, for example, detail the source and purity of the water or its biochemical components or how much consumers should drink every day (Hawkins, 2011). In other words, brands did far more than stand for the product or deceive consumers. They were, as Lury (2004) argues, complex ontological objects and translation mediums that actively reshaped relations between water and consumers, and created fields for various social actions beyond exchange from health awareness to the valorization of nature. As another key market device, brands interacted with the package, reframing what was once ordinary and cheaply available into something that was singularized, distinctive – and far more expensive. The whole possibility of this market, of making water into a commodity, was dependent on being able to distinguish water in bottles from ordinary water flowing from taps. Packaging and branding were central to facilitating this new commodity and the subsequent economy of qualities for water. It could not have happened without them.

In terms of disposability the PET bottle prompted new ways to drink and discard. Mobile drinking practices were not unique to bottled water: they had been in place long before in fast food and beverages markets, with their focus on convenience and what is referred to in the industry as 'immediate consumption'. The PET package, however, changed these existing dynamics in significant ways. Unlike glass or aluminium, PET's light and transparent materiality generated new meanings for disposability that have had significant waste and environmental impacts.

Disposability generates a complex socio-material and economic paradox. Packages for single-use items have to perform as both tough *and* expendable. In the logics of commodity supply chains and retail storage, they have to be sturdy enough to withstand the movements and long temporalities of circulation. But in the act of instant gratification that is mobile consumption, they have to be almost superfluous; they have to facilitate immediate access to the product without too much interference. PET bottles appear to negotiate this paradox well. Their affordances of physical strength, translucence and remarkable lightness are not just valued for their technical attributes but because they also enhance the practice of single use. As plastic packaging, PET generates a material semiotics of impermanence and transience, quite unlike glass and cans. This is a package that does not simply contain and frame water, it also suggests the ways in which it can be drunk: on the move, convenience sipping with a light almost ethereal container made to throw away. Despite all the time spent sitting in containers or supermarket fridges, in the act of

The Sociological Review, 69:S2, pp. 66–83 (2013), DOI: 10.1111/1467-954X.12038

consumption the plastic bottle seems barely there; barely used before it is done with.

But it is not really done with. Its role as a market device may be exhausted but its brute material presence remains. Here, the shadow reality of disposability emerges: the persistence of the package. While the consumer may have thrown away the bottle and severed all relations with it, it still has capacities and generates effects because the bottle is *at once* cheap and disposable packaging and also *non*-biodegradable and *non*-disposable recalcitrant matter. Classifying the empty bottle as 'waste' is ineffective in capturing this paradox. It assumes that this new identity is easily acquired and stabilized; that becoming waste is a seamless linear transition. It is not. Disposable items whose value is exhausted after a single use manifest the absolute banality of fast-food consumption as both plenitude and rapid transience. They also manifest the problem of material endurance; the reality of an endless afterlife that is congealed in the unbreakable plastic container even before the contents are consumed. The work of marketing is to suppress this overflowing or shadow reality, to amplify the instant pleasures of the product, and to make packaging into a material we see but do not see.

Crucially, PET's performative agency as a disposable package not only gave new meaning to packaging as ephemeral, but also seriously interfered with existing waste management regimes. While glass bottles and cans had already established the practice of throw-away containers, discarding them often required a certain amount of care. Many, of course, entered waste streams, contributing to the massive growth in waste as the use of disposable objects post-World War II increased. However, the fact that these forms of packaging had been around for a long time meant that, in many developed economies, recycling or container deposit systems had developed as an alternative to thoughtless discarding. Both glass and aluminium presented effective opportunities for recycling as these materials could be reused in the making of new containers. PET bottles disrupted these arrangements. At the time that they entered the market, systems for recycling plastic were very underdeveloped. As Mathews notes:

> The development of PET bottles to replace the heavier more easily breakable glass variety, coupled with an early lack of facilities to recover and recycle the containers in a similar manner to glass, has undoubtedly contributed to public concern about the apparent waste of resource and rejection of the containers to landfills. Public concern is eventually manifest in political interest and related activity to regulate, control and, if possible, eliminate the case of concern. (Mathews, 2002: 315)

The absence of effective waste management systems beyond the bin helped fuel connotations of plastic packaging as ephemeral and disposable. That is to say, the lack of any obvious pathway for the afterlife of the bottle and the affordances of PET plastic as 'barely there' led to an equation of lightness with litter. The PET bottle therefore invited cavalier waste practices rather than careful recycling. It gave new meaning to the temporality of disposability, to the idea of fleeting utility. So, while PET was rapidly taken up as a replacement for glass, its material performance generated new disposal practices that were increasingly problematic: it looked the same as glass, but felt and behaved quite differently. Its troubling afterlife as a rapidly growing waste problem clearly constituted an unexpected performative effect.

This example of disposability highlights the paradoxical and multiple realities of packaging. While there is no question that the enactment of the PET bottle as a market device has had significant effects on assembling new qualities for water, as well as new mobile drinking practices, as a single-use or throw-away item it has also had phenomenal waste effects. In other words, the bottle's performative agency overflows beyond the market frame into a range of other fields where it enacts different effects, not least environmental and political ones. Such overflows or externalities are an outcome of all markets. As Callon *et al.* (2009) argue, markets cannot exist without frames that actively exclude anything not relevant to the calculation of profits and benefits. In the case of food packaging, its material enactment as future waste has to be aggressively kept out of market frames. However, despite these efforts, food packaging has a counter-performativity, a recalcitrant material presence that has made it impossible to ignore. In the next section I investigate how this counter-performativity became a matter of concern and how food packaging became emblematic of 'the waste crisis'.

The counter-performativity of packaging: the emergence of the waste crisis

In an earlier study (Hawkins, 2006) I outlined the major discursive and material shifts that prefigured the rise of contemporary recycling. Unlike the nineteenth century, when cultures of reuse were shaped by notions of thrift, household efficiency and scarcity, from the 1960s onwards the reinvention of recycling was connected to very different debates about the problem of excessive waste and what to do with it. Much of this excessive waste was packaging. As Gandy (1994) notes, since World War II packaging has emerged as the largest component of household waste and a major problem for urban authorities. Most of this packaging comes from food purchases:

> Trends within retailing over the post-war period associated with the growth of super-markets and the rise of mass consumption have led to the increased use of smaller one-way containers for food and beverages which formerly would have been sold in larger returnable containers or, in the case of many bakeries and greengrocers with minimal packaging. *Over 80 per cent of packaging waste in developed economies is now calculated to be derived from food and beverages.* (Gandy, 1994: 25; emphasis added)

In response to post-war changes in waste materials specifically, the accumulation of discarded packaging in household bins and as litter and urban pollution, a range of discursive and policy shifts in relation to waste management emerged.

While some of these discourses did not explicitly address food packaging, they were nevertheless crucial in creating a wider field of controversy and problematization in terms of the state of cities and the environment. These discourses were not simply describing a new reality: they were also helping to construct it. This is the performative dimension of discourse – the way in which it is not outside the reality it describes but actively participates in shaping it. As Foucault (2002) reminds us, discourse creates its own object: in this instance a variety of discourses from very different sectors coalesced around the idea that cities were facing a waste crisis and the ever-accumulating presence of food packaging was a significant cause.[3]

Three key discourses were involved in enacting the counter-performativity of packaging waste as a serious problem and in making household recycling 'thinkable'. The first, in the 1960s, came from various environmental movements that emerged to contest the impacts of rapid economic growth on nature. These movements initially targeted industrial pollution and its contaminating effects on environments, urban air quality and similar issues. The key political effects of this discourse were increased regulations and restrictions on industry in the name of environmental protection. In this way, 'the environment' emerged as a field separate from humans and vulnerable to exploitation and destruction (Castree and Braun, 2001).

The second parallel discourse emerging at around the same time focused on the post-war rise of cultures of consumption and the problem of abundance. Vance Packard's 1963 book *The Waste Makers* is often cited as a key source of this critique. Packard exposed consumption to sweeping moral condemnation – and central to this was his depiction of shoppers as too easily seduced by the cult of the new and too ready to discard perfectly useful things. Hedonism and material abundance, evident in homes groaning with 'stuff', had produced a population blind to the effects of self-indulgent, conspicuous consumption (Hawkins, 2006: 101).

Finally, a 'waste crisis' facing cities was specifically identified. As Melosi (1981) and Strasser (1999) have shown, the affluent society of the post-World War II period generated an overwhelming volume of waste in most developed economies. While representations of this crisis varied according to different locales and political structures, the basic plot remained the same. Cities could no longer cope with escalating amounts of urban waste which were not only polluting environments but also putting immense pressure on budgets and waste infrastructures. Packaging waste presented very specific problems not only because of its sheer quantity but also because it was so heterogeneous, with much of it completely defying disposal. Increased amounts of plastic in solid waste streams, for example, created problems for landfill and incineration. Plastic is, clearly, non-biodegradable and some forms burn at such high temperatures they damage incinerators (Melosi, 1981). Technocratic approaches to waste management, based on efficient removal and disposal, were not only becoming increasingly expensive but also having little impact on waste reduction. Numerous reports and policy documents began discussing the effects of wasteful everyday practices – from littering to overconsumption; the burden of accumulating waste on fragile environments; and the need to shift from a focus on disposal to 'management' and 'reduction'. Waste could no longer be seen as the exclusive focus of engineering or transport systems, it was, rather, a problem of household practices and ways of living. In problematizing waste in this way, a key shift was enacted. For householders waste was no longer 'out of sight and out of mind': it was becoming a matter of concern, something in which they were now implicated in managing more carefully.

Discourses about the environment, overconsumption and the 'waste crisis' were central to making food packaging visible as a major urban problem. These discourses, which emerged in multiple sites – from government inquires to local government leaflets – did not simply represent packaging as waste, they also made it available for governmental action. As Rose and Miller (1992: 182) argue, government is a problematizing activity: 'Governing a sphere requires that it can be represented, depicted in a way which both grasps its truth and re-presents it in a form in which it can enter the sphere of conscious political calculation.' In the process of problematizing packaging, governmental technologies also identified programmes to address it and ways to act on it. The introduction of mass kerbside recycling programmes in the 1970s in many developed economies, for instance, emerged in this context. Recycling was hailed as a new way to both manage and reduce waste. It offered a changed political rationality for waste management; one both attentive to the rise of environmental concerns (MacBride, 2012; Hawkins, 2006) and focused on new moral justifications for changed householder practices in the handling of packaging – 'doing the right thing'.

Making a recycler: packaging as a 'political material'

The waste crisis and the dynamics of problematization show how packaging became an object of government. However, this analysis can still imply that packaging was a passive material subject to various political processes and deliberations. In seeking to understand the performative role of packaging in *making* a new identity, 'the recycler', recent work in materiality and political theory is particularly valuable. The concept of 'political matter' extends governmentality analyses of waste in important ways – specifically, by investigating the active material presence of waste as a political participant not just a problem or object of government. Emerging from recent debates between political theory and science and technology studies, this approach investigates how the micro-physical workings of modern forms of rule are enacted in and through artefacts, architectures and settings. These material 'things' are not simply tacit supporters of, or constraints on, rule: rather, they are actants actively involved in the constitution of political processes and subjects (Marres and Lezuan, 2011). Developing this argument further, Braun and Whatmore (2010) claim that politics is increasingly 'more-than-human'.[4] In critiquing the anthropocentrism of mainstream political theory, they argue that the effect of this has been 'to cast anything nonhuman out of the political fold or to relegate it to the status of resources or tools, entering political theory only to the extent that it has *instrumental* value but not in terms of its *constitutive* powers (2010: xv; emphasis in original). The issue is not that all matter is inherently political, but rather that in specific contexts and associations matter can acquire political capacities: it can invite forms of action and engagement that have political effects.

This focus on how matter acquires distinctively political agency resonates with the idea of market devices. Many analyses of political matter are 'device-centred' (Marres and Lezuan, 2011: 491): they pay careful attention to the distinctively material forms of political participation and the ways in which mundane artefacts help generate novel forms of citizenship and publics. As Marres and Lezuan (2011: 493) argue, the purpose of a device-centred approach to political participation is 'to examine more closely what is distinctive or special . . . about participatory objects, settings, devices and stuff . . . that in a particular situation come to play a role in the enactment of public participation'.

What does it mean, then, to investigate food packaging as political materials or as devices for enacting political processes? First, it means resisting seeing packaging waste as an *a priori* political problem. Instead, it is necessary to investigate exactly how packaging becomes relevant to political action; in what situations and settings it acquires the capacity to materialize new forms of political process such as recycling; and to constitute new subjectivities like 'recyclers'. As shown above, discourses about the waste crisis were an important step in problematizing packaging and prompting a range of new policies and governmental calculations. However, this analysis only takes us so far, for it can implicitly reinforce the notion that politics is primarily about state institutions and interventions and the negotiation of conflicting interests. Beyond the dynamics of problematization and policies it is necessary to see how food packaging is constitutive of *everyday* or ordinary forms of political engagement and participation. In what ways does packaging waste make mundane activities like putting out the rubbish an encounter with materials invested with moral and political capacities, materials with the 'powers of engagement' (Marres and Lezuan, 2011: 495)?

The implementation of domestic recycling schemes has involved an immense variety of institutional, political and economic arrangements that are outside the scope of this paper. What is relevant is the ways in which these arrangements involve changes in the everyday performance of waste management in households and the effects of these changes. Recycling schemes mean that waste must be handled differently. No longer the cavalier chucking in the bin: as separate bins for recyclables have been distributed to households – along with mountains of information about rubbish as a resource and the environment under pressure – discarded food packaging becomes invested with new values and capacities. In assembling recycling numerous material, technical and human elements are brought into new associations, and in these associations food packaging becomes a crucial participant in prompting changed practices and forms of political participation. Rather than throw out the empty Italian peeled tomato tin without a second thought, the tin now presents itself as a morally charged object capable of slowing things down and posing questions to the householder: where will this end up? In carefully rinsing and putting it in the special bin for recyclables the householder responds to this moral capacity, to the power of the tin to suggest new forms of engagement and action.

In the performance of household recycling it is difficult to argue that food packaging is the passive object of the virtuous gestures of subjects. My claim is that food packaging has helped *constitute* a recycling subject. Its capacity to engage householders in new responses to waste and new senses of responsibility makes it political matter. Food packaging becomes a political device not simply by scripting new practices in association with other technical objects – from special garbage bins to recyclable logos on the bottom of containers – but also by entangling householders in wider networks of ethical concern about the environment and the afterlife of packaging. It is not a tacit enabler of a new political subjectivity; it is, rather, a device for materializing new forms of political participation and citizenship.

While these new forms of participation might be minor changes in household habits, they still constitute a very precise form of politics. A better term, perhaps, is 'micropolitics'. For Connolly (1999), micropolitics involve the ways in which habits and self-cultivation emerge through our relations with things and the world. When those relations are disrupted, when things enact or suggest different material realities, they can catch subjects in new networks of reflexivity. Packaging waste's capacity to disrupt comes not only from being connected to wider political discourses of environmental decline or new garbage collection rules, but also from the ways in which it demands new *effort* on the part of the householder. In contrast to cavalier disposal, recycling involves certain forms of work: sorting waste items and putting them in the correct bin, rinsing, crushing and more. Of course, this effort may be experienced as coercive duty or as a nuisance but it can also be experienced as a form of political participation, validating the work of recycling in terms of making a contribution to a less polluted world or being environmentally aware.[5] This work also *requalifies* food packaging, making its speculative value as a potential resource (rather than as useless rubbish) present and potent. In understanding the making of a recycler it is impossible to say that this political identity is simply produced by external policies or forms of rule in which the subject has little say. This identity is made by the subject's active engagement with the messy residues of food, the stuff of packaging and the effort it demands.

Conclusion

There are many ways to tell the story of the rise and impacts of food packaging. Celebratory accounts of packaging as a technical innovation are one way.

Another is prescriptive political analysis about the massive environmental burden of discarded food packaging. These stories, however, have already been told, and in many senses they can blind us to the material performance and affordances of packaging as actants. Here the focus has been on the performative agency of packaging's multiple material realities; the ways in which it is enrolled and behaves in different settings. As a market device, packaging has had phenomenal economic effects in terms of transforming the production, distribution and consumption of food. But packaging's capacity to enhance the economization of food cannot be separated from its impacts on mediating and reordering the economy of qualities of what we eat or drink and the way we do it. As a market device, packaging's effects have been multiple and often unexpected. As the invention of the PET bottle has shown, this container has been central to reconfiguring the values of water, how it is drunk, and the phenomenal growth in disposable objects and consumer comfort with single-use items. The rise of disposability contributed significantly to the emergence of a major waste burden in cities. While the origins of the 1960s' waste crisis were diverse and complex, mountains of accumulating single-use food containers and wrapping were at the heart of it. In responding to this material reality, the problematizing dynamics of government made packaging waste into a sphere of political calculation and action. The rise of recycling programmes is a key example of this. However, as I have argued, food packaging is also a key example of 'political matter': of a material that has become implicated in the organization of everyday forms of political participation. One of the places where this performative agency has been most keenly felt is in households where packaging began capturing householders in new circuits of duty and obligation to the environment. In the effort of recycling, discarded food packaging revealed itself as a device capable of materializing new forms of political participation and engagement.

Notes

1 See the special issue of the *Journal of Cultural Economy*, on 'Performativity, economics and politics' for an excellent discussion of this field (Cochoy *et al.*, 2010).
2 Freinkel (2011: 173) says: 'The fastest growing segment of that chug-on-the go market is bottled water – a controversial product that arguably owes its existence to the PET bottle.'
3 The argument in this section is drawn from my book *The Ethics of Waste* (Hawkins, 2006).
4 See Hawkins (2009) for an extended discussion of the more than human politics of anti-plastic bag campaigns.
5 See Marres and Lezuan (2011: 501–502) for an excellent discussion of the complexities of effort in public engagement.

References

Bailey, A. R., Shaw, G., Alexander, A. and Nell, D., (2010), 'Consumer behaviour and the life course: shopper reactions to self-service grocery shops and supermarkets in England c. 1947–75', *Environment and Planning A*, 42 (6): 1496–1512.

Borgstrom, G., (1967), 'Food processing and packaging', in M. Kranzberg and C. Pursell Jr (eds), *Technology in Western Civilization Vol. 11*, 386–402, London: Oxford University Press.

Braun, B. and Whatmore, S. (eds), (2010), 'The stuff of politics: an introduction', in *Political Matter*, ix–xl, Minneapolis: University of Minnesota Press.

Brooks, D. and Giles, A., (2002), *PET Packaging Technology*, Sheffield: Sheffield Academic Press and CRC Press.

Butler, J., (2010), 'Performative agency', *Journal of Cultural Economy*, 3 (2): 147–161.

Callon, M. (ed.), (1998), *The Laws of Markets*, London: Blackwell.

Callon, M., Lascoumes, P. and Barthe, Y., (2009), *Acting in an Uncertain World: An Essay on Technical Democracy* (trans. G. Burchell), Cambridge, MA: MIT Press.

Castree, N. and Braun, B. (eds), (2001), *Social Nature*, London: Blackwell.

Cochoy, F., (2007), 'A sociology of market-things: on tending the garden of choices in mass retailing', in M. Callon, Y. Millo and F. Muniesa (eds), *Market Devices*, 109–129, London: Blackwell.

Cochoy, F., Giraudeu, M. and McFall, L., (2010), 'Performativity, economics and politics', *Journal of Cultural Economy*, 3 (2): 139–146.

Cochoy, F. and Grandclément-Chaffy, C., (2005), 'Publicizing Goldilocks' Choice at the Supermarket: The Political Work of Shopping Packs, Carts and Talk', in B. Latour and P. Weibel (eds), *Making Things Public: Atmospheres of Democracy*, 646–657, Cambridge, MA: ZKM and MIT Press.

Connolly, W., (1999), *Why I Am Not a Secularist*, Minneapolis: University of Minnesota Press.

Cook, M. L. and Chaddad, F. R., (2000), 'Agroindustrialization of the global agrifood economy: bridging development economics and agribusiness research', *Agricultural Economics*, 23 (3): 207–218.

Fisher, T. and Shipton, J., (2010), *Designing for Re-Use: The Life of Consumer Packaging*, London: Earthscan.

Foucault, M., (2002), *The Archaeology of Knowledge* (trans. A. M. Sheridan-Smith), London: Routledge.

Freinkel, S., (2011), *Plastic: A Toxic Love Story*, Melbourne: Text Publishing.

Gandy, M., (1994), *Recycling and the Politics of Urban Waste*, New York: St Martin's Press.

Geiser, K., (2001), *Materials Matter: Toward a Sustainable Materials Policy*, Cambridge, MA: MIT Press.

Hawkins, G., (2006), *The Ethics of Waste*, Lanham, MD: Rowman and Littlefield.

Hawkins, G., (2009) 'More than human politics – the case of plastic bags', *Australian Humanities Review* (May), http://www.australianhumanitiesreview.org/archive/Issue-May-2009/hawkins.htm

Hawkins, G., (2011), 'The politics of bottled water: assembling bottled water as brand, waste and oil', in T. Bennett and C. Healy (eds), *Assembling Culture*, 177–189, London: Routledge.

Imhoff, D., (2005), *Paper or Plastic: Searching for Solutions to an Overpackaged World*, San Francisco: Sierra Club Books.

Lang, T., (2003), 'Food industrialization and food power: implications for food governance', *Development Policy Review*, 21 (5/6): 555–568.

Lang, T., Barling, D. and Caraher, M., (2009), *Food Policy: Integrating Health, Environment and Society*, Oxford: Oxford University Press.

Latour, B., (1996), 'On actor-network theory: a few clarifications', *Soziale Welt*, 47 (4): 369–381.

Law, J. and Lien, M., (2010), 'Slippery: field notes on empirical ontology', unpublished essay available at: http://heterogeneities.net/projects.htm

Lury, C., (2004), *Brands: The Logos of the Global Economy*, London: Routledge.

MacBride, S., (2012), *Recycling Reconsidered: The Present Failure and Future Promise of Environmental Action in the United States*, Cambridge, MA: The MIT Press.

Mackenzie, D. and Millo, Y., (2003), 'Constructing a market, performing theory: the historical sociology of financial derivatives exchange', *American Journal of Sociology*, 109: 107–145.

Marres, N. and Lezuan, J., (2011), 'Materials and devices of the public: an introduction', *Economy and Society*, 40 (4): 489–509.

The Sociological Review, 69:S2, pp. 66–83 (2013), DOI: 10.1111/1467-954X.12038
© 2013 The Author. Editorial organisation © 2013 The Editorial Board of the Sociological Review

Mathews, V., (2002), 'Environmental and recycling considerations', in D. Brooks and A. Giles (eds), *PET Packaging Technology*, 315–364, Sheffield: Sheffield Academic Press and CRC Press.

Melosi, M., (1981), *Garbage in the Cities: Refuse, Reform and the Environment, 1880–1980*, College Station: Texas A&M University Press.

Montanari, M., (1996), *The Culture of Food*, Oxford: Wiley-Blackwell.

Muniesa, F., Millo, Y. and Callon, M. (eds), (2007), 'An introduction to market devices', in *Market Devices*, 1–12, Oxford: Blackwell.

Packard, V., (1963), *The Waste Makers*, London: Penguin.

Pinkham, M., (2002), 'Aluminium cans – history, development and market', *Aluminum International Today*, April/May: 37–38.

Risch, S. J., (2009), 'Food packaging history and innovations', *Journal of Agriculture and Food Chemistry*, 57 (18): 8089–8092.

Robertson, G. L., (2010), *Food Packaging and Shelf Life: A Practical Guide*, Boca Raton: Taylor & Francis.

Rose, N. and Miller, P., (1992), 'Political power beyond the state: the problematics of government', *British Journal of Sociology*, 43 (2): 173–208.

Shephard, S., (2000), *Pickled, Potted and Canned*, London: Headline.

Shiva, V., (2000), *Stolen Harvest: The Hijacking of the Global Food Supply*, London: Zed Books.

Shove, E., Watson, M., Hand, M. and Ingram, J., (2007), *The Design of Everyday Life*, London: Berg.

Strasser, S., (1999), *Waste and Want*, New York: Metropolitan Books.

Testin, R. and Vergano, P., (1991), 'Food packaging', *Food Review*, 14 (2): 31.

Thorne, S., (1986), *The History of Food Preservation*, Kirby Lonsdale: Parthenon.

Wilk, R., (2006), 'Bottled water – the pure commodity in the age of branding', *Journal of Consumer Culture*, 6 (3): 303–325.

Arbiters of waste: date labels, the consumer and knowing good, safe food

Richard Milne

Abstract: The importance of date labelling in informing both retailers and consumers how long a food will remain edible, safe and of sufficient quality makes it a prime site for the identification of, and intervention in, food waste. This paper examines the historical and spatial evolution of the date labelling system in the UK. The paper shows how reforms to date marking have occurred in response to shifting concerns about food quality, safety and latterly waste. It distinguishes four periods during which labels moved from an internal stock control mechanism to a consumer protection mechanism, a food safety device and recently emerged as a key element in the fight against food waste. Contributing to recent sociological studies of food labelling, the paper charts changing understandings of the role of the label in mediating between consumers, the food industry and regulators. It shows how regulatory objects such as date labels materialize societal concerns about food and situates contemporary efforts to reform date labelling in relation to prior articulations of consumer, government and industry interests.

Keywords: food, regulation, labelling, consumption, waste

Introduction

Food labelling is a key instrument of food policy, and sits between production, retailing and consumption. Labelling is the site at which the roles and responsibilities of governments, the food industry and consumers in contemporary food systems are defined and distributed (Morgan *et al.*, 2006; Frohlich, 2011). However, labels exist in a diverse and rapidly evolving array of forms. In the UK, discussions of food waste have pointed to labels as contributing to the unnecessary disposal of edible food by consumers (eg Stuart, 2009; Waste and Resources Action Programme (WRAP), 2008; Benn, 2009). In September 2011, the government minister responsible for food, Caroline Spelman, introduced new expiry date labelling guidelines for food businesses as a contribution to preventing the yearly waste of an estimated £750 million of food. She described how the guidance would 'end the food labelling confusion' and 'make it clear once and for all when food is good and safe to eat' (Department for Environment, Food and Rural Affairs (DEFRA), 2011a).

The Sociological Review, 60:S2, pp. 84–101 (2013), DOI: 10.1111/1467-954X.12039
© 2013 The Author. Editorial organisation © 2013 The Editorial Board of the Sociological Review. Published by John Wiley & Sons Ltd, 9600 Garsington Road, Oxford OX4 2DQ, UK and 350 Main Street, Malden, MA 02148, USA

Despite the proliferation of labelling and its potential culpability in the production of waste, it has been subject to little research attention. Building on the work of Frohlich (2011) and others (eg Eden *et al.*, 2008), who have started to 'open the black box' of food labelling, this paper explores the evolution of the expiry date labelling system in the UK. It situates concerns about the role of date labelling in the production of food waste in relation to shifting understandings of the role not only of the label itself but also of the consumer, and of knowledge associated with the 'end of food'.

As Frank Trentmann (2006) demonstrates, the 'consumer' is not a stable figure, but emerges in dynamic relations with other actors, authorities and experts. The figure of 'the consumer' is mobilized differently at different times, its boundaries drawn and redrawn and its authority and interests appropriated by different groups. This is evident in the evolution of food labelling. For example, Frohlich (2011) considers how the nutrition label represents changing understandings of the consumer within the US Food and Drugs Administration (FDA). He describes how US regulators in the 1950s and 60s concentrated on the 'ordinary consumer' – embodied by the quality-concerned housewife – and represented in an institutional focus on standardized, quality products. In the 1970s, this construction gave way to the model of the 'informed consumer' as the FDA moved towards the loosely standardized provision of *information* and a labelling discourse that emphasized 'consumer empowerment'. By the 1990s, however, Frohlich shows this next version had given way to standardized nutrition information that attempted to balance the interests of food and health lobbies, alongside a model of public *education* in which consumers were – and continue to be – brought into agreement – commensurated – with nutritional guidelines.

Frohlich's discussion of the changing roles taken by actors in relation to labels and their association with differing distributions of knowledge and expertise is instructive for the analysis of date labelling. This paper explores the historical and spatial evolution of the date marking system of food in the UK as a project designed to define and capture 'good' and 'safe' food. Expiration date marks are obligatory on pre-packed foodstuffs both in the UK and across the EU. They currently take the form of 'best-before' or 'use-by' dates. The latter communicates food safety risks and risk management practices to the consumer. It represents 'the date up to and including which the food may be used safely (e.g. cooked or processed or consumed) if it has been stored correctly' (Food Standards Agency (FSA), 2003). 'Best-before' dating of food refers to the predicted longevity of quality characteristics (flavour, appearance, texture etc.). Other labels such as 'display until' are used by stores in stock control.

This paper describes how the date labelling system reflects societal anxieties about the food system and incorporates changing understandings of the consumer role – from concerned housewife, to neo-liberal agent of food safety, to environmentally responsible actor. It draws attention to the recurrent problematization of what constitutes 'reliable' knowledge about shelf-life and consumer behaviour within date labelling debates. This paper examines four specific periods in the history of date labelling: a period prior to the late 1960s, where periodic demands for mandatory expiry labels were deemed impractical; the introduction of the first mandatory system in the 1970s for the purposes of consumer protection; the inclusion of date labelling in food safety reforms in the 1980s; and its place in early twenty-first-century debates on food waste.

Freshness and stock management

The first suggestions that some form of date marking should be applied to food reflected the value attached to 'freshness' as an ideal in late nineteenth- and early twentieth-century 'consumer capitalism' (Freidberg, 2009: 484). As Freidberg describes, 'freshness' is ambiguous and frequently contested and, in this particular period, new food packaging and transport technologies prompted both concern about the authenticity of freshness and suggestions that the government should intervene to protect the customer from retailer malpractice. In 1913, proposals were introduced in the UK to mark cans of condensed milk with dates of manufacture. These were never enacted, primarily because of the intervention of World War I, but also because of explicit resistance to marking or labelling schemes from the food industry. This opposition emphasized the uncertain connection between labels and the labelled contents. It also reflected the attitude in 1930s' UK food governance that 'market forces', rather than intervention, represented the best form of regulation (Phillips and French, 1998). Consequently, in 1939, the President of the UK Board of Trade stated in Parliament that:

> as at present advised, I am not satisfied that the advantages which might result from [mandatory date marking] would outweigh the administrative and technical difficulties involved. (House of Commons 26/4/39)

Despite these difficulties, coded date marking was widely used for stock management of tinned food by the late 1940s, and its use expanded as prepared, packaged product lines became increasingly common. Retailers also introduced new systems to manage the freshness of their baked and prepared products. The visibility of these coded systems led to pressure for decoded, 'open' date marking, as described by Marks and Spencer's technologist Norman Robson:

> *NR*: We'd done a lot of work on this cherry Genoa cake, and when you make it you make it in a big slab, because to make it smaller affects the quality of it . . . So, what we did was to build in to the sheets of film a coloured strip, and the colour represented the day on which the girl cut and wrapped the cake, and then the store would know when the cake was cut and wrapped and hence they received it, 'cause they always received it on the same day as it was cut and wrapped, and how long they'd got to sell it. And that was really the starting point for real control. And the magic word was 'Progby'. Purple, red, orange, green, blue, yellow. Six days of the week. And if you wrapped it on a Monday, you had film with a purple streak in it, and so it went on.

And that was the first real attempt, certainly for us, to label a perishable food with the date of packing.

I: But there was no indication on that that would tell the customers to eat within a week or two days or . . . ?

NR: No, there wasn't initially, but customers started asking questions and so we told them. And we issued a little ticket which was put on the display explaining what the coloured strip was . . . Because you really need to come clean with customers – they spot these things and they ask questions and you should answer them . . . But I mean that was the beginning, as I say, of this freshness story and this dating business that's now so terribly important.
(Marks and Spencer's food technologist Norman Robson, n.d.[1])

Marks and Spencer's in-house labelling codes were gradually opened up in response to emerging consumer demand. Making dates of packing or manufacture 'readable' in the form of the sell-by date represented the food industry 'coming clean' with the consumer, a valuable element in a transparent, honest relationship between the retailer and their customers.

As Marks and Spencer's and other manufacturers began making their labelling schemes more understandable, open date labelling regulations were also being introduced across Europe. Indeed, by the early 1970s, the UK was one of only three European countries *not* to have some form of mandatory open date marking system (along with Belgium and Sweden; Trenchard, 1973). This pressure for labelling illustrated the growing importance of objective, transparent standards in post-war definitions of quality (Cochoy, 2005) as well as the emerging power of consumer organizations and of the consumer's 'right to know'.

Mobilizing the consumer's right to know

As labelling became widespread, the direct consumer pressure described by Robson became accompanied in policy circles by various 'mobilizations' of consumer concerns and anxieties (cf. Miller and Rose, 1997). Both proponents and opponents of labelling – together with those of particular forms of labelling – drew on their relationship with, and knowledge of, the consumer to support their position. Thus supporters of labelling within Parliament, such as Conservative MP Sally Oppenheim (later Minister for Consumer Affairs and chair of the National Consumer Council) invoked the figure of the 'British housewife' in support of labelling, to argue that:

> it is an insult to the housewife to put coded date stamping on food when she can buy French yoghurt in any shop in England with the date clearly marked on it *not* in code. (House of Commons 21/11/72, emphasis added)

Although a 1964 government review reiterated that labelling was technically impractical and might actually result in a 'false sense of security' among consumers (Turner, 1995), the Food Standards Committee was asked to revisit the question in the early 1970s. Its final report reflected wider assertions of the consumer's 'right to know' (cf. Trentmann, 2006) in recommending the introduction of mandatory labelling. For the *British Food Journal*, the decision to introduce date labelling was:

> a timely reminder of what public pressure can achieve these days; how sustained advocacy and publicity by interested sectors of society . . . can secure legislative changes which . . . run counter to trade opinions. (Anon., 1973: 71)

The *British Food Journal* editorial reflected the transformation of the consumer 'questions' posed to Marks and Spencer's into an organized campaign led by *The Sunday Times,* consumer-oriented MPs in Parliament and newly formed consumer organizations. In response, the government established the 'Steering Group on Food Freshness' (SGFF) to advise on labelling under the leadership of Patricia McLaughlin, ex-MP and co-founder of consumer organization the Housewives' Trust. The steering group's report (SGFF, 1976) formed the basis not only for subsequent regulation but also for the British position within European negotiations over the harmonization of labelling.

The SGFF report reflected the continuing consensus that the safety of food was sufficiently covered by existing legislation and that the important task for new regulation was to ensure the taste, texture and acceptability of food (cf. Cooter and Fulton, 2001). It separated foods into four groups on the basis of their shelf-life, in which greatest concern is for those products with very short shelf-lives, such as sausages, pies, soft cheese and cream cakes. The focus of the report was overwhelmingly on freshness and quality, and the reference to the potentially 'serious adverse effects' of these products was the only time that it concerned itself with food safety.

Even once a decision had been taken to introduce labelling, the structure and content of the labels continued to be contested. The consumer may have had the 'right to know', but *what* they needed to know, and *how* this was established, had not been determined. For example, a commentary on food labelling from dietician Jenny Salmon in the *Journal of Nutrition and Food Science* argued that the labelling system would not fulfil the consumer's requirements for freshness:

> because people have been told for years that old food is stale food and may be 'off' *the consumer's demand is interpreted by some people* as meaning she wants date stamps, dates of production or eat by dates. *How wrong can you be? She doesn't really want any of those.* They are simply the inadequate terms she uses to express her wish for fresh food. No date stamp is going to guarantee that. (Salmon, 1977: 4; my emphasis)

For Salmon, date labels were an ineffective proxy for freshness, and reflected the inability of the consumer to clearly represent their own demands. Salmon's concerns illustrate how the introduction of labelling opened up a space for a range of interest groups to emphasize their own ability to 'interpret' consumer demand and introduce their own representations of the consumer. As the system focused on providing consumers with knowledge, those who could establish that

The Sociological Review, 60:S2, pp. 84–101 (2013), DOI: 10.1111/1467-954X.12039

they best knew or best represented the consumer interest were able to comment most authoritatively on the suitability of different labels.

In line with the 1973 recommendations of the Food Standards Committee, a 'sell-by' date label had been widely adopted on a voluntary basis by food businesses concerned with pre-empting regulatory intervention. This wording was recommended by the SGFF and represented the food industry's preferred option, and was one aimed at the retailer. However, with the UK's accession to the European Union in 1973 and participation in efforts at regulatory harmonization, its food politics became entwined with those of Europe. Other European member states and consumer groups favoured the adoption of a 'best-before' or 'eat by' date – dates aimed at the consumer rather than at businesses.

As the debate developed, each actor focused on their (assumed) superior ability to act as spokespersons for the 'concerned consumer'. For example, in a House of Lords debate in March 1977, Lord Mottistone, Director of the Cake and Biscuit Alliance, challenged the ability of 'consumer interests' to represent the consumer, arguing that:

> *manufacturers listen to what the consumers say.* After all, their livelihood depends upon the consumers; so there is not much problem there. The fact of the matter is that *there is sometimes a tendency to listen to people who say they are consumers rather than to representatives of consumers* . . . it is very important to make the distinction. One would suggest to the Government that *the manufacturer probably knows his consumers better than the Government do, or possibly sometimes the organisations which purport to represent them.* (House of Lords 17/3/77, emphasis added).

In the House of Commons a month later, MP Giles Shaw focused on Lord Mottistone's continued questioning in this particular session to mobilize his own authority to represent the consumer. Shaw concentrated on an exchange with Dr Roberts of the Consumers' Association, who argued that consumers supported the adoption of 'best before' labelling. Roberts' argument – which was challenged – was based on consumer research:

> *Giles Shaw*: Lord Mottistone asked: Do you have a methodical way of doing that or is it done rather generally by the officials and people like yourself talking to their wives or meeting a consumer from time to time? Dr Roberts replied: I certainly do talk to my wife about this problem, but we have just spent £6,000 on a very large survey finding out *not what Consumers' Association members think, but what the general public think.* We have carried out very large surveys of about 800 people. I am sure that that is reasonable research, but . . . *we should have evidence based upon substantial research.* (House of Commons 21/4/1977, emphasis added)

Lord Mottistone's attack on the Consumers' Association (CA) problematized their authority to mobilize the consumer. For Roberts, the authority of the CA was based on their ability to interpret the consumer through quantitative research. Similarly, by repeating Roberts' response to Lord Mottistone in the House of Commons, Shaw established the value of consumer research in the face of industry's experiential knowledge of the consumer. Having introduced the CA to validate the need for research, Shaw then introduced a further survey, sponsored by a 'major meat producer', which trumped that of the CA by suggesting that the public supported the industry preference for 'sell-by' rather than 'eat-by' or 'best-before' dating.

The contested knowledge associated with introduction of date labels corresponded not only to the use of labels and the representation of the consumer, but the definition of labels themselves and the representation of material changes in food products. Early resistance to labels had focused on the difficulties of ensuring correspondence between the label and the qualities of the product. Mandatory labels, therefore, required the production of reliable knowledge about product longevity, or shelf life. The SGFF report argued that this had to be the responsibility of manufacturers, as the food retail sector was too diverse to ensure accurate checking. The report suggested that while the larger supermarket retailers might be able to undertake ongoing checks for freshness, such company stores were too few and far between for this to be practical. Consequently, food manufacturers required a stable definition of freshness that could be applied at the point foods left the production line. However, as described in a 1973 article in the *British Food Journal*:

> when we come to such items as sandwich cakes and swiss rolls, which deteriorate gradually . . . it is not so easy to know where to draw the line . . . It is in the manufacturers' interests to carry out tests to ascertain the stage at which the cakes will no longer appeal to customers. (Stafford, 1973: 146)

As shelf-life literally could not be determined 'on the shelf', actors from without the production system had to be incorporated, namely via 'a tasting panel with members drawn from both production and sales departments, together with some housewives' (Stafford, 1973: 146). The recommendations from this panel place the consumer within the definition of shelf life and the bounding of freshness, highlighting the in-folding of linear production-consumption relations as the consumer now became physically as well as virtually present within quality assessment. Tasting panels, therefore, enabled date labels to reflect a specific representation of consumers' tastes and expectations.

Establishing and asserting freshness immediately raised concerns about the waste of stock, and thus the loss of profits, for food businesses. As a *British Food Journal* editorial described in 1971:

> The main objection by the trade against actual date stamping is that shoppers will naturally take the freshest, according to the date, leaving the later packets, with resultant losses. (Anon., 1971: 72)

The concern of the industry was that by (re-)introducing visible differences in freshness, date labelling would lead to new forms of consumer selection – an unsought-for consequence of the exercise of informed consumer choice. Similarly, the SGFF report introduced concerns about wastage and consumer understanding, specifically highlighting that waste would be borne disproportionately by those products where freshness was most valued (SGFF, 1976).

The Sociological Review, 60:S2, pp. 84–101 (2013), DOI: 10.1111/1467-954X.12039
© 2013 The Author. Editorial organisation © 2013 The Editorial Board of the Sociological Review

In the Lords debate outlined above, Lord Sainsbury, chairman of the national supermarket group, argued that 'best before' dates which tried to capture the full lifespan of foods would result in over-cautious labelling as manufacturers attempted to 'safeguard' themselves (House of Lords 17/3/77), and consequently lead to waste. Where Lord Mottistone questioned the type of knowledge of the consumer embedded in the choice of labels, Lord Sainsbury challenged knowledge of expiration, suggesting that sell-by dates which worked to the point of sale would more accurately capture the deterioration of food within directly controllable parts of the food system.

The date labelling system was finally introduced in the UK in 1980 when the Food Labelling Regulations harmonized UK law with the 1979 EC Labelling Directive (79/112/EC). The regulation called for a 'date of minimum durability' – the 'best-before' date – but provided member states with derogations to use their own terms, thus allowing the UK to use the sell-by system.

While the introduction of labelling reflected a successful exercise of the 'consumer interest', the form in which date labels appeared showed the influence of industrial interests. Moreover, it was not illegal for food to be sold after the date mark. Effectively, labels were enrolled into the neo-liberal project of the new Thatcher government: that is, consumers, having 'pushed' for the introduction of labelling and mobilized in its calculation, were now enrolled to make it work. An education campaign, for example, encouraged them to challenge retailers found to be selling out-of-date food (Collins, 1983) before reporting it to Trading Standards officers.

Ensuring food safety

The third stage in the evolution of the date labelling system involved a shift in focus from food quality and the representation of the consumer interest, to food safety and the protection of consumer health. It involved direct government intervention as labels became tools of enforcement as well as guidance, and incorporated a redefinition of the knowledge-base associated with the definition of the end of food.

In the mid-1980s the 'food scare' became the defining feature of the British food system, referring to episodes of 'acute collective anxiety' sparked by reports of risks posed by invisible chemical hazards or food-borne pathogens (Beardsworth, 1990). The 'food scare' had significant consequences for the general regulation of food safety in Britain and for the expiry date labelling of pre-packed food in particular. At this time, the safety of the British food supply became the focus of widespread public disquiet and calls for reform to a regulatory system that had remained predominantly unchanged since the Food and Drugs Act of 1955. This 1955 Act had replaced the 1875 Sale of Food and Drugs Act (SFDA) – introduced to protect the 'public' from fraud and adulteration (Phillips and French, 1998; Draper and Green 2002) – and established a Ministry of Agriculture, Fisheries and Food (MAFF), which assumed control of standards for food and food labelling jointly with the Ministry of Health.

Although they led ultimately to a widespread questioning of the productivist paradigm of the UK food system in light of BSE, the first 'food scares' of the 1980s were primarily associated with changes in food preparation and retail, particularly the spread of cook/chill foods. Such foods were seen as introducing new – and serious – microbiological risks to the food supply. The first major food scare was an outbreak of Salmonella in 1988 which infected people throughout the country, including 120 members of the House of Lords. It was closely followed by what was termed 'Listeria hysteria': several outbreaks of listeriosis, with the bacteria consequently found to be widespread in cheeses, cooked meats and pâtés.

As food scares seemed to proliferate through Britain, the regulatory framework for food, and the role of MAFF, understandably came under heavy scrutiny. Date labelling – suddenly shifting from being a tool of consumer information and protection – became newly problematized as a failing element in the regulation of pre-packed foods. Consequently, as the regulatory system was reworked, date labels moved from being a consumer-oriented tool primarily concerned with ensuring food quality to be at the heart of the regulation of food safety throughout systems of food production and consumption.

In February 1989, the Institute of Environmental Health Officers warned that sell-by dates on perishable chilled products did not represent 'safety', and called for the introduction of 'eat by' dates (Hall, 1989), thus resurrecting the wording debates of a decade earlier. Later in the same year, as concerns about food safety continued to mount, the *Guardian*'s resident poet Simon Rae positioned date labelling among the myriad problems of the British food system:

Another day, another chef's selection
Fresh from the current Bad Food Guide;
And then the accusations, counter-claims
As someone totals up who died:
The elderly, the weak, the unarrived
(The fit and strong, quite unconcerned, survive).

The experts wring their hands and mutter darkly,
'There is a lot of it about.
The dose-response relationship's not known,
However, there can be no doubt
We need to spend more on research, not less,
If we are going to overcome this mess.'

The Government is getting quite defensive
At having to explain away
What seems to absolutely everyone
An inexplicable delay
In warning people of the risk they take
When eating almost anything but steak.

The Sociological Review, 60:S2, pp. 84–101 (2013), DOI: 10.1111/1467-954X.12039
© 2013 The Author. Editorial organisation © 2013 The Editorial Board of the Sociological Review

(All members of advisory committees
To do with food – it is a fact –
Are willy-nilly now required to sign
The old Official Secrets Act.
If Gorby knew the secrets of listeria
There would, I'm sure, be national hysteria).

What's clear is that the whole thing needs reviewing,
From Old MacDonald's lethal sprays
Through hygiene standards in the shops, to what
The product packaging displays.
The sell-by date is past its sell-by date
As is, perhaps, the Secretary of State.
(Rae, 1989)

Pressure for reform resulted in changes to the labelling system. The UK not only implemented new EC Directives (89/395/EEC), but also went further both with its own specific hygiene and labelling requirements in 1989 and in the later 1990 Food Safety Act. The EU directive, however, removed the UK's derogation and signalled the end of the 'sell-by date'. Instead, it introduced 'use-by' dating for foods deemed hazardous to health after a short period of time (Turner, 1995). 'Best-before' labelling was also extended to a wider range of long-life products and frozen foods, while hygiene regulations created a 'chill chain' requiring food businesses to store chilled short-life foods between 0 and 8°C.

The food scares also prompted the commissioning of the Richmond Report on the Microbiological Safety of Food. The first volume of this report, published in 1990, welcomed the changes to the labelling system:

> the introduction of the 'use by' date . . . will mean that microbiological considerations must be taken into account. This should in turn ensure that *the dates shown on food are far more directly related to the assurance of food safety than has been the case hitherto.*
> (Richmond, 1990: 144; my emphasis)

With the introduction of the 'use by' framework, the labelling system extended to explicitly cover food safety. As Rae's poem suggests, the food safety concerns of the 1980s prompted changes in the institutional knowledge requirements associated with the regulation of food. In a publication in early 1989, the National Consumer Council (NCC), led by the now Baroness Oppenheim-Barnes, argued that while consumers had a duty to observe date marks,

> above all, [they] need to know the degree of risk, if there is any, of food contamination. They need consistent and reliable information. They need to know that research is adequate. (cited in Hornsby, 1989)

By this time the dominant concern of the NCC, ostensibly spokesperson for 'the consumer' had become the risk of contamination rather than the threat of deception. This redefinition of food in terms of risk and safety correspondingly required new definitions of the limits of food that could reflect the shifting constituency of date labelling. While the 1979 system involved freshness sampling based on the mobilization of consumer taste by manufacturers, the use-by system, with its focus on safety, required research that could establish degrees of risk and independent verification of this data. Government food safety research, which had been on the wane, was reinvigorated as food safety became a matter of national focus and the limits of existing knowledge were recognized in the establishment of the Advisory Committee on the Microbiological Safety of Food (Cooter and Fulton, 2001).

Guidance on shelf-life determination in the late 1970s had been provided by the *BFJ* alongside industry representatives. In contrast, the Richmond Report called for government guidance that:

> might need to stress that shelf-lives for individual products can only be determined in light of proper consideration of the particular product by a suitably qualified microbiologist. (Richmond, 1990: 144)

The 'use-by' labelling regime introduced new forms of knowledge and expertise and rigorous requirements for testing, as well as an enhanced role for 'qualified' experts. Specifically, it introduced endpoints for food defined in terms of its 'microbiological load' rather than consumer taste.

The changes to date labels, together with their association with new forms of knowledge production, fundamentally changed the role and responsibilities of the consumer. In the pursuit of food safety for 'the population', the views and tastes of 'consumers' were subordinated to microbiological expertise. Consumer bodies such as the NCC also shifted their focus onto the systemic, invisible and unavoidable risks posed by food – as opposed to the more visible threat of the untrustworthy shopkeeper. Whereas consumer tastes had earlier been virtually, and sometimes physically, present within quality definition, the new food safety regimes in contrast constructed consumer behaviour as an object of concern. For the 'use-by' system to work, for example, the Richmond report stressed that government would need to '. . . remind consumers from time to time of the meaning of the 'use by' date and of the risks of not observing it' (Richmond, 1990: 144).

The report also stressed that consumers were part of the solution as well as the problem, describing their responsibility to check for 'poor practices at the point of sale', such as food past its date mark (Richmond, 1990: 145). However, while the 'sell-by' date had historically stopped at the retailer, the new regulations moved the site at which food safety was seen by the state – that is, the point at which the life of food 'officially' ended – into the consumer home. 'Use-by' labelling thus represented part of the re-imagining of the home as the arena of food safety management, resonantly captured in the description of the domestic kitchen as 'the last line of defence in the food chain' (Richmond, 1990: 145).

Waste and uncertainty

The changes introduced in 1989 were reasserted in both the Food Labelling Regulations of 1996, in subsequent amendments to European legislation in 2000

(2000/13/EEC) and the EU Food Information Regulation of 2011. Recently, however, the terms under which date labels are discussed has undergone a further change, moving away from quality and safety to focus on waste. This in turn has resulted in new understandings of the role of the consumer and in the relations of knowledge and expertise associated with defining the 'end of food'.

The use and meanings of date labels have become central to UK debates about food waste and the balance of power and responsibility between consumers, retailers, manufacturers and government. As described earlier, worries about food waste were present as an industry-raised concern about the loss of retailer stock in the background of the 1970s date labelling debate. In the 1990s, companies such as Marks and Spencer's made a virtue of this loss, highlighting their donations of out-of-date food to redistribution charities. In the late 2000s, however, attention has shifted to focus on the role of labels in 'unnecessary' food waste in the retail and domestic context.

In June 2009 Hilary Benn, Spelman's Labour predecessor as Minister for Food, the Environment and Rural Affairs, gave a speech to the Chartered Institute of Waste Management in which he argued that:

> When we buy food it should be easy to know how long we should keep it for and how we should store it. Too many of us are putting things in the bin simply because we're not sure, we're confused by the label, or were just playing safe. (Benn, 2009)

Benn's speech highlighted key features of discussions around food waste in contemporary Britain and distributed blame for waste between retailers, consumers and the labelling system. The speech took place at the peak of a wave of attention to food waste sparked by WRAP's influential *The Food We Waste* report (2008) and Tristram Stuart's *Waste* (2009). WRAP (2008) suggested that almost a quarter of waste food was disposed of because it was 'past its date', but also argued that significant quantities of food were thrown away 'in date'. Similarly, Stuart devoted a chapter to how 'the sell-by date mythology' contributed to food waste.

Concerns about consumers echoed the recommendations of the Richmond Report and the SGFF about the ability of consumers to use labels as they are intended. However, they also reflect the post-1989 movement of labels into the domestic context, and the relocation not only of safety, but of quality and waste concerns. Along with FSA surveys (2007), WRAP's work (2008) suggests that confusion exists about the correct meanings of 'use-by' and 'best-before' labels, and that this potentially contributes to food waste and to risky food practices. Similarly, Stuart described the public as 'in utter confusion' (2009: 62) over these issues. In each case, re-educating or re-skilling consumers in the use of labels is proposed as part of the solution to the waste problem. As the chief executive of Leatherhead Food Research, one of the major sources of expert advice on shelf-life, argued:

> the distinction between 'use by' and 'best before' is very useful. One is about safety, the other is about quality. The key is to ensure that consumers understand the distinction. (Berryman, 2010)

Unlike previous debates around date labelling – which pushed reform of labels themselves – these discussions focus on the consumer and reflect a wider problematization of consumer behaviour and knowledge related to food. In the 1970s debates on labelling, knowledge of food quality was considered as something that had been unfairly taken away from the British consumer, as in Oppenheim's comparison with the French and in campaigns by the then-new consumer organizations. In contrast, by the 2000s, a lack of knowledge about food has become the consumer's responsibility, while the role of the state is to provide the information required for the exercise of responsible citizenship and effective self-governance (see Draper and Green, 2002; Frohlich, 2011; Watson and Meah, this volume).

Concerns about consumers are again tied up with the long-standing challenge of knowing how long food lasts, and on what terms it can be deemed to be inedible. For Stuart, WRAP, Benn and Spelman, consumer confusion is exacerbated by inconsistent and/or unnecessary labelling. Indeed, Stuart (2009) approvingly quotes US industry body the Food Marketing Institute in their opposition to 'overly-complex' date labels, citing this as 'the reign of common sense'. WRAP point to the case of four Cheddar cheeses to demonstrate the vagaries of the labelling system (Parry, 2009). Within the same product group, they highlight the variation in the application of 'use-by' or 'best-before' labels – that is, between the definition of the product as either potentially unsafe or as simply likely to lose quality. This perceived unreliability of date labelling has prompted the commissioning of the new guidance described earlier (DEFRA, 2011a, 2011b) – together with Spelman's suggestion that such guidance would lead to the clear identification of 'good', 'safe' food.

The DEFRA guidance (2011b) addresses variation by introducing a programmatic 'decision tree' for labelling. This starts from an initial distinction between microbiologically perishable and non-perishable goods. However, as a worked example of yoghurt provided in Figure 1 shows, this line is difficult to maintain.

The final distinction between 'use-by' and 'best-before' for Yoghurt B depends on judgements made at a series of stages. The decision tree suggests this is related to the intrinsic qualities of the product. However, the accompanying documentation makes it clear that labelling decisions also reflect the material and social contexts of food manufacture. Making a judgement between a 'use-by' date (which may lead to unnecessary waste) or a 'best-before' date (which may lead to unnecessary risk) requires the manufacturer to be confident in their knowledge not only of the product, but also – perhaps more importantly – their control of the production environment. Thus, at Q2, a 'best-before' label is applied to Yoghurt A, a similar product to Yoghurt B. This decision is not made on the certainty that B will represent a risk, but on proxies including the manufacturer's record of hygiene and knowledge of the behaviour of *Listeria monocytogenes* in the product. The manufacturer of Yoghurt B has only had 'very occasional' detection of *L. monocytogenes*, yet has no evidence that it will *not* grow in the product (DEFRA, 2011b: 16). Consequently, yoghurt produced

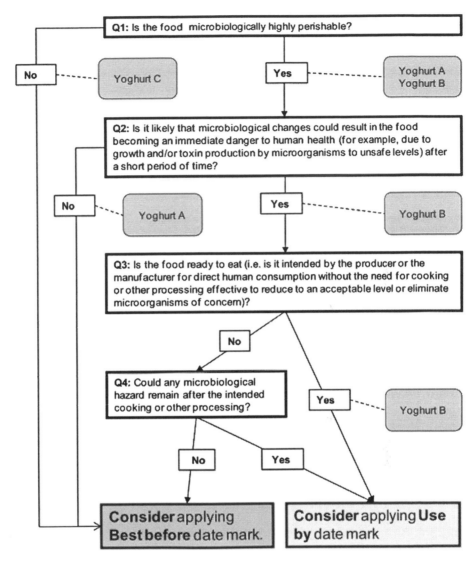

Figure 1: *Decision tree for date labelling of yoghurts from DEFRA (2011b).*

by this manufacturer is deemed a potential threat regardless of its own inherent characteristics. The choice of label is therefore determined by the manufacturers' past control over production and their access to appropriate forms of microbiological evidence and expertise.

Moreover, in debates about food waste, the ability or inability of the science of shelf-life to provide accurate guides to food decay and deterioration has also become a key point of contest. These contested (in)abilities reopen the closures of the 1970s and 1980s related to the appropriate production of knowledge. For

The Sociological Review, 60:S2, pp. 84–101 (2013), DOI: 10.1111/1467-954X.12039

example, once a quality-defined 'best-before' label is applied, the question remains as to whether calculated sensory shelf-lives accurately correspond to the everyday experiences and sensitivities of consumer taste (Hough, 2010). Similarly, the example of yoghurts shows how a microbiologically safe product may still be labelled with a 'use-by date' and potentially wasted. The history of date labelling presented here suggests these debates can be understood as a further iteration of the politics of knowing and representing the consumer and foodstuffs.

Conclusions: date labels and the consumer

Clearly, as date labelling has evolved, distinct roles have been attributed to the consumer; roles which echo both government judgements about the relation between the interests of consumers and the food industry and also different approaches to food governance in general. Equally clearly, these changing roles draw attention to the diversity of knowledge practices and expertises associated with consumption.

In the first period outlined above, consumers were judged to be well protected by existing law, and the emphasis of government was on improving the profitability of British food companies. At this stage, date labelling was rejected on the basis that the complexity of the food supply made it infeasible to effectively calculate how long foods would remain edible. The systems that did exist were primarily used for stock control. These systems were also coded, making them inaccessible to the uninitiated.

By the second period, dating from the early 1960s, we see that change was spurred by socio-technical shifts in food preparation and retailing that made the freshness of food more difficult to ascertain first-hand. As large retailers such as Marks and Spencer's expanded their food ranges, they also began to introduce stock control systems on short-life foods and open these controls up to 'reading' by the consumer. Pressure to expand this system came from both consumers themselves and the bodies claiming to represent them, who had dually begun to play an increasingly visible role in parliamentary debates about food. This new 'presence' – coupled with diversifying company structures – ultimately produced a labelling system that (ideally) balanced the desire to protect consumers from misleading retailing and avoided loading the food industry with onerous legislation. It also coincided with neo-liberal moves to endow the consumer with responsibilities for the governance of the food system. However, the form of such labels became the subject of considerable debate as the ability to know and represent both the consumer and the edible life of foodstuffs were contested.

In the late 1980s, date labelling was again placed at the heart of efforts to protect consumers. The initial labelling system had focused on quality, and thus ideologically represented a continuing consensus that existing food safety legislation effectively protected the consumer from food-borne illnesses. As the 'food scare' became a feature of the British food supply specifically associated with the

The Sociological Review, 60:S2, pp. 84–101 (2013), DOI: 10.1111/1467-954X.12039

introduction of chilled foods, date labels became a means of protecting the health of the public from unseen microbiological threats. The consumer now became a responsibilized and cooperative member of a threatened population. The legal requirement that food be taken off sale after a certain date provided government and retailers with a means of managing the risks posed by, in particular, *Listeria* up to the point of sale, while the demand that consumer *'Use By'* attempted to extend this control into the home. In turn, this labelling relied on a new nexus of microbiological expertise and endpoints of edibility that became tightly defined in terms of the microbiological 'load' of food.

Finally, in the late twentieth and early twenty-first centuries, date labels have become central to debates about food waste. While the reforms of the 1980s introduced a dual labelling system of 'best-before' and 'use-by' dates, this system is now considered to confuse consumers, a situation not helped by the continuing use of the deprecated term 'sell-by' in popular discourse. The reduction of food waste thus represents a new problematization of date labelling in which consumers are considered as abjuring the responsibilities given to them in the 1980s. Politicians, industry and waste activists such as Tristram Stuart have all emphasized the need for better 'consumer understanding' of the labelling system. The 'proper use' of date labels thus becomes part of the exercise of environmentally conscious consumer-citizenship. However, as in previous periods, the very debates that arise over date labelling and waste highlight the politics of knowledge associated with representing consumer interests and food expiration. Efforts to reform the system involve disentangling the quality and safety roles of the labelling system, and establishing the appropriate basis for doing so. As the introduction of government guidance shows, though, this is not simply a question of applying certain knowledge of food. Instead, it is inextricable from the confidence food businesses have in both their production systems, and in their own and regulatory bodies' understandings of consumer behaviour.

More broadly, this paper highlights how regulatory objects such as date labels increase the shelf-life of social anxieties about food by carrying them into the future. They introduce a path-dependency to regulatory interventions; a dependency grounded in responses to past articulations of consumer, government and industry interests and of technological change. Labels coalesce and preserve the social and material relations of food. Every 'best-before' label, for instance, carries the legacy of consumer organizations' campaigns to prevent the sale of stale food to the housewife following the emergence of prepared, packaged foods. Equally influentially, 'use-by' dates embody the lasting consequences of the microbiological menace of the 1980s; mediatized food scares; the introduction of chilled foods; and the unpredictability of consumer behaviour.

Acknowledgements

Thanks are due to the editors and anonymous reviewers for their helpful and insightful comments and suggestions on previous versions of this paper. Thanks also to Peter Jackson and the 'Consumer Culture in an Age of Anxiety' (CONANX) group at the University of Sheffield for their discussions of date labelling and food safety. This research was funded by an Advanced Investigator Grant awarded to Peter Jackson by the European Research Council (ERC-2008-AdG-230287-CONANX).

Note

1 Interview in British Library Food Stories archive, http://www.bl.uk/learning/resources/pdf/foodstories/robsoncaketranscript.pdf (accessed 11 November 2011).

References

Anon., (1971), 'Date stamping of food', *British Food Journal*, May/June: 68–72.
Anon., (1973), 'Compulsory date marking of foods', *British Food Journal*, May/June: 71.
Beardsworth, A.D., (1990), 'Trans-science and moral panics: understanding food scares', *British Food Journal*, 92 (5): 11–16.
Benn, H., (2009), *A World without Waste?* Speech by Hilary Benn at the Futuresource conference at the Excel Centre in London, 9 June, http://www.defra.gov.uk/corporate/about/who/ministers/speeches/hilary-benn/hb090609.htm
Berryman, P., (2010), 'Are date marks approaching their sell by date? Food manufacture', http://www.foodmanufacture.co.uk/Ingredients/Are-date-marks-approaching-their-sell-by-date (accessed 1 March 2010).
Cochoy, F., (2005), 'A brief history of "customers," or the gradual standardization of markets and organizations', *Sociologie du Travail*, 47: e36–e56.
Collins, R., (1983), 'Now you can tell what is food and what is hydroxybenzoate', *The Guardian*, 29 January: 23.
Cooter, R., and Fulton, R., (2001), 'Food matters: food safety research in the UK public sector, 1917–1990', *Food Industry Journal*, 4 (3): 251–262.
DEFRA (Department for Environment, Food and Rural Affairs), (2011a). 'Expiry date for confusing date labels', DEFRA press release, http://www.defra.gov.uk/news/2011/09/15/expiry-date-for-confusing-date-labels/ (accessed 15 September 2011).
DEFRA, (2011b), 'Guidance on the application of date labels to food', http://www.defra.gov.uk/publications/files/pb132629-food-date-labelling-110915.pdf (accessed 16 May 2012).
Draper, A. and Green, J., (2002), 'Food safety and consumers: constructions of choice and risk', *Social Policy and Administration*, 36: 610–625.
Eden, S., Bear, C., and Walker, G. (2008), 'Mucky carrots and other proxies: problematising the knowledge-fix for sustainable and ethical consumption', *Geoforum*, 1044–1057.
Freidberg, S., (2009), *Fresh: A Perishable History*, Cambridge, MA: Belknap Press.
Frohlich, X., (2011), 'Imaginer des consommateurs, constituer les sujets: l'étiquetage nutritionnel aux États Unis, 1945–1995', *Sciences de la société*, 80 (Mai): 11–27.
FSA (Food Standards Agency), (2003), 'Use by date Guidance Notes', http://www.food.gov.uk/foodindustry/guidancenotes/labelregsguidance/usebydateguid (accessed 6 May 2010). Archived version available at http://webarchive.nationalarchives.gov.uk/20100817075455/http://www.food.gov.uk/foodindustry/guidancenotes/labelregsguidance/usebydateguid
FSA, (2007), *Consumer Attitudes to Food Standards: Wave 7*, Report prepared by TNS for the Food Standards Agency, London: FSA.
Hall, C., (1989), 'Sell-by on food "not reliable" ', *The Independent*, 21 February: 2.

The Sociological Review, 60:S2, pp. 84–101 (2013), DOI: 10.1111/1467-954X.12039
© 2013 The Author. Editorial organisation © 2013 The Editorial Board of the Sociological Review

Hornsby, M., (1989), 'Consumer council presses for charter to ensure food safety', *The Times*, 15 March.

Hough, G., (2010), *Sensory Shelf Life Estimation of Food Products*, Boca Raton, FL: CRC Press.

Miller, P. and Rose, N., (1997), 'Mobilizing the consumer: assembling the subject of consumption', *Theory, Culture and Society*, 14 (1): 1–36.

Morgan, K., Marsden, T., and Murdoch, J., (2006), *Worlds of Food: Place, Power, and Provenance in the Food Chain*, Oxford: Oxford University Press.

Parry, A., (2009), 'Date labels: what could we do differently?' A presentation for WRAP, www.wrap.org.uk/document.rm?id=7216 (accessed 19 November 2011).

Phillips, J. and French, M., (1998), 'Adulteration and food law, 1899–1939', *Twentieth Century British History*, 9 (3): 350–369.

Rae, S., (1989), 'Thought for food', *The Guardian*, 22 July.

Richmond, M., (1990), *The Microbiological Safety of Food*, Report of the Committee on the Microbiological Safety of Food, London: HMSO.

Salmon, J., (1977), 'The consumer and the food label', *Nutrition and Food Science*, 77 (1), L 2–4.

SGFF (Steering Group on Food Freshness), (1976), *Final Report of the Steering Group on Food Freshness to the Ministry of Agriculture, Fisheries and Food*, London: HMSO.

Stafford, H., (1973), 'Date marking of food', *British Food Journal*, September/October: 146–148.

Stuart, T., (2009), *Waste: Uncovering the Global Food Scandal*, London: Penguin.

Trenchard, L., (1973), 'Potential effect of E.E.C. membership on the character of our foods: (a) Will competition still be the consumer's best friend?', *The Journal of the Royal Society for the Promotion of Health*, 93 (5), 233–237.

Trentmann, F., (2006), 'Knowing consumers: histories, identities, practices: an introduction', in F. Trentmann (ed.), *The Making of the Consumer: Knowledge, Power and Identity in the Modern World*, 1–31, London: Berg.

Turner, A., (1995), 'Prepacked food labelling: past, present and future', *British Food Journal*, 97 (5): 23–31.

WRAP (Waste and Resources Action Programme), (2008), *The Food We Waste*, Banbury: WRAP.

101

Food, waste and safety: negotiating conflicting social anxieties into the practices of domestic provisioning

Matt Watson and Angela Meah

Abstract: Two significant realms of social anxiety, visible in the discourses of media and public policy, potentially pull practices of home food provisioning in conflicting directions. On the one hand, campaigns to reduce the astonishing levels of food waste generated in the UK moralize acts of both food saving (such as keeping and finding creative culinary uses for leftovers) and food disposal. On the other hand, agencies concerned with food safety, including food-poisoning, problematize common practices of thrift, saving and reuse around provisioning. The tensions that arise as these public discourses are negotiated together into domestic practices open up moments in which 'stuff' crosses the line from being food to being waste. This paper pursues this through the lens of qualitative and ethnographic data collected as part of a four-year European research programme concerned with consumer anxieties about food. Through focus groups, life-history interviews and observations, data emerged which give critical insights into processes from which food waste results. With a particular focus on how research participants negotiate use-by dates, we argue that interventions to reduce food waste can be enhanced by appreciating how food *becomes* waste through everyday practices.

Keywords: food waste practices, food safety, social anxiety, domestic provisioning, ethnographic methods

Introduction

A host of potential social anxieties can be part of what gets cooked up in the domestic kitchen (Meah and Watson, 2011). Two of these – which pull the practices of domestic provisioning in different directions – are the often competing moral imperatives to avoid food waste, on the one hand, and to ensure food safety on the other. These two competing realms of concern can be followed from the immediacy of the kitchen to relative abstractions of public policy. On one hand, the significant role of food waste in greenhouse gas emissions from household waste treatment is the primary impetus in the UK for a public policy push to reduce the startling proportion of the food that house-

The Sociological Review, 60:S2, pp. 102–120 (2013), DOI: 10.1111/1467-954X.12040

holds buy which then ends up in the waste stream (DEFRA, 2011). On the other hand, compelling arguments for reducing the incidence of foodborne diseases underpin both education and technologies, such as use-by dates, which impel people to throw out food which has passed a point in time at which it is considered to become unsafe to eat. These public discourses represent real tensions that all those involved in the provisioning of food have to negotiate into practice. Whether from concern about the global climate, for household budgets or some vestigial moral imperative for thrift and the avoidance of waste, cultural logics exist that can make us feel guilty about throwing food out. Conversely, whether through scientifically informed concerns about *E.coli* or *Salmonella*, or because finding space in the fridge and a recipe for safely using up leftovers is inconvenient, concerns which could be identified with food safety make their presence felt.

In this article, we use this fundamental tension between food waste and food safety as a distinctive means of cutting through and exposing the mess of practices from which food waste is produced. We do so on the basis of our current research project, which explores continuity and change in families' domestic kitchen practices over the last century as a means of interrogating how differing, and often competing, discourses and sources of knowledge around food are negotiated into quotidian routines. We follow how relatively clear normative public discourses around safety and waste are uneasily translated into the mundane actions of shopping and cooking. This, we contend, distinctively illuminates the challenges of conventional policy approaches in tackling both food waste and food safety in households.

Recently, research has begun to go beyond the stark statistics of domestic food waste and the inferences of profligacy that follow them, to unpick the complex social relations from which food waste emerges (Evans, 2011a, 2012). Two fields of recent research can be drawn together to begin to address what remains a gap in social scientific understanding of food waste.

First, consideration of food waste can clearly be informed by work on waste in a more general sense. From sporadic earlier engagements (Thompson, 1979; Rathje and Murphy, 1992; Gandy, 1994), work on the cultural locations of waste and wasting began to burgeon with the turn of the century (Strasser, 2000; Hawkins and Muecke, 2003; Scanlan, 2005; O'Brien, 2007). Social research on waste has moved from focus on materials that have already been categorized as waste towards understanding of the processes through which materials end up being so categorized. This has been pursued substantially through engagement with work on consumer culture, particularly with debates around material culture, and around everyday practice (Hawkins, 2006; Gregson *et al.*, 2007; Bulkeley and Gregson, 2009). Selected strands of this work have moved more thoroughly into relational materialist perspectives, through which the *matter* that is wasted is an active force in the situations in which it becomes waste (Hawkins, 2009; Gregson *et al.*, 2010).

A similar intellectual trajectory can be traced in a second major field of research, namely, studies focusing on food and its location in everyday life and sociality. In comparison to waste, engagement with food in this register has a longer and more continuous history. Nevertheless, recent years have seen parallel trends with those identified above in waste scholarship, both with a growing location of food research in relation to theories of practice (Warde *et al.*, 2007; Halkier, 2009), and with the emergence of relational materialist approaches which enable exploration of the active role of the stuff of food (Roe, 2006; Bennett, 2007). Bennett (2007) explores the relational agency of food stuffs through the different affordances the vital materiality of foods offer to both situations of consumption and to the flesh and being of humans who ingest it. Drawing on Harris (1985), Roe (2006: 112) sets out to illuminate the question, 'how do things like rancid mammary gland secretions, fungi and rock under particular circumstances become cheese, mushrooms and salt?' Through a relational materialist approach, she argues that 'things become food through how they are handled by humans, not by how they are described and named' (2006: 112).

The easy location of food waste between these two strands of current research enables identification of clear lines of inquiry. In particular, the recognition that matter *becomes* waste, or *becomes* food, within situations of doing makes clear a pressing question of inquiry: how does matter which is food become matter which is waste? What goes on in these moments has been neglected until recent work from David Evans (2011a, 2012). Evans starts from a recognition that food becomes waste through situations of doing as the rationale for ethnographic exploration of food wasting in Manchester households, revealing much about the ways in which the organization of daily life results in wasted food. These moments can bear considerably more study yet, being both intellectually challenging and empirically important. For the total food thrown away by UK households each year – around 8 million tonnes (Quested and Parry, 2011) – results only from the innumerable moments in millions of kitchens in which something passes a line which differentiates 'food' from 'waste'. Reducing domestic food waste ultimately depends on intervention into these moments, for which we need to better understand what relations and processes are significant in making food into waste. Analysis of these moments reveals food waste as fallout from the organization of daily life, both individually and collectively.

In what follows, we begin by outlining key expressions of public discourses encouraging the avoidance of food waste and concern for food safety in the UK. This provides the backdrop against which we explore how such discourses are translated into domestic routines. We draw out the ranges of entities and relationships which converge into the moments in which matter is categorized either as food or as waste. How people negotiate the technology of date labels, such as 'best before' and 'use-by' provides a ready empirical hook around which to explore this process of categorization, not least through exploration of the tensions which open up around this process between members of the same household, or different generations of the same family. What becomes clear in how people talk about these processes – and consistent with how they are observed to act – is how public discourses of environmental responsibility (in

The Sociological Review, 60:S2, pp. 102–120 (2013), DOI: 10.1111/1467-954X.12040

relation to waste) together with responsibility to self and immediate others (in respect of safety) each have to be negotiated into more immediately meaningful discourses of responsibility. Within these, a sense of *thrift* is part of an over-whelming purpose of performing care for self and immediate others enacted through the everyday business of cooking and feeding (Miller, 2001; Evans, 2011b; Meah and Watson, in press).

Public discourses of food waste and food safety

Food waste has had a late but rapid ascendancy in public policy. The statistics of food waste are astonishing in themselves, but when held against the backdrop of issues of climate change, peak oil and global food security (Foresight, 2011), the matter of food waste takes on a pressing urgency. Estimates of total food waste throughout the global food system range from 30 per cent to 50 per cent (Godfray *et al.*, 2010; Foresight, 2011). According to surveys undertaken by and for the UK's Waste and Resources Action Programme (WRAP), the average UK household throws out about 25 per cent of food purchased. Further, 15 per cent of food and drink wasted is categorized by WRAP as 'easily avoidable', at a typical cost for a household with children of £680 per year (Quested and Parry, 2011). With the food system estimated to contribute as much as one-third of anthropogenic greenhouse gas emissions (Pretty *et al.*, 2010), alongside the chal-lenges of feeding an expected global population of 9 billion by 2050, reducing food waste is an obvious policy priority.

However, within the UK, the key legislative impetus for tackling domestic food waste has been the effects of its decomposition following landfill disposal. In the wake of landmark legislation in the EU Landfill Directive 1999, the 'modes of governing' household waste in the UK have undergone a radical shift, from a mode shaped around the disposal of waste – primarily to landfill – to a mode of *diversion* (Bulkeley *et al.*, 2007). Diversion here refers to ensuring as much material as possible is diverted away from landfill. After more than a decade of serious action on municipal waste in the wake of the Directive, the easiest 'wins' in diverting waste from landfill have been 'won', most obviously through the rollout of kerbside recycling of dry wastes and, to a lesser extent, green waste.

With the continuing obligations of the Directive focusing on biodegradable waste, food waste has come decidedly onto the agenda in recent years. However, this target for changing waste practices is not an easy win. Recycling focuses simply on shifting what happens to some materials after they have been used, rather than tackling the much greater challenges of reducing overall flows of material through the household, or keeping products in use. This has been argued to be a significant part of the reasons why recycling has been prioritized through policy measures, despite political declarations of commitment to the waste hierarchy in which reuse and waste minimization are given precedence over recycling as targets for action (Watson *et al.*, 2008). Attacking food waste adds a messy extra element to the demands of recycling – rather than cleaned tins and bottles, getting food waste into the recycling means sorting and storing materials that threaten disgust and putrefaction. But campaigns on food waste seek to go further, pushing political intervention further up the waste hierarchy. While minimization of domestic waste (rather than recycling) has had little policy push in general, minimization is a major theme in campaigns to reduce food waste. For example, WRAP launched the campaign 'Love Food Hate Waste' in 2007 (WRAP, n.d.). The campaign's website has sections on portion sizing, storage advice, menu planning, shopping and recipe ideas for using up leftovers. A section educating readers about use-by and best-before dates indicates the intersection with a different realm of public policy discourse, linking through to the National Health Service (NHS) 'Goodfood' site (NHS, n.d.).

While concern for environmental responsibility means getting people to throw less food out, a concern for preventing foodborne illness means, in part, getting people to do precisely the opposite. In the UK, it is estimated that foodborne illnesses affect around one million people, causing around 20,000 people to receive hospital treatment, and around 500 deaths (FSA, 2011). Food storage practices have emerged as a key area of concern and a Dutch study concerning storage and disposal (Terpstra *et al.*, 2005) points toward a gap between consumer knowledge, reported via interviews, and observed practices, with fridge temperatures also implicated as cause for concern. Consequently, the Food Standards Agency (FSA) has led its consumer-facing work with a strategy focusing on the '4 Cs' (cleaning, cross-contamination, cooking and cooling) and has also commissioned a piece of research exploring domestic 'Kitchen Life' (FSA, 2012) in which the second author is involved. Similarly, the NHS Goodfood site is one small part of public health endeavours around food in the UK. It features a similar range of advice to Love Food Hate Waste – on preparation, cooking, cleaning, storing and shopping – but focused around food safety, rather than waste. Its pages explaining food dates indicate both the significance of this technology in the prevention of food-borne illness, and the confusions that cluster around it. The two agencies and their websites do not directly conflict – both agree that food that has gone beyond its use-by date should not be eaten. However, as realms of public discourse, they nevertheless pull in different directions when followed through to actual realms of domestic practice.

Negotiating public discourses to domestic practices

It is how these discourses are negotiated into practices and performances that we explore below. We do so by drawing upon fieldwork conducted predominantly in South Yorkshire and Derbyshire, UK, between February 2010 and August 2011. Fieldwork followed two stages: first it involved a series of focus groups segmented by age and household types, with additional subsidiary dimensions of difference;[1] second – and the primary empirical focus of the project – was an

The Sociological Review, 60:S2, pp. 102–120 (2013), DOI: 10.1111/1467-954X.12040
© 2013 The Authors. Editorial organisation © 2013 The Editorial Board of the Sociological Review

ethnographic household study. While previous studies have highlighted the complexities of household provisioning (see Charles and Kerr, 1988; DeVault, 1991), these have relied on interviews, where reports of what people say they do have been taken as proxies for what they actually do (Murcott, 2000). Our study sought to explore the gap in understanding the differences between *sayings* and *doings* by going beyond the discursive focus of the focus groups and the narrative interviews, to explore the actual *doings* of cooks as they interact with food and other materials and technologies, in the shop and in their own kitchens. Food-focused life history interviews were combined with observational work, including provisioning 'go-alongs' (Kusenbach, 2003) on shopping trips, and observation, including both video and photographic recording, of kitchen tours and meal preparation.[2] Interviews were undertaken before the ethnographic work as a way of establishing rapport with participants in order that they might feel more comfortable with the more 'intrusive' aspects of the ethnographic work, which quite literally involved poking about and photographing inside cupboards and fridges, as well as filming respondents' practices.

Ethnographic methods which draw upon the visual have been highlighted as potentially important in enabling us to move beyond the limitations of purely text-based approaches, which cannot fully capture lived experiences (Power, 2003). Our choice of methods sought to facilitate an exploration of respondents' 'stream of experiences and practices as they move[d] through, and interact[ed] with, their physical and social environment' (Kusenbach, 2003: 463), including material objects in their kitchens and the spaces beyond, but also their engagement with a range of discourses which exist around food.

Unlike Evans (2012), whose decision to 'hang out' in participants' homes and communities was motivated by a specific interest in food waste, our study had a much broader focus. To this end a very open brief was used in the ethnographic work, and it was explained to respondents that we were interested in all of the processes through which food arrived in their cupboards and fridges, as well as what happened to it in the home. The second author filmed participants cooking meals of various degrees of complexity while other household members came and went through the kitchen. During these visits, she would also photograph the kitchen: the appliances, cupboards, fridge and freezer and their contents, inquiring about the design and layout, the role of various technologies and uses by different members of the household. Engaging with respondents while they undertook everyday routines and practices, surrounded by the material objects which constitute their own domestic spaces, proved to be a valuable form of elicitation – the image of the wrinkled orange peel in one respondents' fridge, for instance, which led to a discussion of a life beyond the normal point of disposal (see below) – and enabled them to unconsciously demonstrate practices which are so habitual that they would perhaps not think them relevant in an interview (here, the washing of meat provided one example).

In pursuing our interest in decisions regarding the what, when, how and why of food shopping, the second author also accompanied respondents while they did their shopping. For one woman, this meant the observation of her regular online procedure, supplemented by trips to the local shops by her husband. In some cases, a trip to the supermarket was done solely for the purposes of speculative 'top-up' shopping, while others did the 'big shop' equipped with shopping lists which would enable them to deliver planned meals designed to accommodate the tastes and preferences of different members of the household, as well as making use of what might already be in the fridge/freezer. Browsing the aisles with respondents provided an opportunity to understand the situated nature of the processes which contribute to respondents' provisioning decisions – what is important to them, and why. More often than not, the discussions would be driven by the respondent, who might pick up an item and comment on an issue of ethics, quality, price, provenance or the environment. Of course, this method does not give some unmediated access to empirical reality devoid of researcher influence. It does, however, enable exploration of subtleties of practice which go beyond what could be gained through interviews alone. 'Being there', hanging out with them while they did their shopping, facilitated an awareness of the dilemmas consumers are faced with, for example in the simple act of buying a litre of milk.

These methods were undertaken with at least two – and up to four – generations in each of eight extended families, comprising a total of 17 households. In all, 23 participants were interviewed, and ethnographic work was completed with 15 of the 17 households. The vast majority of respondents were white British, with one white Irish respondent within an otherwise British family, and a Pakistani family, the younger generation of which was British-born. The white British respondents were predominantly middle class, though social mobility, especially amongst older generations, is significant. Households worked with included an all-male house-share, a childless couple, families with young children, a family with teenagers, retired couples, multi-generational and lone households. As is inevitable for in-depth qualitative and ethnographic research, there can be no claims to be representative of a broader population. Rather, discussion and conclusions drawn from the study reported here are based upon exploration of the complex details of provisioning practices which are only accessible through methodological approaches which demand a relatively small number of households.

Food safety in practice

From the perspective of a food safety expert, the standards of some of our respondents may be so far below what policy and guidance seek to promote that they appear almost non-existent. Key examples here came from focus-group discussions between house-sharers, where more overtly 'cavalier' (Kennedy *et al.*, 2005) food safety practices were reported. These included the drunken late-night preparation of food after a weekend of partying which involved cutting up vegetables and meat on a 'filthy worktop'. Another participant reflects that:

Our fridge is rubbish, it's really not cold enough I don't think, so I'm kind of particularly more careful with milk . . . not that I smell it like, I have to pour it out and see if there's any bits in it before we use it. (Chris, 28)

Here, while Chris showed what may well be considered a relatively low level of concern, he nevertheless demonstrated that, however low, he still has boundaries of acceptability. Indeed, while standards varied widely, all respondents necessarily recognize boundaries of food safety. While in general respondents did not clearly articulate ideas of food safety strictly in line with the sort of guidance offered by food safety professionals, a number were able to demonstrate an awareness of expert advice about particular food safety issues, including being able to identify the sources of their knowledge. For example, in a group of older, working-class, respondents, an 84-year old man pointed out that 'you've to watch chicken', while a 78-year old woman explained that she has seen information videos, while waiting at the doctor's surgery, which highlight risks concerning chicken, listeria and fridges. Similarly, in a focus group with Somali and Indian mothers, these women expressed particular concerns regarding the safety of fresh food which may have been left out of the fridge overnight.

So, for all respondents boundaries exist, even if they are often defined by the affective experience of disgust more than cognitive reflection on bacterial risks. This distinction is most clearly articulated by one older woman who, in recounting the disposal of large quantities of dry goods, like porridge oats and pulses, as a result of finding them infested with meal moths, implies that the decision to dispose of food is not so much a matter of cognitive implementation of expert advice as a result of a more visceral response: 'I wouldn't sort of think about it making me ill particularly, it's more of a just a disgust thing.' Here, there is evidence of the role of disgust within the cultural processes through which waste emerges, as informed by Douglas's (1966) contention that we should think of 'dirt as disorder'. Douglas's understandings have been applied to waste across a range of contexts, including to thoroughly durable and inorganic matter (Lucas, 2002; Gregson and Crang, 2010). Food, with its necessary relation to bodies, its capacity to degrade over relatively short time periods, and often to degrade in ways which unarguably threaten one's health, makes the role of disgust in the cultural classification of food as waste far more obvious than in many other fields of wasting.

While discussion – in interviews and more especially in focus groups – could result in relatively clear engagement with issues of food safety, more often than not food safety as a theme emerges in relation to other concerns and priorities, and more ethnographic methods quickly showed the limits of analytically distilling out insights into specific concerns, such as those around particular bacteria.

(Not) Wasting food

Frequently, issues of food safety arose in relation to concerns which can be framed as concerns about 'waste'. Just as all respondents have boundaries that relate to acceptable safety, so too did these exist in relation to waste. Some respondents did recognize that they were perhaps more ready to waste food than is perceived to be desirable. Yet it can be argued that no respondent sees himself/herself as profligate. In one family, for example, a range of attitudes were expressed concerning waste. During his interview, Jonathan Anderson (38) stated that 'there's not many things that I would treat as worthy leftovers', but also said that 'I never like putting it in the bin, I always quite like to pass it on to [parents] if they – you know they'll take anything, you know, a few bits of cabbage in a bowl (.)³completely different attitude'. However, during a tour of his kitchen, he drew the second author's attention ('Good timing – are you watching?') as he deposited a range of half empty jars of food into the kitchen bin. As suggested by Jonathan, his parents, Ted (66) and Laura (64), demonstrate a very different approach to food waste. Laura articulated this in terms of their having been children who grew up in the aftermath of the Second World War. During one of several observations of Ted cooking, the second author picked up on Ted's practices concerning waste reduction. The following excerpt from her field-notes highlights how his practices are, to an extent, a legacy of those observed in his own mother's kitchen, and an acknowledgement of both different attitudes to, or motivations for, avoiding food waste within, and without, the family:

> 'Polly [daughter-in-law] doesn't mind wasting stuff'. He says: 'It's not a big concern. Waste is a negative state. There's waste that's technically useless, and waste that's wasting stuff'. I mention Jonathan's thing about passing on bits of cabbage and Laura joins in: 'We'd be cross if it gets thrown away.' (Field-notes)

What the example of this extended family illustrates, through both the changes in relation to food and its value over generations within a family and the intergenerational tensions that result, is the profoundly contextual and pragmatic contingency of categorizing matter as waste. As emphasized by recent scholarship on waste (Hetherington, 2004; Gregson *et al.*, 2007; Evans, 2012), matter becomes waste through the moment of disposal rather than as a consequence of its innate material properties. There is no stable, universal line differentiating matter which is food from that which is waste. Rather, matter crosses that line, turning from food to waste, as a result of the convergence of diverse concerns and pressures, including of routine, anxieties, care, time and space. These convergences come across clearly in the different ways in which our respondents negotiate the tensions that arise around date labels on food.

Negotiating food date labels

Date labels can be understood as innovations to fill gaps of trust, responsibility and control in increasingly extended food production chains. This was implicit in a focus group discussion between older people. In turning to use-by and sell-by dates, one participant pointed out that 'our mother's didn't have 'em'. The discussion went on to recognize the different routes through which food was acquired: 'they didn't have them pre-wrapped. You went to the proper butchers and you knew that food was alright.' As situations of purchase and consumption have become ever more remote from locations of production (Ilbery and Maye, 2005; Renting *et al.*, 2003), with industrial supply chains opaque to consumers, retailer practices, consumer confidence and food safety concerns have increasingly required technological intervention. Over time, date labels in the UK became stabilized, with 'use-by' dates applied to foods with limited shelf life and which are potentially hazardous to health when degraded; 'best before' dates to indicate when qualities of a food product may begin to deteriorate; and 'sell-by' – later 'display until' – dates enabling retailers to manage stock. Collectively, these date labels offer 'mediation of anxieties through a bundle of texts [and] materials' (Milne *et al.*, 2011: 186), a simple technology attempting to intervene in practice to enhance both confidence and safety. They seek, in effect, to redistribute responsibility, away from the direct relation between consumer and retailer and, more crucially, away from the consumer and their capacity to assess the safety of food through direct sensory engagement. Responsibility is instead assumed by institutional processes of risk assessment and knowledge production.

Our fieldwork certainly found instances where date labels were effective in shaping consumer practices. For example, one woman stated that when she sees a use-by date 'I take that it that there's something in there that can go off and make you sick, and I tend to pretty well stick by use-by dates' (Mary Green, 67). Elsewhere, a rural focus group participant, Marie (42), protested that:

> . . . my daughter [aged 11] is absolutely obsessed with sell-by dates . . . everything she eats I see her check it . . . 'Have you checked the sell-by date?', 'Yes'. 'Mum you put some crisps in my lunch box today, they were out of date, I could have eaten some' [laughs].

To fulfil their function of communication to consumers, and through that communication to shape practice, date labels have to be simple, clear and certain. Indeed, in order to shape practice in diverse locales, they have to have properties of what Latour (1987) terms 'immutable mobiles', in that they have to carry stable and transparent meaning in order to influence action across space. Date labels accomplish this with the clear indication of a single day date, leaving a minimum of space for the label reader's interpretation. The didactic certainty of the date label, together with its opaque institutional origins, are part of what causes many of our respondents to resist the discipline implied by use-by dates, and the redistribution of responsibility they represent. Our interviews and observations revealed some of the complexities and contingencies which lie behind a recent survey finding that only 25 per cent of respondents considered the use-by date a primary way of telling whether food is safe to eat (Prior *et al.*, 2011).

Some respondents see food dates as cynical manipulations. For example, 85-year-old focus group participant Bert thinks they are 'a manufacturer's gimmick', while Carmen (38), a pregnant mother taking part in a discussion with mothers of young children, said she thinks date labelling is a mechanism to 'have you back in the shops' and that shops are 'preying on your insecurities in looking at use-by dates'. Others place date labels in broader patterns of the state assuming responsibilities on behalf of its citizens. Farmer's wife Marie blamed what she saw as the reliance of young people on date labels on the emergence of the 'nanny state' and children's reliance on guidance from above.

This is not, however, to suggest that any of our respondents would entirely ignore use-by dates. Rather, the dates are one piece of information assimilated alongside many others in assessing whether something is still food, or has become waste. Through their own experience of working with and eating food, people know that foods change gradually, and according to a wide range of factors concerning the ways in which they are stored. For some respondents, the idea implicit within the label – namely, that someone in the production process can fix a future time at which a food turns to waste – is not credible in the face of their experience of working with food. For example, contributing to a discussion among malehouse-sharers, one participant, Steve (30), expressed cynicism regarding the processes by which date labels are produced:

> . . . first of all, who decides? I refuse to believe that it's always exactly the same period of time from slaughter to being packaged when they presumably print the date on it. They might keep really close records of it, but I doubt it. Surely, all like different meats are gonna . . . different pieces of the same meat, are gonna, er, from different animals, are gonna age at a different rate, and then there's all the factors of how it's stored, what temperature it's stored, how long it's (. . .) left, not in the fridge when it arrives, you know, there's *so* many factors.

Resistance to the institutional imperative implicit in use-by dates can have a variety of sources, but one which emerged as fundamental is the conflict between that imperative and people's antipathy towards wasting food. This tension emerges clearly when people reflect on what goes on in those moments when matter is assessed to see if it is still food. For Jonathan Anderson:

> I mean the one thing we're probably guilty of is . . . throwing stuff away because it is very obviously just, nothing to do with the date on the pack, it's fresh stuff that's, a bag of herbs that haven't got used that's black in the bag, and so it gets thrown away for that reason. (. . .) I suppose things that typically we end up 'umming' and 'aahing' about, things like (.) half pots of crème fraiche, opened packs of ham where they're 'once opened eat inside three days' . . . Packs of cheap arsed . . . ham, and I'm usually more inclined to smell and look (. . .) sort of trust my senses a little bit. Things like cream I tend to be a bit funny if it's (. . .) like been opened (. . .) it's not so much the date it's this 'Once opened consumed within'. I'm a bit of a sucker for that.

What comes across first here is some sense of guilt ('the one thing we're probably guilty of') about wasting food. More generally, this statement reflects the process of tacit reckoning that consumers practise during which direct sensory evaluation ('I'm more inclined to smell and look . . . Sort of trust my senses a little bit') is negotiated together with formal information (like 'the date on the

The Sociological Review, 60:S2, pp. 102–120 (2013), DOI: 10.1111/1467-954X.12040
© 2013 The Authors. Editorial organisation © 2013 The Editorial Board of the Sociological Review

pack' and the 'once opened . . .' guidelines). These different modes of assessment, along with issues of institutional trust, are negotiated together differently depending on the specifics of the situation, including the specificities of the foodstuff itself.

Exploration of the ways in which people follow, use and resist date labels thus reveals a seemingly innate resistance to wasting. The desire to keep food as food rather than consign it to waste is a major factor which pulls people away from following the discipline of use-by dates. However, this resistance to waste itself requires interrogation.

What stops food crossing the line?

> I don't like wasting food . . . it annoys me when I have to throw stuff away 'cause firstly, I've wasted my money on it, and second of all you've just, just (. . .) I've, I've had, I don't know, I don't like wasting stuff.

Andy (24) is not unusual in finding it difficult to articulate his resistance to wasting food. Across different research encounters, this resistance is generally found to arise from the convergence of a number of different concerns. However, even where respondents were articulate about their relations to wasting food, these different concerns rarely connect at all with the global environment. Not one respondent brought up the greenhouse gas emissions that result from consigning food waste to landfill. None explicitly connected the disposal of food with the material resources that it took to get the food grown, processed, packaged and transported. While a few identified enduring guilt from childhood admonishments about starving children in other parts of the world, most concerns seem closer to home. Rather than an expression of global citizenship, resistance to wasting food is primarily rooted in *thrift*.

Thrift is concerned with responsible and conservative use of resources. As Miller (2001) argues, thrift is a ubiquitous characteristic of shopping, as part of the performance of care and responsibility for the household. So, part of what keeps food from crossing the line is simple household economics. Food uses up finite supplies of money; as in Andy's clearest articulation, 'I've wasted my money on it'. Time can be as finite as money for a household, and provisioning food takes time and is often fitted in as people negotiate their days. It seems reasonable to suppose that food is much less likely to be consigned to waste when the food in question is an essential component in the only meal that presents itself as possible from what happens to be in the fridge and cupboards that night.

Beyond pragmatic concern for time and money, there is ample evidence, too, of a sense of responsibility to food itself. Laura Anderson, for instance, was articulate about her aversion to wasting and identified its roots in her own childhood experience of relative scarcity:

> . . . the idea of wasting . . . I mean that's like a thread right through from you know, being a kid after the war, you just didn't waste anything. It's always like a big worry

about food, in terms of food hygiene, it's the idea of not letting your food go off 'cause then you'd waste it.

Her husband Ted explained his own mother's hatred of waste as a result of material necessity in the face of scarcity: 'the reason she did it is because she had to stretch food out'. However, recognizing that his own affluence means there is no scarcity, he identified his own resistance to waste in a more general sense of responsibility: 'the reason someone like me does it is because this stuff's precious, it shouldn't be thrown away. It's been grown and nurtured and cooked.'

For others, these different forms of responsibility – for money, time and the food itself – are expressed more through the satisfactions they find in the skills of *doing* thrift. In one focus group, Carmen readily articulated her approach to effective planning and shopping to ensure sufficiency without surplus, and of avoiding waste by preparing 'make do' dishes with leftovers – 'turning something into some other dish . . . like bubble and squeak'. She talked about her confidence in preparing meals 'from scratch', but acknowledged that not everyone has the time or the confidence to do that. Joe Green (45) talked of his regular Monday risotto-night, with the defining ingredients of the risotto determined by what was left over from the Sunday roast. Observation led our research into more esoteric practices of keeping foodstuff as food, when it might easily cross the line to become waste:

> While photographing the interior of [Ted and Laura Anderson's] fridge I spotted what appeared – to me – to be a bit of scabby orange peel. When quizzed about this, he said, it was 'free rubbish' and produced a jar of something even scabbier looking, explaining that he dried orange peel in the oven to produce this intensely citrusy, crisp snack which tasted 'wonderful' dipped in chocolate. He said that he liked to put it in with his coffee beans, infusing them with its flavour. However, its principal use was as an ingredient in meat-based Moroccan dishes, in which the peel would help bring out the flavours of the meat. (Field-notes)

So, participants spoke of, or enacted, different ways in which they maintained an acceptable limit to the amount of food they wasted. Specific routines and techniques had evolved within the rhythms of their own lives that enabled them to police the line between food and waste, and to minimize what crossed it in order to fall within their own acceptable limits. Forms of thrift with food, whether expressed through classic home economics of planning and stock control, or through culinary adventurism, emerge as ubiquitous to domestic food consumption.

This finding clearly contests the implications of careless profligacy that follow from the stark statistics of household food waste (Evans, 2012) and connects debates about food waste to broader debates about consumption and profligacy. Over recent years, a range of researchers have found an ethics of care towards consumer goods that undermines characterizations of a 'throwaway society' (Watson, 2011; Lane and Watson, 2012). These studies have focused on durable consumer goods, such as the care people take to pass on rather than dispose of possessions like furniture (Gregson and Crewe, 2003; Gregson *et al.*, 2007) or

The Sociological Review, 60:S2, pp. 102–120 (2013), DOI: 10.1111/1467-954X.12040

for the longevity and after-life of white goods (Cooper, 2005). Finding the practices of responsibility and thrift amongst our own research participants indicates that the ethics of care towards materials extends from durable goods to the troublingly mutable matter of food. However, research undermining easy narratives of profligacy and disposability has to confront the stark statistics that give rise to those narratives. If people care so much about food – as shown through their resistance to following the date label, or in their satisfaction in their skilled management and use of food – then how come so much is thrown away?

How food becomes waste

As Miller (2001) makes clear, there is no necessary alignment between impulses of thrift and concern for the global environment and future generations. Evans (2011b) draws out how thrift does not provide restraint on total resource consumption, but instead frees up resources to enable further consumption. This is not, however, to suggest that thrift does not have its own morality, as excavated by Lucas (2002) through a historical perspective on the productive tension between moralities of hygiene and thrift from the nineteenth century. Clearly, the practices of thrift represented by our participants are not a direct translation of public and policy discourses about food waste and its consequences for global environment and food security. Rather, they are enactments of a combination of concerns – from pragmatic conservation of household time and money to a culturally embedded sense of responsibility to the food itself – which are situated within the mess of practices and routines through which food provisioning is accomplished within a household. This ongoing accomplishment demands coordination of complex flows and relations between foods, products, technologies, skills, meanings, values and purposes, all within the spatial and temporal conditions of people's lived days. Incorporated in this, concerns like thrift, or indeed food safety, are subsumed within and subordinated to a more fundamental ethic: that of responsibility to and care for self and immediate others (Miller, 1998; Meah and Watson, in press).

Hannah Faulkner, mother of two young daughters, gave a strong sense of how provisioning practice is pulled in conflicting directions as she talks about food and waste:

> Well I compost food and I, and I try to look in the, in the fridge to see what we've got and make meals around what we've got and use leftovers, but again because everything is so, there's so many compromises when I'm trying to compromise between doing something else for the kids, healthy food, whatever. Ideally I would like to not waste any food but sometimes if it's, if it's the choice between erm, thinking 'Oh actually I haven't got time to cook that particular vegetable that I've bought, I've ran out of time to do it', well actually it'll just have to go to waste because something else is more important. So in an ideal world I wouldn't waste anything but, I am aware

that I probably do waste things because I'm trying to, because it's part of the compromise.

Hannah conveyed how food becomes waste within the specific flow of doing, and shifting distributions of time, risk and responsibility. Her aversion to wasting is over-ridden in a process of compromise where, so often, 'something else is more important' in the context of getting the family fed in the midst of the rest of life. As Evans (2012) showed from his ethnographic work with south Manchester householders, food waste emerges from the intersection of 'time, tastes, conventions, family relations and domestic divisions of labour' within 'the material context . . . of domestic technologies, infrastructures of provision and the materiality properties of food itself' (2012: 12).

As matter becomes food through practice (Roe, 2006), so matter that is food becomes waste through practice. This is not to say that the processes through which food is re-categorized as waste are somehow solely cultural, purified of the role of the matter itself. As contemporary theorizations of practice make clear, materials are constituent parts of practices (Shove *et al.*, 2012). With food – more than with most materials that households consign to waste streams – the very properties of the materials play a clear role. Food degrades over time, often with clearly sensible changes to the material itself, such as when mould and putrefaction take hold. For Roe (2006), the stuff of food, its form and affordances, have an active role to play in the situations of purchase, preparation and eating through which it becomes food. Bennett (2007) places still more emphasis on the relational agency of the vital materials of food in eating and ingestion. Consideration of the processes and practices which result in food becoming waste, particularly when considered alongside considerations of food safety, therefore, shows that the matter of food plays an active role in its own status, not least through the changes it does and can undergo.

Conclusion

The dynamic material properties of foodstuff are only one component of the moments in which food becomes waste. Through exploring the tensions between concerns for food waste and for food safety when translated to domestic practice, it has been made apparent that food becomes waste through the convergence of diverse relationships in the flow of people's days. Food waste is in this way the fallout of the organization of everyday life. The location of practices of household food provisioning within broader patterns and rhythms through which everyday life is accomplished can easily work to displace enactment of concerns to avoid waste.

On one hand, the message from this research for policy interventions intended to reduce food waste is bleak. Interventions aimed at raising consciousness about the social and environmental impacts of food waste, for example, cannot hope for much purchase when the production of that waste is an almost

The Sociological Review, 60:S2, pp. 102–120 (2013), DOI: 10.1111/1467-954X.12040

inherent part of the complex processes of coordination through which a household is kept well fed. On the other hand, this research adds to the growing evidence for the value of contemporary academic debates around food, waste, materiality and practice for better understanding policy issues rooted in the detail of the organization of everyday life. It does so by bringing to light different potential points of intervention in pursuit of reducing food waste.

Whilst our research suggests that campaigns emphasizing issues of environmental responsibility have limited potential for reducing food waste, a strong finding from our research is the presence of an innate resistance to wasting food as an expression of an ethic of thrift. While thrift remains as a seemingly ubiquitous feature of food consumption, the practices which constitute thrift are clearly reshaped by the relatively low necessary costs – in terms of share of income and demands on time – of acquiring food in historical perspective.[4] This aspect of the collective organization of daily life interacts with broader restructuring of the temporal ordering of daily life (Shove, 2003; Southerton, 2003) and of changing divisions of labour that have resulted in a growing sense of fragmentation of time and demands of coordination in the accomplishment of daily life. Consequently, there is often 'something more important' than the feats of planning and coordination required to manage the flows of food and feeding through the home which would be required to at once perform adequate levels of care for self and immediate others while eliminating 'avoidable' food waste. Just how these demands play out in any kitchen depends on specific contextual factors, of time, household composition and divisions of labour, space, technologies and more. Nevertheless, thrift has been apparent in our respondents' talk and actions. While not generally framing their reasons within the themes of climate change or food security which drive governing interventions into food waste, people are nevertheless averse to wasting food.

This then suggests a different focus for interventions to reduce food waste, through seeking opportunities to enable people to enact thriftiness. It has not been unusual for our respondents to speak with some satisfaction about their skills in canny or thrifty food consumption, emphasizing the role of competence and skills as part of what is required to reduce the frequency with which food becomes waste. Rather than sharp interventions into people's knowledge and attitudes, policy interventions to reduce food waste are better understood as a means of changing the social and cultural gradients that come together to determine whether or not stuff ends up sliding over the line to become waste.

Acknowledgements

The research discussed in this chapter derives from a project that is part of an international programme of research on 'Consumer Culture in an Age of Anxiety' (CONANX) funded by an Advanced Investigator Grant awarded to Peter Jackson by the European Research Council (ERC-2008-AdG-230287-CONANX). We are very grateful to the participants in this research who have opened up their homes and their provisioning routines to our research, and to the editors and anonymous reviewers, whose helpful comments and suggestions have considerably improved this paper.

Notes

1 Thirty-seven participants contributed to the seven focus groups, including thirteen men. In addition to a mixed pilot group, one group was with young male house-sharers aged 23–30; another with older people aged 63–89 living in a former mining village; one was comprised of Indian and Somali women with school-aged children; one of low-income mothers aged 27–38; one with married or cohabiting couples aged 29–41; one with people aged 39–79 living in rural Derbyshire. The research was approved through ethical review at the University of Sheffield.

2 Selected images from the go-alongs and kitchen tours can be accessed via the project's online photo-gallery: http://www.flickr.com/photos/52548860@N08/sets/

3 (.) Indicates a short pause or hesitation; (. . .) indicates a longer pause; ( ) indicates an indistinguishable utterance or uncertain reading.

4 While recent years have seen substantial food price rises, in historical terms food is still very cheap in the UK as a proportion of household income; Zuke (2012) estimates that, in 2012, food was 13 times cheaper than in 1862, thanks to both production changes and rising incomes. The time needed for the process of provisioning has in principle reduced over the decades thanks to changes to systems of provision (rise of supermarkets, of chilled and frozen supply chains and technologies, convenience foods, etc.) and domestic technologies (including microwaves and freezers).

References

Bennett, J., (2007), 'Edible matter', *New Left Review*, 45: 133–145.

Bulkeley, H. and Gregson, N., (2009), 'Crossing the threshold: municipal waste policy and household waste generation', *Environment and Planning A*, 41 (4): 929–945.

Bulkeley, H., Watson, M. and Hudson, R., (2007), 'Modes of governing municipal waste', *Environment and Planning A*, 39: 2733–2753.

Charles, N. and Kerr, M., (1988), *Women, Food and Families*, Manchester: Manchester University Press.

Cooper, T., (2005), 'Slower consumption: reflections on product life spans and the "throwaway society" ', *Journal of Industrial Ecology*, 9 (1/2): 51–67.

DEFRA (Department for Environment, Food and Rural Affairs), (2011), *Government Review of Waste Policy in England 2011*, London: DEFRA.

DeVault, M., (1991), *Feeding the Family: The Social Organisation of Caring as Gendered Work*, Chicago: University of Chicago Press.

Douglas, M., (1966), *Purity and Danger: An Analysis of Concepts of Pollution and Taboo*, London: Routledge & Kegan Paul.

Evans, D., (2011a), 'Blaming the consumer – once again: the social and material contexts of everyday food waste practices in some English households', *Critical Public Health*, 21 (4): 429–440.

Evans, D., (2011b), 'Thrifty, green or frugal: reflections on sustainable consumption in a changing economic climate', *Geoforum*, 42 (5): 550–557.

Evans, D., (2012), 'Beyond the throwaway society to ordinary domestic practice: what can sociology say about food waste?' *Sociology*, 46 (1): 41–56.

Foresight, (2011), *The Future of Food and Farming*, Final Project Report, London: The Government Office for Science.

The Sociological Review, 60:S2, pp. 102–120 (2013), DOI: 10.1111/1467-954X.12040
© 2013 The Authors. Editorial organisation © 2013 The Editorial Board of the Sociological Review

FSA (Food Standards Agency), (2011), *Foodborne Disease Strategy 2010–15*, An FSA Programme for the Reduction of Foodborne Disease in the UK, London: FSA.

FSA, (2012), *Research Exploring Domestic Kitchen Practices*, http://www.food.gov.uk/science/socsci/ssres/foodsafetyss/fs244026/ (accessed 30 April 2012).

Gandy, M., (1994), *Recycling and the Politics of Urban Waste*, London: Earthscan.

Godfray, H. C. J., Beddington, J. R., Crute, I. R., Haddad, L., Lawrence, D., Muir, J. F., Pretty, J., Robinson, S., Thomas, S. M. and Toulmin, C., (2010), 'Food security: the challenge of feeding 9 billion people', *Science*, 327 (5967): 812–818.

Gregson, N. and Crang, M., (2010), 'Materiality and waste: inorganic vitality in a networked world', *Environment and Planning A*, 42 (5): 1026–1032.

Gregson, N. and Crewe, L., (2003), *Second-hand Cultures*, Oxford: Berg.

Gregson, N., Metcalfe, A. and Crewe, L., (2007), 'Identity, mobility, and the throwaway society', *Environment and Planning D*, 25 (4): 682–700.

Gregson, N., Watkins, H. and Calestani, M., (2010), 'Inextinguishable fibres: demolition and the vital materialisms of asbestos', *Environment and Planning A*, 42 (5): 1065–1083.

Halkier, B., (2009), 'A practice theoretical perspective on everyday dealings with environmental challenges of food consumption', *Anthropology of Food*, (S5) http://aof.revues.org/index6405.html (29 April 2012).

Harris, M., (1985), *Good to Eat: Riddles of Food and Culture*, London: Simon and Schuster.

Hawkins, G., (2006), *The Ethics of Waste: How We Relate to Rubbish*, Plymouth: Rowman & Littlefield.

Hawkins, G., (2009), 'The politics of bottled water', *Journal of Cultural Economy*, 2 (1–2): 183–195.

Hawkins, G. and Muecke, S., (2003), *Culture and Waste: The Creation and Destruction of Value*, Plymouth: Rowman & Littlefield.

Hetherington, K., (2004), 'Secondhandedness: consumption, disposal and absent presence', *Environment and Planning D: Society and Space*, 22: 157–173.

Ilbery, B., and Maye, D., (2005), 'Alternative (shorter) food supply chains and specialist livestock products in the Scottish-English borders', *Environment and Planning A*, 37 (5): 823–844.

Kennedy, J., Jackson, V., Cowan, C., Blair, I., McDowell, D., and Bolton, D., (2005), 'Consumer food safety knowledge: segmentation of Irish home food preparers based on food safety knowledge and practice', *British Food Journal*, 107: 441–452.

Kusenbach, M., (2003), 'Street phenomenology: the go-along as ethnographic research tool', *Ethnography*, 4 (3): 445–485.

Lane, R. and Watson, M., (2012), 'Stewardship of things: the radical potential of product stewardship for re-framing responsibilities and relationships to products and materials', *Geoforum*, 43: 1254–1265.

Latour, B., (1987), *Science in Action: How to Follow Scientists and Engineers Through Society*, Cambridge, MA: Harvard University Press.

Lucas, G., (2002), 'Disposability and dispossession in the twentieth century', *Journal of Material Culture*, 7 (1): 5–22.

Meah, A. and Watson, M., (2011), 'Saints and slackers: challenging discourses about the decline of domestic cooking', *Sociological Research Online*, 16 (2): 6.

Meah, A. and Watson, M., (in press), 'Cooking up consumer anxieties about 'provenance' and 'ethics': why it sometimes matters where foods come from in domestic provisioning', *Food, Culture and Society*.

Miller, D., (1998), *A Theory of Shopping*, Cambridge: Polity.

Miller, D., (2001), *The Dialectics of Shopping*, Chicago: University of Chicago Press.

Milne, R., Wenzer, J., Brembeck, H. and Brodin, M., (2011), 'Fraught cuisine: food scares and the modulation of anxieties', *Distinktion: Scandinavian Journal of Social Theory*, 12 (2): 177–192.

Murcott, A., (2000), 'Is it still a pleasure to cook for him? Social changes in the household and the family', *Journal of Consumer Culture*, 24: 78–84.

NHS, (n.d.), 'Food labelling terms', *Livewell/Goodfood*, http://www.nhs.uk/Livewell/Goodfood/Pages/food-labelling-terms.aspx (accessed 24 October 2011).

119

O'Brien, M., (2007), *A Crisis of Waste? Understanding the Rubbish Society*, London: Routledge.

Power, E. M., (2003), 'De-centering the text: exploring the potential for visual methods in the sociology of food', *Journal for the Study of Food and Society*, 6: 9–20.

Pretty, J., Sutherland, W. J., Ashby, J., Auburn, J., Baulcombe, D., Bell, M., Bentley, J., Bickersteth, S., Brown, K. and Burke, J., (2010), 'The top 100 questions of importance to the future of global agriculture', *International Journal of Agricultural Sustainability*, 8 (4): 219–236.

Prior, G., Hall, L., Morris, S. and Draper, A., (2011), *Exploring Food Attitudes and Behaviours: Findings from the Food and You Survey 2010*, London: FSA.

Quested, T. and Parry, A., (2011), *New Estimates for Household Food and Drink Waste in the UK*, Banbury: WRAP.

Rathje, W. and Murphy, C., (1992), *Rubbish! The Archaeology of Garbage*, New York: Harper Collins.

Renting, H., Marsden, T. K. and Banks, J., (2003), 'Understanding alternative food networks: exploring the role of short food supply chains in rural development', *Environment and Planning A*, 35 (3): 393–412.

Roe, E. J., (2006), 'Things becoming food and the embodied, material practices of an organic food consumer', *Sociologia Ruralis*, 46 (2): 104–121.

Scanlan, J., (2005), *On Garbage*, London: Reaktion Books.

Shove, E., (2003), *Comfort, Cleanliness and Convenience: The Social Organisation of Normality*, Oxford: Berg.

Shove, E., Pantzar, M. and Watson, M., (2012), *The Dynamics of Social Practice*, London: Sage.

Southerton, D., (2003), ' "Squeezing time" – allocating practices, coordinating networks and scheduling society', *Time and Society*, 12 (1): 5–25.

Strasser, S., (2000), *Waste and Want: A Social History of Trash*, New York: Owl Books.

Terpstra, M. J., Steenbekkers, L. P. A., de Maertelaere, N. C. M. and Nijhuis, S., (2005). 'Food storage and disposal: consumer practice and knowledge', *British Food Journal*, 107 (7): 526–533.

Thompson, M., (1979), *Rubbish Theory: The Creation and Destruction of Value*, Oxford: Oxford University Press.

Warde, A., Cheng, S. L., Olsen, W. and Southerton, D., (2007), 'Changes in the practice of eating', *Acta Sociologica*, 50 (4): 363–385.

Watson, M., (2011), 'Mapping geographies of reuse in Sheffield and Melbourne', in R. Lane and A. Gorman-Murray (eds), *Material Geographies of Household Sustainability*, 133–156, Farnham: Ashgate.

Watson, M., Bulkeley, H. and Hudson, R., (2008), 'Unpicking environmental policy integration with tales from waste management', *Environment and Planning C: Government and Policy*, 26: 481–498.

WRAP (Waste and Resources Action Programme), (n.d.), 'Love Food Hate Waste', http://www.lovefoodhatewaste.com/ (accessed 24 October 2011).

Zuke, E., (2012), 'Food shop is 13 times cheaper than 1862', *The Grocer*, 7 July, http://www.thegrocer.co.uk/food-shop-is-13-times-cheaper-than-in-1862/224815.article

The Sociological Review, 60:S2, pp. 102–120 (2013), DOI: 10.1111/1467-954X.12040
© 2013 The Authors. Editorial organisation © 2013 The Editorial Board of the Sociological Review

Practising thrift at dinnertime: mealtime leftovers, sacrifice and family membership

Benedetta Cappellini and Elizabeth Parsons

Abstract: Exploring our relationship with mealtime leftovers tells us a lot about not only our relationships with waste, but with one another, in the home. In our study of British mealtimes we explore how leftovers are transformed and reused as meals. We refer to theories of disposal in exploring the skills involved in transforming leftovers. We also explore the motivations behind these transformations. Drawing on the work of Miller (1998) we examine how the reuse of leftovers involves sacrifice by individual family members for the greater good of the whole family. We also find that reusing and eating up leftovers involves a collective sacrifice by family members which marks out their membership to the family unit.

Keywords: food, leftovers, family, thrift, membership, sacrifice

Introduction

Sociological and consumer research reveals the importance of the family meal for reinforcing individual identities as well as perpetuating and reshaping family relationships (Murcott, 1983; Charles and Kerr, 1986, 1988; DeVault, 1991; Jansson, 1995; Brown and Miller, 2002). This literature recognizes that it is not only the consumption of the meal that has significance for the shaping of identities, but the series of practices surrounding the business of feeding the family – including planning (Cappellini and Parsons, 2012a), shopping (Carrigan and Szmigin, 2006), and cooking and serving the meal (DeVault, 1991). However, these studies still seem to view the actual consumption of the meal as the end of the story. With a few exceptions (Munro, 1995; Cappellini, 2009; Evans, 2012), there is very little work that looks at the series of practices that revolve around the disposal, and potential revaluing and reuse, of the meal. In this paper we examine the practices of revaluing leftovers as a specific conduit of disposing of food surplus, giving such food a 'second chance' (Soderman and Carter, 2008: 22) and thus rather than moving it out of the house as waste, we look at the ways it is 'moved along' (see Gregson *et al.*, 2007) within the house and (eventually) re-transformed into a new meal or snack. It is our contention that these practices have as much, if not more, significance in signalling family

The Sociological Review, 60:S2, pp. 121–134 (2013), DOI: 10.1111/1467-954X.12041

membership and intimacy than practices more traditionally associated with the 'front end' of meal consumption. The few studies that do explore domestic food disposal are attempts at theorizing disposal either in relation to wider consumption and production practices (Munro, 1995), or in relation to wider debates surrounding sustainability[1] (Evans, 2011a, 2011b). As yet, little has been said about the intersection of these practices with *collective* family identity and membership (although see Cappellini, 2009). Responding to this gap, this study explores practices of reusing and revaluing leftovers, and the implications for collective family identity. We have positioned these practices of reusing and revaluing food as 'thrift practices'. This positioning enables us to explore the skills and competencies involved in the reuse of food while at the same time exploring the motivations behind these practices (ie viewing thrift as an ideal or disposition). In doing so we build on the thesis that thrift practices are not only about saving resources per se, but about saving in order to spend at a future date (Miller, 1998).

Thrift practices, sacrifice and family membership

The concept of thrift embodies both a set of practices and also a set of moral ideals and dispositions. Arguing that thrift is distinct from mere frugality, Hunter and Yates (2011) observe that its meaning can be traced back to mid-seventeenth-century Puritanical understandings of thrift as a condition of thriving: 'Thrift in this deeper sense moves beyond the instrumentalities of "more or less" and begs the question: *what does it mean to thrive?* In short, thrift for what? More or less of what, and for what end? Such questions locate thrift's distinctive moral gravity' (2011: 11; emphasis in the original). Having roots in mutual aid societies, municipal savings banks and credit unions, thrift was not only about *individual* saving and frugality but was about people coming together to save for the greater good of the membership. It is this *collective* dimension of thrift that seems to be absent from contemporary debates.

In his *Theory of Shopping* (1998) Miller has a particular take on thrift, linking it with theories of sacrifice. In his analysis of households he shows how mothers save money in their everyday shopping in order to spend such savings on treats and presents for their family, mainly their children. Thrifty consumption epitomizes consumer society, as mothers' everyday thrift is in fact a temporary saving of economic resources to be spent in the future for the household. Thus, thrifty consumption has a circular nature: saving resources (by mothers) and spending resources (by mothers for their children). This circular movement of saving and spending is analogous to the process of sacrifice. Following classic anthropological works on sacrifice, including Hubert and Mauss (1964 [1899]) and Bataille (1988 [1949]), Miller argues that sacrifice is a process of communication between individuals and their deities. This communication operates through a *do ut des* system, wherein individuals donate their best resources and in return make specific requests of their deities for help and protection. Individuals demonstrate self-abnegation in renouncing their precious objects and giving them to their deities. This does not simply perpetuate the importance of the deities in their lives, but 'in fact sustains their ideal existence' (Hubert and Mauss, 1964: 102).

The thrift practices we are interested in involve the reuse of foodstuffs. As Munro (1995: 313) observes when it comes to food, 'Far from "choosing" what we eat, as is the presumption in both the "production" view and the "consumption" view, eating is governed in part by an availability of "conduits" for disposal'. These conduits are varying and diverse in the context of food – they could be the waste bin or the recycling bin, or conduits with more potential for 'revaluation as meal', such as the fridge. Theorists observe that there is a distinct geography to processes of (re)valuation here, in that dealing with disposal is a process of 'moving things along'; in other words moving them between sites or 'conduits for disposal' (Munro, 1995; Gregson *et al.*, 2007). The process of moving objects along requires skills and competencies in classifying, re-evaluating and ordering objects (Parsons, 2008), as well as the spatial knowledge involved in moving them to a specific elsewhere (Gregson *et al.*, 2007). If, in the process of sacrifice outlined by Miller, mothers are competent shoppers, evaluating the best bargains for saving resources, in the matter of reusing food it is the cook (often also the mother) who must be competent in evaluating leftovers, determining both the means of storing them, and potential future meals to be made with them. The ambiguous nature of food leftovers requires competence in dealing with foodstuffs that are neither meal nor ingredients, neither fresh nor completely spoiled; as such, they do not belong on the plate but neither do they yet belong in the waste bin. They are considered surplus, and not yet waste (Evans, 2011a), they muddy the waters of classification and introduce a sense of disorder (Munro, 1995; Edensor, 2005). Usefully reordering food leftovers requires knowledge of the materiality of the food, for example how long it will remain safely and tastily edible (Terpstra *et al.*, 2005), as well as the different conduits available for disposal. Such knowledge has consequences for the sorting and ordering of foodstuffs as excess (to be placed in the waste bin or food recycling box) or as surplus – potential ingredients for future consumption (to be placed in the fridge). Potential ingredients do not always make the transition into new meals; instead, as Evans (2012) found, other considerations intervene or they are forgotten about and their destination is instead the waste bin.

In the specific case of dealing with food disposal in the household, consumers are not simply dealing with the life of the objects and their placement, but also with the tastes, expectations and desires of other members of the family (Cappellini, 2009; Evans, 2012). As such, practices of reclassification and ordering are always constrained by those of accommodation. Studies on domestic food consumption show that feeding the family is demanding work whereby what mothers provide 'cannot just be any food, but must be food that will satisfy them [the family]' (DeVault, 1991: 40). Mothers do not simply cook for the family, but provide food that the family likes (DeVault, 1991), and that fits in with their schedules and priorities. Commensality is often a guiding principle in the design of meals (Sobal, 2000; Sobal and Nelson, 2003) and women often deny their own tastes in deference to other family members (Murcott, 1983; Charles and Kerr, 1986, 1988; Jansson, 1995; Brown and Miller, 2002). As such, in dealing with leftovers the schedules, desires and expectations of other members of the family need to be taken into consideration (Cappellini, 2009; Evans, 2011a). Although we recognize mothers' tireless work in feeding the family as an unbalanced gift exchange (see Ruskola, 2005) – since mothers give more than they receive – we think that there is also a collective family identity (see Epp and Price, 2008) to be considered when looking at the food shared in the household. With a few exceptions (Marshall, 2005; Cappellini and Parsons, 2012b), studies looking at sharing the meal do not necessarily explore the micro practices involved. In addition, studies are mostly focused on extraordinary meals (Wallendorf and Arnould, 1991) as opposed to ordinary and mundane meals wherein familial bonds and relationships are reinforced as well as reshaped.

Methodology

This paper is based on an ethnographic study undertaken by the first author between November 2007 and December 2008. The fieldwork was conducted with 20 households living in an ex-industrial city and its surroundings in the Midlands, UK. Most of the participants worked in the education sector and some of them had temporary jobs as research or teaching assistants. The sample might be described as solidly middle class in composition with a relatively high degree of educational capital. The recruited households consisted of nine nuclear families (both parents with children), one single mother living with her three children, five couples without children, two couples whose children had left home, two single people living on their own and a single person sharing a house with friends. With one exception all households were white, and the age range of the adults was early 30s to early 50s.

The ethnographic approach employed consists of a number of methods, including interviews and observation of participants during mealtimes. The person responsible for food provision in the household was interviewed about the organization of everyday meals, practices surrounding the process of having a meal, and the division of work in the household; but also the ideas, emotions and life goals associated with domestic food consumption. Interviews were followed up by observation of participants at mealtimes – planning, preparation, serving, sharing and disposal of the meal were observed. A fieldwork diary was kept which included photographs of mealtimes.

Combining interviews with observations helped us to understand how the family, and not simply mothers, materialize their ideas, know-how and emotions, and how they describe and perform their mealtime practices while a guest (the first author) is present. During fieldwork, the disposal of the meal emerged as a central theme for understanding family relationships as well as the process of having a meal. Because the approach of the research was inductive, the analysis presented here is an attempt to illuminate our data with the existing literature, and the literature with our ethnographic evidence (see Willis, 2000).

Thrifty meals: saving resources at dinnertime

Findings reveal that everyday meals are thrifty meals, as they are driven by the idea of saving resources, including time, money and effort. Elsewhere (Cappellini and Parsons, 2012b) this has been examined in detail, looking at all of the practices surrounding the everyday meal (from the planning to the washing up). Here we want to highlight how the served meal is influenced by the family's likes and dislikes, but also by saving resources. Dishes satisfying both criteria seemed to be repeated on a regular basis, becoming part of the family's meal repertoire. Take, for example, Margaret, a single mum living with her two teenage sons. She explains that 'spag bol' is one of her recurrent dishes, saving not only money but also time and effort from start to finish, including the planning, the cooking and the washing up.

> 'With spag bol you throw everything in a pan. It's very easy and quick . . . that's why I make it at least once a week [. . .] You get a tin of tomatoes, and chop an onion and a few herbs and it is quite simple, an awful lot cheaper, you can put in whatever you have and you don't have lots and lots of washing up.' (Margaret)

Take also David and Kate, a childless couple married for a couple of years. David, the primary cook, explains how his regular dishes have to be 'good for both' as well as 'not too much fuss'. Indeed, cooking for his wife, a 'fussy eater', and finding a meal requiring little fuss, seem to be the two main characteristics of David's dinners.

> 'She is a very fussy eater, so I can't really, I can't just put something on a plate and say "Eat it". If she likes something you can cook it forever. And that's what I am doing at the moment, cooking things she likes and are good for both [. . .] I make twenty dishes regularly so I make sure it is not the same thing every week. I would not cook a thing this week that we had last week. I try to keep things varying all the time. [. . .] On Sunday we have a roast dinner, so a traditional English roast dinner, but different every week [. . .] During the week we have pretty basic stuff, things that you do not have to cook forever and requiring too much fuss.' (David)

Observations reveal that participants have substantially different standards when judging what constitutes a quick, cheap and easy meal. In some households a quick meal is one that does not take more than 10 minutes to prepare, in others no more than 30 minutes. Similarly, in some households a cheap meal is one that costs no more than £10, in others no more than £20. Despite having different standards, participants describe the everyday meal as a thrifty meal. As with Miller's mothers, participants' focus on thrift does not necessarily mean that they save resources – rather that they are motivated by saving resources in order to spend them elsewhere. Eating up leftovers forms part of this saving of resources from ordinary weekday meals: for example, Tracey's weekly Sunday evening 'making do' dinner consists of making a dinner out of what is left in the fridge. Typical 'making do' dishes are sandwiches with some cold meat from the previous lunch, with some salad and pickles. The timing of this meal is significant (Sunday evening) as Tracey also mentions that a cooked family Sunday lunch earlier in the day is an important family appointment which she spends time in planning and cooking. As such, the later evening meal is one that requires little effort from her.

Margaret plans ahead when making her spag bol not only for future meals that she will prepare but to make things easy for her son so that he can prepare a healthy meal when she is not at home:

> 'When I make this sauce I tend to do it in large quantity, enough for another couple of times. Usually one lot goes straight to the freezer and one goes to the fridge so the guys can use it when I am out [. . .] On Wednesday night I teach until 6 and I am at home not before 7, 7.30. Michael [her oldest son] takes care of the dinner. I usually tell him what to prepare for him and John [her younger son]. He makes basic stuff . . . If I get round to making some sauce they usually go for that with some rice or pasta.'

At other times meals based on leftovers are more complex than the one Margaret's son prepares, since they require time and effort in using parts of the old dish to make a completely new one. David's reuse of the Sunday leftovers is in fact quite a complex process which involves sorting the food into different conduits for disposal.

> 'If I made a roast chicken, then I will make a chicken salad on Sunday night, but we will have it on Monday at lunch time. I tend to prepare a nice stock with the carcass of the chicken and some vegetables and I freeze it to make risotto during the week. If I made roast beef I tend to make a stew on Monday night, occasionally I can come up with something more unusual like a beef curry, but it's really rare. We do not usually have lamb, I am not that keen on lamb, but when we have it I leave the remainder for Kate. She will have a sandwich or something like that for her lunch.'
> 'What do you do with the rest of the chicken?'
> 'There is no rest, we use all of it.'
> 'What about the skin?'
> 'It goes in the bin. Skin is very bad for you.'

In describing his conduits for disposal of the meal, David seems to apply a similar strategy and set of competencies to those used by Gregson *et al.*'s (2007) participants in their disposal of household durables. Their participants demonstrated that disposal is not simply a matter of moving things out of the house, but rather classifying them and consequently moving them on through specific conduits (for example, a charity shop or the recycling bin). In a similar way, David divides the leftovers into various parts such as food surplus (meat) to be moved into the fridge and food waste (skin) to be moved to the bin. The

The Sociological Review, 60:S2, pp. 121–134 (2013), DOI: 10.1111/1467-954X.12041

way David chooses different conduits for the remains of the meal shows that his classification is not based on an intrinsic value of the different parts, but rather on his differing orientations towards their possible reuse. Planning the reuse of leftovers is a complex process that requires both knowledge of the material qualities of the food, and forward thinking as to the likely contexts of its reuse. These practices might also be seen as 'moving thrift along', as one thrifty meal often provides for another.

Food's particular nature as being subject to spoiling or decay shows that the classification between waste and surplus is not definitive, since what has been previously classified as surplus can be reclassified as waste – food is always 'in process' and requires ongoing effort to reclassify and rework it. When it is not reworked within a certain amount of time, plans for reusing leftovers can go awry. Our participants describe their routine as a mixture of plans that go ahead and others that are thwarted by unexpected events, like the urge to have a takeaway.

> 'We tend to be fairly organised and not have leftovers, mainly because I do not like eating the same stuff again. When there are leftovers we tend to eat them very soon otherwise we forget about them and they go bad. Like yesterday I planned to make a pie with the chicken left from Monday night, but we then decide to have a takeaway, and this morning when I looked at the chicken in the fridge I thought: 'Mmmm, this looks too bad'.'
>
> 'What did you do then?'
>
> 'Bin' [laughing].

Anne's story highlights that although participants see their leftovers as a form of thrift (ie devices for saving resources), such saving does not always take place and food often only temporarily escapes the bin. Others (Bardhi and Arnould, 2005) have shown how, despite participants' intention to be thrifty and reuse objects, the complexity of the everyday organization of the household often prevents them from doing so. We do not know how many times David makes the stock with the chicken bones or how many times 'making do' at Tracey's consists of a cold meat sandwich rather than a 'new' frozen pizza. What matters here is the idea of having saved some resources during ordinary meals – the actual saving becomes somehow less important since 'the general sense of being thrifty becomes abstracted from a specific act of saving' (Miller, 1998: 103).

Sharing thrifty meals: saving together

In the previous section we illustrated the complex work of reordering leftovers, and moving them along. In this section we explore how the everyday thrifty meal reinforces a sense of 'doing family' through the individual cook's (often mother's) sacrifice in abnegating his/her desires, and also through the collective sacrifice of 'saving together'.

Take the case of Tracey. Like other participants, Tracey plans and replans what to do with food leftovers and she moves them through various meals. In doing so she does not simply choose the conduits of disposal, but becomes one of these conduits herself. If some leftovers are shared amongst the family (during the 'making do' Sunday dinner for example), others are consumed entirely by Tracey. In planning her meals, she only shares leftovers with the family that she knows they will like, thus accommodating their tastes and desires. On Monday night Tracey usually makes a risotto if she had made roast chicken the previous day. A dish liked by her husband and children, risotto becomes a family conduit for disposal. However, this does not happen with other parts of Sunday lunch, such as boiled carrots and broccoli. Barely tolerated once a week with a lot of gravy to disguise their flavour, Tracey's husband and children reject any of her attempts to dispose of these leftovers through soups or pies. As a result, if she wishes to reuse the carrots and broccoli she must eat them herself.

> '[At lunch time] I'm usually on my own and I do not bother making a meal for myself. I usually have something quick, a sandwich or something left from the night before, nothing special really. I tend to open the fridge and see what is left and no-one wants anymore.'
> 'Like the carrots that you were telling me about before?'
> 'Yes, like the carrots, like other vegetables left from previous meals or things that are not enough for all of us.'

Here Tracey describes the consumption of leftovers in terms of not being bothered to make a meal for herself and thus consuming leftovers as a matter of convenience. However, on further questioning we discover that they are also food items that 'no-one wants anymore', and as such we might also think of Tracey as sacrificing her own tastes for the wider benefit of the family (DeVault, 1991). The way in which Tracey moves leftovers along and uses some of them for her lunches shows how disposal is part of Tracey's self-abnegation and sacrifice. Such sacrifice is shown through what she gives or does not give to her family, as well as what she prepares or does not prepare for herself. This sacrifice reaffirms Tracey's identity of 'being a mum', as well as reaffirming the relational identity of subjugating her desires to those of the objects of her devotion, her family. Like the mothers in Miller's (1998) and DeVault's (1991) studies, Tracey's sacrifice reaffirms her affiliation to her family and perpetuates her relationship with her children, who are seen as objects of her devotion and therefore the motivation for her self-abnegation.

Although mothers, when in charge of food provision in the household, are the ones who sacrifice themselves, other family members are expected to participate in the sacrifice involved in eating up leftovers. For instance, Katherine remembers how on Monday nights she used to make a pie out of what was left from the weekend. Although this was not always a welcome dish, she did not offer her children any alternative:

> 'They couldn't choose. I cooked it and I put it on the table and they had to eat it. If they. . . [pulls a disgusted face], 'If you don't want it, that's fine, next time you cook

for yourself'. They tried everything, they were too lazy and they had what I put on their plates [. . .] I've never let them decide what to eat for dinner. I was working full time and I did not have the time to make different dishes for four people. My meals were quite simple, nothing exciting, I have to admit, but nice, nice meals. [. . .] I could not throw away all the stuff left over from the Sunday lunch and I could not end up eating it all myself. I used to make pies and casseroles for everybody.' (Katherine)

Being part of Katherine's household includes sharing the 'nice' but thrifty Monday dinner, a family conduit for the disposal of Sunday lunch. Katherine does not portray herself as the sacrificing member of the family – instead, she describes the sacrifice of dealing with leftovers as a family practice. Thus, in her case we can say that disposal of the Sunday meal at the Monday night dinner table constitutes a family sacrifice. Although there are differences from household to household, participants confirm what Katherine and Tracey imply, that sharing the everyday meal is a family practice wherein everybody has to do their bit, including eating dishes made with leftovers. This confirms Belk's (2010) point that sharing reinforces and perpetuates affiliation and membership of a group and our roles within it. Indeed, Katherine's children's contributions to family meals do not simply reciprocate their mothers' sacrifices, but also underscore their obligations and identities as sons and thus their affiliation to the family unit.

Sharing extraordinary meals: spending together

The everyday driving force of saving resources at dinner time, through the reuse of leftovers (amongst other things), can be better understood by looking at times when this norm is interrupted. Indeed the meanings surrounding the process of eating leftovers can only be fully understood if we look at the longer run cosmology of the family meal, in particular the relationship between thrifty everyday meals and more extraordinary (weekend or special occasion) meals. If during the weekday meals all members of the family, although to different degrees, 'do their bit' in order to save 'something', during extraordinary meals resources such as time, money and labour in making a meal are spent considerably. This way of spending resources is usually considered as an exception, an extravagance, or a 'treat' as some of our participants define these meals, since they lie outside the mundane and thrifty provision of the meal. The existence of these treats and deviations from the norm serve to define the mundane and thrifty meal as the norm itself. As Nigel, a middle-aged man living with his wife observes:

> During the week we tend to have basic commodities but at the weekend we tend to say 'Right I am going to make this for this weekend' and cook something like a casserole or more complex like a pheasant so we plan it and take more time for the cooking.

Similarly, Tim, a father of two, observes:

> We are always in a rush, but at the weekend we can do things with more time and we
> have nice food and we sit and chat . . . it's nice, I think the children like it as well!

Nigel's weekend meal is characterized by the expenditure of extra time and labour in the kitchen since he cooks *more complex* dishes using more exotic ingredients such as pheasant which contrasts with the *basic commodities* of thrifty meals. For Tim weekend meals are characterized by nice food requiring more time and labour in its preparation. More time is also spent in sharing the food with the rest of the family. In both households these meals represent an interruption to the norm, since resources such as time and effort are spent considerably. For others the interruption to the norm is marked by extravagant purchases such as a more expensive bottle of wine, a piece of meat from the local farm or a 'special pudding'. The issue here is that what makes these meals special is that they mark a departure from the norm and importantly involve the spending of resources saved during thrifty (typically weekday) mealtimes. It is not surprising to see that leftovers are absent in these extraordinary meals, and more extravagant ingredients make their appearance.

Leftovers are also absent when guests are invited for a meal. Inviting guests into the family home presents an opportunity to display family to outsiders and in doing so, to spend the best resources in the form of an offer of the best food. As Tina, a mother of three in her fifties explains:

> 'I don't serve leftovers to my guests. Let's say you are coming for your observation, I
> will cook something special [. . .] I will cook something that we don't have regularly,
> something special, like a roast meal. [. . .] I will serve the meal at the dining table or at
> the kitchen table, but I'm more likely to serve it at the dining table.'

For Tina, as well as other participants, only family members or close friends are invited to eat everyday thrifty meals, where food previously cooked for other occasions reappears at the table. Carefully prepared as opposed to convenient food, and fresh food as opposed to leftovers, and abundance as opposed to frugality, are important. Indeed, anthropological studies show how sharing thrifty (or low ranked) food implies the most intimate of family relationships (Appadurai, 1981). Sharing leftover food, then, is a means by which boundaries of admission and exclusion to the family are unconsciously marked and perpetuated.

The literature on family meals tells us that it is during extraordinary meals that collective family identity is reinforced and perpetuated. For example, studies on Thanksgiving show how the exceptional nature of the menu, the ritual and the way of sharing the meal show how such a celebration mark family membership as well as the perpetuation of collective family identity (Wallendorf and Arnould, 1991). Similarly Douglas and Isherwood (1980: 88) remind us, 'sharing goods and being made welcome to the hospitable table . . . are the first, closest fields of inclusion'. In our cases it is the thrifty table, rather than the more hospitable one, that implies a deeper level of inclusion: being part of the family and sharing in the everyday saving of resources. Family members are expected to participate in the everyday household sacrifice of saving resources during mealtimes: it marks a level of intimacy and reaffirms family membership. The very process of sacrifice also marks a level of intimacy and inclusion within the family unit that may only be shared by family members or close friends.

Conclusion

In conclusion, we have a series of observations about the operation of thrift in household food practices and the associated implications for both individual and collective family identity. These thrift practices are both grounded in everyday behaviours and at the same time part of a public moral discourse about consumption. While public discourses surrounding food waste have a tendency to blame consumers' '(assumed) profligacy and (imagined) lack of culinary competence' (Evans, 2011a: 429), we have found little evidence of this lack of competence in our sample. Rather we have found the contrary, that using up leftovers is a complex practice that involves a series of skills and competencies which are related to knowledge surrounding both the material elements of the foodstuffs and the likely contexts of their reuse. Leftovers need to be materially managed and accommodated (Munro, 1995). As surplus from earlier consumption events (mealtimes) they need to be dealt with and re-sorted as waste or as potential ingredients, and placed in the fridge, the saucepan or the waste bin accordingly. The creation of leftovers is often also a motivation in the planning of a meal, and as such thrifty meals are often planned with reuse in mind. Here we see an inversion of typical theorizations of consumption leading in a linear fashion to eventual disposal, as planned conduits for disposal shape the choice of meals to cook as well as the choice of foods to be bought in the supermarket.

The flow of value in the household is therefore affected by creative acts of transforming and reframing food. However, these practices need to be located within, and be constrained by, the likes and dislikes of family members. So it is not only the materiality of the food leftovers that needs to be navigated but the daily routines and tastes of other individuals in the household (DeVault, 1991). As such, food provisioning, and in particular the use of leftovers, has to fit in with our wider modes of dwelling, and the routines and rhythms of life (Gregson, 2007).

In exploring leftovers as a form of thrift we have also explored the issues of familial belonging and membership, highlighting the sacrifice made by individual family members as well as the family as a whole. The primary cook within the home typically makes a sacrifice of time and effort in preparing the meal, so that the meal is a gift to other family members for which they are often required to reciprocate. This might involve setting the table or clearing away the dishes. It might also involve being prepared to sit down to the meal in a formal setting, express enjoyment of the meal or make conversation during mealtimes. In all of these cases the cook requires some reciprocation for the time and effort they have put into planning and preparing the meal. Mothers have typically been identified as sacrificing more than other family members in the preparation of meals, and we found this often to be the case amongst our participants. In putting the likes and dislikes of other family members first, it was often the mother who ended up consuming leftovers in order that other family members might enjoy fresh food. Such a practice clearly reveals the micro-economy of household food provisioning, in particular the way in which members are co-dependent, and how one individual's consumption decision nearly always impacts on the others.

However, we also found that through the consumption of thrifty meals, other family members were expected to share in this sacrifice, and that this was a key mechanism of marking membership to the family. Returning to Hunter and Yates' (2011: 11) questions relating to thrift: *'What does it mean to thrive?* In short, thrift for what? More or less of what, and for what end?' we see that practising thrift in the family unit is all about thriving as a family. Here thrift practices are directed towards reinforcing family membership. Family membership means saving and spending together for the greater good of the family unit. This focus on thriving views the household as a relatively closed unit in which the resources of time and energy saved in both the production and consumption of thrifty meals are spent in more extravagant meals in the longer term. We can see that saving occurs in going without, forsaking or sacrificing for the greater good of the family. Preparing and eating Sunday dinner every day simply would not be possible or practical given the resources of time and effort required. Thus, we see a longer-run cycle of saving to spend in future mealtime practices. There is a balance here between immediate and longer-term gratification, for example saving resources in everyday meals for more elaborate meals in the immediate (ie Sunday dinner), and longer-term (ie Christmas dinner) future.

As well as a set of practices, thrift can also be seen as a moral disposition which tells us something about our relationship to material goods. What we have observed in our small sample of households is likely to be indicative of broader shifts in contemporary consumption towards sustainability and doing more with less in times of economic crisis. Further research is needed, with a much wider socio-economic spread of households. However, for the middle-class families in our sample we speculate that practising thrift at mealtimes is not only a reaction to economic hardship: for these families it is certainly more than a just form of belt tightening. Rather, we posit that thrift is still somewhat of a *middle-class disposition* in the UK, and as such it is as much about identity as economics (see Morrison and Dunlap, 1986, for a similar view regarding environmentalism). Practising thrift represents a form of control over the flow of resources in the household, even if this does not equate to a reduction in overall resource usage and/or wastage. As Miller observes, 'The general sense of being thrifty becomes abstracted from a specific act of saving' (1998: 103). As such, participants' disposition towards thrift may in fact merely be masking what is really going on in terms of food use. These participants may be wasting quite a volume of food in the long run but this gets lost in their focus on 'being thrifty' on a day-to-day basis. This orientation towards thrift is a way of regulating and controlling the spending of resources in the household, and has a significant moral symbolic dimension which is arguably central to moral economies of the self in the context of contemporary capitalism.

Note

1 Reducing food waste at household level is currently high on the UK government's agenda. It is estimated that British households throw away around a fifth of the food they buy, costing the average family with children around £680 a year (WRAP, 2011a). A series of social marketing initiatives have been introduced to 're-educate' the consumer in using up leftovers (ie WRAP, 2011b).

References

Appadurai, A., (1981), 'Gastro-politics in Hindu South Asia', *American Ethnologist*, 8 (3): 494–511.

Bardhi, F. and Arnould, E. J., (2005), 'Thrift shopping: combining utilitarian thrift and hedonic treat benefits', *Journal of Consumer Behaviour*, 4 (4): 223–233.

Bataille, G., (1988 [1949]), *The Accursed Share*, New York: Zone Books.

Belk, R. W., (2010), 'Sharing', *Journal of Consumer Research*, 36 (5): 715–734.

Brown, L. J. and Miller, D., (2002), 'Couples' gender role preferences and management of family food preferences', *Journal of Nutrition Education and Behavior*, 34, 215–223.

Cappellini, B., (2009), 'The sacrifice of re-use: the travels of leftovers and family relations', *Journal of Consumer Behaviour*, 8 (6): 365–375.

Cappellini, B. and Parsons, E., (2012a), '(Re)enacting motherhood: self-sacrifice and abnegation in the kitchen', in R. Belk and A. Ruvio (eds), *Identity and Consumption*, London: Routledge.

Cappellini, B. and Parsons, E., (2012b), 'Sharing the meal: food consumption and family identity', *Research in Consumer Behaviour*, 13: 109–128.

Carrigan, M. and Szmigin, I., (2006), ' "Mothers of invention": maternal empowerment and convenience consumption', *European Journal of Marketing*, 40 (9/10): 1122–1142.

Charles, N. and Kerr, M., (1986), 'Food for feminist thought', *The Sociological Review*, 34 (1): 547–572.

Charles, N. and Kerr, M., (1988), *Women, Food and Families*, Manchester: Manchester University Press.

DeVault, M. L., (1991), *Feeding the Family: The Social Organisation of Caring as Gendered Work*, Chicago: University of Chicago Press.

Douglas, M. and Isherwood, B., (1980), *The World of Goods towards an Anthropology of Consumption*, London: Allen Lane.

Edensor, T., (2005), 'Waste matter – the debris of industrial ruins and the disordering of the material world', *Journal of Material Culture*, 10 (3): 311–332.

Epp, M. A. and Price, L., (2008), 'Family identity: a framework of identity interplay in consumption practices', *Journal of Consumer Research*, 35 (1): 50–70.

Evans, D., (2011a), 'Blaming the consumer – once again: the social and material contexts of everyday food waste practices in some English households', *Critical Public Health*, 21 (4): 429–440.

Evans, D., (2011b), 'Thrifty, green or frugal: reflections on sustainable consumption in a changing economic climate', *Geoforum*, 42 (5): 550–557.

Evans, D., (2012), 'Beyond the throwaway society: ordinary domestic practice and a sociological approach to household food waste', *Sociology*, 46 (1): 41–56.

Gregson, N., (2007), *Living with Things: Ridding, Accommodation, Dwelling*, Wantage: Sean Kingston Publishing.

Gregson, N., Metcalfe, A. and Crewe, L., (2007), 'Moving things along: the conduits and practices of divestment in consumption', *Transactions of the Institute of British Geographers*, 32 (2): 187–200.

Hubert, H. and Mauss, M., (1964 [1899]), *Sacrifice: Its Nature and Functions*, Chicago: University of Chicago Press.

Hunter, J. D. and Yates, J. J., (2011), 'Introduction: the question of thrift', in J. J. Yates and J. D. Hunter (eds), *Thrift and Thriving in America: Capitalism and Moral Order from the Puritans to the Present*, 3–36, Oxford: Oxford University Press.

Jansson, S., (1995), 'Food practices and the division of domestic labor', *The Sociological Review*, 43, 462–477.

Marshall, D., (2005), 'Food as ritual, routine or convention', *Consumption, Markets and Culture*, 8 (1): 69–85.

Miller, D., (1998), *A Theory of Shopping*, New York: Cornell University Press.

Morrison, D. E. and Dunlap, R. E., (1986), 'Environmentalism and elitism: a conceptual and empirical analysis', *Environmental Management*, 10 (5): 581–589.

Munro, R., (1995), 'The disposal of the meal', in D. Marshall (ed.), *Food Choices and the Consumer*, 313–325, London: Blackie Academic and Professional.

Murcott, A., (1983), ' "It's a pleasure to cook for him": food, mealtimes and gender in some South Wales households', in E. Gamarnikow, D. H. J. Morgan, J. Purvis and D. Taylorson (eds), *The Public and the Private*, 78–90, London: Heinemann.

Parsons, E., (2008), 'Thompsons' rubbish theory: exploring the practices of value creation', *European Advances in Consumer Research*, 8: 390–393.

Ruskola, T., (2005), 'Home economics: what is the difference between a family and a corporation?' in M. Ertman and M. Williams (eds), *Rethinking Commodification: Cases and Readings in Law and Culture*, 324–344, New York: New York University Press.

Sobal, J., (2000), 'Sociability and meals: facilitation, commensality, and interaction', in H. L. Meiselman (ed.), *Dimensions of the Meal: The Science, Culture, Business, and Art of Eating*, 119–133, Gaithersburg, MD: Aspen Publications.

Sobal, J. and Nelson, M. K., (2003), 'Commensal eating patterns: a community study', *Appetite*, 41 (2): 181–190.

Soderman, B. and Carter, R., (2008), 'The auto salvage: a space of second chances', *Space and Culture*, 11 (1): 20–38.

Terpstra, M. J., Steenbekkers, L. P. A., de Maertelaere, N. C. M. and Nijhuis, S., (2005), 'Food storage and disposal: consumer practices and knowledge', *British Food Journal*, 107 (7): 526–533.

Wallendorf, M. and Arnould, E. J. (1991), ' "We gather together": consumption and rituals of Thanksgiving Day,' *Journal of Consumer Research*, 18 (1): 13–31.

Willis, P., (2000), *The Ethnographic Imagination*, Cambridge: Polity.

WRAP (Waste and Resources Action Programme), (2011a), *New Estimates for Household Food and Drink Waste in the UK* http://www.wrap.org.uk/retail_supply_chain/research_tools/research/report_new.html

WRAP, (2011b), *Love Food Hate Waste* campaign, http://www.lovefoodhatewaste.com/recipes.

The Sociological Review, 60:S2, pp. 121–134 (2013), DOI: 10.1111/1467-954X.12041

Food waste bins: bridging infrastructures and practices

Alan Metcalfe, Mark Riley, Stewart Barr,
Terry Tudor, Guy Robinson and Steve Guilbert

Abstract: Recent years have seen an increasing number of councils begin separate food waste collections from domestic premises, a change that has resulted in house-holders having to sort food waste and keep it in separate bins until collection. Yet bins – of any kind – have been subject to little investigation, despite being a central element of the waste infrastructure. This paper attends to this omission by examining food bins. First of all, it explores the ways that bins have agency through an exploration of how their presence has affected waste practices. We find that their agency is three-fold: it is symbolic, relational and, importantly, material – an aspect which has been overlooked all too often in analyses of material culture and consumption. Secondly, we show how this material agency can be troubling: we explore how this agency is managed by households through practices of accommodation and resistance. Exam-ining the food bin's agency and how it is consumed gives an insight into the imple-mentation of, and engagement with, waste policy 'on the ground'. This allows us to make some suggestions for how to improve the implementation of this policy. This paper also opens up two new areas of study: first, a more sustained and developed exploration of bins, giving some pointers as to other possible issues. Secondly, and more broadly, the paper examines the extent to which the objects that materialize policy can be useful in the implementation of that policy, especially if the policy seeks 'behaviour change'.

Keywords: bins, food, waste, object agency, material culture, consumption, policy

Introduction

Food waste has risen up the waste policy agenda recently to become, according to the 2011 Waste Review, a 'priority waste stream' (Department of the Environment, Food and Rural Affairs (DEFRA), 2011: 58). Although largely ignored in the explosion of interest in recycling in the 1990s and early 2000s, much recent effort has been turned towards the food waste stream. First of all, there has been a focus on prevention (Waste and Resources Action Programme (WRAP), 2010; Sharp *et al.*, 2010a, 2010b), with households encouraged to waste less food through campaigns such as WRAP's *Love Food, Hate Waste*

The Sociological Review, 60:S2, pp. 135–155 (2013), DOI: 10.1111/1467-954X.12042

campaign.[1] However, as WRAP (2009) themselves recognize, this is a difficult task, not least because – as Evans (2012a) has shown – food waste is caused not so much by irrational excess that can be cut, but through competent, everyday domestic practices. Given these difficulties, a second approach is to manage the disposal and treatment of food waste. This has, until recently, involved councils (re)organizing the local waste infrastructure so that an increase on the 2006 figure of 2 per cent of food waste produced is collected for composting or anaerobic digestion (Hogg *et al.*, 2007). This has required not only the deployment of appropriate treatment technologies[2] but also an effective collection system. Pivotal to such a renewed waste infrastructure is the presence of a food bin alongside recycling and residual waste bins. This paper focuses specifically on the food bin.

Bins, as Chappells and Shove (1999: 268) make clear, are 'a gateway between domestic waste arrangements and systems of public provision'. Exploring how waste receptacles have changed over time, these authors show how bins are 'moulded by the interests of specific constellations of actors' while they simultaneously 'promise to reframe our everyday waste practices' (1999: 268). Though avoiding a linear, top-down determinism of a bin both shaped and then in turn shaping, their analysis does not take account of how bins' agency escapes the interests of the 'constellation of actors', nor does it explore how households manage this 'reframing'. Although they do stress the need to think about whether and how bins will have, what they see as, the right effects, they do not draw on empirical research to examine contemporary bins. In this they are not alone. Despite the fact that since Chappells and Shove's publication there has been a veritable explosion in the study of waste (Hawkins and Meucke, 2003; Hawkins, 2006; Scanlan, 2005; Clarke, 2007; Gille, 2007; Cooper, 2008, 2010; O'Brien, 2008; Riley, 2008; Reno, 2009; Gregson *et al.*, 2010), few have focused attention on the bin itself.

Where bins have featured in academic research, they have tended to be subsumed within wider discussions. Within social psychology, for instance, most studies have examined attitudes to explain differential participation rates in recycling, with only a few considering 'situational' factors such as bins. Even then bins are not directly considered, instead they are only explored as an aspect of the wider waste service and the available bin storage space within dwellings (Barr *et al.*, 2003; Derksen and Gartrell, 1993; Guagnano *et al.*, 1995). Similarly, the examination of waste governance (Bulkeley *et al.*, 2005, 2007; Davies, 2005, 2008; Davoudi, 2009; Davoudi and Evans, 2005; Fagan, 2003) has focused on macro factors that affect waste infrastructures, including the provision of bins. However, it has failed to address the impacts of waste policy 'on the ground' (Davies, 2003). Those who have studied waste 'on the ground' – examining domestic waste and disposal practices – have similarly omitted the bin itself from direct examination, often using disposal diaries as a proxy (Gregson, 2007; Gregson *et al.*, 2007a, 2007b; Evans, 2012a). With the focus on consumption and disposal, the bin was just one of a range of conduits through which unwanted material could be moved on (Munro, 1995; Hetherington, 2004).

The Sociological Review, 60:S2, pp. 135–155 (2013), DOI: 10.1111/1467-954X.12042

We found only two papers that directly examined bins (Bulkeley and Gregson, 2009; Evans, 2012b). Yet even in these they have remained marginal; secondary to the primary argument they are discussed in just one section of each paper. Bulkeley and Gregson (2009) are primarily interested in policy. Coming from the governance and consumption approaches respectively they identify bins as situated at the interface between waste infrastructure and waste practices. Drawing on reflections from previous work conducted separately, they argue that policy could be improved by connecting infrastructure to everyday and regular practices of consumption and disposal, such as events like moving house. Regarding bins, they suggest possible reasons for low participation rates in recycling schemes within certain areas, including a general resistance to the state and its apparent creeping intrusion into the home (cf. Miller, 1988), and local cultural concerns regarding cleanliness, aesthetics, order and respectability (Madigan and Munro, 1996; O'Brien, 1999). These tantalizing suggestions are supported by the empirical research of Evans (2012b). However, even here the bin is not the focus of the study as Evans is primarily concerned with food-waste practices and the 'passage of "food" to "waste" ' (2012b: n. 2). At the end point of the process, the bin is one of several conduits that are incorporated into the performance of these practices. It becomes an object for analysis when, towards the end of the study, food caddies are distributed by the council and Evans reflects upon the first impressions of his participants. Echoing Bulkeley and Gregson (2009), these participants voice concerns about aesthetics, littering and mistrust of the council, though some are grateful for the caddies as the food-waste will be recycled – its value salvaged along with their conscience.

This review shows that work from a range of conceptual directions – all with different agendas, making different points about waste and recycling – have recognized the importance of the bin, yet direct empirical examination of bins, their place in the household and between the private and public realms, has remained curiously absent. This paper, in contrast, attends to this omission of the bin from waste research. In doing so it makes a significant and original contribution to debates in studies of waste by providing the first and much-needed empirically grounded exploration of the bin. It does this through a rigorous examination of one specific type of bin pivotal to the separation of a distinct waste stream: the food caddy. Here, the food bin is conceptualized not as a second order object, appropriated to enable the performance of waste practices, but as an object with which people have a relationship: it is an object of consumption. Households may not have chosen or even wanted any kind of food bin for their home, but it remains subject to the same processes and practices of consumption, use and display, accommodation, appropriation and resistance as any consumer good (Gregson, 2007).

By taking this object seriously, this paper focuses on two inter-related aspects of its place between the home and the wider waste infrastructure. First of all, we argue that the food bin has agency. An agency that calls householders to undertake particular waste practices. This agency is an effect of an interweaving of the bin's symbolic qualities, its relationalities and its material capacities.

Symbolically the bin represents waste and the environment on the one hand, and cultural cleanliness, order and pollution on the other; relationally, it is one aspect of a broader waste infrastructure without which it would not exist as a conduit of unwanted material; and materially it has capacities and affordances (Gibson, 1977), and as such affects waste practices. Secondly, we argue that people engage with and seek to manage this agency. They do this through placing the bin in certain areas of the kitchen, by instigating cleansing and emptying routines, and/or if it proves too troublesome by rejecting the bin. However, such rejection does not necessarily mean non-participation in the food-waste collection scheme; instead we found that some households replaced the troublesome caddy with another receptacle more suited to their needs, a receptacle that then took on the same symbolic and infrastructural agency of the rejected caddy. To demonstrate these points we rigorously examine the empirical material to show how a reluctant recycler was drawn into undertaking food-waste collection, and then more generally how households manage the food bin and its agency through accommodation and resistance.

Examining the food bin and how it is consumed enables us to draw several conclusions. First of all, we argue that consumption and material culture studies need to examine the three aspects of an object's representational, infrastructural and material qualities and how these interweave. There has been a tendency to focus on the representational and relational aspects, and to by-pass the material (Olsen, 2010); to counter this, the paper focuses especially on the material aspect of the bin, an approach that is gaining ground (Dant, 2008; Watson, 2008; Gregson *et al.*, 2009; Olsen, 2010). Secondly, this research suggests that a more sustained and developed exploration of bins would contribute much to material culture studies, waste studies and so on; and we give some pointers as to other possible issues. Thirdly, the insight provided by these case studies exploring the implementation of, and engagement with, waste policy 'on the ground' allows us to make some suggestions for how to improve policy implementation. Finally, and more broadly, this study suggests a potentially fruitful examination of the extent to which objects that materialize policy can be useful in the implementation of that policy, especially if the policy seeks 'behaviour change'.

Before this discussion and conclusion we outline the research project upon which this paper is based, documenting its aims and methods, the location of the study and the changing waste regime in this location. It is to this that we now turn.

The research

This paper is based on a Leverhulme Trust funded project entitled 'Lifestyles and Life-course: The Social Context of Household Waste Management'. The central aim of this project was to explore people's relationships with waste, in particular how these relationships have changed over time; how they currently manage their household wastes; and how this links to broader environmental issues, concerns and actions. The research focused on one local authority area, Kingston upon Thames in south London (UK) and used a mixed methods approach, initially undertaking a survey of 10 per cent of resident households followed by interviews with a cross-section of respondents.

For the survey, 6,000 households were sent a questionnaire asking what they did with their unwanted and waste materials as well as how they saw their broader environmental attitudes and behaviours. A cluster analysis of the 1,627 responses delineated six groups: 'reusers', 'normative wasters', 'hidden waste managers', 'refusenics', 'conscious consumers and disposers' and 'eco-angels'.[3] Interviews with 27 of the households followed using semi-structured interviews and object elicitation. Potential participants were distinguished so that a range of social characteristics were covered such as age, household size, occupation, education, housing tenure, income, ethnicity and fundamentally their 'waste grouping', that is, 'composters', 'garden wasters', and so on. The interviews focused on three areas: waste biographies, current waste practices, and broader environmental attitudes and practices. This was supplemented by object-elicitation as a means of further drawing out current waste practices. For this, waste material from different bins was emptied out, items photographed and interviewees were asked to reflect upon the objects found, what they were and why and how they had ended up where they had. Repeat interviews were undertaken with many of the participants. Interviews were then transcribed and analysed literally, interpretively and reflexively (Mason, 2002).

Kingston upon Thames is a relatively wealthy suburb of south London[4] marked by low crime rates, excellent schools, and a particular ethnic mix (77 per cent white with Sri Lankan and Korean[5] its largest minority ethnic groups). In terms of waste, Kingston went through a fundamental transformation in its waste regime in 2008–2009. New bins, bags and boxes were distributed to all houses and to most flats as the council sought to separate paper, cardboard, plastics, textiles, tins, batteries, garden trimmings and food into distinct recycling streams separate from the general waste for landfill. Recycling was also encouraged by implementing new collection timings: recycling would be collected every week while residual waste for landfill would be collected fortnightly. Table 1 indicates the changed waste flows as a result of the new regime.

The table shows that two dramatic changes took place as a result of the new waste regime. First there was a huge reduction in the proportion of municipal solid waste (MSW) sent for landfilling, and secondly there was an increase in the range of routes available for that portion not landfilled. The proportion of waste landfilled declined from over 90 per cent prior to 2008–2009 to around 55 per cent per annum from 2009–2010. Although there was a significant decrease in the amount of MSW collected over the period (2006–2011), from 56,351 to 51,771 tonnes, this still left a large amount of waste that needed to be handled in ways other than landfilling. In 2006–2007 the only alternative to landfilling was Windrow (open air composting) only suitable for organic garden waste. Over the following few years new conduits and technologies were added to the options, including materials recovery facilities (MRFs) to which around one-

The Sociological Review, 60:S2, pp. 135–155 (2013), DOI: 10.1111/1467-954X.12042

Table 1: *Kingston upon Thames destination of municipal solid waste (MSW) 2006–2011*

	2006–2007		2007–2008		2008–2009		2009–2010		2010–2011	
	Tonnes	%	Tonnes	%	Tonnes	%	Tonnes	%	Tonnes	%
Non-hazardous landfill	52,564	93.3	49,580	91.9	40,373	74.9	27,619	53.5	29,014	56.0
Hazardous landfill	27	0	22	0	8	0	83	0.2	91	0.2
Incineration with energy recovery							4,805	9.3	2,747	5.3
Incineration without energy recovery							2	0	2	0
Materials recovery facility					6,737	12.5	9,551	18.5	9,812	19.0
In-vessel composting			447	0.8	2,417	4.5	5,159	10.0	5,213	10.1
Windrow or other composting	3,760	6.7	3,911	7.2	4,392	8.1	4,399	8.5	4,892	9.5
Total tonnages input	56,351		53,960		53,927		51,618		51,771	

Source: adapted from data retrieved from wastedataflow.org.

(a)   (b)

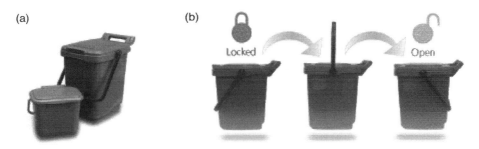

Figure 1: *(a) The large and the small caddies (b) Showing how caddies lock and open © Kingston upon Thames.*[7]

fifth of MSW was sent; in-vessel composting (IVC) which received about 10 per cent of MSW collected; and incineration with energy recovery (EfW) to which a sporadic increase then decrease in material was sent. Key for this paper is the increase in IVC. If food is to be recycled it must go to IVC. Although not all waste going to IVC has to be food, it is safe to assume that the vast majority of the 5,213 tonnes will be made up of food waste. The fundamental point is clear: Kingston upon Thames' new waste regime has had a dramatic effect on the proportions of materials landfilled and recycled.

Food bins are at the heart of this waste transformation in Kingston. There are two plastic food-waste caddies distributed to most households in the borough,[6] and 52 biodegradable bags are also delivered each year. The smaller of the two caddies – the 'kitchen caddy' – has a 5 litre capacity, which means that it is less obtrusive and can be kept in the kitchen, on work surfaces or in cupboards. It also means it fills up relatively quickly so requires frequent emptying into the larger caddy. This 23-litre box stores food waste for up to a week and is kept outside. Both bins lock when the handle is down at the front to prevent vermin getting in (see Figure 1). The bags are to line the larger caddy, and it is these that the waste collectors generally take to the collection truck rather than the caddy itself. In terms of use by households, it is the smaller 'kitchen caddy' with which they have a closer relationship, as they are likely to keep this in their kitchen and use it every day. The rest of the paper draws on illustrative case studies to explore and analyse these relations in more detail. In the next section we consider the agency of this small caddy and its effects on a 'reluctant recycler'.

The agency of the food caddy: the reluctant recycler

What soon became apparent within the research was that bins in general, and food-waste bins in particular, were not simply neutral containers that enabled willing householders to act. Instead, bins clearly had a capacity to affect the waste practices of respondents. To illustrate this agency, we draw on the case of

Karen and Damian.[8] In their early forties, they are married, with two young children and live in a semi-detached house on a post-war private estate. Damian is a regional sales manager and Karen, formerly in sales, is now a full-time mother and housewife. Karen spoke explicitly of her reluctance to participate in the food waste separation scheme when it was first introduced, yet she tells of how the presence of the kitchen caddy nevertheless affected her waste practices:

> I remember being very resistant to a food receptacle, 'I'm not having, I'm not having a receptacle full of dirty old food sitting on my countertop, forget about it, that's not going to happen.'

Karen's indignation stemmed from her association of waste food with 'dirt'. As such it felt inappropriate to put the caddy on the countertops, a place of food preparation and cleanliness: she felt anxious about 'dirty old food' that could contaminate surfaces and food to be eaten. Because the food bin contained waste, or was designed to, it thereby represented or 'spoke of' such waste. Having the bin (and its contents) on the countertop disrupted the ideal of cleanliness and order in the kitchen. It was 'matter out of place' (Douglas, 1984).

Her resistance to the food bin dissipated over time and the kitchen caddy is now kept on the countertop. Karen acknowledges that 'the aesthetics bothered me but with familiarity you just, it just becomes the norm'. The caddy's presence on the countertop has also had a real effect on her actions, as she explains:

> That initial change, behaviour change was quite tricky because you were so used to just throwing tea bags or whatever in the bin, suddenly you're on your own in the house but the voice is going 'well it should go in there', and you're going [whispering] 'well no I can't be bothered, just throw it in the bin', the sense of guilt around that. Maybe it's because of the way I'm built I couldn't go against the [unclear] no-one was there to tell me off, no-one would necessarily know.

Effectively, the presence of the caddy hailed her, it called her to action. In Karen's explanation of her relationship with the bin – of how it affected her actions – its power was in making her reflect on what was the 'right' thing to do. Perhaps, she suggests, this was because of the way she is '*built*', that she finds it hard to go against authority. The effects, though, seemed more thorough-going. Being pressed into doing the recycling led her, she says, to develop an '*environmental conscience*'. She went on to explain that this was her first 'encounter with being environmentally friendly really, my first conscious contact with it in any way'. Having made contact she now took the responsibility of recycling seriously, doing what she could. However, undertaking these waste practices not only appeared to reveal her prior ignorance to herself but also to provide redemption that she need do nothing more, recycling was enough:

> I began to have this environmental conscience and doing nothing else toward saving the planet this became my only outlet, so then I got on board and got on board strongly 'cause it sort of appeased my guilt maybe in other areas, or I realised I'd been so ignorant for so long.

The food caddy thus seemed to have two effects: it 'made' her do the recycling, especially the food waste, despite her reluctance, and it triggered an environmental conscience – albeit one limited to recycling as this redeemed her prior inaction and absolved her of performing other environmental friendly actions.

So how could the bin have such effects? Where did its power and capacity, its agency originate? We contend that such agency lay in the fact that the food caddy was multiple. It had powerful representational, relational and material qualities, working together and apart constituted its effect. In terms of its representational qualities it acted as a compelling metaphor for authority, waste and the environment. As Karen said, she found it hard to refuse the council's request given the way she is 'built'. Beyond this, it also brought her into contact with ideas about – and meanings of – waste and 'the environment', ideas that, seemingly, she had barely acknowledged prior to this. In representing an external other judging her (in)actions, the bin seemed to open up these inactions to reflection. This reflection, this inner voice of a judging other, meant that she not only succumbed and began to use the food caddy but that she 'bought into' the idea of recycling as *her way* of being environmentally friendly. This recycling, however, did not lead to her undertaking other environmental actions. Doing the difficult and dirty food-waste, along with the rest of the recycling, meant that she was 'doing her bit' (Gilg and Barr, 2005). This act absolved her of further action; it stood for environmental acts in the wider sense and meant that she did not have to do anything else: recycling made her, and thereby the household, 'environmentally friendly'.

A second way in which the caddy operated metaphorically was by representing dirt and pollution, and in this sense it was more troubling and more difficult than representing the environment. This was something that, initially at least, threatened to disrupt the cleanliness and order of the kitchen, not because of what it was but because of what it contained, or was designed to contain (food waste). The bin was thus doubled: it contained this pollutant, and through containing it, it became 'infected' and could pollute. The food waste could stick to the caddy, making it dirty or as Lucy (an interviewee discussed below) said, it became 'icky' to handle.

The object though, is not just representational of something else, a constant deferral to some other idea or ideal that invokes action, it is also an infrastructural and a material thing – both of which also attribute it with agency. As an infrastructural object, its agency is a relational effect of a network of waste technologies, policies, contracts, collection routes and routines; it is only this interconnection with the waste infrastructure that gives the container its qualities *qua* a food-waste bin. For instance, the kitchen caddy is entwined with the other bins, including the landfill bin. This landfill bin is meant for residual material; it is half the size of the old landfill bin and is now collected fortnightly – in effect giving one quarter the capacity for material to be landfilled. This effects a displacement of material to the recycling bins, including the food caddy. However, while the changing capacities of these containers might all but force recycling of bulky items such as bottles, card and paper, there is less need with regard to food waste. Food waste is not bulky and falls between the gaps left in the residual bin by unrecyclable packaging. Moreover, many interviewees said their landfill bin was only half full every collection day. This would suggest there was not really a *practical need* to recycle their food waste: they could easily continue to put it in the (semi-filled) landfill bin. The presence of the different bins, however, was key, as their presence *invited* certain actions. It is at this point that we see the material agency of the bin.

As a material object a bin may initially appear inanimate, something that merely enables the human agent to act and to achieve their ends. As a material thing, however, it is an object with capacities and affordances that invite rather than just enable action (Gibson, 1977; Olsen, 2010). As Olsen argues, 'things make a difference not because of the sake of difference itself . . . they are real entities that possess their own unique qualities and competences which they bring to our cohabitation to them' (2010: 156). At its simplest, the caddy is a small, brown plastic box with a hinged lid into which material might be placed and kept. Its size and shape mean that it can be placed relatively unobtrusively on countertops or inside cupboards. Its capacity means that it holds a limited amount of material. Its construction, colour and functional design means it is considered ugly by some, not an object households want to have on show. However, it contains rotting food which may begin to smell, it may become unpleasant to handle, need frequent cleansing, and – in terms of the external caddies in particular – it can attract vermin and mischievous youths (cf. Bulkeley and Gregson, 2009; Evans, 2012b). While these material aspects of the object and its agency may appear obvious, the phenomenological aspects of objects are often 'missed out' as writers look for their agency in the representational and relational domains (Olsen, 2010). The importance of material agency is demonstrated below as we show how its materiality becomes troublesome. In the next section, therefore, we explore how people managed to accommodate this materiality, and then discuss how this material agency was inherently so troubling it was resisted.

Managing agency through accommodation

In Karen's story the bin's initially troublesome nature seemed to dissipate as she got used to it. We contend, however, that something else was going on. The caddy became part of the kitchen not by just being there, but rather by the ways in which it was handled and managed. Karen, for example, did indeed place it on the kitchen top (exactly where she initially did not want it), but she placed it in a specific spot on the countertop – in a corner between the sink and a cupboard, not only away from food storage and preparation areas but close to areas dealing with cleansing and expulsion (see centre photo, Figure 3) (Roderick, 1997). By this placing, she managed its potentially troubling qualities, containing its potential as a pollutant. This practice of 'making space' for the caddy, placing it in

The Sociological Review, 60:S2, pp. 135–155 (2013), DOI: 10.1111/1467-954X.12042

Figure 2: *Keeping food caddies in cupboards:*
(Left) Priti and Deepak: using a clear plastic tub for their food bin
(Middle) Simon and Carol – using their own food bin, lined with a blue
plastic bag and containing flowers (Right) Nicola and Matt's kitchen caddy
in a cupboard.

Figure 3: *Food caddies on the work surface in 'non-food zones'*
(Left) Harry: Keeps his next to the draining board and near cleaning materials
(Middle) Karen and Damian's caddy is kept in the far corner near the sink
(Right) Lara and Keith also keep theirs in the corner, along with some recycling.

'dirty' or 'non-food' zones spatially distinct from 'clean' or 'food' areas in the kitchen was something relatively common in the households we visited. Looking closely at the placing of the food bin in the different kitchens, we found that 18 of the 22 households using a food caddy made clear spatial distinctions. Most placed them in corners, next to the sink or with the washing up, while a few made the spatial distinction even clearer by putting them on the floor or in a cupboard (see Figures 2 and 3). This spatial division is a clear manifestation of Douglas's analysis of dirt and pollution (1984), in which order is disrupted by matter out of place, and is maintained by placing it 'back' in place, or, here, devising a new and appropriate place where this matter can be kept.

While this spatial division may have been found in most households, it was not true of all. A few kept their food bins on the kitchen worktop but in less distinct spaces, close to food preparation areas. Rather than marginalizing the

Figure 4: *Caddies kept in more indistinct spaces, near to food storage and preparation areas*
(Left) Carl and Penny; (Middle) John and Gabriela; (Right) Peter and Sue.

bin itself, these households emphasized cleansing routines and practices to counter any potential problems. Yet this did not always effectively prevent smell intruding on food preparation; instead it was accepted that smell was something that they would occasionally have to manage 'in the moment'. This acceptance was not necessarily an attitude of the whole household, as different tolerances could be found within households. For instance, John and Gabriela's kitchen caddy, though pushed to the back wall, is kept between the microwave, kettle and toaster, which together frame the food preparation area (see Figure 4). The kitchen is small in their three-bedroom Victorian semi-detached house, shared with three daughters aged 8–12, but another countertop alongside the sink and draining board could be used for the caddy to maintain the sort of spatial distinction discussed above. However, John, who usually prepares the food, prefers it close to hand. Having retired, he is the one who takes care of the children and performs the domestic chores – according to Gabriela, who works as a school Spanish teacher, he is a '*househusband*'. The placement of the caddy here led to the question of whether this caused any problems:

Gabriela [If] you are careful and you wash that thing [the caddy] every day, every time that you change that thing it doesn't smell, but if you leave without washing, like he does, it smells. If you are careful, if you wash it, change every day, answering your question, it doesn't,

John I tend to keep stuff in until it's full up, so that's every three days . . . well it does smell a bit, but it's not, it doesn't get any flies, which is surprising, it's well designed, isn't it,

Gabriela I think it's efficient, as long as you are careful, but if you leave it for every day it doesn't work

[. . .]

Alan Mmm, OK, and what about having [it] on the work surface

Gabriela It's not a problem because a lid, it has a lid and as he said, if you're not careful and everything I said before, if you leave like 3, 4, 5 days [. . .] then that smell comes and the mess happens, but [. . .] it's easy to change the bag, empty that, put a new bag, like you do with the bin when it's full, it's not a problem.

The Sociological Review, 60:S2, pp. 135–155 (2013), DOI: 10.1111/1467-954X.12042

In answer to the question of whether the caddy's placement on the countertop created problems, Gabriela and John give somewhat different responses. Gabriela emphasizes care, and frequent emptying and cleaning of the box: only if you leave it '3, 4, 5 days' without getting rid of the contents or failing to wash it will it begin to smell. But she does not deal with the food caddy. For the most part it is John who does so, and while her answers are about what one *should* do, his are more about what he *actually does*: he empties it when it is full, about every three days. He concedes that 'it does smell a bit' (supporting her accusation that he leaves the box without washing it), but at least, he continues, 'it doesn't get any flies, which is surprising'. John seems, if not unconcerned, then certainly much more relaxed about smells. Any smells are not too bad, as it only smells 'a bit', and they can be managed. If it does smell then it can be emptied and washed out, but it is not worth constantly cleansing to prevent any possibility of smell.

One possible reason for this difference between their answers is that even though John is the one who takes care of this, Gabriela still feels that she may be seen as the one responsible, as the one who will be judged by others – here by the interviewer – and so she tells the interviewer how the box 'should' be managed. John, in contrast, tells how it is managed in practice, something that has fewer consequences in terms of how he might be judged. There is an issue of gendered respectability at play here. This gendered talk *about* the bin demonstrates a further point that the household is a far from ubiquitous 'unit' with one, unified approach to waste; instead it is a space in which individuals may perform different, sometimes conflicting, sometimes complementary, practices.

Managing agency through resistance

Not everyone was persuaded to participate in recycling food waste simply because of the presence of the bin and what it symbolized. This research included four households that refused or failed to participate. On the surface these households' reasons chimed with the findings of a study by WRAP (2009), which examined why people refused to participate in food-waste collection trials.[9] Two composting households believed they lacked food waste; a third was disdainful of the council and so saw its failure to send compostable bags as a reason to refuse to participate; and a fourth household refused because the smell and hygiene were too troublesome. It is this fourth household that we will focus on as their concern about smell and the 'ickiness' of the food bin is most pertinent to the real and imagined problems of food caddies, reflecting the main reason for non-participation according to WRAP (2009).

Lucy, Andy and Michael resisted the food waste element of the recycling regime because Lucy has a strong dislike, even 'hatred', of the food bin. The two others accede to her wishes and support her in different ways. Originally from Australia, all three are in their late twenties and work respectively as a communications manager, a science teacher and an environmental consultant. Since migrating to the UK they have lived together and currently share a three-bedroomed flat in a modern low-rise block. Principally it was Lucy's visceral response to food-waste and to the caddy that meant food-waste was simply put in the main kitchen bin:

Lucy   Where we lived before [. . .] we had the little brown [. . .] caddy that used to sit in the kitchen. But that used to, it smelt
Andy   You see we were on ground level there so we actually, a lot of the time, kept it outside.
Lucy   Yeah
Andy   Whereas here we're not on ground level, so we've got one of those brown bins, it's just on the balcony. But because we're not, we can't put it away and get the smell out of reach, we don't want to use it, certainly I don't want to use it.

[. . .]

Andy   But I think if we were on the ground floor [. . .] and there was a little garden where we could keep a bin, we'd do it, because it's not a lot of effort. But none of us want a smell of rotting food on our balcony.

[. . .]

Lucy   For me it's a laziness thing. Because I hate it. Because we had the smaller caddy that could sit on the counter, and [our landlady] said 'well that's OK, because it's small that gets you to then take it to the [. . .] one outside', but, you know, sometimes you'd put a little bit in there and then nothing for days and then when you went to go and empty it out, it was just icky to handle, it was mouldy, and then when you washed it out every time it was soaking it in bleach for a while in the sink.
Andy   To be fair, unless we do a roast we very rarely have any leftovers.

Here, the fundamental issue is the smell and their capacity to manage it. Lucy's starting point recalling their past experience of having a food bin in their last kitchen flat is then picked up by Andy, who reiterates that the difficulty is in 'putting [the bin] away and getting the smell out of reach' and not wanting 'the smell of rotting food on our balcony'. The problem, as Andy sees it, is that they do not live on the ground floor. He repeats three times that if they did then they would recycle food waste in the caddy; after all, he admits, 'it's not a lot of effort'. Lucy, however, makes a further point. While she chastizes herself, thinking it is 'laziness' on her part, her language seems more visceral: after all, it is something that she 'hates'. She explains that when they did do it, their lifestyle – often not eating at home for days at a time – meant that food would go 'mouldy' in the bin as it did not get emptied. This, continuing to evoke a visceral disdain for the practice, made the bin 'icky to handle'. It then had to be cleaned, in bleach, which disturbed the kitchen as it was left to soak in the sink. Finally, Andy, once again picking up Lucy's point about not putting food in for days at a time, claims that they hardly have any leftovers anyway, unless they make a roast. The implication being that doing the food-waste would hardly be worth the hassle, as they would divert precious little into this waste stream.

While Andy is vocally supportive, confirming and supplementing Lucy's discussion, Michael's silence is telling. As an environmental consultant, Michael is aware of green issues and there was an indication that he would have used the caddy. However, because Lucy is so set against it and because he is away a lot with work and the Territorial Army, his insistence on its use may have caused tensions within the household, especially if his flatmates were left to deal with his food waste while he was away. Lucy's strength of feeling is thus given precedence, and their non-participation is the – understandable – settlement within this household.

What is demonstrated here is how the troubling qualities of the bin cannot always be managed through the processes of accommodation described above. It appears that the material spaces and the nature of their associated routines make the troubling qualities of the bin difficult to accommodate. Whereas participants in the previous sections appeared satisfied that the polluting nature of the bin could be managed through the specific placing of the bin or the instigation of cleansing routines, this was not possible here. Living on the top floor of a block of flats meant that it was too much effort to take the bin out every day, while their lifestyles also meant that food waste would sit in the caddy for prolonged periods, increasing in potency and threatening greater contamination of the caddy and their home. The waste and the bin cannot be managed within their current everyday spaces and routines so they have resisted the food bin and its call to recycle. Such a resistance to the food caddy does not necessarily mean a rejection of food recycling though, as the final case study illustrates.

Several other households did not like the bin either. However, rather than rejecting the waste collection scheme wholesale they replaced the caddy with another container in which to sort, separate and store food waste. Deepak and Priti, British Asians originally from East Africa, represented one such household. They are a middle-aged, married couple with two boys aged 16 and 8 living in an extended four-bedroom semi-detached house on a post-war suburban estate. Priti is a part-time optician and Deepak is an IT consultant. They rejected the small brown food caddy, but not the infrastructure or the idea of food recycling. Instead, they used a small plastic tub that was kept under the sink alongside a small kitchen bin. Asked whether they would countenance having the tub on the countertop, Priti made the situation plain:

Priti   No
Deepak   That's a no-no. That's a non-negotiable.
Priti   I've got space there, I'll put it in the cupboard so I don't need to see it really.

Recalling the earlier discussion of the symbolic qualities of the food bin, if it was 'on display' it would disrupt not only the aesthetic and the order of the kitchen (Evans, 2012b) but also the sense of respectability (Bulkeley and Gregson, 2009). As the housewife, this respectability is something that Priti manages through cooking, cleaning and overseeing the kitchen. The use of an alternative food-waste container that can be hidden under the sink relates inherently to the maintenance of order and respectability.

This is highlighted in a discussion of the larger bins that are often found in British kitchens. Priti explains her dislike of them: 'I don't like that sort of bin, we've always had this tiny one and then it gets put outside straightaway.' What is interesting here is how she talks about the effect of the bin – how the small size of both her kitchen bin and food tub – means that the contents are 'put outside straightaway'. The imagination of immediacy is belied by the reality of the bin and its contents. When we looked through the food tub it held several biscuits and a tea bag. So 'straightaway' does not simply mean immediately, rather some things can hang around under the sink, but not many and not for long, as there is simply no room. Effectively, the bin size ensures that it is attended to regularly; it imposes itself on household waste practices. These are more likely to be performed at certain times of the day, such as after the evening meal when Priti takes the bin from its hiding place and places it on the countertop while she cleans up, scraping leftovers into it, a routine that is completed when the tub is emptied into the larger caddy outside.

What is rejected here, then, is the material agency of the council distributed kitchen caddy. Priti and Deepak deem the caddy too large for their domestic waste practices: its size means that it might not be emptied often enough, leaving food waste to fester and rot, generating smells, making the kitchen unhygienic, and possibly attracting vermin – an anxiety they attribute to their Indian heritage and their upbringing in East Africa. In replacing it with a smaller tub the aim was to determine their everyday waste practices, namely to ensure its frequent removal outside. What was not rejected was the infrastructural and symbolic aspects of the bin's agency: replacing the bin simply transferred these qualities to the smaller tub. While they had recycled before the council collected materials from the kerbside, this had not included food waste, so the bin service was an extension of an idea they already valued. It enabled what was waste to be reused for little effort on their part. Such participation was something that had become the norm within much of Kingston, at least within the settled, middle-class portion of the district, as indicated by both the interviews and the high recycling rates. To reject it because of the trouble with the caddy would not have 'fitted' with the identity of households such as this one, with their sense of family and their relationship with the council – a markedly different relationship to those identified by Miller (1988) and Bulkeley and Gregson (2009). Indeed, the food-waste tub demanded routines and vigilance about smell such that respectability becomes embodied. In accommodating the waste infrastructure, materials need to be mobilized, routines developed and meanings articulated. In the case of Deepak and Priti these elements were mobilized by replacing the kitchen caddy with a small tub that, because of its size, demanded daily attention. This small tub sits symbolically between the waste infrastructure and household waste practices, holding the two together. The material, the representational and the relational all interconnect.

Conclusion: food bins and beyond

We began our analysis by looking at the food caddy and how it affected waste practices, and we have ended it by witnessing its removal from the kitchen. This narrative has revealed two principal points: that bins have agency and that households both engage with and manage this agency. In particular, the paper has focused attention on the material aspects of the bins' agency for two reasons. First, this is what has most troubled people. We saw, for example, how both Deepak and Priti and Lucy and her flatmates resisted the smell and 'ickiness' of the caddy. We also saw, however, how Priti mobilized a different receptacle with the 'right' material qualities to enable separation and storage of food waste on her terms, thus keeping the kitchen ordered and respectability intact. More generally we saw how households accommodated the caddies through placing them in non-food zones, and/or instigating cleansing and emptying routines. Smells and 'ickiness' were managed, even accepted, by these means. A second reason for the focus on material agency is because writers on material culture and consumption have tended to foreground the representational and relational, sidelining the material and phenomenological (Olsen, 2010). However, it is impossible to draw on material aspects without the relational and representational facets looming large. The insistence on articulating these as a 'three-fold' – that is, recognizing them as distinct aspects that inevitably interweave to constitute an object's agency – marks the theoretical contribution of the paper to material culture and consumption studies.

This examination of the distribution and use of food caddies as part of a broader transformation of the waste infrastructure has lessons for municipalities considering such a move to increase recycling rates. The accommodation and use of food bins does not simply flow from a positive pro-environmental view: as we have seen, even those with pro-environmental attitudes may be put off if using the bin proves too troublesome a task. It would seem that the conclusion to draw from this observation is not to work at changing hearts and minds but to put a system in place whereby the multiple agency of the bin does not disrupt households. Regarding infrastructural and representational agency, the clear message is 'invest in infrastructure, get that right – and then communicate how the scheme works'. The bins can themselves represent the issues. As noted, it was the material agency of the bin that proved most troublesome, particularly in terms of smell, hygiene, size, aesthetics, order and respectability. One solution would be to offer different caddies, by size, shape and colour, perhaps charging for some less basic models. Injecting some flexibility into the material agency of the bin – for instance, by giving a choice of caddy – would be a way of allowing people some control over troublesome issues. It might also be worthwhile distributing compostable bags for the kitchen caddies as well as for the large ones; and/or to explain how newspaper can be used to wrap food and to line the small caddy, thus containing smell and reducing 'ickiness'.

This analysis leads us to make two further points. First of all, in opening up the bin for study there are many more issues to explore than we can cover here, several of which are already being examined by others. While this paper has focused on the kitchen caddy, other domestic bins also need consideration, primarily as a set of inter-related containers rather than just as single entities – 'obligatory points of passage'[10] between households and the waste sector. Other issues include, first, how households account for a bin's contents: what the difference is, and what the differential effects are, between household bins and communal dwelling bins, bins in public spaces and in institutions, and how these can be managed. Secondly, how bins and their collection tap into prevailing notions of respectability and responsibility – for instance, through the use of clear plastic bags (Parizeau, 2012). Thirdly, how waste collectors manage bins and the material disposed of at the kerbside, an issue that is especially pertinent in countries where informal intermediaries collect recycling direct from general waste bins potentially putting their health at risk (Binion, 2012). Fourthly, how waste authorities communicate and manage bins and their contents to measure and improve quantities and qualities of recycling. Finally, we need to examine issues of the ownership[11] of waste when in the bin and on the margins of properties, an issue especially pertinent to the recent phenomenon of 'dumpster diving' (Abrahamsson and De Vries, 2012).

A different and broader question concerns the extent to which devices have the potential to implement policy. As seen in this study, food bins appear to have encouraged recycling, even by those more reticent. However, it could be argued that such devices may have detrimental – even contradictory – effects as they salve consciences on a relatively superficial level, so preventing further and more fundamental 'behaviour change'. A counter argument, however, would suggest that those people who did think that recycling was enough, and who felt that they were now 'doing their bit', would typically mobilize anything to justify their (in)activity. At least these bins, calling on their sense of citizenship, have entailed them doing something they otherwise would not do. There is unlikely to be a simple answer: the potential of any device will be dependent upon its agency, and on how it is then consumed. In different policy arenas, objects may have more troublesome representational qualities, or the object itself may have little infrastructural agency so there may be little need for people to pay attention to the object (eg an electricity usage monitor can be put in a drawer and forgotten about). Nevertheless, this study of 'the bin' suggests a new field of examination, one that chimes with the recent interest in 'nudge theory'. We may now ask: what 'policy-objects' could be designed to materialize policy and in what ways do they effect 'behaviour change', if at all? Clearly, this constitutes a field that demands an examination of the object, its agency and how both are consumed.

Acknowledgements

Thanks go to David, Anne and Hugh for the invitation to contribute to this special edition; to the referees for their insightful comments; to Joseph Burridge for his comments on an earlier draft of the paper; and to audiences at the Association of American Geographers and British Sociological Association conferences 2012 for their feedback on versions presented. All have helped develop and improve the paper markedly.

Notes

1 This was a national press advertising campaign making the point that British households 'waste' 7.2 million tonnes of food each year. It has continued in an online form offering visitors advice on planning their shopping and meal preparation in order that they may generate less food waste – see http://www.lovefoodhatewaste.com/

2 The principal technologies for treating general waste are landfills, Energy from Waste incinerators (EfWs) and Mechanical Biological Treatment plants (MBTs) (which separates and treats mixed materials). These can all 'treat' food waste, but only as part of general waste; it does not undergo any separation. If food waste is to be treated separately then it can either go to an In-Vessel Composter (IVC) or Anaerobic Digestor (AD). Both of these technologies can also treat green waste with food waste and so the two can be collected together as one waste stream. However, it is sometimes decided to compost green waste separately using the Windrow or open-air method, because, requiring little infrastructure, it is much cheaper. However, food cannot be composted using this method as the Animal By-products regulations have banned this due to the dangers of spreading pathogens.

3 These are simply summaries and the typologies are more defined than is perhaps suggested here. 'The reusers': individuals who have a higher tendency to reuse, restore, store, repair and sell/donate items; 'Normative wasters': individuals who are 'middle of the road'; they recycle moderately large amounts of waste, as well as making some conscious decisions about reduction and reuse; 'Hidden waste managers': respondents who recycle relatively low levels of waste in the municipal scheme, but who have high levels of reuse, restoration and repair of products and arrange for dedicated collections of waste for recycling or composting; 'The refusenics': low levels of participation across all waste practices; 'Conscious consumers and disposers': respondents who have a high tendency to make conscious choices about purchasing specific 'low waste' products, alongside disposing of products responsibly; 'Eco-angels': all-round environmentally conscious behaviours.

4 It is one of the 20 per cent least deprived areas in the UK, and is the third least deprived area in London behind the City of London and Richmond (Royal Borough of Kingston upon Thames (RBK), 2011).

5 It is believed the largest Korean population in Europe (RBK, 2011).

6 Some flats still do not have them, though most now do. Two households in this study had no recycling collection, a third had collection of dry recycling but no food-waste collection – all flats.

7 Images taken from website: http://www.kingston.gov.uk/browse/environment/recycling/household_collections.htm. Permission has been requested.

8 All names are pseudonyms.

9 Twenty-four per cent of households stated that issues of hygiene, smell and/or vermin were the reason for their reticence, while 21 per cent did not participate because they believed that they did not produce enough food waste to make it worthwhile.

10 Thanks to Robert Dingwall for pointing this out.

11 A point noted by Josh Lepawsky at the Geographies of Waste panel at the Association of American Geographers, 2012.

References

Abrahamsson, S. and De Vries, E., (2012), ' "I may be looking for waste, but I eat food": on the legal and organic limits of eating wasted food', paper presented at the Association of American Geographers Annual Conference, New York, 24–28 February, available at: discardstudies.wordpress.com/2012/03/27/dumpsters-muffins-waste-and-law/

Barr, S., Ford, N. J. and Gilg, A. W., (2003), 'Attitudes towards recycling household waste in Exeter, Devon: quantitative and qualitative approaches', *Local Environment*, 8. 407–421.

Binion, E., (2012), ' "Yeah, I am good. I am still standing" – A study of the perceptions of health and injuries associated with informal recycling in Buenos Aires, Argentina', paper presented at the Association of American Geographers Annual Conference, New York, 24–28 February.

Bulkeley, H. and Gregson, N., (2009), 'Crossing the threshold: municipal waste policy and household waste generation', *Environment and Planning A*, 41: 929–945.

Bulkeley, H., Watson, M. and Hudson, R., (2007), 'Modes of governing municipal waste', *Environment and Planning A*, 39: 2733–2753.

Bulkeley, H., Watson, M., Hudson, R. and Weaver, P., (2005), 'Governing municipal waste: towards a new analytical framework', *Journal of Environmental Policy and Planning*, 7: 1–23.

Chappells, H. and Shove, E., (1999), 'The dustbin: a study of domestic waste, household practices and utility services', *International Planning Studies*, 4: 267–280.

Clarke, J. F. M., (2007), ' "The incineration of refuse is beautiful": Torquay and the introduction of municipal refuse destructors', *Urban History*, 34: 254–276.

Cooper, T., (2008), 'Challenging the "refuse revolution": war, waste and the rediscovery of recycling, 1900–1950', *Historical Research*, 81: 710–731.

Cooper, T., (2010), 'Burying the "refuse revolution": the rise of controlled tipping in Britain 1920–1960', *Environment and Planning A*, 42: 1033–1048.

Dant, T., (2008), 'The "pragmatics" of material interaction', *Journal of Consumer Culture*, 8: 11–33.

Davies, A. R., (2003), 'Waste wars public attitudes and the politics of place in waste management strategies', *Irish Geography*, 361: 77–92.

Davies, A. R., (2005), 'Incineration politics and the geographies of waste governance: a burning issue for Ireland?' *Environment and Planning C: Government and Policy*, 23: 375–397.

Davies, A. R., (2008), *The Geographies of Garbage Governance: Interventions, Interactions, and Outcomes*, London: Ashgate.

Davoudi, S., (2009), 'Governing waste: introduction to the special issue', *Journal of Environmental Planning and Management*, 52: 131–136.

Davoudi, S. and Evans, N., (2005), 'The challenge of governance in regional waste planning', *Environment and Planning C: Government and Policy*, 23: 493–517.

Department of the Environment, Food and Rural Affairs (DEFRA), (2011), *Waste Strategy 2011*, London: The Stationery Office.

Derksen, L. and Gartrell, J., (1993), 'The social context of recycling', *American Sociological Review*, 58: 434–442.

Douglas, M., (1984), *Purity and Danger*, London: Ark.

Evans, D., (2012a), 'Beyond the throwaway society: ordinary domestic practice and a sociological approach to household food waste', *Sociology*, 46: 43–58.

Evans, D., (2012b), 'Binning, gifting and recovery: the conduits of disposal in household food consumption', *Environment and Planning D: Society and Space*, 30: 1123–1137.

Fagan, H., (2003), 'Sociological reflections on governing waste', *Irish Journal of Sociology*, 12: 67–85.

Gibson, J. J., (1977), 'The theory of affordances', in R. Shaw and J. Bransford (eds), *Perceiving, Acting, and Knowing*, 67–82, Mahwah, NJ: Erlbaum.

Gilg, A. and Barr, S., (2005), 'Encouraging "environmental action" by exhortation: evidence from a study in Devon', *Journal of Environmental Planning and Management*, 48: 593–618.

Gille, Z., (2007), *From the Cult of Waste to the Trash Heap of History: The Politics of Waste in Socialist and Post-Socialist Hungary*, Bloomington: Indiana University Press.

Gregson, N., (2007), *Living with Things: Ridding, Accommodation, Dwelling*, London: Sean Kingston Publishing.

Gregson, N., Metcalfe, A. and Crewe, L., (2007a), 'Identity, mobility, and the throwaway society', *Environment and Planning D: Society and Space*, 25: 682–700.

Gregson, N., Metcalfe, A. and Crewe, L., (2007b), 'Moving things along: the conduits and practices of divestment in consumption', *Transactions of the Institute of British Geographers*, 32: 187–200.

Gregson, N., Metcalfe, A. and Crewe, L., (2009), 'Practices of object maintenance and repair', *Journal of Consumer Culture*, 9 (2): 248–272.

The Sociological Review, 60:S2, pp. 135–155 (2013), DOI: 10.1111/1467-954X.12042

Gregson, N., Watkins, H. and Calestani, M., (2010), 'Inextinguishable fibres: demolition and the vital materialisms of asbestos', *Environment and Planning A*, 42: 1065–1083.

Guagnano, G. A., Stern, P. C. and Dietz, T., (1995), 'Influences on attitude-behavior relationships', *Environment and Behavior*, 27: 699–718.

Hawkins, G., (2006), *The Ethics of Waste: How We Relate to Rubbish*, Sydney: University of New South Wales Press.

Hawkins, G. and Meucke, S. (eds), (2003), *Culture and Waste: The Creation and Destruction of Value*, Lanham, MD: Rowman and Littlefield.

Hetherington, K., (2004), 'Second-handedness: consumption, disposal and absent presence', *Environment and Planning D: Society and Space*, 22 (1): 157–173.

Hogg, D., Barth, J., Schleiss, K. and Favoino, E., (2007), 'Dealing with food waste in the UK', Eunomia Research and Consulting Limited, http://www.wrap.org.uk/sites/files/wrap/Dealing_with_Food_Waste_-_Final_-_2_March_07.pdf.

Madigan, R. and Munro, M., (1996), 'House beautiful: style and consumption in the home', *Sociology*, 30 (1): 41–57.

Mason, J., (2002), *Qualitative Researching*, 2nd edn, London: Sage.

Miller, D., (1988), 'Appropriating the state on the council estate', *Man*, 23: 354–372.

Munro, R., (1995), 'Disposal of the meal', in D. Marshall (ed.), *Food Choice and the Consumer*, 313–326, Glasgow: Blackie Academic.

O'Brien, M., (1999), 'Rubbish-power: towards a sociology of the rubbish society', in J. Hearn and S. Roseneil (eds), *Consuming Cultures*, 262–277, Basingstoke: Macmillan.

O'Brien, M., (2008), *A Crisis of Waste: Understanding the Rubbish Society*, London: Routledge.

Olsen, B., (2010), *In Defence of Things: Archaeology and the Ontology of Objects*, Plymouth: Rowman and Littlefield.

Parizeau, K., (2012), 'The public/private natures of waste production and disposal', paper presented at the Association of American Geographers Annual Conference, New York, 24–28 February.

Reno, J., (2009), 'Your trash is someone's treasure: the politics of value at a Michigan Landfill', *Journal of Material Culture*, 14: 29–46.

Riley, M., (2008), 'From salvage to recycling: new agendas or same old rubbish?' *Area*, 40 (1): 79–89.

Roderick, I., (1997), 'Household sanitation and the flow of domestic space', *Space and Culture*, 1 (1): 105–132.

Royal Borough of Kingston upon Thames (RBK), (2011), *Borough Profile*. http://www.kingston.gov.uk/borough_profile_2011-4.pdf (accessed 14 Feb 2012).

Scanlan, J., (2005), *On Garbage*, London: Reaktion Books.

Sharp, V., Giorgi, S. and Wilson, D. C., (2010a), 'Delivery and impact of household waste prevention campaigns (at the local level)', *Waste Management and Research*, 28: 256–268.

Sharp, V., Giorgi, S. and Wilson, D. C., (2010b), 'Methods to monitor and evaluate household waste prevention', *Waste Management and Research*, 28: 269–280.

Waste and Resources Action Programme (WRAP), (2009), *Evaluation of the WRAP Separate Food Waste Collection Trials*, availableat: http://www.wrap.org.uk/local_authorities/research_guidance/food_waste/ (accessed 14 February 2012).

Waste and Resources Action Programme (WRAP), (2010), *Improving the Performance of Waste Diversion Schemes: A Good Practice Guide to Monitoring and Evaluation*, available at: http://www.wrap.org.uk/local_authorities/research_guidance/monitoring_and_evaluation_guidance/ (accessed 14 February 2012).

Watson, M., (2008), 'The materials of consumption', *Journal of Consumer Culture*, 8: 5–10.

Eating from the bin: salmon heads, waste and the markets that make them

Benjamin Coles and Lucius Hallett IV

Abstract: Recent scholarship in the social sciences has begun to question the cultural contingencies that demarcate waste from 'stuff worth keeping' (Watson and Meah, this volume). This scholarship has problematized linear discourses of production, consumption and disposal, and interrogated the relationships between objects, commodities and value but has yet to investigate the ways in which place and place-making are complicit in constituting these relationships. This paper explores where and how the lines between foodstuff and food waste are drawn, as well as the role of place and processes of place-making in contesting and reproducing them. Focusing on salmon heads and salmon, this paper examines not only how food becomes waste, but also on the issue of how waste becomes food. Specifically, we analyse the geographical processes through which salmon heads are valued as foodstuffs in some places but waste in others. We argue further that these valuations extend beyond the place of one market to encompass an assembled geography of markets. Further, we suggest that by tracing out the geographies of salmon heads and salmon – and the markets where each can be found – we can better articulate where as well as how it is that waste can become food. Ultimately, we argue that questions of food and waste are not just questions of materiality, but questions of the ways in which the material intersects relations of place, place-making and geography. Salmon heads, we argue, become a matter of geography.

Keywords: food, waste, commodities, material culture, place

Material evaluations: Opening proposition

We are in the indoor portion of Birmingham's Bull Ring Market, standing in front of a fishmonger, some way away from the main centre-aisle. One vendor tells us that either the very poor or the idle rich come to this market to shop. This is one of the out-of-the-way stalls: less shiny, smelling like old fish, cheaper, with various fish from different parts of the world – more than the turbot, cod, sea bass or salmon that mainstream fishmongers located in a more convenient position within the market might sell. This place seems to specialize in what the industry sometimes calls 'trash' fish, pompano, rockfish or conger eel – those that get caught in the nets but have little commercial demand beyond what a fisherman might be able to get for them on the

The Sociological Review, 60:S2, pp. 156–173 (2013), DOI: 10.1111/1467-954X.12043

quayside. In this marketplace someone will find a use for it, buy it and eat it. The fish are layered out in rows and packed on ice. In the corner of the display, off to the side, there are buckets full of fish parts, bones, carcasses, off cuts, and startling for us, salmon heads. A very thin black man with a vaguely Caribbean accent is arguing with the fishmonger over the price of salmon heads; apparently they're now 55 pence a pound. He complains that this is too expensive; they used to be 35 pence apiece. When asked if they were for his cat, he says no, they were for dinner. 35p is not much money, but for the man arguing it is the difference between buying one fish head or two – the difference between possibly having enough to eat or not. (Excerpt from field diary 2006).

We begin this paper with two opening propositions: first, that waste and rubbish are not food, and second, that salmon heads, along with the rest of its carcass and other such discarded materials usually found in skips and bins, even if edible, are 'waste'. Waste is 'matter that has crossed a contingent cultural line that separates it from stuff that is worth keeping' (Watson and Meah, forth-coming) while food is a ' "thing" caught up in the process of being eaten by a consumer' after being valued as a foodstuff (Roe, 2006: 112). In some instances, owing to particular materialities of particular objects as well as to fundamental properties of their geographies, waste crosses back over the 'culturally contin-gent line'. It is (re)valued as foodstuffs – objects with the potential to become food. It is (re)formed into food. This paper interrogates the material processes through which waste can become food and the geographical relationships that underpin its transformation. Through the objective correlatives of salmon heads and salmon; their peculiar material properties; the marketplaces where they are (re)valued; and the geographies into which these places and objects are assem-bled, this paper provides an account of what needs to happen to waste for it (once again) to become food.

We are geographers, and thus attuned to questions of 'place'. This paper therefore engages with where and how the lines that delineate food-waste from foodstuff are drawn, as well as where and how these lines are contested, trans-gressed and otherwise reproduced through and within processes of place and place-making, with a particular focus on food markets. The opening vignette illustrates some of the ways in which the relations that comprise Birmingham's Bull Ring Market challenge normative distinctions between food and waste and transform the market into a place where a waste-stuff – such as salmon heads – can be revalued and commoditized into foodstuffs. We argue that the relations through which waste becomes food extend beyond the place of this market (where waste-stuff like salmon heads are materialized into food-stuffs) to other places where salmon heads are dismissed as waste and separated from the rest of the valuable flesh. By tracing out the geographies not only of salmon heads but also of salmon (the fish and flesh), we can better understand and articulate 'where' as well as 'how' waste can become food. We further argue that these are not simply questions of materiality, but also questions about the ways in which the material and the places into which the material is embedded are assembled into a kind of geography.

The empirical research on which this paper is based was carried out in three distinctive UK food markets. Birmingham's Bull Ring Market is a retail market located in the city centre but on its social and economic margins. London's Billingsgate Market is primarily a wholesale market that was located on the River Thames in the City of London until 1982 when it was moved to the East London Docklands. London's Borough Market at the southern end of London Bridge is both wholesale and retail – and increasingly noted both for its high-end, 'ethical' and 'alternative' foods and for its reproduction of a kind of 'foodie' culture (Coles and Crang, 2011). We focus on markets because, we argue, they are the key sites in which definitions of food and waste are contested. Although 'market' and 'marketplace' may refer to discursive spaces of the 'economy' (see Abolafia, 1998; Callon, 1998), as Bestor (2001: 91) comments, flows of 'stuff' (capital, fish, etc.) organized at a global scale work 'hand in glove' with locally embedded agents through the interaction of market and place. Here we first consider markets individually as places that value food, waste, salmon and salmon heads, before connecting them into their broader geographies. As marketplaces, each represents an assemblage of people, things and ideas, organized around the buying, selling and exchange of goods. They are places where 'actions' such as commoditization and 'things' such as commodity fetishes are produced, consumed and/or otherwise invoked. As markets, and as places, each of these three markets is linked materially, socially and discursively to each other, as well as to other places that constitute their 'geographies'. The salmon heads and salmon upon which this paper focuses comprise one-such relation.

Conceptually the paper is organized into three interconnected and interrelated parts that weave their way through the body of the text. First it relates a narrative of our own encounters with salmon heads and salmon as they materialize at a variety of different sites – akin to 'following the things' (see Marcus, 1995; Cook et al., 2004a). Rather than constructing a biography of salmon heads and salmon, which implies looking 'back' at the negotiation(s) of their value(s) (see Kopytoff, 2005 [1986]; Appadurai, 2005 [1986]), this paper constructs a 'geography' that also looks 'forward' (and side-to-side) at some of the different places where salmon heads and salmon can be found in order to elucidate the object's material, social and discursive possibilities. We suggest that this topographic perspective (see Coles, 2013a; Coles and Crang, 2011) is necessary to deal with a transitory assemblage of mutable objects (eg the fish before, during and after it has been parcelled out into its constituent parts). These objects could become food or waste, or indeed, based on the organization of its geographies, these objects flit between these two culturally contingent categories.

Second, through this geographical narrative, the paper demonstrates the importance of an object's geography (assembled through place-making and the interrelatedness of place) in shaping its multiple possibilities. We contend that whether or not salmon heads become food is contingent upon relations that extend beyond those between salmon head consumers and the places where salmon heads are available for consumption. Our expanded geographical

The Sociological Review, 60:S2, pp. 156–173 (2013), DOI: 10.1111/1467-954X.12043
© 2013 The Authors. Editorial organisation © 2013 The Editorial Board of the Sociological Review

analysis includes relations surrounding salmon production more generally but also relations surrounding the valuing and consumption of salmon flesh, which subsequently leads to the dismissal of salmon heads as waste. In short we argue that salmon heads are transformed into food in one set of places and waste in others because salmon flesh itself is valued and consumed as a foodstuff. The value of the rest of the fish is left to be negotiated. Finally, we use this geographical framework to make a moral critique of food waste. We are not so much interested in the usual ways that food production and consumption lead to waste or the supposed moral implications that come with wasting food (see Evans, 2011b; Godfray *et al.*, 2010), but rather the moral implications that underlie place and place-making as they relate to consumption (Sack, 1992, 1997). Particularly we are concerned with the ways in which place and place-making shape where and how foodstuffs are demarcated from waste-stuffs and the ways in which some places, such as markets, eclipse 'geographical awareness' and make it so the normative boundaries between food and waste can be transgressed.

Material evaluations: Salmon and salmon heads

A fishy smelling puddle of icy water covers nearly the entire floor of Billingsgate Market. It's cold; it's wet; it's slippery, and we're standing in the middle of it. We would find later, long after departure that a certain lingering fishiness seemed to follow us around. Billingsgate Market is the City of London's main fish market and at one time the largest in the world. It is open to the public, but the market's primary business is with the city's caterers and fishmongers. It is a busy place. There are forty or so vendors, each with their seafood on display. Stalls are laid out to show off a wide variety of fish and shellfish. Everything is displayed on ice, and fish is packed in polystyrene cartons that all seem to be a standardized size. Given the tremendous volume of fish that are on display we can only wonder at how many of these cartons are used each week, and how many of them make their ways into skips and landfills at the end. We hazard guesses about the amount of ice the fish market uses in a year.

This market has no stylized 'marketing'. The architecture of the building resembles an aluminium Quonset hut. The fish here are traded on price, quality and the skill of negotiators. Buyers and sellers haggle to get the best prices for the commodities before porters ferry them to waiting vehicles that transport the fish to London's fishmongers', retail food markets and restaurants. This is an everyday place of food but one that hides within a vast food system. We're here looking for salmon heads. Billingsgate has an extraordinary variety of fish available, including numerous types and 'configurations' of salmon – filets, 'steaks', whole fish, but we've yet to spot just their heads here. Given their retail value (somewhere between 40 and 55 pence) their absence at a mostly wholesale market is unsurprising (Excerpt from field diary, 2010).

Salmon heads begin their 'lives' as waste. Before they are separated from the rest of the fish, salmon heads are part of an assemblage of materialities that comprise a fish called 'salmon'. Individually, salmon's materialities embody specific biophysical characteristics and portray particular socially and culturally derived values that conspire to make some parts of the fish, its flank for instance, a foodstuff and some parts, such as the head and carcass, a waste-stuff. These assembled materialities inhabit discrete geographical locales, ranging from the sea, to a fishing boat, to a collection of markets before finally arriving at the body as food, or the bin as waste. These locales further assemble into a geography that comprises salmon and salmon heads. As the whole 'thing' moves from place to place, however, this assemblage is cut apart. Some parts are valued as foodstuffs and begin their own 'lives' where they have the potential to become food. Others parts, such as the heads and carcasses, are not valued as foodstuffs. They begin a different 'life' where they might become by-products for which applications can be found, or they might become waste and subject to disposal. The places where these assemblages and dis-assemblages occur are critical in determining the shape, direction and indeed geography of their various future material lives.

Salmon are cold-water fish from the North Atlantic and the North Pacific. Unlike cod or halibut – familiar to those who frequent the UK's fish and chip shops, and whose carcasses, like those of other white fish, are often prized by restaurants because they can be used for making fish stock – salmon is an oily fish. This is important, because oily fish not only spoil faster than lean white fish, but when they do begin to spoil it is obvious because of the smell. One of the reasons why salmon carcasses are not used for fish stock is that boiling water has a similar effect to the bacteria growth of spoilage. Both quickly break down salmon's fatty acids and proteins into nitrogen and sulphur compounds, which are ultimately the chemicals that make fish smell 'fishy' in the first place (McGee, 2004: 205). These bio-physical properties are one reason why the recent history of salmon as a food source is marked by technological capabilities (such as ice, flash freezing and refrigeration) that keep the fish as 'fresh' as possible – these inhibit such chemicals from forming, thus preventing the fish from going off and to keep it from smelling and tasting 'fishy' (or worse) (Freidberg, 2009).

As a food and as a commodity, salmon is available for purchase almost everywhere that sells food in the UK, and comes in many forms. At the fishmonger, it is available fresh, whole, in fillets, cut into steaks, wild or farmed, and also smoked. In supermarkets, it can be displayed 'fresh' at the fish counter, in plastic packs in freezer cabinets or tinned in the canned goods aisles. Often it can be found frozen in Cryovac bags in the freezer aisles along with other fish associated with the 'world' food system, such as tilapia. In broad terms, salmon can be divided into two classes: 'market salmon' and 'industrial' salmon. Market salmon are those that appear for sale in the world's retail and wholesale markets and are destined for restaurants and fishmongers, and ultimately domestic kitchens and dining rooms. Market fish can be either wild or farmed (factors that impact their price and position within the market), and they are sold through a variety of marketing systems where prices are set through negotiations that take into consideration the fish's provenance, quality and size, as well as secondary factors such as season and availability – all of which trickle down to impact the

The Sociological Review, 60:S2, pp. 156–173 (2013), DOI: 10.1111/1467-954X.12043

price and value of salmon. Salmon are also part of industrialized and mechanized fishing systems in which the movement of salmon from ocean to saleable item is created in on-board factory-fishing ships or in the pens where they are farmed. These systems rely on economies of scale and typically supply supermarkets with 'fresh frozen' filets and steaks. The processes are largely mechanized to remove as much flesh as possible from the carcass, with even remaining flesh being mechanically separated from the carcass to be ground up and tinned. The bones and heads are packed separately, and typically sold frozen *en masse* in one-ton blocks to fertilizer manufacturers – a recent price check showed the going rate for a block of salmon heads to be about US\$950 per ton (we were unable to find anyone who would deal in smaller quantities of heads, and, given the equipment necessary to deal with such a quantity, one ton of salmon heads can probably be considered 'for industrial use only').

The critical difference between market and industrial salmon is that market fish enter markets as whole objects (minus the guts, which end up in the sea). Only later down the 'chain' is their flesh separated from carcasses and the edible bits parcelled out from waste pieces. Much of the work surrounding market salmon is done in geographically disparate locales by skilled labourers such as fishermen (and women), market traders and porters, fishmongers and cooks. Each of these labourers occupies a particular locale within a salmon's 'life', and each contributes to the fish's 'added value' – added values that make the fish more edible through capturing, portering, filleting and cooking. These are the values that are reified into the commodity form. Salmon gets more valuable as it moves from sea to fork (or bin), is repeatedly bought and sold in markets, and paradoxically as it is parcelled into smaller and smaller pieces.

Market fish, or those found at most retail fish markets and fishmongers, are part of a wide variety of commercial fishing operations that range from seine- and gill-net trawler fishing, to line-caught day fishing, to fish farming on a variety of scales. These operations, however, are not as industrialized as the factory fishing model. Seine-nets scoop up entire schools of fish after they are located by sonar; everything in the water is captured, and all fish in the net are ultimately sent to different markets – the valuable fish to places such as Billingsgate, less valuable 'trash' to the wholesalers that supply fishmongers in markets such as Birmingham's. Gillnets only capture fish large enough to become entangled in the nets by their gill plates (hence the name). Smaller fish can swim through, while larger fish (such as tuna) do not get caught. Setting the net sizes generates a consistent size of fish, and with gillnets it is also possible to fish for particular species – all elements that make it possible for fishing boat skippers to more closely control where their fish might end up, such as markets like Billingsgate that promise the greatest chance of profitability. Salmon taken off day boats, for example, are caught with individual lines and usually end up in specialty markets (such as Borough Market), or they are sold directly to local restaurants where their extreme freshness, together with associated claims to 'wildness', commands premium prices – which restaurateurs are willing to pay. All market salmon arrive in markets packed whole in ice, fresh-frozen and gutted. Once at the wholesale market the entire fish is sold to restaurateurs and suppliers, to fishmongers or possibly to members of the public based on either a daily market price or via face-to-face negotiation when they are sold.

Fishmongers and cooks are the ones who then display and market the fish to end consumers, and who also prepare the fish for cooking. At a fishmonger, salmon are displayed on ice along with other fish so shoppers may choose for themselves what they might want to buy. Because whole salmon are usually large, customers typically tell the fishmonger what cut they want and how they want it. For a fillet, the fishmonger scales the fish, removes the head, and then slices the flesh free of the main skeleton, and sometimes skins the resulting fillet. The fillet is cut to the customer's requirements, and then wrapped in greased paper before being placed in a plastic carrier bag. Preparing a salmon for the table in this way clearly creates a lot of waste: skin, bones, heads. The cost of this wastage, along with the cost of everything else (transport, labour, packaging and so on), is bound up in the price of the commodity and passed on to the shopper. The materiality of wastage goes into the bin because these aspects of the salmon no longer incorporate the part that makes 'salmon' valuable. In Birmingham's Market, this bin is a parts bucket where carcasses and heads await (re)sale and (re)consumption – or, in other words, revaluation. Other bones, such as those of white fish, might await resale as a value-added product such as fish stock, but, because of their material properties (outlined above), salmon heads and bones are not desirable for stock, so they remain in the bucket until someone buys them to eat, or until the fishmonger puts them out with the rest of the rubbish at the end of the day. When they are in the parts bin, salmon heads enter into a kind of liminality because even here, they might cross back over into 'food'.

Material evaluations: Place and commodities

We are in Borough Market, London. The market floor is hectic. Customers and tourists consume Borough Market's material and affective commodities (see Coles and Crang, 2011). A fishmonger is selling the usual variety of high quality, extremely fresh fish arranged on ice and around a display comprised of driftwood sculptures and fishing bric-a-brac (old nets, lures, lobster pots). Colourful trash-fish are arranged in comic poses around the other bits: a shark's mouth is propped open with plastic diver figurine from an aquarium; a large octopus is wrapped around one of the sculptures, and large salmon heads are splayed on hooks and hung from the back of the stall giving the whole place a 'fishy' feel . . . A couple of hours later – it's 3:35 and Borough Market has reached a critical moment where customers and vendors are in a further frenzy of buying and selling. During this time, stuff that does not sell ends up in the skips out back, so vendors are keen to bargain and customers keen to haggle. We stop back by the fishmonger and see the salmon heads placed alongside a rapidly depleting stock of other fish. The ice is melting fast and everything is for sale. 'How much are these?' '£1.50' each. 'What are they good for?' 'Stock,' 'You can't make stock with salmon heads, it goes funny'. 'Okay £1 each'. 'Done! back in 30 minutes, keep 'em here?' 'Fine!' We take a walk around the market for about half an hour and buy a

The Sociological Review, 60:S2, pp. 156–173 (2013), DOI: 10.1111/1467-954X.12043

lemon, some celery stalks, parsley and some spring onions – the usual ingredients for fish stock. 'Let's see if we can make stock with salmon heads'. It's 2 minutes before the closing bell. The vendor's gone. Only his assistant remains. 'How much for the salmon heads?' She glances at her watch and back at me, 'a quid [£1]'. 'For the lot?' 'Yep,' 'Done!' 'What are you going to do with those?' 'Gonna try to make fish stock . . .' 'Ha!' (Excerpt from field diary, 2008).

Reclaiming salmon heads depends on renegotiating their value(s). In this case, their reclamation from some type of symbolic value as an artefact of a visual economy to a potential foodstuff occurs because of the commodity relations at Borough Market, which are negotiated after the rest of the fish is valued and commoditized. Salmon heads in this market start as a waste-stuff that is produced when a whole salmon is butchered into 'useable' and therefore saleable parts, and whatever is left over. The heads become useful only so far as they help constitute the market's visual material culture, but they are no longer food-stuffs nor are they commodities. As the market begins to close and the relations holding it together begin to weaken, the usefulness of salmon heads as part of the display diminishes, and, had the authors not sought to renegotiate their values, the salmon heads would become 'stuff not worth keeping'. At this point in time and space, the salmon heads are essentially waste and only become commodities as their potential to become a foodstuff is recognized by the authors and their values summarily renegotiated. The analysis of salmon heads therefore depends on more than following the thing and examining its materialities. Materialities are important, but only so far as they are bracketed by the material, social and discursive relations that comprise Borough Market, or indeed the other markets and places where salmon heads may be found. The limitations to just following the thing when it comes to salmon heads lies in identifying which 'thing' to follow. Following salmon does not necessarily lead to a salmon head: as we have suggested, salmon heads as food signify an unexpected outcome of both the commodity relations and geographical relations that underlie salmon as food. Salmon heads are not bound up in the same processes as the commoditization and fetishization as salmon. Rather, their commoditization happens within the peculiar, yet all-too-normal relations of the markets that either make salmon heads available for sale as foodstuff, or, subsequently and specifically, do not, unless as the above vignette demonstrates, the usual ordering of things is explicitly renegotiated.

Within the processes that define an object, such as those that define commodities, or those that delimit waste and food, the question of 'where' is often overlooked (Castree, 2004). Appadurai (2005: 13) argues that alongside other 'aspects of commodity-hood' – including 'phase' and 'candidacy' – 'commodity context' requires 'explication'. 'Context' for us suggests place and place-making, which are processes that involve the internal organization of material, social and discursive relations as well as the external ordering of a constellation of other places into a 'geography'. Although the desirability of salmon flesh as a foodstuff is socially and culturally mediated through a variety of sites and places, the contexts that help to demarcate the valuable salmon from salmon heads are generally markets, which are produced as places when people, things and ideas come together through their own culturally contingent relations *in situ* (Caliskan, 2007; Abolafia, 2002; Taussig, 1980; Geertz, 1978). Specific markets, such as Borough, Billingsgate or the Bull Ring, however, are also defined through their relations with each other.

Internal and external relations of place define salmon and salmon heads as well as 'govern' their commoditization (Callon, 1998). Externally both salmon and salmon heads are produced through the relations that define a variety of commercial fishing operations and link the different sites that handle and add value to the fish. Internally, however, as the vignette above suggests, salmon and salmon heads are subjected to relations that are defined by the place(s) where their values are further negotiated – relations which establish, for instance, the things that are available for commoditization as a foodstuff, and the things that are positioned as waste. This field encounter suggests a different trajectory for fish leftovers. The salmon heads in Borough Market are cast aside; 'liberated' as rubbish (Min'an, 2011); and hung on hooks to be reclaimed as part of Borough Market's 'material semiotic' fabric (Coles, 2013a). They are not destined to be eaten unless a customer really wants them. In this vein, anything in a market is negotiable. The fishmonger in Borough Market uses salmon carcasses and heads and other 'trash fish' (sharks, eels, octopus, among others) to decorate the stall, alongside lobster traps, old fishing nets and other bric-a-brac associated with fishing, to produce some kind of geographical knowledge and imagination of 'fishing'. The decoration of this stall, along with all the other stalls in the market, assembles into a visual material culture that is ultimately consumed as part of Borough Market's visual economy. The fishmonger will sell the heads, and he even recognizes an option for their use as a foodstuff. Mostly, to him, however, the value of salmon heads is to make his stall look more like a fish stall so he can sell more valuable parts of the salmon. Rubbish, after all, is not normally consumed here.

Relations within the market do more than make commodities. They also obscure geographical relations and truncate geographical awareness. In the case of Borough Market, these relations produce an imaginative geography that replaces the market's external relations that define the food supply/commodity chain with a collection of geographical discourses about food, markets and consumption. Borough Market is a high-end London retail food market that positions itself as an 'alternative' and otherwise 'ethical' marketplace that specializes in retailing foodstuffs that are rich in their declared provenance. These foodstuffs are variously 'local', 'fair', 'organic', and each have some kind of geographical story or knowledge associated with them that seemingly unveils the fetish of the commodity but in practice effectively evokes a kind of 'double' commodity fetish in which the value of the commodity is partially derived from production of geographical knowledge (Cook and Crang, 1996). Vendors in Borough Market produce these knowledges by 'revealing' some narratives of production through devices such as labels designating geographical origin, small object biographies, stall displays and other materials that assemble into a

The Sociological Review, 60:S2, pp. 156–173 (2013), DOI: 10.1111/1467-954X.12043
© 2013 The Authors. Editorial organisation © 2013 The Editorial Board of the Sociological Review

material-semiotic locating of Borough Market and its foods within an idealized geographical imaginary of food consumption that only includes partial and mediated geographies (Coles, 2013a, 2013b).

These imaginative geographies do not include the market's own waste, which remains largely invisible, except during critical moments such as near the end of the trading day when the relations holding the market together are already unstable, and therefore allow for the renegotiation of its materialities. More significantly, while these imaginary geographies may or may not aid consumers in unveiling the commodity fetish that obscures production, they certainly are not orientated as such to allow consumers to see or imagine the effects that their consumption might have on what others might consume elsewhere. The market for salmon in Borough necessitates the production of salmon waste. Buying salmon in Borough Market displaces its head and leaves them to be disposed of by someone or someplace else.

Moral evaluations: Waste, objects and geography

Recent literatures have sought to problematize waste. In particular, these literatures focus on the ways in which wasting and rubbishing are active processes of disposal bound to the maintenance of social and cultural order (see Douglas, 1994 [1966]; Douglas and Isherwood, 1996; Hetherington, 2004); the ways that processes of disposal are often incomplete, conditional and otherwise fraught (Munro, 2001); and, the ways these processes effectively respatialize more-or-less 'traditional' notions of political economy to incorporate multiple productions and multiple consumptions of 'waste' (Gregson *et al.*, 2010a). This scholarship not only complicates 'typical' production/consumption narratives of objects and commodities, but also highlights the processes of material as well as ephemeral production implicit within commodity processes and the processes of waste. Hetherington (2004: 159), for instance, disrupts such linear narratives of production, consumption and disposal by suggesting that 'waste' signifies too final 'an act of closure': disposal, he argues, does not necessarily represent some 'final state of rubbishing' but rather constitutes an act that signals the 'closure of a particular sequence of production-consumption events'. This allows us to consider the binning of salmon heads not as a final act of rubbishing but as a suspension of their 'lives' into a liminal period of possibility. Should they enter into particular geographical relationships they might become food, they might become objects of visual economy – or they might stay in the bin, where they remain waste.

The relationship between consumption and waste and the liminal possibilities they possess are further problematized by examining and understanding the ways in which consumers variously produce, consume and re-produce objects that might be classed as waste. Notions of 'second hand cultures' suggest that – rather than a final act of rubbishing that signifies a complete devaluation – disposal constitutes the renegotiation and subsequent transference of value

(Gregson and Crewe, 1999, 2003). Moreover, reconfiguring and theorizing spaces of consumption in order to challenge the discourses of so-called 'consumerism' broadens the ways in which rubbish and waste are, and can be, spatialized to provide fuller accounts of initial production to presumed 'end-of-life' and 'final' burial (Gregson *et al.*, 2002, 2007, 2010a, 2010b). The negotiation of salmon in Billingsgate, the (re)negotiation of salmon heads in Birmingham, and the various negotiations of salmon and their heads in Borough Market suggest a broadening of salmon's spatialities as a foodstuff and as a commodity.

Working from the perspective of material entropy and decay, Edensor (2005) and DeSilvey (2006) conceptualize the affective, ephemeral and material productions that come alongside waste and wastage. Both deploy notions of material memory and monument. Edensor (2005), drawing from Neville and Villeneuve's (2002) work, for instance, considers the absent presences contained within 'ruins'. Specifically, he comments that whilst ruins 'disassemble and rot' and 'seem to have lost any value they may once have possessed ... ruinous matter has not been consigned to burial or erasure, and still bears the vague traces of its previous use and context' (Edensor, 2005: 317). Using this lens, salmon heads contain value as food because they bear traces of the fish's previous material assemblages, in the form of some nutritional content, and contexts through their presence as part of the broader salmon system. One way to consider a salmon head, therefore, is to consider its absent salmon body – if the body is edible, then why not the head? DeSilvey (2006) examines ecological processes of 'dis-assemblage' and decay and argues that, as well as being destructive, waste can also be a part of productive processes leading to new life. For her, as for us with salmon heads, notions of 'new life' can be taken very literally as organisms ingest 'waste' as part of their own bodily reproduction. We are not convinced that eating waste is acceptable – even if it is edible and fulfils basic biological requirements for bodily reproduction. An understanding of geography where place-making is a moral act and places are evaluated based on the ways in which they promote geographical awareness informs this position (Sack, 2003). Our argument is that ingesting 'waste' happens because the place-making processes in markets obscure the circulation of – and therefore the possibilities for – multiple materialities. We thus position the consumption of salmon within a broader narrative of consumerism that requires salmon's disassembly into constituent parts, some of which are valued as foodstuffs and some devalued as waste, and binds it to processes of place and place-making.

Evans (2011b, 2011a, 2012) aligns debates about food and food consumption with those of waste to examine the 'conduits' of food as it moves through the household, but also the household practices that simultaneously reproduce and contest a discourse of a 'throwaway society'. Drawing from a range of anthropological literatures Evans (2012) considers first and second 'burials' of food in refrigerators, and positions food waste as existing in a kind of liminal space as its owners decide its fate: the rubbish bin, a gift or a material transformation into compost. Crucially, this work acknowledges that food and foodstuffs are different from other objects that might one day become waste.

Food provides for biological nourishment and reproduction, but it also constitutes a site where politics and ethics are contested and contestable (Goodman *et al.*, 2010). Salmon heads are buried in bins or hung on display, and they can be exhumed as food depending on the internal and external relations that define place and its geographies. In any case, the paths that salmon heads take raise ethical and political questions about where they go and how they get there.

Food also differs from other objects because it has a definite shelf-life. Its ability to sustain life not only diminishes when it ages, and – should ageing not be managed properly, for example through poor refrigeration, inappropriate preservation, and so on – food can be transformed into a poison that takes life away. Food's very material properties make its values as a foodstuff fragile. If not ingested, foodstuffs are destined to become waste: only through some kind of material reconfiguration and respatialization (such as that presented in Evans's 2012 description of composting) can some value be (re)claimed from food-waste. Even the value of waste in this case, however, lies not in that it is/was food, *per se*, but that compost itself has some value as organic matter, which can be used as fertilizer. In a roundabout way this links back to DeSilvey's (2006) commentary about organic reproduction, and to arguments about 'micro-ecology' and the 'force of things' (Sage, 2007; Bennett, 2004).

Prolonging the 'life' of the object and highlighting the particular ways that old objects can be reconfigured into new ones with new conduits and values and (that may or may not bear spectral resemblance to the old), centres on reconstituting value to reclaim objects from their normative categorization as waste and placing them into new material and social contexts. In other words, 'new' places must be made to accommodate the newly valued object (that was once 'waste'), but these new places are on pre-existing material and geographical conditions. What we mean by this is that the possibility to revalue salmon heads as food, and thereby reclaim them from their normative categorization as waste, exists because there is a pre-existing demand for salmon flesh; the material properties of the fish allow it to be split up and its multiple parts to be sent down multiple conduits, and there is a geography to accommodate these relationships. Salmon do not enter the food system because of their heads.

A more expansive understanding of salmon's material and geographical organization is especially important to debates about the relationships between value, decay, reconfiguration and revaluation as applied to salmon. Because of its bio-physical properties, salmon, like all food, is already in a state of decay. Once fished and killed, the biological processes that keep salmon alive and fresh are disrupted. From this point, the materialities that make the fish a potential foodstuff only remain applicable for a short time – after which they dissolve into other 'stuff'. Much of the food industry is, in fact, organized around preventing, slowing or otherwise managing decay to preserve freshness and to allow food-stuffs as much time as possible before they (once again) 'die' (Godley and Williams, 2009; Freidberg, 2009). But, while salmon will become waste if not first configured into a foodstuff and then eaten, salmon heads are already 'waste'. They may have some possible uses should the geographies be in a position to exploit them, but salmon heads are neither surplus nor oversupply. They simply 'happen' because salmon are valuable as foodstuffs, and they may then become commodities because traders seek to exploit their value after the value of salmon flesh (as food) has been extracted.

Salmon heads may just 'happen', but their revaluation and eventual consumption as food comes near the end of a geographical 'life' that is enveloped by interconnecting politics of production and of consumption. Food – obviously – is valued for its ability to sustain life and reproduce the body. This makes it, along with its production and consumption, intensely political. However, much of what we eat circulates as part of a commodity system that works to obscure these same political relations behind a commodity fetish that hides the social conditions of production from consumers. Harvey (1990: 423) uses this concept as a starting point to encourage researchers to uncover, unravel, or otherwise 'to get behind the veil, the fetishism of the market and the commodity, in order to tell the full story of social reproduction'. This 'full story' can be traced by 'following' consumption to production (and production to consumption) (Cook et al., 2004a, 2006).

Unveiling the fetish that hides these relations, however, does not account for all the relations that allow for waste to turn into food nor the types of places where such transgression can occur:

> Standard analysis of the commodity fetish sets out to lay bare the process of production, but this is only the first step. The really effective trick of the commodity fetish is to suggest that it is enough to stop at this point, to conclude that by unveiling the mystery of the content of the commodity then the mystery of the commodity has been dispensed with. (Page, 2005: 304)

Engaging solely with the commodity 'fetish' overlooks what happens after the commodity is consumed, and similarly fails to account for waste, wasting or possible reclamation. Consuming salmon produces salmon heads, and this waste goes somewhere. Understanding the conduits of salmon heads and their geographical reproduction thus becomes a matter of starting where the salmon ends, particularly when exploring the geographies required to bring objects back from the dead – and never more so than when these 'dead' objects are then used to feed the living.

One way to start is to reconsider the geographies of commodities so that they incorporate the life of the object before commodification and, particularly in our case, to then consider the lives that the object might have after it has been consumed. Page (2005: 298) suggests 'that there is no single momentous shift from non-commodity to commodity, but there is . . . the suggestion that there are endless other narratives that could be traced through the biography'. He goes on to identify a 'new geography of commodities' that considers such broader narratives (Page, 2005; for an example of these 'new' geographies, see Cook and Crang, 1996; Whatmore and Thorne, 1997; Leslie and Reimer, 1999; Hughes, 2005; Castree, 2001, 2004; Jackson *et al.*, 2006, 2009; Cook *et al.*,

The Sociological Review, 60:S2, pp. 156–173 (2013), DOI: 10.1111/1467-954X.12043

2004a, 2006). The life of the salmon, for instance, is traceable back from fork to sea: its fetish can therefore be unravelled by turning back and re-examining this trip, which is what the material culture of Borough Market attempts to evoke. Salmon heads, however, are only along for part of this journey. When it comes to aligning questions of waste with those of their materiality and their geographies, insights into the commodity fetish must also take into considera-tion the mutability of objects, and the multiple possible futures that consider what the object might become. While questions of material becoming – such as old ships becoming 'new' 'chocky-chocky furniture' (Gregson *et al.*, 2010b) or old food becoming compost (Evans, 2012) – are centrally important, so are the questions about the geographies that enable these transformations.

Moral evaluations: Closing proclamations

Much of the food we eat is the product of industrial food systems in which foodstuffs are manufactured for profit and circulated as commodities in a market economy (Goodman and Watts, 1997). As a result, when thinking about food and waste, it is tempting to focus an analysis and critique of waste as something systemic and structural within industrialized capitalism. Such analy-sis might consider the tonnes of food discarded each year (Godfray *et al.*, 2010); the ecological and ethical cost of particular foods, such as meat, in terms of 'lost' (or wasted) trophic energy and environmental degradation (de Bakker and Dagevos, 2012); or the material resources mobilized to produce and transport foods as part of an internationalized system of trade (Marsh and Bugusu, 2007; Pretty *et al.*, 2005). At the centre of such critiques (and something that Evans, 2011b, seeks to problematize in his own examination of the complex politics that bind food consumption, waste and blame in such a system to consumers in the home) is a sense of moral outrage that surrounds the notion of food waste in which wasting food becomes tantamount to all that is wrong with capitalism in the first place. We do not mean to suggest that there should be no moral critique when it comes to issues of food, waste and wasted food; rather, we argue that such critiques come with a moral imperative, not to not waste food, but rather to construct places and geographies where the impacts of consumption on the places affected by food waste are more apparent.

Such geographies and their implicit moral imperative go beyond the implied ethics and political positioning that comes along with appeals to 'unveil' or otherwise 'get with' the fetish of the commodity (see Harvey, 1990; Cook *et al.*, 2004b) and lead to notions of 'alternative' and 'ethical' consumption (Eden *et al.*, 2008). We extend our moral critique of the geographies of consumption to consider the ways in which the relations of consumption in one place, such as valuing and eating salmon flesh, prescribe the relations of consumption in other places and lead to the revaluing and eating of waste in the form of salmon heads. This shift in perspective positions a moral imperative onto consumption that includes not just matters surrounding the material *production* of commodities and their social and discursive reproduction as they relate to places of consumption, but also to matters surrounding the material *consumption* of commodities and their social, discursive and material effects as they extend to other places of *consumption*. This makes consumers responsible for not only the production of the things they consume but also responsible as producers of the waste that their consumption generates as well as responsible for what sometimes happens to make it to go away.

The consumption of salmon heads demonstrates the unsettling realization that 'the outcome of disposal is placing rather than rubbishing' (Hetherington, 2004: 163). The transformation from waste to foodstuff to food means 'reaching into the bin' in order to reclaim, revalue and (re)consume its contents. This account of salmon and salmon heads suggests that reaching into the bin 'happens' because of the ordering of particular places into a particular geography. The transformation of waste into food is further complicated when it takes place within the market. Markets are sites where market-relations define the use and exchange-values of objects; they are effectively where, amongst other things, objects become commodities and where commodities are consumed. As places, markets actively obscure the geographic relations that bring objects into their midst and they disavow an understanding of the processes that send objects away. Salmon heads are 'things' caught up in the relations of the market; they are reified as commodities, valued as foodstuffs, and they are normalized to become food. Often missing from their narrative, however, is that the salmon heads Bull Ring Market are also caught up in the relations of other markets, such as Billingsgate, or Borough where they are not normally consumed. Displacing salmon heads from these markets replaces them to Birmingham where they are deposited as food.

The disconcerting encounter that begins this paper compels us to join in with others to contradict or otherwise 'queer' the normalizing discourses and interpretations of economic practice more generally (Pollard *et al.*, 2009: 138). Such a geographical perspective, moreover, permits multi-sited gazes and engages with the multiple spatialities and temporalities that come with objects in motion. Part of this 'queering' involves momentarily suspending the uncomfortable encounters (Rosenberg, 2011; Butler, 2006) that an analysis of eating waste such as salmon heads necessarily entails in order to trace the ways in which the geographies that lead to such encounters come to outline their underlying and unequal materialities. This takes the 'rhizomic' nature of 'thing-power' at face value to consider the ways in which power reverberates through a geographical assemblage of places (Bennett, 2004). Articulating a 'multi-sited' geographical account, one that brings together a concern for the material with a concern for their geographies, interrogates not just the places where the object goes or has been, but also the places where the object has not been, will not, or should not go – yet somehow ends up anyway. We argue that objects like salmon heads end up in certain places based partly on their valuation in one place and partly on their valuation(s) in others. Even this interrogation is incomplete until it goes so far as to examine why the materialities of these objects-in-motion happen the

The Sociological Review, 60:S2, pp. 156–173 (2013), DOI: 10.1111/1467-954X.12043

way they do. This means 'following the thing', but it also means following the geography, and following it to unexpected, unsavoury and uncomfortable places where other things, like salmon heads, might be eaten.

Acknowledgements

The authors would like to thank European Research Council (ERC), the University of Leicester, the University of Western Michigan and the University of Sheffield for supporting this research project. In addition we would like to thank Peter Jackson and Nicky Gregson for comments on an earlier draft of this paper and an anonymous reviewer for commentary on a later version. We would especially like to thank David Evans, Hugh Campbell and Anne Murcott for both their insightful comments and endless patience. Mistakes, omissions and all other shortcomings are ours and ours alone.

References

Abolafia, M. Y., (1998), 'Market's as cultures: an ethnographic approach', in M. Callon (ed.), *The Laws of Markets*, 69–85, Oxford: Blackwell.

Abolafia, M. Y., (2002), 'Making markets: opportunism and restraint on Wall Street', in B. N. Woolsey Biggart (ed.), *Readings in Economic Sociology*, 94–111, Malden, MA: Blackwell.

Appadurai, A., (2005 [1986]), 'Introduction: commodities and the politics of value', in A. Appadurai (ed.), *The Social Lives of Things: Commodities in Cultural Perspective*, Cambridge: Cambridge University Press.

Bennett, J., (2004), 'The force of things: steps toward an ecology of matter', *Political Theory*, 32: 347–372.

Bestor, T., (2001), 'Supply-side suchi: commodity, market, and the global city', *American Anthropologist*, 103 (1): 76–95.

Butler, J., (2006), *Precarious Life: The Powers of Mourning and Violence*, London: Verso.

Caliskan, K., (2007), 'Price as a market device: cotton trading in Izmir Mercantile Exchange', *Sociological Review*, 55 (2): 241–260.

Callon, M., (1998), 'Introduction: the embeddedness of economic markets in economics', in M. Callon (ed.), *The Laws of Markets*, Oxford: Blackwell.

Castree, N., (2001), 'Commentary: commodity fetishism, geographical imaginations and imaginative geographies', *Environment and Planning A*, 33: 7.

Castree, N., (2004), 'The geographical lives of commodities: problems of analysis and critique', *Social and Cultural Geography*, 5: 15.

Coles, B., (2013a), 'Consuming coffees and producing places: from the intimate to the global – and everywhere in between', in E.-J. Abbotts and A. Lavis (eds), *Why We Eat How We Eat*, London: Ashgate.

Coles, B., (2013b), 'Making the market place: a topography of Borough Market, London'. *Cultural Geographies*, online first, doi: 10.1177/1474474013479845.

Coles, B. and Crang, P., (2011), 'Placing alternative consumption: commodity fetishism in Borough Fine Foods Market, London', T. Lewis and E. Potter (eds), *Ethical Consumption: A Critical Introduction*, 87–102, London: Routledge.

Cook, I. *et al.*, (2004a), 'Follow the thing: Papaya', *Antipode*, 36: 642–664.

Cook, I. *et al.*, (2006), 'Geographies of food: following', *Progress in Human Geography*, 30, 655–666.

Cook, I. and Crang, P., (1996), 'The world on a plate', *Journal of Material Culture*, 1: 22.

Cook, I., Crang, P. and Thorpe, M., (2004b), 'Tropics of consumption: "getting with the fetish" of "exotic" fruit', in A. Hughes and S. Reimer (eds), *Geographies of Commodity Chains*, 173–192, London: Routledge.

De Bakker, E. and Dagevos, H. (2012), 'Reducing meat consumption in today's consumer society: questioning the citizen-consumer gap', *Journal of Agricultural and Environmental Ethics*, 25: 877–894.

DeSilvey, C., (2006), 'Observed decay: telling stories with mutable things', *Journal of Material Culture*, 11: 318–338.

Douglas, M., (1994 [1966]), *Purity and Danger: An Analysis of the Concept of Pollution and Taboo*, London: Routledge.

Douglas, M. and Isherwood, B., (1996), *The World of Goods: Towards and Anthropology of Consumption*, London: Routledge.

Eden, S., Bear, C. and Walker, G., (2008), 'Mucky carrots and other proxies: problematising the knowledge-fix for sustainable and ethical consumption', *Geoforum*, 39(2): 1044–1057.

Edensor, T., (2005), 'Waste matter: the debris of industrial ruins and the disordering of the material world', *Journal of Material Culture*, 10: 311–332.

Evans, D., (2011a), 'Beyond the throwaway society: ordinary domestic practice and a sociological approach to household food waste', *Sociology*, 46: 41–56.

Evans, D., (2011b), 'Blaming the consumer – once again: the social and material contexts of everyday food waste practices in some English households', *Critical Public Health*, 21: 429–440.

Evans, D., (2012), 'Binning, gifting and recovery: the conduits of disposal in household food consumption', *Environment and Planning D: Society and Space*, 30 (6): 1123–1137.

Freidberg, S., (2009), *Fresh: A Perishable History*, London: Belknap Press of Harvard University Press.

Geertz, C., (1978), 'The bazaar economy: information and search in peasant marketing', *The American Economic Review*, 68 (2): 28–32.

Godfray, H. C. J., Beddington, J. R., Crute, I. R. *et al.*, (2010), 'Food security: the challenge of feeding 9 billion people', *Science*, 327: 812–818.

Godley, A. and Williams, B., (2009), 'Democratizing luxury and the contentious "invention of the technological chicken" in Britain', *Business History Review*, 83: 267–290.

Goodman, D. and Watts, M., (1997), *Globalising Food: Agrarian Questions and Global Restructuring*, London: Routledge.

Goodman, M. K., Maye, D. and Holloway, L., (2010), 'Ethical foodscapes? premises, promises, possibilities', *Environment and Planning A*, 42: 1782–1796.

Gregson, N., Crang, M., Ahamed, F., Akhter, N. and Ferdous, R., (2010a), 'Following things of rubbish value: end-of-life ships, "chock-chocky" furniture and the Bangladeshi middle class consumer', *Geoforum*, 41: 846–854.

Gregson, N. and Crewe, L., (1999), 'Beyond the highstreet', *Area*, 26: 261–267.

Gregson, N. and Crewe, L., (2003), *Second Hand Cultures*, London: Berg.

Gregson, N., Crewe, L. and Brooks, K., (2002), 'Shopping, space and practice', *Environment and Planning D: Society and Space*, 20: 597–617.

Gregson, N., Metcalfe, A. and Crewe, L., (2007), 'Identity, mobility, and the throwaway society', *Environment and Planning A*, 25: 682–700.

Gregson, N., Watkins, H. and Calestani, M., (2010b), 'Inextinguishable fibres: demolition and the vital materialisms of asbestos', *Environment and Planning A*, 42: 1065–1083.

Harvey, D., (1990), 'Between space and time: reflections on the geographical imagination', *Annals of the Association of American Geographers*, 80: 418–434.

Hetherington, K., (2004), 'Secondhandedness: consumption, disposal, and absent presence', *Environment and Planning D: Society and Space*, 22: 157–173.

Hughes, A., (2005), 'Geographies of exhange and circulation: alternative trading spaces', *Progress in Human Geography*, 29: 9.

The Sociological Review, 60:S2, pp. 156–173 (2013), DOI: 10.1111/1467-954X.12043

Jackson, P., Ward, N. and Russell, P., (2006), 'Mobilising the commodity chain concept in the politics of food and farming', *Journal of Rural Studies*, 22: 13.

Jackson, P., Ward, N. and Russell, P., (2009), 'Moral economies of food and geographies of responsibility', *Transactions of the Institute of British Geographers*, 34: 12–24.

Kopytoff, I., (2005 [1986]), 'The cultural biography of things', in A. Appadurai (ed.), *The Social Life of Things: Commodities in Cultural Perspective*, Cambridge: Cambridge University Press.

Leslie, D. and Reimer, D., (1999), 'Spatializing commodity chains', *Progress in Human Geography*, 23: 201–220.

Marcus, G. E., (1995), 'Ethnography in/of the world system: the emergence of multi-sited ethnography', *Annual Review of Anthropology*, 24: 95–117.

Marsh, K. and Bugusu, B., (2007), 'Food packaging – roles, materials, and environmental issues', *Journal of Food Science*, 72: R39–R55.

McGee, H., (2004), *On Food and Cooking: The Science and Lore of the Kitchen*, New York: Scribner.

Min'an, W., (2011), 'On rubbish', *Theory, Culture and Society*, 28: 340–353.

Munro, R., (2001), 'Disposal of the body: upending postmodernism', *Ephemera*, 1: 108–130.

Neville, B. and Villeneuve, J., (2002), 'Introduction: in lieu of waste', in B. Neville and J. Villeneuve (eds), *Waste-Site Stories: The Recycling of Memory*, Albany, NY: State University of New York Press.

Page, B., (2005), 'Paying for water and the geography of commodities', *Transactions of the Institute of British Geography*, 30: 14.

Pollard, J., McEwan, C., Laurie, N. and Stenning, A., (2009), 'Economic geography under postcolonial scrutiny', *Transactions of the Institute of British Geographers*, 34: 137–142.

Pretty, J. N., Ball, A. S., Lang, T. and Morison, J. I. L., (2005), 'Farm costs and food miles: an assessment of the full cost of the UK weekly food basket', *Food Policy*, 30: 1–19.

Roe, E., (2006), 'Things becoming food and the embodied, material practices of an organic food consumer', *Sociologia Ruralis*, 46: 104–121.

Rosenberg, S., (2011), 'Facing losses/losing gurantees: a meditation on openings to traumatic ignorance as constitutive demand', in R. Crownshaw, J. Kilby and A. Rowland (eds), *The Future of Memory*, 245–264, Oxford: Berghahn Books.

Sack, R., (1992), *Place, Modernity and the Consumer's World: A Relational Framework for Geographical Analysis*, Baltimore, MD: Johns Hopkins University Press.

Sack, R., (1997), *Homogeographicus: A Framework for Action, Awareness and Moral Concern*, Baltimore, MD: Johns Hopkins University Press.

Sack, R., (2003), *A Geographical Guide to the Real and the Good*. London: Routledge.

Sage, C., (2007), ' "Bending science to match their convictions": Hygienist conceptions of food safety as a challenge to alternative food enterprises in Ireland', in D. Maye, B. W. Ilbery and M. Kneafsey (eds), *Alternative Food Geographies: Representation and Practice*, 203–222, London: Elsevier.

Taussig, M., (1980), *The Devil and Commodity Fetishism in South America*, Chapel Hill, NC: University of North Carolina Press.

Whatmore, S. and Thorne, L., (1997), 'Nourishing networks: alternative geographies of food', in D. Goodman and M. Watts (eds), *Globalising food: Agrarian Questions and Global Restructuring*, London: Routledge.

Food waste in Australia: the freegan response

Ferne Edwards and Dave Mercer

Abstract: A common problem in all affluent societies, particularly in the retail sector, is the burgeoning issue of food waste. In this, Australia is no exception. However, to a large extent, the main focus of research in Australia to date has been on food waste at the household level. This paper focuses on the previous stage in the food life-cycle and examines the freegan practice of collecting and redistributing food discarded as 'worthless' by supermarket chains, in particular. For freegans, this is an act of choice, not need, to protest against issues of overconsumption and waste. The practice of freeganism has had multiple manifestations throughout history. It represents an alternative ethics of consumption and has multiple forms, embracing such issues as pesticide contamination, excessive labour exploitation, packaging and more. This paper reports on ongoing ethnographic research into two freegan subcultures in Australia: dumpster-divers and participation in the activities associated with 'Food Not Bombs'. It complements freegan research conducted across the world while its analysis, applying theories of alternative food networks, food justice, diverse economies and concepts of autonomy, provides insights into contemporary forms of activism and social change around issues of food waste in Australia.

Keywords: freeganism, free food, waste, punk, urban social movements

Introduction

> The possession of wealth is shown by the wasting of time, effort and goods. In order to be conspicuous it must be wasteful . . . what happens in the neo-liberal phase of capitalism is the transformation of whole cities', regions' or islands' economies/societies into centres of 'wasteful' production and consumption (Urry 2010: 206).

Urry's words are clearly designed to emphasize how central he considers the concept of waste to be in late capitalism, and he is by no means alone in this judgement. Gidwani and Reddy (2011: 1625), for example, have characterized waste as 'the political other of capitalist "value" . . . the things, places and lives that are cast outside the pale of "value" at particular moments as superfluity, remnant, excess, or detritus'. Needless to add, there are many, especially in the so-called 'developing' world, who see considerable value in 'detritus'. One

The Sociological Review, 60:S2, pp. 174–191 (2013), DOI: 10.1111/1467-954X.12044

estimate suggests that around 1 per cent of urban dwellers (or 15 million people) in 'developing' countries survive by scavenging (Medina, 2007). However – especially since the 2008 global financial crisis – the practice is by no means confined to less affluent societies.

Parallel to a broader focus on overconsumption and materialism in the West[1] (Hamilton and Denniss, 2005; Humphery, 2010), recent years in Australia have witnessed growing academic and policy interest in the issues of food, food waste and alternative food networks (AFNs) (Farmar-Bowers *et al.*, 2013). In numerous innovative ways, individuals and groups outside the 'mainstream' have sought to provide their own solutions to 'extra-market' food provision. In Australia, responses range from domestic and community garden production, to food exchange and sharing, to 'direct action' in the form of 'guerrilla' gardening and dumpster diving/skip dipping (also referred to as bin diving) to retrieve edible food discarded by supermarkets, shops and restaurants (Edwards, 2011).

This paper contributes to this debate both by building on recent literature (Daskalaki and Mould, 2013; Wilson, 2012) and focusing attention on the ethical stance and activities of the contemporary freegan subculture in urban Australia. As suggested by the conjunction of the words 'free' and 'vegan', 'freegan' food choices are ethical ones that centre on the issue of waste. According to the freegan.info website:[2]

> Freegans are people who employ alternative strategies for living based on limited participation in the conventional economy and minimal consumption of resources. . . . they embrace community, generosity, social concern, freedom, cooperation and sharing in opposition to a society based on materialism, moral apathy, competition, conformity and greed.

As a political statement against overconsumption, waste and corporate greed, the origins of freeganism have been traced back to the 'food-gifting' activities of the San Francisco-based Diggers' street theatre collective in the 1960s. However, elements of a much longer historical heritage are also apparent. For hundreds of years, many, so-called 'peasant' societies have actively embraced an ethic of cooperation, conservation and sharing.[3] Similarly, all the world's major religions promote values of charity towards the less fortunate, including food donation. Freeganism also accords with many of the central values of the contemporary 'Occupy Wall Street' movement, along with other 'money-less' movements such as squatting (Cattaneo, 2011) and the myriad of subversive urban social formations analysed by Daskalaki and Mould (2013).

This paper reports on ethnographic research conducted in Australian cities into what many may regard as socially marginal – even abhorrent – practice (Black, 2007). The freegans in this research adopt two forms of practice: 'dumpster-diving' ('dumpster divers' or DD) or participating in the activist soup kitchen called 'Food Not Bombs' (FNB). These forms differ from each other in their sourcing and distribution of food from waste. DD either go out alone or as part of a small team to rummage through supermarket dumpster bins and other commercial food waste outlets for their produce, while FNB members collect food *before* it hits the bins, often from fresh produce markets, to redistribute to those in need. Such radical, informal freegan activities complement formal, organized, institutional responses to waste, while also drawing attention to often overlooked commercial waste sources (Australian Government, 2010; Barilla Center for Food and Nutrition, 2012).

This study sits firmly within the now rapidly growing agri-food research field focusing on 'consumers as active participants in food provisioning' (Holloway *et al.*, 2007a: 2; Wilson, 2012). Through the lens of 'alternative food network' theory (or AFN) it highlights alternatives to the standardization, globalization, and typically unethical nature of the global industrial food system (Dixon, 2011). Freeganism represents an anti- or non- capitalist AFN, linking into a wider research agenda in Australia and elsewhere on food justice (Levkoe, 2006), urban social movements (Daskalaki and Mould, 2013), diverse economies (Gibson-Graham, 2006; Pusey, 2010), and autonomy (Chatterton, 2005; Leyshon *et al.*, 2003; Pickerill and Chatterton, 2006; Wilson, 2012). The emergence of freeganism not only introduces food waste into AFN literature but also refocuses attention on the commercial retail sector's crucial role in producing the waste in the first place – an oversight that often puts excessive blame on the consumer (Barilla Center for Food and Nutrition, 2012; Evans, 2011, 2012; Princen *et al.*, 2002).

Waste and food waste in Australia

Food waste is a growing area of concern yet to be adequately addressed in Australia. The National Food Plan (Ludwig, 2010) a document currently in draft stage, aims 'to foster a sustainable, globally competitive, resilient food supply that supports access to nutritious and affordable food'.[4] As part of this process, a lengthy 'Green Paper' was published in July 2012 (Commonwealth of Australia, 2012) as a preliminary to the final 'White Paper'. Notably, only 5 of the Green Paper's 274 pages were devoted (cursorily) to food waste. We regard this as a serious omission due to the corresponding – and highly pertinent – issues such as food insecurity where people do not have regular access to safe, nutritionally adequate, affordable and culturally acceptable food, as well as environmental concerns and shrinking domestic agricultural production in Australia (Farmar-Bowers *et al.*, 2013).

These issues require expanding in a little more detail. First, in what is ostensibly one of the world's most affluent nations, there is mounting evidence of the widespread incidence of 'food deserts' (ie households living more than 500 metres from a fresh fruit and vegetable retail outlet)[5] in Australia (Rosier, 2011). In a country where three major corporations alone have an unprecedented 90 per cent share of the food retail market that some consider a stranglehold (Ferguson, 2012),[6] grocery prices have risen by 40 per cent in the ten years to 2010, higher than in any other developed nation – in some cases, double the average. Given that people living on low incomes, such as pensions and student

The Sociological Review, 60:S2, pp. 174–191 (2013), DOI: 10.1111/1467-954X.12044

allowances, often spend as much as 20–30 per cent of their household income on food purchases (in comparison with the national average of 8 per cent), such inflation clearly generates significant hardship (ABC Radio National, 2011). A survey of 81 food relief agencies in Victoria and Tasmania, following the global financial crisis, found a marked increase in demand for their services. Over 21 per cent of the agencies, for example, reported not only a rise of at least 75 per cent in the previous 12 months, but also a significant shift in the demographic profile towards more younger and elderly people and families (SecondBite, 2010). In addition, an earlier study found that, nationally, 11 per cent of the population suffered from food insecurity (NSW Centre for Public Health Nutrition, 2003), while a more recent Victorian investigation confirmed similar proportions for certain local government areas in that State (Department of Health, 2008). These data roughly approximate to estimates of the percentage of the Australian population living in poverty (totalling around 2.2 million people).[7] Needless to add, research by Foodbank[8] found that 77 per cent of the population are either unaware of the issue or refuse to believe that a hunger 'problem' exists in Australia.[9]

Second, the collection and disposal of domestic and municipal waste in landfill sites – around 50 per cent of which consists of organic material – is becoming an increasingly expensive exercise (Australian Government, 2010; Baker *et al.*, 2009). Potential new landfill sites close to major urban centres are rare, with transportation distances consequently increasing. As it degrades, that domestic waste which is collected and transported to landfill becomes a major source of methane gas emissions. Methane – a far more potent greenhouse gas than carbon dioxide – currently accounts for some 4 per cent of Australia's total emissions, with food waste as the second largest contributor to this.[10] Perhaps unsurprisingly, Australia has the highest per capita level of greenhouse gas emissions in the developed world. The introduction of carbon taxes in July 2012 increases economic concern on the part of local municipalities and landfill site operators. Waste disposal charges currently average around AU$75 per tonne and it is anticipated that the carbon tax will add $25 to this. One possible solution for food waste management is a renewed emphasis on aerobic home composting (see Lundie and Peters, 2005).

Finally, although Australia is a very large country, the proportion that has fertile soils and sufficient rainfall for productive agriculture is not only severely limited but is also rapidly decreasing due to urban expansion and foreign takeovers (6 per cent of farmland is now majority-owned by overseas interests). The country is now, for example, a net importer of vegetables and fruit. This means that efficiency concerns around agricultural production and consumption are of growing significance. Wasted food, clearly, does not just involve lost nutritional value, but also the water, energy and other resources that go into its production.[11]

With per capita waste generation rates in excess of 2 tonnes per day, low recycling rates and the aforementioned high levels of greenhouse gas emissions, means that by any measure, Australia is a 'wasteful' society. Moreover, as concluded in a recent Senate Standing Committee inquiry, there is a glaring lack of political will to tackle the problem (Senate Standing Committee on Environment, Communication and the Arts, 2008). Prior to the introduction of a weak *National Waste Policy* in 2009,[12] the period 2002–2007 had witnessed a 31 per cent increase in waste generation – now 43.8 million tonnes was going to landfill.[13] Approximately a third of this total waste stream was either domestic or municipal waste. Again unsurprisingly, a recent solid waste management audit by Victoria's Auditor-General was highly critical of the lack of progress towards reducing the amount of waste going to landfill in that State (Victorian Auditor-General, 2011).

Since 2004 researchers at the Australia Institute have been monitoring 'wasteful consumption', defined as 'spending on goods and services that are not subsequently consumed' (Hamilton *et al.*, 2005: vii). Their 2004 survey of the spending habits of 1,644 respondents found that the average household wasted AU$1226 per year on products that they did not use. This amounted to AU$10.5 million nationally, with food being by far the most commonly wasted item:

> Overall Australians threw away $2.9 billion of fresh food, $630 million of uneaten take-away food, $876 million of leftovers, $596 million of unfinished drinks and $241 million of frozen food, a total of $5.3 billion on all forms of food in 2004 (Hamilton *et al.*, 2005: vii–viii).

In 2009, the Institute followed up this project with a more focused study on the purchase, consumption and 'waste' of food by a similar-sized, nationwide sample (Baker *et al.*, 2009). The authors concluded that, valued at an estimated AU$5 billion per year, food discarded by households – especially more affluent and single-person households – continued to be a major problem. It is estimated that households discard some 4.45 million tonnes of food each year, alongside the 3 million tonnes discarded by commercial enterprises. 'Food retailers', they argue, 'represent a major barrier to implementing effective waste policies, since their profits are contingent on the amount of food sold rather than the amount of food consumed' (Baker *et al.*, 2009: 1).

Following Evans (2011), we should emphasize at this point that we have no intention of pointing the finger of blame wholly at individual consumers for excessive household food waste. As we suggest above, much of the problem has its root cause in the underlying structures of contemporary food production, retailing and consumption in Western societies. Stuart (2009), for example, is unrelenting in his attack on British supermarkets for their excessive production of food waste and their lack of transparency on this issue.[14] His arguments apply with equal force in Australia. However, as Black (2007) further reminds us, in most affluent countries waste on this scale is a relatively recent phenomenon. Following the two World Wars, entire generations grew up espousing the core values of frugality and efficiency in food preparation, while the 1930s Depression in Australia out of necessity fuelled many innovative strategies for sourcing and sharing food. These ranged from widespread foraging in urban and rural environments to reducing waste and the expansion of charitable donation.

The Sociological Review, 60:S2, pp. 174–191 (2013), DOI: 10.1111/1467-954X.12044

Institutional responses

Historically in Australia, church and other charity organizations have been the main suppliers of emergency food aid to families and individuals in need. More recently, governments at all levels, as well as the three major supermarket chains, have come under mounting pressure from the community to reduce waste, to become more 'sustainable' in their practices, and to take a more active role in providing relief for the growing population of the 'food insecure'. However, in neoliberal Australia, where *private governance* of the food chain is now firmly entrenched, the state, retail chains and peak interest group agencies such as the Australian Food and Grocery Council have all consistently shown a marked reluctance to become involved in hunger relief other than at the most marginal of scales[15] (Busch, 2011). The widening emergency gap has been filled by food rescue charities and not-for-profit organizations such as OzHarvest and Foodbank nation-wide, and FareShare and SecondBite in Victoria (Farmar-Bowers *et al.*, 2013). Over the last decade – and following years of active lobbying by the not-for-profit sector – the work of such agencies has been increasingly facilitated by the passage of so-called 'Good Samaritan' legislation in most States. Starting with Victoria in 2002,[16] this legislation allows not-for-profit organizations to distribute donated food without the fear of being prosecuted by consumers who may subsequently fall ill.

Freeganism – a counter-institutional response

Freegans complement institutional responses to food waste and hunger by targeting discarded food to feed themselves and others in need. Over the last decade, there has been a rise in freegan consciousness – and hence food-waste awareness – with many news articles, books, web, blog sites and wikis[17] widely publicizing what was once a little-known underground subculture. This is illustrated in US-based ethnographies, including, for example, Ferrell (2006), Gross (2009), Barnard (2011) and More (2011). Australian contributions include Rush (2006), Singer and Mason (2006), Edwards (2005) and Edwards and Mercer (2007). This emerging coverage reveals a variety of 'freegans', or people who rescue – and, in the process, revalue – food from waste for human consumption.

Freegans across the world

Over recent years, the practice of 'freeganism' has extended to include broader food sources, social groups, locations and activities. Freegans may choose to eat food sourced from supermarket and other retail outlets' dumpster bins (as already noted, commonly referred to as 'dumpster divers' or 'skip dippers'), to collect, or receive, donated food before it hits the bins from open fresh food markets (such as members of 'Food Not Bombs'). Alternatively, they may choose to forage wild foods from their surrounding locales. As such, the sources of waste determine their diet, with vegans, or vegetarian freegans, eating meat if found in supermarket bins, while other diets include what have become known as 'dumpsterian', 'frego', 'raw foodism' and 'veganic' diets.

The most commonly researched freegans are university students who are drawn to the practice not least for the free food, fun and excitement but who often also endorse environmental and social justice ethics. Other accounts range from activists involved in 'new cooperativism' in the UK and Europe (Pusey, 2010; Cattaneo, 2011), to the practice of 'DIY-punk' (Edwards, 2005), to Barnard's (2011) New Yorker freegans who participate in dumpstering and other activities organized by the group, freegan.info, with the explicit purpose of educating the public about issues of food waste. This range of participants also extends across gender, from males who enjoy 'playing' in the bins, to More's (2011) female freegans who are often well-educated graduates or university students.

Regardless of the diversity of approaches, these participants share an ethical and political commitment to reduce the amount of food waste produced by the industrial, capitalist food system. In other words, food has become the means by which to enact this political and ethical belief. Additional motivations include not contributing to the demand for ethically unacceptable products of industrial agriculture, including pesticides, excessive packaging, labour exploitation and animal cruelty.

Freegans in Australia

As noted, this paper is based upon ethnographic research. It was conducted in 2005 in two Australian cities in which 30 freegans were interviewed and their activities and events observed. The participants were a far cry from the (often elderly) 'food insecure', urban poor identified above. Rather, they were often well-educated males in their mid-20s from middle-class backgrounds practising two, often interrelated, activities: dumpster-diving on the one hand and involvement in FNB on the other.

DD is the most widely-publicized form of freeganism. DD food is for individual or small-group consumption, with DD households enjoying what Hoffman (1993: 8) calls a 'maximum diving lifestyle', which does not mean all income and possessions are obtained from dumpsters, but rather that participants are able to enjoy the greatest benefits possible.

FNB's history, that basically represents an anarchist, autonomous soup kitchen, began in the United States in 1980, when a group of friends were protesting against the Seabrook nuclear power project in Cambridge, Massachusetts. The movement originally coalesced around issues of nuclear power, militarism and food, but has since expanded throughout the world to

The Sociological Review, 60:S2, pp. 174–191 (2013), DOI: 10.1111/1467-954X.12044

redistribute food that otherwise would go to waste in areas where it is most needed (Butler and McHenry, 2000). Today, volunteers who share similar political beliefs gather to cook vegan meals to distribute to the poor on the streets of Melbourne. This city has one of the most regular, ongoing FNB chapters in Australia, one that has maintained a regular presence since its inception in the Easter of 1996. The organization regularly operates three soup kitchens, distributes fruit and vegetables to charities, and occasionally supports benefits for causes such as indigenous issues, veganism and anarchism.

In Australia, people who participate in either of these two above activities can be broadly categorized into one of four activist subcultures delineated as (i) *purist university food co-op hippies* ('They'll be more into organic food and being healthy and good to your body, but there's edges of that community that will also be into squatting and DD'[18]); (ii) *anarcho-punk or pc-punks* ('Different from the crusty punks, as they are generally more politically aware and intellectual, but there's often a lot of overlap between the two groups'); (iii) the *autonomistas* ('They're all into being really intellectual about their politics and they're autonomist socialists and all . . . and are often involved in independent media projects'); and (iv) the *forest ferals* (often sporting 'a shaved head with crusty hair out the back, kinda anti-intellectual').

Since this original Australian research (Edwards, 2005), recent media and literature suggests that while these activist subcultures have persisted, some also have merged and evolved into new affiliations in line with Daskalaki and Mould's (2013) conceptualization of 'rhizomatic' social formations. As such, 'freeganism' has grown to encompass both genders, a range of subcultures, and a wider range of practices. Freegans therefore occupy one segment in a broad spectrum of AFNs, providing accessible food to those in need, fulfilling a sense of freedom, fun (Mair and Sumner, 2008) and self-empowerment to those who desire it, while simultaneously contesting the justice, efficiency and values embedded within the industrial food system. They join a wider net of others who participate in alternative food economies, often in cities, where people grow, glean and exchange their food outside of capitalist relations. 'Freegans' are thus more than simply radical, punk and/or male university students, but also include ethical, anti-consumer citizens of all ages, backgrounds and a variety of locations – effectively adding a modern layer to the biblical 'gleaners' of earlier eras.

Freegan food

So what do freegans actually eat? Those who DD often eat food that has been discarded due to 'best-before' or 'use-by' dates, that are either tarnished or that have broken packaging, from restaurants, bakeries, supermarkets and markets at the end of the day's trading. Supermarkets are particularly good sources as a consequence of their deliberate overstocking to give an illusion of 'cornucopian choice' (Stuart, 2009: 27). Godinho (2009) calculated that, at any given time, there are around 25 tonnes of food on the shelves of the average Australian supermarket. He has also estimated that in Victoria, alone, each year sees food dumped in landfills to fully stock 30,000 supermarkets. Food that is dumpster-dived from supermarkets then, consists of a wide choice, as explained by one diver:

> Basically, when it comes to food, anything you can think of that the supermarket stocks, you can get it in the bin from organic macadamia nuts to apples to laundry detergent to fertiliser to jars of olives to feta cheese . . .

General foods collected (in declining order of popularity) include vegetables and fruit, damaged packaged goods (including rice and canned food), bread, eggs and cheese. Although the bins contain a disproportionate amount of 'junk' food – such as packets of potato chips and sugary sweets – many DD opt for more healthy items, such as fresh fruit and vegetables. A key level of enjoyment for DD activists is the element of surprise, with the experience akin to a treasure hunt. Best 'scores' found by participants include shopping trolleys full of pasta, several large jars of vegemite, boxes of coco-pops, a bottle of Absolut vodka, 12 bottles of Chivas Regal scotch whisky, 23 slabs of beer, 12 packs of Guinness stout, and 200 boxes of Ferrero Rocher chocolates (Edwards, 2005).

Contrary to what would be expected, few people fall sick from DD food. This is because of the wide selection of produce available, the common adherence to a vegan or vegetarian diet, careful food preparation knowledge, and the sensible application of the senses of touch, taste and smell in product selection and preparation. The wide choice and knowledge of the best times for collection (for example, when ice-cream is still solid), allow foragers to pick and choose the best produce on offer. As one diver explains:

> When you do dumpster a lot, you end up eating mainly supermarket food which is not food that you would choose to eat if you had to pay for it. So you do get quite fussy . . . If you are fussy, you have the time to search for what you want. . . . Like we won't take [anything that's] fully opened and exposed . . . You don't have to take the zucchini with a bit of mould on it because there's a perfectly good one there . . . Just because you got it from the dumpster, doesn't mean that people are going to want to eat it.

The vegan or vegetarian diet preference helps prevent food poisoning as more risky, perishable products are not sourced. This dietary selection is especially important in warmer climates where decomposition occurs at a faster rate. Furthermore, many DD have moderate to high levels of food preparation knowledge and skills, as many, often being students or youth starting out in life, work in commercial kitchens, cafes or food-related industries.[19] By personally selecting produce using the senses of touch, taste and smell, dumpster divers no longer rely on supermarket labels to gauge food safety. This marks a conscious shift away from corporate control, enabling divers to reclaim a connection to their senses.

In terms of FNB, food comes directly from the leftovers at organic fresh food markets, consisting of fruit and vegetables that would normally be highly priced. The state of such food is explained by a FNB participant:

There's no high risk food [because there is no meat or dairy] and the food's at its point where it's at its height in ripeness and it's the most nutritionally good when the shops would throw it away. . . . It's because of its shelf life – you can't have something there that would be rotten by the end of the next day . . .

The FNB soup kitchen menu considers the nutritional content of the food, the physical state of its clients (nothing too spicy and providing a variety of dishes to cater for those with allergies), and the clientele's established food tastes (for example, baked potatoes are offered as a healthy alternative to hot chips).

Such alternative consumption practices by both DD and FNB questions conventional food safety boundaries. So, while Morgan (2009: 15) argues that we need to recognize a tripartite definition of *avoidable* food losses (ie truly edible foods); *possibly avoidable* (discarded but potentially edible food); and *unavoidable* losses, the freegans' diet demonstrates that such categories are highly subjective. By reaching beyond 'acceptable' food choices in the consumption of wasted food – and creating a space where no rules or regulations except the human senses of touch, taste, sight and smell apply – freegans access a layer of food waste that remains qualitatively out of bounds for institutionalized food rescue organizations.

Dumpster etiquette

Freegan ethics are also practised in the collection of food. Freegans make their own rules and these rules reflect an ethics of care for other freegans, for others in need, and for the environment. These ethics occur at many levels. 'Dumpster etiquette' expresses the three most common rules of dumpster diving as revealed from ethnographic accounts:

1. To come and go quietly and not leave a mess. Bins should be left as if they were never touched (some people even go to the extent of carrying a small broom and dustpan to sweep the area upon departure). This rule aims to prevent attracting negative attention to the activity, which includes raising issues of public liability that may result in security lockdowns.
2. First come, first served – if someone is in the dumpster upon arrival, their space and right to food must be respected. Patience and sharing are core values.
3. To remember that, although there is not much competition, some people rely upon this alternative food source. As such, it is important to not trash foods: this includes not ripping bags unnecessarily and re-tying bags after initial investigation, and only taking what is needed so as to leave a good quality and range of food for DD or the homeless who may arrive later.

Eating on the edge

The location of freegan practices also serves an important role in revealing both an ethics and politics behind wasteful consumption. Australian DD are generally secretive about their 'premium' DD spots, often due to concern about possible actions by authorities that may damage or lessen their supplies. The selection of favoured locations for Australian DD takes into consideration the quality and quantity of food, as well as proximity to, and ease of food collection. Ethical factors also impinge upon source selection, such as company histories, labour conditions, the environmental and social background of the products they sell, and the sheer volume of waste generated. Large supermarket chains are generally favoured over smaller independent stores because of their support for large-scale industrial farming. Their practice of importing foodstuffs from poorer, overseas countries to the detriment of local farmers is also a concern.[20] Multinational chains are similarly targeted due to their impersonal nature and their use of in-store, micro-management techniques to encourage citizens to consume beyond need. By targeting large multinational corporations, dumpster divers act as modern-day 'Robin Hoods', redistributing wealth:

> When we found thirty frypans in the dumpster . . . [we thought] that the public should have those frypans . . . we put them all in a trolley and took them all down to the Brotherhood[21] . . .

People also DD from smaller retail outlets, but for different reasons. These stores often discard gourmet- or health-related produce, highly valued by those who 'dive'. Given the shops' smaller size, they are often more resourceful with their stock than larger stores, producing less waste overall and investing more time in shop details. As one participant explains:

> The bigger the stores, the less likely they are to have these policies – like smaller organic bakeries will give food . . . Whereas bigger ones will say it's too much of an effort and chuck it out.

This secrecy of DD location in Australia contrasts to Barnard's (2011) study in New York City, where an organized group of freegans choose to draw public attention to their activities by participating in 'public trash tours' in which they inspect local dumpsters and place their produce on footpaths accompanied by open lectures to highlight issues of capitalist overconsumption and waste.

FNB serving sites in many ways parallel this placement for public protest, as food servings occur in politically specific places – that is, not simply where they are most needed, but also where they are likely to be seen. Two of the Australian sites, for example, are located beside high-rise, low-income housing complexes, while the third is located in a low-income suburb. The first two sites represent the permaculture concept of the 'edge' (Crabtree, 1999), or the fertile interface or overlap between two ecosystems, as they are situated between 'up-market' shopping districts in full view of trams that run along both these streets into the central city, effectively conveying the activists' identity and message to a diversity of citizens within this communicative zone. This 'audience' ranges from business commuters, to people going out to dinner or art

The Sociological Review, 60:S2, pp. 174–191 (2013), DOI: 10.1111/1467-954X.12044

exhibitions, to university students and travellers. FNB participants thus occupy 'fringe' territories on street corners between poor and affluent communities, feeding themselves and their friends – a blend of anarcho- and crusty punks and 'ferals' – alongside the homeless and hungry.

Hetherington (2004: 159) recognizes this spatial (and temporal) aspect of 'waste' by talking of 'disposal', where disposal, in a fluid and never quite final state, is defined as the 'continual practice of engaging with making and holding things in a state of absence'. Hence, objects do not follow a neat, linear path travelling from production to consumption but instead can loop back through space and time to acquire new value (see also Evans, 2012). Drawing on the work of Douglas (1984) among others, Hetherington argues that this placement of absence has consequences both for social relations and for creating modes of representational order. The public display of eating food that would have been wasted while people go hungry is akin to 'unfinished disposal', where 'first burial', such as disposal of food at the end of the market day, has either 'failed, been hurried, or has not been carried out to its full effect' (Hetherington, 2004: 170). Freegans effectively introduce an extra step before the final stage of 'waste', forming a space where new values, identities and social categorizations are drawn.

For DD, this transition occurs during the process of collecting, cleaning and cooking dumpstered cuisine. This reassignment of value is similar to that of 'punk cuisine', in which punk subculture defines industrially processed (or 'cooked') food as corporate-capitalist 'junk food', supporting cash-cropping, causing cancer and leading to the commodification of nature. As researched by Clark (2004), 'punks' – people who critique privilege and challenge social hierarchies as encountered in their participation in the Black Cat cafe in Seattle – choose to eat either 'raw' (unprocessed) or 'rotten' foods (such as stolen natural foods from health shops or dumpstered food) rather than 'civilized' (cooked) foods. By appropriating provisions outside of the marketplace, these punks – like freegans – symbolically returned blemished 'cooked' food to a 'raw' status, rendering it acceptable for politicized consumption.

Similarly, by halting 'final burial', participants in FNB direct attention to the two interlinked issues of food waste and hunger. At this juncture, freegans extend the life of the product, they value 'use' over 'exchange' value, and they re-embed 'waste' as a nutritional substance that is socially exchanged. Through their practices, freegans draw new boundaries of what is acceptable, adding dimensions of social and environmental justice to material value to challenge both the ethics of the industrial food system and Western society's definition of 'waste'. The reappropriation and redistribution of food by FNB in the public sphere acknowledges 'unfinished, unmanaged disposal', expressed by Hetherington as 'haunting' (also see Gordon, 1997). By exposing, and even performing, what would have been 'waste', freegans convey a message of capitalist impotence, pointing out the government's mismanagement of resources and their inability to protect their citizens from hunger

More than a free meal

Returning to Urry (2010), quoted in our introduction, we suggest that freegans go beyond rescuing food to also revalue and reuse other aspects of transport, work, leisure and housing, via their lifestyle choices. Preferred transport, for instance, includes cycling, public transport and the use of alternative fuels such as biodiesel. In accordance with their 'anti-consumerist' beliefs, rather than choosing more mainstream, 'green' or 'ethical' commercial options, many freegans choose to reduce their dependence on paid work in order to lessen their participation in the capitalist system. Unable to live completely without money, many freegans work part-time in food cooperatives or organic foodstores or choose to pursue more ethical careers, such as social support in housing or community development. Recreational activities often equate to activist activities, with freegans participating in events such as *Critical Mass*, a communal bicycle ride that reclaims the streets from cars, and *Reclaim the Streets*, a political street party.

The Australian research also revealed that many freegans also shared a 'DIY-punk' ('do-it-yourself'-punk) ethos, namely, to reject the values inherent in capitalism by living outside the capitalist system as much as possible by not making or spending money. This lifestyle choice neither supports nor contributes to environmental exploitation or social injustices deemed embedded within capitalist power structures. Freegans often take part in such DIY-punk activities including squatting, scavenging, using community warehouses, cycling, second-hand clothes' shopping, fare evasion, 'zine' (magazine) production and making clothes or music (Edwards, 2005; Edwards and Mercer, 2007). One FNB participant explains the rationale behind DIY-punk and how it relates to time, work and DD:

> DIY is taking something into your own hands and out of other peoples' hands. In the case of shoplifting, the corporations will try to charge as much as they can . . . So when you shoplift, you're taking that back and the reason why that's so important is because if you don't work, you don't get money and that means . . . you could starve to death. Another way of breaking that down is every hour you spend working, you're basically paid with an hour of your life so you can survive. So I work 10 hours a day, someone decides that my time is worth $8.50 an hour – they're buying bits of my life for $8.50. . . . With dumpster-diving you're taking that back in your own hands, your own life back in your own hands. That's your DIY – if I do it myself and spend less, essentially the more of my life I'm able to spend doing what I'd love to do . . . Stuff that's beneficial to myself and to the community . . . It could be about putting out a record that's not a label . . . I would really like to try and get my own sustainable vegie garden. I make my own clothes, I listen to mainly DIY music.

Aside from DD, squatting – the occupation of privately owned buildings that are not being used – is another key example of an Australian DIY-punk activity. One dumpster diver comments:

The Sociological Review, 60:S2, pp. 174–191 (2013), DOI: 10.1111/1467-954X.12044

Yep, [there's] definitely a correlation between dumpster diving and squatting – they've basically let the house become a bin . . . Thrown it away . . . You make use of all the shit you find . . . We used to have a joke that the house was just a big dumpster . . . We had all these appliances we DD as well, like sandwich grills, grinders, juicers and stuff. We used to joke that we'd get this garbage and spread it with this garbage, put some garbage in it, stick in the hot garbage . . . All the ingredients in the toasted sandwich were dumpstered, including the appliance.

These activities; freeganism, DD, FNB and DIY-punk, all fit concepts of 'autonomy' such as autonomous economic spaces (Leyshon *et al.*, 2003) autonomous geographies (Chatterton, 2005; Pickerill and Chatterton 2006) and autonomous food spaces (Wilson, 2012). Pickerill and Chatterton's definition of autonomous geographies – places in which people seek to constitute 'non-capitalist, egalitarian and solidaristic forms of political, social and economic organization through a combination of resistance and creation' (2006: 730) fits well with the freegan ethic.

Conclusion: freegans and food waste

This study of freegans contributes to the literature on food waste, AFNs, diverse economies and autonomy in several ways. Both freegans and formal food-rescue organizations, through their processes of respatialization and revaluing, redefine what society considers as 'waste'. Freegans add an extra dimension by accessing a controversial food source to redistribute free food (or what may be seen as 'waste') both to people who follow their political beliefs, to the general community, and to people in need. Their actions, couched in overt political and ethical discourse, are demonstrated or performed in 'edge' locations, further visualizing issues of retail food waste and hunger. Once an underground – and, some would consider, legally marginal activity – the media have increasingly drawn attention to the act of reappropriating food still fit for human consumption that would otherwise have been discarded. This has certainly struck a moral chord with the public, and, if not perceiving freegans as the 'Robin Hoods' they would like to be seen as, many endorse their right to 'glean' food if they so choose. Although not everyone relates positively to such a diet, and while freegans may not resolve issues as they consume rather than produce their own food outside of neoliberalism, freegan ethics and actions nevertheless reveal capitalism's contradictions and serve to reconnect people, place and produce in new ways.

Freeganism, lying as it does at the radical end of AFN examples, fits within a network of activities that foster innovative processes endorsing characteristics of the local, of quality and of ethics, while simultaneously establishing new relationships between producers and consumers. By introducing new sources and processes, those who participate in this movement serve to embed meanings and trust through proximate place-based relations (Feagan, 2007; Renting *et al.*, 2003). As Goodman (2009) explains, the moral economy of AFNs represents a double movement that disconnects one from the current system in order to critically reflect on established truths and to form new moral understandings for (re)connection. The recent emergence of freeganism contributes to non-capitalist AFN literature, a discourse which has grown in definition, range and practice over recent years to include, amongst others, activists in New York and food foragers who re-read city spaces to consume kerbside weeds and the produce of wild fruit and nut trees (Kramer, 2011). Perhaps, as Urry claims, our cities have been 'wasted'. Within them, however, there are many who are redefining and revaluing the world around us – and eating it for dinner!

Notes

1 By contrast, for a recent, controversial view challenging the 'overconsumption' rhetoric and arguing that the world is now undergoing a substantial consumption 'paradigm shift', see Pearce (2012).

2 http://www.freegan.info (accessed 3 August 2012). See also Kurutz (2007).

3 One example is the 'gold coat' ceremony in Nagaland, India. A person hosts a village feast that may last for days until they have divested themselves of all their assets. They are then awarded the gold coat in recognition of the 'feast of merit'.

4 http://www.daff.gov.au/nationalfoodplan/national-food-plan (accessed 20 August 2012).

5 See www.fooddeserts.org.

6 As in the UK, Australia does not have an independent watchdog overseeing the activities of supermarket chains. (Editors' note: A supermarket ombudsman was appointed by the UK government on 22 January 2013; see http://www.bbc.co.uk/news/business-21141841, accessed 23 January 2013.)

7 However, findings inevitably are coloured by the statistical techniques used to measure 'insecurity'. Another recent study, utilizing a more robust and sophisticated US measuring tool, uncovered much higher rates of food insecurity in three disadvantaged Sydney suburbs (Nolan *et al.*, 2006).

8 www.foodbank.com.au. In an attempt to raise the level of awareness, Foodbank constructed a giant, replica sculpture of the Sydney Harbour Bridge made out of donated food alongside that structure on World Food Day, 16 October 2011.

9 In common with 'waste', there are serious measurement problems as many definitions conflate 'severe' and 'moderate' forms of food insecurity (Temple, 2008).

10 Some researchers differentiate between 'food waste' and 'food loss' (eg fruit and vegetable skins or food scraps). Food wastage has been found to be the largest source of organic matter in landfill sites (see Rathje, 1986; Schapper and Chan, 2010).

11 For example, over 3 million tonnes of food are dumped in Australian landfill sites each year. The embedded water is enough to supply Melbourne and Sydney for a year. Similarly, dumping a kilogram of beef equates to the 50,000 litres of water involved in production (www.secondbite.org). A detailed assessment of the environmental performance of one food rescue organization (FareShare) found that for every kilogram of food recovered there were savings of 56 litres of water and 1.5 kg of greenhouse gases (Hyder Consulting, 2008; see also Ridoutt *et al.*, 2010).

12 An earlier national waste policy had been launched in 1992 but it was largely symbolic.

13 www.environment.gov.au/wastepolicy/about (accessed 21 September 2011).

14 The author of this hard-hitting book lived for a year solely on food products gleaned from supermarket bins.

15 Note, for example, that the 13-person, Working Group established to formulate a National Food Plan (NFP) has strong representation from the food and grocery and agriculture industries, but little or no representation from environmental, health, or community groups and the welfare sector.

16 *Wrongs and Other Acts (Public Liability Insurance Reform) 2002 ('Good Samaritan Law) (Vic)*.
  New South Wales enacted similar legislation in 2005, the Australian Capital Territory in 2008
  and South Australia and Queensland in 2009.
17 For example, http://trashwiki.org/en/Main_Page
18 Quotations are from Edwards (2005) and Edwards and Mercer (2007).
19 One respondent is a trained chef, two others work in hospitality, four work in food cooperatives,
  and nearly all participants commented that they enjoy cooking.
20 One DD participant noted this discrepancy of wealth and its consequences for the developing
  world when she established a FNB site at Cancun, Mexico, in defiance against the World Trade
  Organization conference. See also, the chronicle of the Brazilian artist, Vik Muniz's work in the
  Oscar-nominated film, *Waste Land* (www.vikmuniz.net).
21 The Brotherhood of St Laurence is a large welfare charity organization in Australia.

References

ABC Radio National, (2011), 'Who's winning the supermarket discounting wars?', *Saturday Extra*,
  8 October.
Australian Government, (2010), *National Waste Report*, Department of the Environment, Water,
  Heritage and the Arts, Canberra.
Baker, D., Fear, J. and Denniss, R., (2009), *What a Waste: An Analysis of Household Expenditure on
  Food*, Policy Brief No. 6, Canberra: The Australia Institute.
Barilla Center for Food and Nutrition, (2012), *Food Waste: Causes, Impacts and Proposals*, Parma,
  Italy. BCFN.
Barnard, A., (2011), ' "Waving the banana" at capitalism: political theater and social movement
  strategy among New York's "freegan" dumpster divers, *Ethnography* 12 (4): 419–444.
Black, R., (2007), 'Eating garbage: socially marginal food provisioning practices', in J. MacClancy,
  J. Henry and H. Macbeth (eds), *Consuming the Inedible: Neglected Dimensions of Food Choice*,
  141–150, New York: Berghan Books.
Busch, L., (2011), 'The private governance of food: equitable exchange or bizarre bazaar?', *Agri-
  culture and Human Values*, 28: 345–352.
Butler, C. T. L. and McHenry, K., (2000), *Food Not Bombs*, Tucson, AZ: Sea Sharp Press.
Cattaneo, C., (2011), 'The money-free autonomy of Spanish squatters', in A. Nelson and F.
  Timmerman (eds), *Life without Money: Building Fair and Sustainable Economies*, 192–213,
  London: Pluto.
Chatterton, P., (2005), 'Making autonomous geographies: Argentina's popular uprising and the
  Movimiento de Trabajadores Desocupados (Unemployed Workers Movement)', *Geoforum*, 36:
  545–561.
Commonwealth of Australia, (2012), *National Food Plan Green Paper*, Canberra: Department of
  Agriculture, Fisheries and Forestry.
Clark, D., (2004), 'The raw and the rotten: punk cusine', *Ethnology*, 43 (1): 19–31.
Crabtree, L., (1999), 'Sustainability as seen from a vegetable garden', unpublished Honours thesis,
  Department of Human Geography, Macquarie University, Sydney.
Daskalaki, M. and Mould, O., (2013), 'Beyond urban subcultures: urban subversions as rhizomatic
  social formations', *International Journal of Urban and Regional Research*, 37(1): 1–18.
Department of Health (Victoria), (2008), *Population Health Survey*, Melbourne, Victoria.
Dixon, J., (2011), 'Diverse food economies, multivariant capitalism, and the community dynamic
  shaping contemporary food systems', *Community Development Journal*, 46: 120–135.
Douglas, M., (1984 [1966]), *Purity and Danger*, London: Ark.
Edwards, F., (2005), *Gleaning from Gluttony: How a Youth Subculture Consumes Food Waste to
  Ascribe Identity and Attain Social Change*, Master of Social Science thesis, Melbourne: RMIT
  University.

Edwards, F., (2011), 'Small, slow and shared: emerging social innovations in urban Australian foodscapes', *Australian Humanities Review*, available at: http://www. australianhumanitiesreview.org/archive/Issue-November-2011/edwards.html.

Edwards, F. and Mercer, D., (2007), 'Gleaning from gluttony: an Australian youth subculture confronts the ethics of waste', *Australian Geographer*, 38 (3): 279–296.

Evans, D., (2011), 'Blaming the consumer – once again: the social and material contexts of everyday food waste practices in some English households', *Critical Public Health*, 1–12.

Evans, D., (2012), 'Binning, gifting and recovery: the conduits of disposal in household food consumption', *Environment and Planning D: Society and Space*, 30: 1123–1137.

Farmar-Bowers, Q., Higgins, V. and Millar, J. (eds), (2013), *Food Security in Australia: Challenges and Prospects for the Future*, New York: Springer.

Feagan, R., (2007), 'The place of food: mapping out the "local" in local food systems', *Progress in Human Geography*, 31 (1): 23–42.

Ferguson, A., (2012), 'The all-consuming market for markets', *The Saturday Age* (Melbourne), 29 July: 8–9.

Ferrell, J., (2006), *Empire of Scrounge: Inside the Urban Underground of Dumpster Diving, Trash Picking, and Street Scavenging*, New York: New York University Press.

Gibson-Graham, J. K., (2006), *A Post-Capitalist Politics*, Minneapolis: University of Minnesota Press.

Gidwani, V. and Reddy, R. N., (2011), 'The afterlives of "waste": notes from India for a minor history of capitalist surplus', *Antipode*, 43 (5): 1625–1658.

Godinho, M., (2009), 'Let's waste not while others are wanting', *The Age* (Melbourne), 1 May: 12.

Goodman, D., (2009), *Place and Space in Alternative Food Networks: Connecting Production and Consumption*, Paper 21, Environment, Politics and Development Working Paper Series, King's College, London: Department of Geography.

Gordon, A., (1997), *Ghostly Matters*, Minneapolis: University of Minnesota Press.

Gross, J., (2009), 'Capitalism and its discontents: back-to-the-lander and freegan foodways in rural Oregon', *Food and Foodways*, 17 (2): 57–79.

Hamilton, C. and Denniss, R., (2005), *Affluenza: When Too Much Is Never Enough*, Sydney: Allen & Unwin.

Hamilton, C., Denniss, R., and Baker, D., (2005), *Wasteful Consumption in Australia*, Discussion Paper No. 77, Canberra: Australia Institute.

Hetherington, K., (2004), 'Secondhandedness: consumption, disposal, and absent presence', *Environment and Planning D: Society and Space*, 22: 157–173.

Hoffman, J., (1993), *The Art and Science of Dumpster Diving*. Washington: Loompanics Unlimited.

Holloway, L., Kneafsey, M., Venn, L., Cox, R., Dowler, E. and Tuomainen, H., (2007a), 'Possible food economies: a methodological framework for exploring food production-consumption relationships', *Sociologia Ruralis*, 47 (1): 1–19.

Humphery, K., (2010), *Excess: Anti-Consumerism in the West*, Cambridge: Polity Press.

Hyder Consulting, (2008), *Sustainability Gains through the Recovery of Unsold or Off-Specification Food*, Melbourne.

Kramer, J., (2011), 'The food at our feet: Why is foraging all the rage?' *The New Yorker*, 21 November: 1–7.

Kurutz, S., (2007), 'Not buying it', *New York Times*, 21 June, http://www.nytimes.com/2007/06/21/garden/21freegan.html

Levkoe, C. Z., (2006), 'Learning democracy through food justice movements', *Agriculture and Human Values*, 23: 89–98.

Leyshon, A., Lee, R. and Williams, C. C. (eds), (2003), *Alternative Economic Spaces*, London: Sage.

Ludwig, J., (2010), 'Government begins work on Australia's first National Food Plan', media release, Minister for Agriculture, Fisheries and Forestry, 1 December: Parliament House, Canberra.

Lundie, S., and Peters, G. M., (2005), 'Life cycle assessment of food waste management options', *Journal of Cleaner Production*, 13: 275–286.

The Sociological Review, 60:S2, pp. 174–191 (2013), DOI: 10.1111/1467-954X.12044

Mair, H. and Sumner, J., (2008), 'The politics of eating: food practices as critically reflexive leisure', *Leisure/Loisir*, 32 (2): 379–405.

Medina, M., (2007), *The World's Scavengers: Salvaging for Sustainable Consumption and Production*, Lanham, MD: Altamira Press.

More, V., (2011), 'Dumpster dinners: an ethnographic study of freeganism', *The Journal of Undergraduate Ethnography*, 1: 43–55.

Morgan, E., (2009), *Fruit and Vegetable Consumption and Waste in Australia*, Melbourne: VicHealth.

Nolan, M., Rikard-Bell, G., Mohsin, M. and Williams, M., (2006), 'Food insecurity in three socially disadvantaged localities in Sydney, Australia', *Health Promotion Journal of Australia*, 17 (3): 247–254.

NSW Centre for Public Health Nutrition, (2003), *Food Security Options Paper: A Planning Framework and Menu of Options for Policy and Practice Interventions*, Sydney: University of Sydney.

Pearce, F., (2012), 'Over the top', *New Scientist*, 2869, 16 June: 38–43.

Pickerill, J. and Chatterton, P., (2006), 'Notes towards autonomous geographies: creation, resistance, and self-management as survival tactics', *Progress in Human Geography*, 30 (6): 730–746.

Princen, T., Maniates, M. and Conca, K. (eds), (2002), *Confronting Consumption*, Boston: MIT Press.

Pusey, A., (2010), 'Social centres and the new cooperativism of the common', *Affinities: A Journal of Radical Theory, Culture and Action*, 4 (1): 176–198.

Rathje, W., (1986), 'Why we throw food away', *The Atlantic*, 257: 14–16.

Renting, H., Marsden, T. K. and Banks, J., (2003), 'Understanding alternative food networks: exploring the role of short food supply chains in rural development', *Environment and Planning A*, 35 (3): 393–411.

Ridoutt, B. G., Juliano, P., Sanguansri, P. and Sellahewa, J., (2010), 'The water footprint of food waste: case study of fresh mango in Australia', *Journal of Cleaner Production*, 18: 1714–1721.

Rosier, K., (2011), *Food Insecurity in Australia*, Australian Institute of Family Studies, Melbourne: Communities and Families Clearinghouse Australia.

Rush, E., (2006), *Skip Dipping in Australia*, Canberra: The Australia Institute.

Schapper, J. and Chan, S., (2010), 'Food waste in Australia', *Food Australia*, 62 (7): 307–310.

SecondBite, (2010), *More Hunger, More Waste: A Report on the Experiences of Emergency Food relief Agencies in Melbourne and Hobart in 2009*, Melbourne.

Senate Standing Committee on Environment, Communication and the Arts, (2008), *Management of Australia's Waste Streams*, Canberra: SSCECA.

Singer, P. and Mason, J., (2006), *The Ethics of What We Eat*, Melbourne: Text.

Stuart, T., (2009), *Waste: Uncovering the Global Food Scandal*, London: Penguin.

Temple, J. B., (2008), 'Severe and moderate forms of food insecurity in Australia: are they distinguishable?', *Australian Journal of Social Issues*, 43 (4): 649–668.

Urry, J., (2010), 'Consuming the planet to excess', *Theory, Culture and Society*, 2–3: 191–212.

Victorian Auditor-General, (2011), *Municipal Solid Waste Management*, Report to Parliament, 29 June, Melbourne.

Wilson, A. D., (2012), 'Beyond alternative: exploring the potential for autonomous food spaces', *Antipode*, DOI: 10.1111/j.1467.8330.2012.01020.x

A 'lasting transformation' of capitalist surplus: from food stocks to feedstocks

Martin O'Brien

Abstract: In this article I link surplus food with the politics of capitalist production and consumption in order to shed some useful light on the strange case of food not being food once it has been discarded but not thrown away. I develop an analysis of waste policy as a dimension of capitalist surplus management (after Sweezy, 1962) by reconfiguring Claus Offe's (1984) essay on the state and social policy and construe waste policy as effecting a 'lasting transformation' of non-accumulating capital into accumulating capital. My intention is to provide a sketch of the labyrinthine semantic and political structures emerging around waste (in general) and waste food (in particular). I show that transforming waste food into capitalist surplus is a multi-layered and multi-stranded endeavour embedded in larger political, economic and cultural arrangements and cosmologies. I undertake this analysis of the transformation of waste into surplus by exploring, first, waste as an imaginary construct; second, the strange case of discarded food not being 'discarded' (and not being 'food', either); third, the convoluted cosmology of European waste policy; and, fourth, aspects of political sociology which help to reveal the status of waste as a source of capital accumulation. I conclude by proposing a sociological account of food waste that situates the critique of excess not in the ignorant, sordid voraciousness of individual citizens but in the structures and institutions of capitalist accumulation.

Keywords: food, discard, feedstock, surplus, value

Introduction

In this article I consider some aspects of waste policy and the conflicting and contradictory political processes that these exhibit. Specifically, I read waste policy as a dimension of capitalist surplus management (after Sweezy, 1962) by reconfiguring Claus Offe's (1984) essay on the state and social policy. I do not suggest that this neo-Marxist outlook exhausts the sociology of waste (or of waste policy) or subsumes within it the various dimensions of the ethnography of waste food (Evans, 2011, 2012), the activist critique of food waste (Stuart, 2009), or all aspects of sustainable food planning and analysis (see Viljoen and Wiskerke, 2012). Instead, I suggest that linking surplus food with the politics of capitalist production and consumption sheds some useful light on the strange

The Sociological Review, 60:S2, pp. 192–211 (2013), DOI: 10.1111/1467-954X.12045
© 2013 The Author. Editorial organisation © 2013 The Editorial Board of the Sociological Review. Published by John Wiley & Sons Ltd, 9600 Garsington Road, Oxford OX4 2DQ, UK and 350 Main Street, Malden, MA 02148, USA

case of food not being food once it has been discarded but not thrown away. To this end I begin with some comments on the imagination of waste before illustrating the ambivalent quality of discarded/not discarded food/not food by reference to two criminal cases brought against (perhaps unintentional) freegans. I then go on to outline the intricate web of semantic and political strands that underpin these strange circumstances by exploring key elements of European waste policy. The final section presents a means of construing that policy as effecting a 'lasting transformation' of non-accumulating capital into accumulating capital.

The central question underpinning the article is: what does it mean to 'discard food'? In order to answer this question, the article does not focus on the dispersion of meanings or household practices around different social groups but rather on the political and institutional arrangements that, with increasing vigour, are rearticulating waste food as a sustainable resource and redefining the meaning of both 'discard' and 'food' in the process.

Imagining waste

Researching waste of any description is always a journey: a convoluted, multi-directional and always fascinating expedition into twistedly dense worlds of definition, classification, meaning and, above all, imagination. The world of waste is a world in which imagination has to run riot in order to stand any chance at all of keeping pace with the bizarre reality of policy and practice. Sometimes what seems, at first sight, entirely commonsensical turns out to be unfathomably obscure, while sometimes what appears to be deeply arcane turns out to be one-dimensionally mundane. This condition is as true of the relationships between food and waste as it is of the relationships between any other substance and waste. To present a sociological account of any kind of waste is to expose an intricate network of social forces and social actions entangling citizens, governments and industries, policies, inventions and profits. To put it another way, it is to pen a portrait of an imagined common life: scenes from a sociological drama of individual lives intertwined with institutions, technologies and practices so that any imagination of waste immediately calls up characteristics of contemporaneous social life.

The reason for this circumstance, partly, is that waste is everywhere. In every nook and cranny of every colonized or yet-to-be colonized landscape and seascape of planet Earth persists the debris of the modern socio-economic order. From the littered trail defining the route to the world's largest peak to the swirling and churning morass that reveals the contours of the Northern Pacific Gyre;[1] from the deteriorating detritus that lines coat pockets to the food-filled skips secreted out of consumer sight behind gleamingly clean supermarkets; from sewage pipes that channel hidden excrement beneath urban highways and rural byways to the lorries and vans that transport the detritus along them: the wastes of modernity seem to stack up to a scathing indictment of profligacy and disdain. All those goods, all those resources, all that energy abandoned, misused, misapplied in a technologically advanced global order with the capacity, in theory at least, to nurture the environment instead of exploiting it, to steward resources carefully instead of destroying them callously. What does it all mean?

To view the world of waste through this kind of lens is to focus on the mismatch between the potential and the actual, on the measurable distance between the world as it should be and the world as it is: the ethical constant that is waste and the lessons it reveals about how people interact with the world around us. It is a lens that has magnified the moral universe of many and diverse scholars – from Dorothy Sayers's (1948) diatribe against Keynesian economics to Vance Packard's (1967) lamentation on compulsive consumption; from Zygmunt Bauman's (2000, 2004) castigation of consumerist logic to John Scanlan's (2005: 129) excoriation of ignorant and absent-minded consumers. Without disputing that waste may exhibit ethical dilemmas, a key problem with this imaginary lens is that it quickly and inevitably morphs into a critique of modern individuals: it becomes a 'we are all to blame' (Tammemagi, 1999: 17; Pearce, 2008) outlook – an outlook which is but a short distance from Chancellor-to-be George Osborne's suggestion that 'we are all in this together'[2] – as the depiction of social order and the reflection on personal action are fused into a single screenplay. It is as if, in this fusion, waste were nothing other than a dead weight dragging society to the depths of depravity and dragging blinded, ignorant, voracious individuals along with it. One consequence of chasing the ethical constant is that there is a tendency to subordinate sociology to moral philosophy: sociological accounts of waste become merely aptly illustrative of the 'existential vacancy' (Ferrell, 2006: 162) into which contemporary citizens have slipped – either unwittingly but spontaneously or under the influence of a dominant ideology of voracious consumption – whilst the state and political economy largely disappear from view.

I have no general disagreement with an ethical approach to the critique of waste; I suggest, however, that important sociological issues can get side-lined when waste is viewed from the ethical high ground. For, the sociological question I want to put is not: is there a lot of waste? Instead, it is: what are the means of dispersion and reconfiguration, what are the policies, procedures and practices that coordinate (or not) the channels and networks that place and displace different wastes in different regional and sectoral locations – not as a single signifier of moral indignation but as materially realized social forms? How is one thing transformed into another through the social process of wasting? To grasp this realization sociologically, I suggest, necessitates a series of engagements with cultures, polities and economies as well as practices, values and beliefs. A sociological approach to waste, as I have argued elsewhere (O'Brien, 1999a, 2008), requires an understanding of the social frameworks through which wasting transpires. This is because there is no such thing as 'waste' as a singular entity or phenomenon – any more than there is such a thing as 'waste policy' as a singular entity or phenomenon. Instead, there are complex, intricate and

The Sociological Review, 60:S2, pp. 192–211 (2013), DOI: 10.1111/1467-954X.12045

contradictory manoeuvres and strategies that define, establish and regulate channels for the flows of material values. Waste exhibits social, political and economic vitality: any and all waste is a fundamental component of social organization that references political and economic interests, establishes (and disrupts) social relations and inspires technological development and bureaucratic regulation. The world of waste is not simply a world marked by abandoned, under-used and callously ejected leftovers – it is not a world emptied or devoid of meaning and value. It is a highly structured and tightly specified world of actions and relationships to which questions of meaning and value are central.

In what follows, I return to an analytical theme I developed in a previous paper (O'Brien, 1999b) on political strategies for coordinating some of the channels and networks that render waste flows available for capitalist exploitation. Here, my focus is on the transformation of waste food into tradable and exploitable commodities – into a *material* capitalist surplus that can be reconstituted to yield surplus *value* – and the political and social scaffolding that is required to define the pathways and permissions, barriers and exclusions that facilitate that transformation. However, as will soon become apparent, those pathways, permissions, barriers and exclusions are embedded elements of larger political, economic and cultural arrangements and cosmologies. Transforming waste food into capitalist surplus is a multi-layered and multi-stranded endeavour that is stitched together through laws, institutions, regulations, subsidies, technologies and markets as well as definitions, plans and discourses.

Let them heat cake

On 22 March 2010, Steven De Geynst (dubbed the 'Muffin Man' by the media) was apprehended taking two bags of muffins from a waste container outside a store in Rupelmonde, Belgium. When confronted by staff he allegedly became aggressive and when subsequently confronted by the police he allegedly tried to resist arrest. For taking two bags of muffins out of a waste container in these circumstances, De Geynst was charged with violent robbery and sent for trial in Dendermonde in April 2011. The judge rejected his defence that the goods belonged to no-one because they had been placed in a waste disposal container and were therefore clearly unwanted by the store in question – as *Flanders Today* put it: 'His lawyer asked the court last week to consider the question of how goods can be stolen when their owner has clearly given them up' – and sentenced him to six months 'adjourned' imprisonment. In February 2012, however, he was acquitted by the Court of Appeal in Ghent on the grounds that no crime had been committed. This was not because the Court of Appeal supported his original defence. Rather, he was acquitted because for several years he had been taking food from the waste container without let or hindrance and had therefore operated with at least the tacit permission of the store which was the rightful owner of its contents, in spite of having discarded them into a waste receptacle.[3]

On 29 January 2011, Sacha Hall, from Chelmsford, England, carried several bags of food across the roofs of adjoining buildings and deposited them, via a window, in her flat. Amongst other things, the bags contained wrapped and unopened pies, cooked ham and potato waffles. These items, already bagged, had been passed to her by one of several men who were rooting through cages containing large quantities of chilled food stored behind a Tesco Express store in the Great Baddow district of Chelmsford. Sacha Hall did not, apparently, enter the cages herself, nor did she bag up the items that she took across the roof. She was charged both with stealing by finding and with handling stolen goods, appeared at Chelmsford Magistrate's Court, but opted for trial by jury at Crown Court (she was dubbed 'the Waffle One' by some protesters at her court appearance). In May 2011, at the Crown Court, the charge of stealing by finding was left to lie on file and no further action was taken but, in June 2011, she was sentenced to twelve months conditional discharge for handling stolen goods. The maximum sentence to which Sacha Hall might have been subjected was seven years in prison.[4]

In both of these cases, the contents of the waste container outside the store in Rupelmonde and the contents of the cages outside the store in Chelmsford had clearly and unequivocally been discarded. None of the participants in either of these incidents disputed that the left-over food items were discards from the stores: in the Rupelmonde case, the muffins were simply noted to be past their best-before date and in the Chelmsford case the store claimed that a power outage had necessitated the removal of stock from the shelves to the cages prior to disposal for health and safety reasons. There are several arguments that might account for the actions against Geynst and Hall – including health and safety issues and the visibility of branded goods circulating at no cost through a sub-freeganic economy, for example – but none of these deflect from the fact that the food items had, blatantly, been discarded. Neither Geynst nor Hall was charged with breaches of health and safety regulations or with brand-infringement or maligning the reputation of the stores. They were charged with the theft of discarded items. This fact alone indicates, empirically, that discarded items have not been abandoned; they are not free of relations of private property or rules of ownership. Items that have been discarded have categorically *not* been thrown away and they are *not* unwanted.

If these discarded items have not been thrown away and are not unwanted then what value underpins their retention? In fact, the kinds of items taken by Geynst and Hall were, to all intents and purposes, very differently valued in economic terms until relatively recently. Before 2008 the overwhelming majority of supermarket food waste was simply dumped in landfill. Since then, however, the major supermarkets have investigated and entered into partnerships with waste management firms to transform surplus food into other commodities – energy, heat and by-products of energy generation such as biofertilizer. This technological response to waste food involves sending leftovers to biowaste-to-energy plants or, more popularly, to anaerobic digestion facilities. In the former, surplus food is burned together with other organic wastes (crop residues, garden wastes, forestry residues, for example) to generate a number of products – notably energy that can be fed into the national grid or used locally, and heat. Anaerobic digestion facilities expose organic wastes to micro-organisms in the absence of oxygen in a temperature range, normally, between 32°C and 45°C. The process produces a 'biogas' (typically 60 per cent methane, 40 per cent carbon dioxide) and a solid digestate that can be used as a fertilizer.[5] The emergence of these energy-product solutions to surplus food can be explained partly by technological developments in the waste management sector, partly by subsidies for 'renewable' energy projects and partly by increases in the landfill tax since 1996. In fact, these solutions have the direct support of the UK government, which, in its 2011 Waste Policy Review, made specific mention of the 'value' of this ambiguously valued substance:

> Food waste that does arise is recognised as a valuable resource, and is processed to produce renewable energy and a biofertiliser so that nutrients are returned to the soil. (Department of the Environment, Food and Rural Affairs (DEFRA), 2011: 58)

On a wider scale, these energy-product responses to organic waste are part of an emerging suite of technologies – including waste-to-energy plants dealing with municipal waste and methane capture from landfill – that have been redefining waste for some time as a renewable energy resource. Whereas early twentieth-century concern about waste centred heavily on the loss and recuperation of physical commodities (see, for example, Talbot, 1919), early twenty-first century policy is dominated by the loss and recuperation of energy: effectively, the energy problem is slowly supplanting the commodities problem as the official value of waste's recuperation. It might be noted in passing, here, that not only is pre-consumed surplus food being brought within the orbit of an energy-generation outlook; post-consumption food, that is, sewage, is also being turned into an energy source using variations on the same technologies described above. In fact, one aspiring company dedicated to supplying power through sewage treatment technologies is called Cake Energy – for whom sewage sludge 'is possibly the most sustainable energy resource on earth'.[6]

From the Muffin Man to sewage cake, the value of 'food' at all stages of its pre- and post-consumption cycle is being realigned and reconstructed as an energy resource, primarily, that brings along with it other environmental and economic benefits. Stealing food from supermarket bins or cages, then, is akin to helping yourself to the contents of a coal pile: what is being taken is not in itself a finished object and nor, incidentally, is it food; it is a raw material to be used in the generation of other commodities. In this sense, surplus food is like the products of extractive industries: it has travelled along the conveyor belt of food supply and consumption chains and been tipped onto an organic mountain ready for use in energy-generation. But for all of this to be possible, a radically new concept of 'discard' must be in place; to discard something can no longer mean to get rid of it, shed it or abandon it. Instead, to 'discard' must now mean 'use for another purpose' or, at least, pass on to another *sanctioned* user. My intention, here, is not simply to point to the variety of networks through which different kinds of waste substances are inventively channelled. I have addressed some of these channellings in previous work (O'Brien, 1999a, 1999b, 2008) and these questions have been imaginatively and more thoroughly taken up by Nicky Gregson and colleagues (see Gregson, 2007; Gregson *et al.*, 2007). My interest here is how food items that have been actually, effectively and uncontestedly discarded *in law* can, simultaneously, be food items that have *not* been discarded *in fact*. The question is, then: under what semantic and political regime of definitions, values, permissions and sanctions does this contradiction persist?

A taxonomy of tripe[7]

There is, in the European Union (EU) Waste Framework Directive, a wondrous and wholly spectral definition of waste, viz:

> Any substance or object in the categories set out in Annex 1 which the holder discards, intends or is required to discard. (Directive 2006/12/EC)

In other words, a waste substance or object is any substance or object contained in a list of waste substances and objects (although, as we shall see, it is even more wondrous than this)! The list provided in Annex 1 refers to the *European Waste Catalogue* (EWC)[8] and, in spite of the fact that the original decision establishing the catalogue (Decision 94/3/EC) has been updated on several occasions, the EWC remains the definitive list of substances and objects to which reference is made whenever a query about the nature of waste arises in EU legal and industrial sectors. It comprises, unsurprisingly for a document generated in committees of the European Union, an entirely regulatory array – most of the contents of the list refer to materials but some refer to industrial sectors or processes. The purpose of the list is not (explicitly, anyway) to philosophize on the ontology or epistemology of waste (even though it does in fact do this). Its purpose is administrative – to apportion substances to more or less well-defined channels of bureaucratic oversight. Its twenty 'chapters' cover mining and quarrying, agriculture, metal treatment, animal and health care, construction and demolition, households and municipalities and waste treatment facilities, amongst many others. The contents of the chapters sum to over 700 items, the most commonly recurring of which is 'wastes not otherwise specified'. This category – as well as having a chapter entirely to itself, Chapter 16: 'Wastes not otherwise specified in the list', comprising 41 items – recurs 70 times, including two mentions in Chapter 16 itself, so that 'wastes not otherwise specified' are listed twice in a chapter entitled 'wastes not otherwise specified'. I cannot help but be reminded of Jorge Luis Borges' essay on 'The Analytical Language of John Wilkins'. Here, Borges tells of 'a certain Chinese Encyclopaedia', the *Celestial Emporium of Benevolent Knowledge*, which divides animals into:

those that belong to the Emperor, embalmed ones, those that are trained, suckling pigs, mermaids, fabulous ones, stray dogs, those included in the present classification, those that tremble as if they were mad, innumerable ones, those drawn with a very fine camelhair brush, others, those that have just broken a flower vase, those that from a long way off look like flies.

Borges writes of Wilkins' analytical language and the purported Chinese Encyclopaedia that 'it is clear that there is no classification of the Universe not being arbitrary and full of conjectures'.[9] The conjectural quality of the EWC appears to open up its semantic universe to a wide range of potential interpretations – indeed, conjecture and arbitrariness is effectively its defining character – but, in fact, its conjectures perform more closures than openings and its arbitrariness both limits and expands the universe of meanings through which waste substances travel.

On top of the ambivalence exhibited by the European Waste catalogue can be added the fact that even if a material is listed in the catalogue it is not necessarily a waste since it is the circumstances, not the material itself, that determine whether or not said material is to be treated as waste. If the catalogue looks anything but straightforward the interpretation of the policy is even more convoluted, partly because the policy is pegged around case law developed through the European Court of Justice. The European Commission issued a communication (COM (2007) 59 final, 21.2.2007)[10] in an effort to facilitate common interpretation of the definition of waste set out in the Waste Framework Directive and its list of waste materials. Here, the Commission declares that:

> ECJ [The European Court of Justice] has set out a three-part test that a production residue must meet in order to be considered as a by-product. The court stated that where the further use of the material was not a mere possibility but a certainty, without any further processing prior to reuse and as part of a continuing process of production, then the material would not be a waste. (s. 3.3, p. 7)

The 'test' is, in fact, cumulative: in order for a substance to be a 'by-product' of a production (or 'pre-consumption') process, and not a waste, all three parts of the test must be passed. Naturally, there are further discussions on the meaning of 'certainty' of further use, 'further reprocessing' and 'continuing process', and these discussions have a particular resonance because of a number of challenges made by member states to the EU definition of waste. The most important of these resulted in an action against the Italian Republic in 2005.[11] The point to which I want to draw attention here is that even when a three-stage test of the essence of non-waste is established, that test itself depends upon further clarifications of terms and those clarifications, in turn, require further clarifications. The final meaning of waste is endlessly deferred in cycles of interpretation of when a waste is not a waste that never settle on any given characteristic, intention, desire or treatment but always contextually determine who will control the material, what its treatment pathway shall be and how that material and that pathway will be regulated.

Instead of a material definition of waste, then, the European Commission establishes a processual definition (in spite of the fact that the EWC is very largely a list of materials) that construes waste as an endlessly deferred chain of channellings, procedures and protocols. However tightly specified and however contextually sensitive these deferrals are, they remain always in a state of partial suspension since '[if] it subsequently turns out that the waste can in fact serve a useful purpose, then the material will lose its waste status when it is ready for use as a recovered product' (s. 3.3.1, p. 7). So, the endless deferral points to the conclusion that any substance or material that fails any or all of the three tests and is, therefore, to be regarded as a waste may actually not be waste after all since it will cease to be waste if and when it becomes a 'recovered product'. On the other hand, any material or substance that passes all of the three tests and is, therefore a by-product and not a waste is, even so, actually a waste if its holder intentionally discards it. In consequence, the communication states, 'the definition of waste essentially turns on the notion of discard' (s. 3.1, p. 6).[12]

But this array of judgments, too, is fundamentally ambivalent since it requires another layer of decisions and policy frameworks in order to ensure that the 'products' and the 'not-products' are sufficiently distinguished and, in particular, to identify waste as part of a stream of products and not simply as a stream of use- or exchange-values. After all, waste substances of very many kinds can be (and are) put to all sorts of different uses and may be exchanged one for another without any guidance from the European Commission or rulings from the European Court of Justice. In fact, as contradictory to ordinary usage as it may appear to be, in European policy waste substances are not waste in any common understanding of that term: instead, they are 'goods'. This definition of waste was confirmed in *Commission of the European Communities* v *Kingdom of Belgium* (the 'Walloon Case', Case C-2/90, 1992, para. 23, 28)[13] in which it was directed that waste is 'to be regarded as "goods" the movement of which, in accordance with Article 30 of the Treaty [of Rome],[14] must in principle not be prevented'. In this case, materials that fail any or all parts of the three-part test and are, consequently, wastes and not products or by-products, nonetheless remain goods. If waste is to be considered goods then it follows that waste is to be treated primarily as an economic, rather than an environmental, issue and, indeed, this is precisely the view offered in draft guidance from the UK's Department of the Environment, Food and Rural Affairs (DEFRA) (2010) on the legal definition of waste and its application – which also refers to the Walloon Case mentioned above. Yet, even here, the clarity offered remains opaque. Given that 'waste' is actually to be treated as 'goods' then why would anyone want to discard it? To give an example, why is it that when someone 'purchases scrap metal with the intention of reprocessing it into steel' that purchaser is still 'taken to have the intention to discard that material even though they may regard it as a valuable secondary raw material' (DEFRA, 2010: 66)?

To even begin an answer to this question it first needs to be noted that whereas the European Waste Catalogue, with its 700-plus entries and its

The Sociological Review, 60:S2, pp. 192–211 (2013), DOI: 10.1111/1467-954X.12045

ambivalence over unspecified substances, lays out an almost messianic material register of waste elements, the interpretation and application of that catalogue orbits around other concepts and practices altogether. The materials in the list do not in any way restrict or solidify the substantial question of what waste comprises. Rather, they make inroads into the conceptual and practical field of waste and provide avenues of sanctioned exploitation, authorized earnings and certified yields. In recognition of the simultaneous semantic limitation and expansion, the ECJ ruled in its dispute with the Italian Republic over food scraps and food waste (*European Commission* v *Italian Republic*, Case C-195/05):

> It should be pointed out at the outset that the list of categories of waste set out in Annex I to the Directive, as well as the disposal and recovery operations listed in Annexes II A and II B thereto, show that there is no type of residue or other substance resulting from the production process which is in principle excluded from the concept of waste. (para. 45)

There is '*no type of residue or other substance resulting from the production process which is in principle excluded from the concept of waste*' (my italics). This bears repetition because it is crucial: the injunction applies to anything at all that is produced during a production process. It applies as much to what a producer intends to produce as to what a producer does not intend to produce. To give an example, Tristram Stuart (2009) writes, in what can only be described as a dumbfounded style, that suppliers of ready-meals and/or sandwiches to giant supermarkets can discard over half of all that they produce and that surplus levels of around 10 per cent are considered normal. The reason for this is that many supermarkets pre-order these goods a week or so in advance based on sales predictions and then change their minds about what and how much of what they are prepared to take just 24 hours before the due delivery date. In this scenario, the producer certainly intended to produce a given quantity of ready-meals and/or sandwiches but now the purchaser no longer wants some portion of them. The restrictive contracts between supplier and supermarket are such that the pallet-loads of unwanted items cannot be sold elsewhere or donated to charities and end up either in landfill or, increasingly (as noted above), in biowaste and anaerobic digestion facilities which turn them into energy, heat, biofertilizer and biogas. Clearly, in this case, the supplier intended to produce these items and intended to do so under a contract with a purchaser. However, since at the pre-consumption stage these intended items are no longer wanted they shift into the category 'waste' as items that the supplier is required to 'discard'.

Waste, it transpires, is not a by-product, not a residue and not a good. At the same time it *is* a by-product, a residue and a good. It is that which is not produced intentionally and that which is produced intentionally. In principle, according to the highest court in the European Union, it is non-exclusive; there is nothing that the category of waste does not address; it covers not only every thing but also every relationship with – and process in – the material world: it is everywhere, not only in its material forms but also in its legal, political and economic forms. To discard waste, then, is emphatically not to abandon it, divest oneself of it or even throw it away; it is to *situate* it in the channels, protocols and procedures of waste management; to place it positively in a politically regulated regime that orchestrates who can profit from it and what can happen to it. In this context, how aptly titled is John Young's (1991) *Discarding the Throwaway Society*! Young could not have foreseen that his proposal would come to be taken literally – but in exactly the opposite semantic framework that he intended. Rather than attacking the procedures and practices that he felt were the cause of waste, contemporary policy simply construes the discarding as a link in the chain of surplus management.

So far, I have developed an analysis that began with the imagination of waste, considered the strange case of discarded food not being discarded at all (and not being food, either), explored aspects of the convoluted cosmology of European waste policy and the contradictory semantic consequences of that convolution. Now, I turn my attention to the theoretical – rather than administrative – question of how surplus materials are constituted as 'surplus' and how waste policy itself is intimately involved in the management of capitalist excess.

A 'lasting transformation'

In a ground-breaking work, first published in 1942, the American economist Paul Sweezy outlined a theory of capitalist development rooted in the process of underconsumption (Sweezy, 1962). In this theory, Sweezy mined Marx for clues to solve the riddle of capitalism's continued world dominance despite its 'periodic crises and occasional lapses into stagnation' (1962: 217). According to Sweezy, the chronic condition of capitalism is a tendency always towards stagnation because there is a contradiction between production capacity and consumption capacity; or, as Sweezy (1962: 175) puts it, production is continually expanded 'without any reference to the consumption which alone can give it meaning'. This situation arises according to Sweezy because, citing Marx:

> The last cause of all real crises always remains the poverty of and restricted consumption of the masses as compared to the tendency of capitalist production to develop the productive forces in such a way that only the absolute power of consumption of the entire society would be their limit. (Capital III, cited in Sweezy, 1962: 177)[15]

In consequence, capitalist societies are permanently scarred in one of two ways: either by a crisis of excess – where there are simply too many goods on the market and the restricted consumption of the masses prevents their sale – or because the productive forces themselves are left to stagnate in order to offset precisely this crisis of underconsumption. In both cases there results a realization crisis: either commodities have been produced but the masses' failure to consume them results in a direct loss of surplus value; or the productive forces are under-utilized and, consequently, fail to generate the commodities that would realize surplus value were they consumed. In this sense, Sweezy follows Marx's understanding of 'waste' as a failure in the efficient use of the productive forces, resulting in a persistent latent or actual surplus of capital.

Later, in *Monopoly Capital* (Baran and Sweezy, 1970), the question of wastefulness takes on a much more central role. The book's focus remains true to Sweezy's original work – the description and explanation of a specific phase of capitalism characterized by monopoly. The book also expands on Sweezy's attempt at a systematic analysis of surplus management, devoting several chapters to the forces that counteract the underconsumption problem. However, much more attention is devoted to an account of why the surplus of capitalism is generated and how it is absorbed in order to stave off the threat of stagnation. In typically straightforward style Baran and Sweezy describe the 'topsy-turvy, and fetishistic' (1970: 326) appearance of monopoly capitalism from the individual's point of view in the following terms:

> The self-contradictory character of monopoly capitalism – its chronic inability to absorb as much surplus as it is capable of producing – impresses itself on the ordinary citizen in a characteristic way. To him, the economic problem appears to be the opposite of what the textbooks say it is: not how best to utilize scarce resources but how to dispose of the products of super-abundant resources. (1970: 114)

It may seem counter-intuitive to construe waste as a consequence of underconsumption when the prevailing outlooks on the contemporary scene almost invariably refer to the overconsumption of the earth's resources. No less an authority than Fred Pearce uses a *New Scientist* column to state baldly that 'overconsumption is the real problem', whilst a Friends of the Earth report surveys resource-use and waste-production to clarify precisely that overconsumption leads inexorably to environmental degradation.[16] Meanwhile, Richard Tucker's (2000) assessment of America's exploitation of the tropics encapsulates the overall perspective neatly in its portentous title *Insatiable Appetite*. Certainly, from the standpoint of the individual citizen, gazing upon the piles of waste generated not only domestically but industrially, the problem does not seem to be one of failing to acquire enough goods but its precise opposite: acquiring too many goods and having to get rid of them. But rapacious overconsumption and the structure of underconsumption are not at all *economically* contradictory. They only appear that way, as Baran and Sweezy note, from the standpoint of the particular instance – here, the standpoint of the 'ordinary citizen'. From the standpoint of the economy as a whole, they are counterweights to capitalism's tipping point – the 'grotesque form of absurd contradiction' that is the 'social form of wealth as a thing external to [the social production of wealth]' (Marx, 1977b: 574). The simultaneous empirical reality of underconsumption and overconsumption is a phenomenon observed not only by Baran and Sweezy but also, characteristically more gnomically, by Bataille (1988: 39) when he writes that:

> As a rule, *particular* existence always risks succumbing for lack of resources. It contrasts with *general* existence whose resources are in excess and for which death has

no meaning. From the *particular* point of view, the problems are posed *in the first instance* by a deficiency of resources. They are posed *in the first instance* by an excess of resources if one starts from the *general* point of view.

Bataille and Baran and Sweezy are, of course, intellectual worlds away from each other, yet both observe that societies are sliced into contradictory polarities by scarcity/restriction and surplus/excess.[17] In Bataille's exposition, 'excess' is a fundamental condition of life originating from the fact that solar energy is given 'without any return' and exemplifies the 'seething energy' that constantly exceeds the possibility of its total consumption (1988: 28, 31). In Sweezy's (and Baran and Sweezy's) account, the 'surplus' is a socially generated glut of commodities (including services) whose deleterious consequences are the result of the anarchic misapplication of the forces of production under capitalism. Bataille, in fact, explicitly denies that his work is a contribution to debates about 'crises of overproduction' (1988: 13) and the political reflections that comprise the final two chapters of *The Accursed Share* veer between Stalinist realpolitik (on the brutality of Soviet collectivization practices) and Hegelian idealism (on 'consciousness of the ultimate end of wealth'). Sweezy, on the other hand, construes the overproduction/underconsumption couplet to exhibit the contours of political rule, of the social regimentation of the material world to service private property and capital accumulation. The generation of capitalist surplus does indeed involve the rapaciously mercenary exploitation of any and all resources, but this 'overconsumption' is precisely one face of capitalism's contradictory coinage whose flip side is the restriction of access to – and control over – those resources in a politically regulated economy of underconsumption. Waste policy, in all its ambiguous and ambivalent appearances, rearticulates again and again the political contradictions of capital accumulation.

Some light can be shed on this politics by reconsidering Claus Offe's (1984) essay on the state and social policy. In that essay, Offe writes that social policy:

> consists of answers to what might be called the *internal* problem of the state apparatus, namely, how it can react *consistently* to the two poles of the 'needs' of labour and capital – in other words, how to make them mutually compatible. (1984: 104; emphasis in original)

The internal problems of the state apparatus arise from the fact that it is pulled in two different directions (or split into two political forms) by the contradictory demands of capitalist accumulation and capitalist socialization – that is, on the one hand the demand for the expansion of surplus value and the development of means of production to achieve this expansion and, on the other, capital's need for a disciplined labour force, compliant with the strictures of wage labour and able to reproduce itself *as* wage labour. In this vision of a split political apparatus, the state is:

> characterized by constitutional and organizational structures whose specific selectivity is designed to reconcile and harmonize the 'privately regulated' capitalist economy with the processes of socialisation this economy triggers. (Offe, 1984: 51)

The Sociological Review, 60:S2, pp. 192–211 (2013), DOI: 10.1111/1467-954X.12045

The push-pull of privatized and socialized supervision plunges the state apparatus into a constant condition of crisis[18] in relation to capitalist accumulation; a crisis which consists in the problem of supplying regulatory services to the economy without politicizing that regulation and thereby opening up the whole capitalist system to social oversight and political scrutiny. In Offe's construction of social policy, the state apparatus transacts welfare transfers with the social sphere for loyalty to – or compliance with – the framework of capitalist accumulation. At the same time, the state apparatus transacts regulatory services with the economic sphere for fiscal inputs to fund the framework of capitalist accumulation. In this system of transactions, the economy needs to be 'insulated' from problems and conflicts that may arise in the social system of family, community, social and trade institutions and unions, and so on. This is achieved, importantly, through the distribution of income transfers from the private sphere of the economy to the public sphere of society. The purpose of these transfers – in the form of welfare services and income support – is to rationalize the framework of social power that underpins capital accumulation. In this circumstance, state social policy is directed towards the task of supplying capital with what it needs to continue and expand private appropriation: labour power. In Offe's (1984: 98) terms, therefore, such policy is not a 'reaction' to the 'problem' of the working class, 'rather it ineluctably contributes to the *constitution* of the working class'. In short:

> social policy is the state's manner of effecting the lasting transformation of non-wage labourers into wage labourers. (Offe, 1984: 92)

The reason I have taken this short sojourn into political sociology is because Offe hints at, but does not develop, a potential route into untangling and overviewing, in sociological terms, the characteristic complexity of waste policy discussed above. For, insofar as labour is constituted, at least in part, through state policies designed to transform dispossessed labour power into 'active' wage labour (1984: 99), then the question immediately arises as to whether state policies, on the other side of the equation, similarly constitute, at least in part, capital. That is, if labour does not lift itself by its own bootstraps into the condition of *wage* labour then it is reasonable to propose that capital does not lift itself by its own bootstraps into *accumulated* capital. In other words, if state policy transforms potential labour into actual labour then it can also be argued that state policy transforms potential capital into actual capital. Thus, Offe's thesis on the constitution of wage labour can be reformulated to apply to the constitution of capital accumulation by noting that the transformation of potential capital into actual capital 'does not occur through the market alone but must be sanctioned by a political structure of rule, through state power' (1984: 99).

The capitalist market cannot be left to effect the transformation by its own mechanisms alone because, in political terms, it is too weakly structured. By this, I mean that the capitalist market is rooted in, but not genetically dominated by, what Offe calls the exchange principle.[19] To the extent that, in theory at least, the market allows exchanges of any kind between any individuals, it lacks a sanctioned mechanism of *compliant* exchange within a capitalist social framework and thus leaves open the possibility for markets themselves to undermine capitalism's normative structures of exchange and distribution. Citizens, left to their own devices and operating only according to a logic of exchange, may decide to build alternative economies by, for example, transforming the redundant resources of capitalist abundance into useable goods. They may decide that the millions of tons of discarded supermarket food supplies represent a fine larder for supplying a hearty Sunday meal. They may, after all, decide that the leftover commodities of capitalist exchange can satisfy a proportion of their material needs sufficient to substitute for a portion of their wage labour, thereby eroding the principle of compliance through which state social policy constitutes wage labour for capitalist exploitation in the first place. These examples are intended to illustrate that if social policy is an attempt to make the needs of labour and capital mutually compatible by intervening in the rights, relationships and arrangements by which (potential) labour power is lastingly transformed into (actual) wage labour in the sphere of compliance then it can be argued that waste policy provides the same kinds of services in the lasting transformation of potential capital into actual capital in the sphere of exchange.

In its regulatory specifications and bureaucratic taxonomies, waste policy defines who can and who cannot profit from the surplus that capitalism produces. The EWC and its surrounding interpretive labyrinth is not merely a 'list' of wastes. Rather, it is a flowchart of allowances and permissions for waste's exploitation. It intervenes into the rights, relationships and arrangements through which capitalism's surplus is configured for exploitation by sanctioned agents whilst at the same time ensuring that the crisis of overproduction in the sphere of exchange does not spill over into a crisis of legitimation in the social sphere and thereby a crisis of capitalist accumulation as a whole. By this analysis, it can be argued that waste policy is not a 'reaction' to the 'problem' of capitalist surplus; rather, it ineluctably contributes to the *constitution* of the surplus and is the state's manner of 'effecting the lasting transformation' of non-accumulating capital into actively accumulating capital.

The regulatory services supplied by the state apparatus not only define (contradictorily and inconsistently) the substances, sectors and industrial processes that surround waste's exploitation: they also define and enforce the exclusions, demarcations and barriers that preclude, criminalize and demonize interference into the cosmological order of capitalist surplus management. Unsurprisingly, in this circumstance, any material substance from which surplus value may be realized is slowly but inexorably drawn into the orbit of capitalist appropriation. The (potentially unintentional) freegans – Steven De Geynst and Sacha Hall – described above may not knowingly constitute the 'forces of socialism' whose 'head-on collision' with state power was, according to Sweezy (1962), the only means of abolishing the institution of private property. They represent, nonetheless, forces of non-capitalist socialization which capital has no choice but to counter. As others have observed (see Ferrell, 2006; Eighner, 1994), scavenging and foraging networks comprise alternative arrangements for exploiting materials of all kinds – they involve *unsanctioned* agents of transformation and distribution of material residues whose actions negate both the compliance mechanisms that effect the 'lasting transformation' of non-wage labour into wage labour and the normative mechanisms by which capitalist exchange accrues surplus value for capitalists.[20] After all, the very reason why 'our friend [the capitalist] has a penal code of his own', according to Marx, is because:

> all wasteful consumption of raw material or instruments of labour is strictly forbidden, because what is so is so wasted, represents labour superfluously expended, labour that does not count in the product or enter into its value. (Marx, 1977a: 190–191)[21]

In a previous paper (O'Brien, 1999b) I quipped that whilst there are UK minerals authorities that control all the minerals beneath the UK there is, currently, no UK waste authority that controls all the rubbish in your attic or your kitchen swing-bin. Yet, from the level of freeganic behaviour to the level of European policy, this possibility is itself slowly becoming a *de facto* reality. There may be no single authority controlling all waste – but government guidelines, European case law and sectoral realignments are inexorably coming to define even surplus food as a resource akin to mineral wealth. There's gold (or, at least, fuel) in them-there waste receptacles[22] – and where there's gold there's a state-supported structure of exploitation that marginalizes, criminalizes and demonizes alternative solutions to capital accumulation. In this structure of exploitation, surplus food stocks are transformed into scarce feedstocks in an economy desperately combating stagnation. As I have shown, this transformation spins webs across national and European legal regimes, waste 'catalogues' and policies, technological developments in materials reprocessing, rearticulations of food as a fuel, the licensing and certification of sanctioned users and the criminalization and exclusion of non-sanctioned users. So, the next time you discard the last half-potato from your plate into the organics box and leave it for your local authority to collect, remember that whilst you may have discarded it you have most certainly not thrown it away. Instead, you have siphoned it into a political economic channel which converts it from a private leftover to a capitalist surplus. In this way, its 'value' can be recharged, revitalized and disbursed to corporations as a counteracting tendency to the depletion of profits established by the structure of underconsumption.

Concluding remarks

The issue in this chapter has been to provide a sociological account of food waste that does not demonize ordinary people; one that situates the critique of excess not in the ignorant, sordid voraciousness of individual citizens but in the structures and institutions of capitalist accumulation. I have considered the mismatch between the potential and the actual through the concrete lens of social transformation rather than the abstract lens of ethical critique: specifically, through the convoluted political and economic strategies for transforming discarded (but not discarded) muffins and waffles into exploitable commodities and services. I do not deny my own or anyone else's wastefulness – I do not deny that I am a statistical entry in a larger measurement of the propensity to eject and exude environmentally damaging quantities of 'stuff'. What I propose is that the over-production of capitalist surplus renders my – and my fellow citizens' – efforts to avoid (where possible) and manage (where not) these wastes worthy at least of proper acknowledgement. I live in a capitalist society that produces much more than it can possibly consume, whilst the surplus value generated by all this stuff accrues as idle capital in the hands of tiny numbers of individuals and millions die from want of basic necessities.

According to Marx, all waste is anathema to capitalism so, rather than reducing the waste, capitalism instead defines it as 'goods' from which surplus value may be realized – and then triumphantly celebrates its technological wizardry in transforming the consequences of underconsumption into scarce energy and fertilizer commodities. The free distribution of food 'represents labour superfluously expended' and cannot, within a capitalist social formation, be permitted to flourish as anything other than a marginal activity.

The imagination of waste is always immediately an imagination of the social conditions of production, distribution and consumption; of social relations and social norms; of moral outlooks on how society is and how it ought to be. To imagine that surplus food stocks are 'renewable' energy feedstocks is to imagine a society in which production is expanded 'without any reference to the consumption which alone can give it meaning'. In this respect, the management of capitalist surplus is a neat shorthand for the monumentally complex contours of waste policy and serves to explain the fierce restrictions on deriving value from that surplus in ways that do not support capital accumulation. So, finally, to 'discard food' means to convert a non- or potential value into a positive or actual value – but *only* within a regulated regime of exploitation in which the alchemists of the rubbish society (O'Brien, 1999b: 280) put a bag of muffins into a political top hat, tap it with a technological stick, and, following a litany of bureaucratic and legal incantations, pull out a shovel of coal.

Notes

1 See   http://www.independent.co.uk/environment/nature/a-mountain-of-trash-china-closes-everest-for-cleanup-857661.html and http://www.ecology.com/2008/08/14/pacific-plastic-waste-dump/ (accessed 21 April 2012).

2 See   http://www.conservatives.com/News/Speeches/2009/10/George_Osborne_We_will_lead_the_economy_out_of_crisis.aspx (accessed 7 May 2012).

3 See http://www.flanderstoday.eu/content/offside-no-such-thing-free-muffin and http://s4ss.org/337/food-for-thought-the-case-of-the-muffin-man/ (accessed 21 April 2012).

4 See 'In court charged with theft by finding, the woman who took food from a Tesco bin' http://www.dailymail.co.uk/news/article-1357741/In-court-charged-theft-finding-woman-took-

food-Tesco-bin.html#ixzz1uw1AzL8f and 'Sentence for "Waffle One" ', *Essex Chronicle*, 23 June 2011. http://www.highbeam.com/doc/1P2-28981984.html (accessed 13 April 2012). See also http://discardstudies.wordpress.com/2012/03/27/dumpsters-muffins-waste-and-law/ (accessed 13 April 2012).

5   See http://www.biogas-info.co.uk/index.php/ad-basics.html (accessed 13 April 2012).

6   See http://www.cakenergy.com/default.aspx and also 'Food waste to provide green gas for carbon-conscious consumers', *The Observer*, Sunday 22 November 2009, http://www. guardian.co.uk/environment/2009/nov/22/food-waste-green-biogas-tariff, (accessed 7 May 2012).

7   Tripe: 1. from the lining of the stomach of some ruminants, used as a source of food. 2. Something, especially speech or writing, that is false or worthless; rubbish. http://dictionary. reference.com/browse/tripe (accessed 4 April 2012).

8   The actual waste catalogue developed in Council Decision 2000/532/EC is different to the list provided in Annex 1 of Directive 2006/12/EC. In fact, Directive 2006/12/EC lists only sixteen Chapters instead of twenty (and omits the detailed list). In spite of this difference, national guidelines invariably refer to the 'List of Wastes' (the LOW) contained in Decision 2000/532/EC. See, for example, Environment Agency (2006) *Using the List of Wastes to Code Waste* (available at http://www.environment-agency.gov.uk/static/documents/ Business/low_guide_v1.2_1397222.pdf). Directive 2006/12/EC updated and emended Decision 94/3/EC which responded to Council Directive 75/442/EEC on waste (accessed 7 May 2012).

9   See http://www.alamut.com/subj/artiface/language/johnWilkins.html (accessed 3 July 2009).

10   See Commission Communication of 21 February 2007 on the Interpretative Communication on waste and by-products [COM(2007) 59 final – not published in the *Official Journal*], http://eur-lex.europa.eu/LexUriServ/site/en/com/2007/com2007_0059en01.pdf.

11   See *Commission v Italy*. Judgment of the Court (Third Chamber), 18 December 2007, http://curia. europa.eu/juris/showPdf.jsf;jsessionid=9ea7d2dc30dbf938d97bdd85423fa56d8d79eac6160e.e34 KaxiLc3qMb40Rch0SaxuKaNr0?text=&docid=71919&pageIndex=0&doclang=en&mode=doc &dir=&occ=first&part=1&cid=1952634 (accessed 7 May 2012).

12   See *Commission v Italy*, para. 34: 'the EWC is 'intended only as guidance . . . and the classification of a substance or object as waste is to be inferred primarily from the holder's actions and the meaning of the term "discard" '.

13   See *Commission v Belgium*, Judgment of the Court, 9 July 1992, Case C-2/90, http://eur-lex.europa.eu/LexUriServ/LexUriServ.do?uri=CELEX:61990CJ0002:EN:PDF (accessed 4 May 2012).

14   Which states that: 'Quantitative restrictions on imports and all measures having equivalent effect shall . . . be prohibited between Member States.'

15   There are different versions of this comment which, originally, was a bracketed aside in Marx's text and was incorporated into the main body by Engels. The version in the 1977 Moore and Aveling translation (which draws extensively on the Charles H. Kerr edition) runs: 'The ultimate reason for all real crises always remains the poverty and restricted consumption of the masses as opposed to the drive of capitalist production to develop the productive forces as though only the absolute consuming power of society constituted their limit'. See Marx (1977b: 484).

16   See 'Population: overconsumption is the real problem', http://www.newscientist.com/article/ mg20327271.700-population-overconsumption-is-the-real-problem.html and 'Overconsumption? Our use of the world's natural resources', http://www.foe.co.uk/resource/reports/over consumption.pdf (accessed 8 April 2012).

17   See Bataille's discussion of 'India's possibilities of industrial growth' (1988: 39): 'On the one hand, there appears the need for an exudation; on the other hand, the need for a growth' – where exudation represents the expenditure of energy without return (or waste) (1988: 23) whilst growth represents the absorption of excess (1988: 21) or 'conformity with the balancing of accounts' (Bataille, 1985: 128).

18   Offe distinguishes between a concept of 'sporadic crisis' – which refers to an event or events that are 'acute, catastrophic, surprising and unforeseeable' and his preferred concept of 'processual

crisis' – which refers to the 'grammar' and 'mechanisms' that generate events. See Offe (1984: 36–37).

19 See Offe (1984) on normative structures, exchange relationships and coercive relationships, and on the elaboration of these terms in his model of the state apparatus.

20 See http://freegan.info/ which announces that freeganism turns essentially on 'strategies for sustainable living beyond capitalism' (accessed 25 June 2012).

21 As Marx observes, capital 'produces essentially capital, and does so only to the extent that it produces surplus value' (Marx, 1977b: 880).

22 'Pots of it' (Swanton, 1998: vii).

References

Baran, P. A. and Sweezy, P. M., (1970 [1966]), *Monopoly Capital: An Essay on the American Economic and Social Order*, Harmondsworth: Penguin.

Bataille, G., (1985), 'The notion of expenditure', in A. Stoekl (ed.), *Visions of Excess: Selected Writings*, trans. A. Stoekl, C. R. Lovitt and D. M. Leslie, Jr, 116–29, Minneapolis, MN: University of Minnesota Press.

Bataille, G., (1988), *The Accursed Share: An Essay on General Economy. Volume I: Consumption*, trans. R. Hurley, New York: Zone Books. Originally published as *La Part Maudite*, 1967 by Les Editions de Minuit.

Bauman, Z., (2000), *Liquid Modernity*, Cambridge: Polity Press.

Bauman, Z., (2004), *Wasted Lives: Modernity and its Outcasts*, Cambridge: Polity Press.

Department of the Environment, Food and Rural Affairs (DEFRA), (2010), *Consultation on the Legal Definition of Waste and its Application*, London: DEFRA. Available at: http://www.defra.gov.uk/corporate/consult/waste-definition/index.htm (accessed 4 May 2012).

Department of the Environment, Food and Rural Affairs (DEFRA), (2011), *Government Review of Waste Policy in England*, London: DEFRA.

Eighner, L., (1994), *Travels with Lizbeth: Three Years on the Road and on the Streets*, New York: Ballantine Books.

Evans, D., (2011), 'Blaming the consumer – once again: the social and material contexts of everyday food waste practices in some English households', *Critical Public Health*, 21 (4): 429–440.

Evans, D., (2012), 'Beyond the throwaway society: ordinary domestic practice and a sociological approach to household food waste', *Sociology*, 46 (1): 43–58.

Ferrell, J., (2006), *Empire of Scrounge: Inside the Urban Underground of Dumpster Diving, Trash Picking and Street Scavenging*, New York: New York University Press.

Gregson, N., (2007), *Living with Things: Ridding, Accommodation, Dwelling*, Wantage: Sean Kingston Publishing.

Gregson, N., Metcalfe, A. and Crewe, L., (2007), 'Moving things along: the conduits and practices of divestment in consumption', *Transactions of the Institute of British Geographers*, 32 (2): 187–200.

Marx, K., (1977a [1867]), *Capital: A Critique of Political Economy*, in F. Engels (ed.), Volume I: *The Process of Production of Capital*, trans. S. Moore and E. Aveling, London: Lawrence & Wishart.

Marx, K., (1977b [1894]), *Capital: A Critique of Political Economy*, in F. Engels (ed.), Volume III: *The Process of Capitalist Production as a Whole*, trans. S. Moore and E. Aveling, London: Lawrence & Wishart.

O'Brien, M., (1999a), 'Rubbish power: towards a sociology of the rubbish society', in J. Hearn and S. Roseneil (eds), *Consuming Cultures: Power and Resistance*, 262–277, Basingstoke: MacMillan.

O'Brien, M., (1999b), 'Rubbish values: reflections on the political economy of waste', *Science as Culture*, 8 (3): 269–295.

O'Brien, M., (2008), *A Crisis of Waste? Understanding the Rubbish Society*, New York: Routledge.

Offe, C., (1984), *Contradictions of the Welfare State*, London: Hutchinson & Co.

Packard, V., (1967 [1960]), *The Waste Makers*, Harmondsworth: Penguin.

The Sociological Review, 60:S2, pp. 192–211 (2013), DOI: 10.1111/1467-954X.12045

Pearce, F., (2008), *Confessions of an Eco-Sinner*, London: Transworld Publishers.

Sayers, D., (1948), *Creed or Chaos? And Other Essays in Popular Theology*, London: The Religious Book Club.

Scanlan, J., (2005), *On Garbage*, London: Reaktion Books.

Stuart, T., (2009), *Waste: Uncovering the Global Food Scandal*, London: Penguin.

Swanton, O., (1998), 'Tips for fortune-seekers', *The Guardian Higher*, 3 February.

Sweezy, P. M., (1962 [1942]), *The Theory of Capitalist Development: Principles of Marxian Political Economy*, London: Dennis Dobson Ltd.

Talbot, F., (1919), *Millions from Waste*, London: T. Fisher Unwin.

Tammemagi, H., (1999), *The Waste Crisis: Landfills, Incinerators, and the Search for a Sustainable Future*, Oxford: Oxford University Press.

Tucker, R. P., (2000), *Insatiable Appetite: The United States and the Ecological Degradation of the Tropical World*, Berkeley, CA: University of California Press.

Viljoen, A. and Wiskerke, H. (eds), (2012), *Sustainable Food Planning: Evolving Theory and Practice*, Wageningen, Netherlands: Wageningen Academic.

Young, J. E., (1991), *Discarding the Throwaway Society* (Worldwatch Paper 101), Washington, DC: Worldwatch Institute.

The disposal of place: facing modernity in the kitchen-diner

Rolland Munro

Abstract: The aim of this paper is to suggest how the material turn in sociology could benefit from a re-theorizing around wider understandings of disposal. The argument is that it is not enough to document how spaces for dwelling are produced and consumed; their building and use also entail a *disposal of place* that has to account for how the materials that make up a dwelling get arranged and 'placed' as moralities. Taking spaces for living and eating as its object of analysis, each section of this paper examines a different aspect of modernity, bringing the kitchen-diner 'front stage'. Avoiding a ubiquitous conflation of disposal with waste – whereby 'excess' is dismissed out of hand as redundant and non-productive to design – the analysis goes on to suggest how modernity advances its orders through our making the 'belongings' of collective identity more detachable and by our thinning the 'stickiness' of cultural institutions.

Keywords: consumption, disposal, dwelling, identity, modernity, moral, order, place, waste

Introduction

This paper explores some material underpinnings to identity in the modern home by attending to the key notion of disposal. Despite indications to the contrary, consideration of materials in sociology is not altogether new – having roots in Marx's historical materialism on the one hand and work like that of Simmel and Mauss on the other. It is fair to say though that if the mainstay of the first settled quickly around the means of *production*, with a focus on domination in the workplace, the second has led to materials being championed as modes of *consumption*, giving heightened attention to custom and ritual over disposable spending in the home and elsewhere (eg Appadurai, 1986; Csikzentmihalyi and Rochberg-Halton, 1981). Certainly the more contemporary emphasis on materials, in its attention to embodiment, actor-networks, and the practices of everyday life, may not only have been unlocking too hard and fast divisions between the workplace and the home, but has opened up questions of domination, both economic and cultural. Yet much analysis

The Sociological Review, 60:S2, pp. 212–231 (2013), DOI: 10.1111/1467-954X.12046

overlooks the priority of disposal as a term for understanding the placing and arranging of materials and debate remains locked into a seesaw of production and consumption perspectives, as if these act as separable functions or exist in different realms. For the purposes of this paper, I take disposal – the placing and arranging of things – to be antecedent therefore to both production and consumption modes and, in what follows, explore how this ongoing placing and re-placing of materials affects the moral framing of our worlds.

The aim of this paper is to suggest how the material turn in sociology, with its close attention to mundane matters from shopping (Shields, 1992) to art in the home (Leach, 2002), might benefit from a re-theorizing around the wider meanings of disposal. Positioned as a mere consequence of consumption, rather than its antecedent, discussion on disposal to date is far too restrictive in both scope and content. Addressing what they take to be profligacy in contemporary society, far too many studies press ethical responsibility onto the consumer (eg Cooper, 2005; Shaw and Newholm, 2002), or restrict disposal to the intricacies of getting rid of things (eg Hawkins, 2000, 2006). It is as if what is 'left over' from the production and consumption process can only register redundancy and inefficiency in society. That waste is prefigured in this way is perhaps no accident.

A particular feature of modernity is the way in which modern ideas of order narrow down to design (Bauman, 2004), expelling what no longer fits into production or consumption as 'rubbish' and 'waste'. In privileging the somewhat old-fashioned term 'disposal' over modernist injunctions of 'order', I am seeking instead to recover a wider range of meanings to disposal than are usually attached by virtue of its contemporary conflation with the problem of 'getting rid of things'. As is conveyed through the concept of 'disposable income', as well as the familiar adage 'Man proposes, God disposes', disposal carries profound meanings about how we exercise discretion over the placing and arranging of things.

Against views that expect markets to arrange everything around individual choice, I take dwelling in modernity (Heidegger, 1993a; Latimer and Munro, 2009) to be 'structured' in preset ways by social institutions. My thinking here owes much to the historical materialism of Marx, but avoids the more grand and overly deterministic interpretations that elide the importance of everyday conduct (see also Miller, 2008). To this end I assume that we exercise *discretion* (Barnes, 1988; Munro, 1999), from moment to moment, in our placing and arranging of materials. Specifically, this continuous exercise of discretion results in our producing and recreating 'places' of identity and belonging that affect our moral sensibilities; inciting us in what we wish to do, by, say, our being in our study, or feel we cannot do, because, say, we are in someone else's office. Or, again, there are places that help us to 'remember' what we want to eat or drink, in the form, say, of a cafe or take-away shop. As such the dispersal and distribution of worlds into 'places' helps activate our enrolments, punctualizes with whom we enjoin (Munro, 2004), and alters (however marginally) expenditure on matters such as comfort, regard and companionship. In this last respect, Alan

Blum's (2003) work on 'scenes' as places 'to be seen' picks up nicely Simmel's (1972) earlier work on the city.

Such affectual work is well caught by the phrase 'to dispose others towards us', found in early novels such as *The Female Quixote* (Lennox, 1989 [1752]). If the phrase has since fallen out of fashion, this should not be understood to signify the absence of such affectual work today. To the contrary, volumes of self-help books and manuals (Hochschild, 2012), including the resilient popularity of Dale Carnegie's (1936) *How to Win Friends and Influence People*, register an *outsourcing* of identity work from institutions to what Goffman (1959) calls 'front' or 'face work' by individuals. What is lost in much discussion of the management of impressions, however, are not only Goffman's own wider meanings of 'face' – in his acute attention to our moment to moment negotiation of social institutions – but other aspects of identity and belonging that either emphasize the materiality of the body (Shilling, 2008) or go beyond face-to-face interaction, such as collective effervescence (Shilling and Mellor, 2001).

In what follows I extend Goffman's meaning of 'front' to the home, using this term to cover our placing and arranging of materials 'to dispose others towards us'. A first point here is to emphasize, over and above what has already been indicated in respect of face work, how much we pre-arrange *material* forms to advertise our identity and belonging. We do not wait to move materials around in response to what is happening in the here and now; but rather, as I go on to discuss later, move materials around in respect of ways that anticipate the future. The second point is to stress how much 'front' can ease face work; much of what follows unpicks how a division between front and face is worked, on occasions, to promote ourselves, variously, as artistic, inclusive, modern, cosmopolitan and democratic. The third point is to indicate how the material forms of modernity incorporate a moral outlook that can nonetheless pre-empt who we think we are. Specifically, I draw attention to how design – in its modern sense – 'outcasts' certain ways of being and that this may, in turn, intensify lines of flight that transform other areas of dwelling into their going backstage.

Disposal beyond waste

Disposal is typically related in the literature – negatively – to waste. Although both Thompson's (1979) typology of different kinds of rubbish and O'Brien's (1999) commentary on the 'rubbish society' are salutary, their analyses fail to go far enough to unpick this unfortunate conflation of disposal with the more reductive notions of waste. Similarly, while important work such as that conducted by Gregson *et al.* (2007) show 'saving' and 'wasting' to be simultaneous practices that are critical to materializing identities and the key social relations of family and home, most writings by-pass Bataille's insights on 'excess' and ignore anthropological work on such matters as the 'potlatch'. Thus the meanings of disposal in its everyday sense of material arrangement and placing

The Sociological Review, 60:S2, pp. 212–231 (2013), DOI: 10.1111/1467-954X.12046

are elided and, with this, much of the moral ordering of place and space is overlooked.

In drawing on Douglas's (1966, 1975) seminal work on the polluting qualities of 'matter out of place', some of my own work also did too little to overthrow this tendency to conflate disposal with waste. Aiming, for instance, to illustrate how disposal is antecedent to consumption, I drew on Marshall's (1990) link between a lack of eating fish in the north-east of England to its smelling in the fridge and stinking in the rubbish bin. While this example was intended to underline how people living in an area with a plentiful supply of cheap and nutritious food might exclude it from their lifeworld (Munro, 1995), my emphasis on the difficulties they experienced in disposing of 'leftovers' appears to have merely reinforced the prevailing view that equates disposal with waste. The same fate awaited another article on disposal (Munro, 1998), inasmuch as Hetherington (2004: 164), while accepting my critique of modern academic research as overly aimed at the disposal of perceived 'gaps' in knowledge, nonetheless read me to be addressing what he took to be the 'problem' of waste.

My writings on disposal, however, have had much larger aims, the first appearing some twenty years ago (Munro, 2001 [1992]). Beginning with the existential problem of our disposing of unwanted meanings (see also Strathern, 1999) rather than materials, I imagined the body as always comporting itself in one 'pose' or another in an ongoing presentation of self in everyday life (Goffman, 1959). Inasmuch as rites of passage, rituals, ceremonies and institutions involve us 'passing' (Garfinkel, 1967) as members who uphold socially available practices and occasions, it is possible to see the body as thus needing to *dis*-pose of itself accordingly. This is to say that one has to conduct oneself appropriately in order to 'duct' oneself through one or another of the ports or passages that institutions and customs open up for everyday conduct.

Picking up on the extent to which this attention to everyday consumption might be revolutionizing the entrenchment of sociology in production perspectives, I then wrote on what I called 'the consumption view' of self. Drawing on Marilyn Strathern's (1991) seminal thinking on the prosthesis of relations, I stressed the importance of considering the endless *detachment* of materials alongside their 'attachment'. Extension, in its Heideggerian sense, I argued, does not entail each of us going out from a core self and back again in a kind of magnification or diminishment of self; to the contrary, extension is something we are always 'in' (Munro, 1996).

Inasmuch as we are always in one kind of material relations or another, it is more than likely that we conduct ourselves in ways that avoid attachments whose disposal might prove problematic (literally and metaphorically) for ducting ourselves mundanely through the 'passages' ahead. For example, although doctors are reputed to wave their stethoscopes at police when stopped by them for speeding, it would be unusual to find any doctor displaying the same item at a social event they intended to enjoy. Beyond these more portable items, however, it is possible to conjecture that we deliberately, if unwittingly, distribute materials in detachable ways that leave a variety of 'places' at our disposal. If this is so, then it would seem that the layout of our dwelling places may be less functional than at first appears and more revealing of the paradoxes in how we live. As a first step in this exploration, it would seem important to clarify the different extensions that are afforded – in terms of attachments and detachments – by the sociological distinction between 'face' and 'front'.

Fronting the place

What then about the contemporary disposal of the home? In asking what a fashionable placing of space displays about eating and entertaining practices, my starting point is with the notion of *front*, a term Erving Goffman (1959) deploys sometimes in place of face. While a child's drawing of a house resembles a face (with the door as the mouth and the windows as eyes), the idea of front allows us to go beneath the surface form and examine how internal changes to the material orderings of space within the home affect consumption (and so in turn structure production). It is in this 'pose' of front that the home can be taken to reflect the dispositions of the family towards hospitality and the intake of food.

The generally accepted story of the house is one of an appropriation of the public space around which the English built their houses in the Middle Ages and its subsequent sub-division into the creation of private places. Over the centuries this re-disposal of space has involved shrinking the great hall – into which everyone was received and ate together – and dividing it up into different kinds of reception rooms. The appearance in the sixteenth century, for instance, of the 'withdrawing' room – into which the family could dispose of itself to gain some privacy – gave way by the eighteenth century to additional separate rooms, such as the library, the morning room and the dining room.

While retaining sleeping quarters as separate bedrooms, recent shifts within architecture reverse this individuation of rooms and reopen up the space inside the skin of any building. Some open-plan rooms even mimic the earlier grandeur of the great halls by having their ceilings lifted upwards to incorporate the erstwhile upper floor, or by displacing lofts in order to create so-called cathedral roofs. In all this the elimination of the reception hall has continued: what was once the fulcrum, around which everything moved (and which remained so even throughout the Tudor, Georgian, Victorian and Edwardian periods), is seen today as redundant; not so much the 'waist of the house' as a 'waste of space'.

Open plan living rooms may also engross themselves today by incorporating the residual space once given over to passageways and corridors – gone are those long, dark inner 'tubes' linking bedrooms to bathrooms or connecting kitchens to dining rooms. Indeed, the tubes of importance are no longer the conduits for people to travel back and forth between the different forms of public and private spaces, but those that pipe in broadband, electricity, water and under-floor heating; each placing the services of light, power and running water at our

The Sociological Review, 60:S2, pp. 212–231 (2013), DOI: 10.1111/1467-954X.12046
© 2013 The Author. Editorial organisatio © 2013 The Editorial Board of the Sociological Review

instant disposal (albeit much traffic for television, telephone and Internet is now 'wireless').

This re-disposal of space in the home is accompanied by a particularly striking shift in the locus for disposable income over the past twenty or so years. What was once lavished on the living area – the so-called 'front room' – is now directed in many homes towards making a kitchen-diner. Such a dramatic change in the locus of spending suggests more is going on than a mere inversion in taste and may indeed reflect something other than a switch in 'lifestyle'. Are families shifting consumption away from a more formal keeping up of appearances? Or, more mundanely perhaps, are they simply redirecting production in the home towards the busy realities of working lives?

The changing face of the kitchen

In focusing on the advent of the kitchen-diner it is tempting to talk about a 'post-tourist' turnabout (Urry, 2002), in which visitors to the home are no longer contained to the public rooms but are taken backstage to witness its workings. Guests are no longer to be kept at the 'front' of house: ushered in through the front door ahead of being received in the front hall, before being ducted onwards into the front room. Today they often go directly into the previously proscribed 'backstage region' (Goffman, 1959) of the kitchen, the very place within which they are able to view the 'production' of the hospitality they anticipate enjoying.

Within this apparent reversion of the reception area for visitors, it is important to note that what is also being signalled is an associated inversion in those areas of the house that are tacitly – or even explicitly – being used as the 'public space'. In reading how the upwardly mobile dispose of both their time and their guests, we can consider the extent to which the former backstage – the kitchen – is now made *front stage*. The well-known author Ian Rankin, for example, in a dramatic break with convention, was reported several years ago as putting his new kitchen into the drawing room of his large house in Edinburgh.

As I recall from childhood visits to mansion houses in the posh residential district of Merchiston, the subsequent home of Rankin and other crime writers, the 'front room' in Scotland was a cold, inhospitable place. Like their distant relation – the 'state rooms' of ducal palaces – the front room was generally reserved for the reception of visitors. Indeed, as the formal 'face' of the family, the place was orientated to hosting the outer world, rather than being open to the consumption of those mainly confined to the remaining rooms. Boasting the best furniture of the house, with prize ornaments standing proudly on a surfeit of surfaces – from mantelpiece to numerous display cabinets – the whole ensemble was veneered towards generating an outward display of opulence.

It is noteworthy that even in the tenement flats of the lower middle class in Edinburgh, the front room was seldom used and often was left unheated except for special occasions, such as Christmas. Kitchens, by comparison, were typically the warmest and busiest room in the house. Even in houses with access to a separate dining room, meals were often taken at the well-scrubbed kitchen table, either for convenience or to keep children away from the ubiquitous ornaments on display on the mahogany table (and from breaking the more expensive crockery and glassware either on display or stored away in sideboards for special occasions). For all this, kitchens were often rather dark cramped places with brown painted walls and mottled linoleum floors. Unlike the light and immaculately dusted front room, whose windows literally fronted onto the street, kitchens were typically placed at the back of the house or tucked out of the way in basements (along with children and servants).

Those working in these 'backstage' regions – typically the daily domestic or female counterpart of the household – looked out through net-curtained windows over giant porcelain sinks onto the backs of other houses. These 'backs' were often grim places, distinguished by coal sheds and oddments of household rubbish including the dustbins, all bordering onto strips of unkempt garden hosting endless washing lines. Inside, the cascades of drying plates and pans, the dusty shelves of endless storage jars, the empty milk bottles in the window, and the wet washing hanging from the pulley above the mangle in a corner all combined to convey the messy ordering of domestic life.

Cosmopolitanism comes home

Modernism, in this sense, can usefully be thought of as a triumph in the aesthetics of disposal. Gone is all that detritus of the old backstage kitchen, now replaced by the 'white goods' that drive much mass production. Yet this is not to claim (with the possible exception of large retro-style American fridges) that this domestic machinery is kept on view. To the contrary, and unlike the refrigerator proudly displayed in the centre of the family living room in V. S. Naipaul's (1957) humorous story, the fridge, freezer, dishwasher and washing machine are now typically hidden away behind fitted units.

While domestic machines necessarily have to be ready-to-hand, their ubiquity in the West removes any need for them to be left on permanent display. Indeed, with only the lack of mess betraying their presence as labour-saving devices, these arrangements do more than conform to a modernist sense of order. To the knowing eye, it is this very effacement of household chores that emphasizes the occasional and intermittent nature of their use: no 'modern' woman or househusband is tied to their chores in the kitchen all day. To the contrary, the kitchen-diner is now somewhere to linger and enjoy; it is a space intended to magnify one's being in the world, rather than diminish it.

Adding to this sense of modernity is the effect of the kitchen-diner being global in reach. Although North American in origin, the contemporary kitchen is a place that also lets its inhabitants celebrate their Western-style centrality as 'cultural omnivores' (Tampubolon, 2010). It is not only the family food that ostensibly comes from 'afar' (Barthes, 1972) in today's worldwide markets –

The Sociological Review, 60:S2, pp. 212–231 (2013), DOI: 10.1111/1467-954X.12046

pizzas replacing pies and curries instead of casseroles. The maple and teak wood from North America and Malaysia, marble and granite worktops from South Africa and Brazil and slate and limestone floors from India and Italy all effortlessly suggest how the 'natural' is being recovered from distant forests and mountains.

Spaces which lie outside the places of modernity – the jungle and the wilderness – are being brought to heel, pressed into service by the technology we think we 'master' (see Heidegger, 1993b). This sense of mastery in the kitchen is reinforced not only by the surfeit of machines, but also by large plate glass doors. These help to unify the paved space of the outside patio with the limestone floors inside; at the press of a button, the doors fold back to dispense with the kitchen boundary and so extend the living space outwards into the open air.

At least for those whose cultural mores might be seen to be included in this particular archetype I am sketching, the outside greenery is thus brought *inside*, where the cosmopolitan feel of the interior granite and wood is harmonized by the sculptural medley of jungle plants from South America, Africa and Asia. With washing lines banished (and green plastic wheelie bins now standing guard at what used to be the front door), the sharp geometry of the kitchen is picked up in the clean modernist lines of wood decking and patio squares – all reflected into the kitchen through the double-glazing.

Temporalizing modernity

In thinking about what an inversion of front stage and backstage might presage, it is helpful to make some further comparisons. In terms of the passage of time, for instance, front rooms had people effectively looking backwards, perhaps to ascertain something of the provenance of the family as well as gauge their 'place' in society. Gilt-edged oil portraits, for example, depicted ancestry; oak furniture and dark mahogany spoke of solid respectability and old money; while silks and Chinese vases suggested a colonial reach. As with the marbled columns of the old style banking halls – today's cafes and gastro-pubs – solidity and respectability were combined intricately with time immemorial.[1]

Yet if kitchens are now to be taken as having come 'front stage', they are a far cry from a former emphasis on heirlooms and a bygone opulence. To note this is not in any way to suggest that the general disposal of wealth and status across society remains anything other than unequal. Rather it is to suggest instead that our attitude to Time is being fundamentally reversed. Stainless steel and geometrical lines combine to have us looking forward: they give a 'space age' ambience, a sense of our being engaged in the projects of progress; of our belonging to the future and our no longer dwelling within monuments of the past.

To be in modernity then is to be facing the future – no longer hanging onto hand-me-downs, or looking backwards into the mists of by-gone places for markers of our identity and belonging. As with the endless sets of newly bought clothes stacked away in bedroom cupboards upstairs, modernist devices place the *future* at our disposal: they stand ready for the next meal and for the next wash. Like those special friends or family who are kept 'on call' to help out on special occasions, or in times of trouble, it is their availability, not their presence, that counts; at least for those fortunate to benefit from an affluent society.

For, after all, it is one's affinity with technology, rather than an enslavement to it, that is a mark of identity – a *pulse* that one is up-to-date and modern rather than stuffy, old-fashioned and caught in a time warp. If the car remains for many (males at least, if not also for increasing numbers of women) a key abode of our engagement with modernity (Latimer and Munro, 2006), the kitchen-diner has become the region in which more and more ordinary people enjoy a sense of their actually having a 'life' in modernity. False consciousness or not, here they can feel they dwell in the future, rather than simply surviving in the long shadows of satanic mills.

The disposal of guests

For many, if hardly most, the 'dream' kitchen of today has become the public face of the house – so much so that some city people have a kitchen-diner in their apartment, even if they never use it. As such it makes sense to show the place off, to bring it into public view rather than hide it away.

As A. N. Whitehead explains (see Strong, 2010), suggestion is critical to reception. While the hearth is absent today from many kitchens (even the beloved Aga being powered by electricity or gas), a welcoming feel is contrived by warm light flooding the room from halogen downlighters or underfloor heating rising from the slate or limestone beneath one's feet. Integral to this effect is the extent to which a combination of fantasy and practicality conveys a sense of 'arrival'. Visitors to the kitchen-diner sense they are where the action is – where things are either happening or are about to happen. However momentarily, we feel we have penetrated to the heart of the house and so gain a sense of our being in the right place at the right time.

Feelings of mobility (see Urry, 2007) are also heightened by the layout of the kitchen-diner, where the open spaces afford visitors a sense of circulation which, when used for parties, makes 'mingling' more possible. To be sure, not everyone cooperates here: there is always John, the businessman who stands in the doorway, as if to stop anyone who wishes to pass. There is also Joan, the local do-gooder who backs the unwary into a far corner of the room. And of course there are smokers standing liminally on the edge of the patio, neither out nor in, keeping the glass doors open to the cold night air while their cigarette smoke drifts back inside.

Indeed, it is not only a physical ease of circulation within the kitchen-diner that is made possible. Introductions between other visitors are also made easy – if indeed anyone bothers with them at all. For example, surnames in many

The Sociological Review, 60:S2, pp. 212–231 (2013), DOI: 10.1111/1467-954X.12046

localities are dispensed with. In 'town' (the code name for the smarter areas of central London), one can meet Ishmael or Sarah, only later to discover they are members of governments or own large businesses. In the country (the code name for homes lying near the better villages), Rubin and Tilly may vie against each other for pre-eminence in local affairs, but are rarely referred to other than by their first name.

Noting these matters is not to suggest social mobility is in any way genuinely enhanced. Rather, it is to note that the kitchen-diner is a space whose putative informality in how we address each other effaces deeper and more widespread inequalities. Like strangers in the night we pass or by-pass each other seemingly at will.

The democracy of informality

For all that this re-disposal of public and private space inside the house may entail an inversion of front stage and backstage, I am also tracing how much of this is brought about through any number of other inversions and reversals. As already anticipated in the previous sections, not the least of these is the way in which the formal is being made informal. At least in the kitchen-diner, no one need stand on ceremony.

Critically any attachment here is temporized by an equal ease of detachment. Unlike the front room, where the expectation was often for everyone to remain seated for the duration of their visit – in obedience to imploratory injunctions of 'Please don't get up!' – today's visitors appear happy to either stand or move about. Should they sit at all, it is to perch on a high bar stool as if they were in a New York club. So no excuses need to be made for leaving; no one has to be trapped with someone they do not like, or make stilted conversation with someone they do not know. Visitors can stay or go, as they like. All this adds to a sense of their occupation of space being *temporary*.

This suggestion of a lack of 'stickiness' in social institutions is likely to enhance feelings of the kitchen-diner being a space of modernity. And 'enter-taining' in the kitchen-diner has particular advantages in this respect. There is, for instance, an air of democracy to the kitchen lacking from the formalities of the dining room. At least among circles where multi-tasking is commonplace, the cook can join in the buzz of conversation while cutting up home-style pizzas or heating up the supermarket's 'finest'. Responsibility for the evening going well is also more likely to be shared. The other partner can be passing around the chardonnay, her or his conversation barely interrupted while reaching for another bottle from the fridge.

In my experience, kitchen suppers are made especially informal by those with kitchen-diners rarely beginning to cook before their first guests arrive. One explanation for this practice is that it preserves informality – easier for the host to cancel or for guests to arrive late. So earlier visitors either wait in a kind of post-tourist mode, observing the spectacle of production, or muck in whenever they like, stirring pots and shifting plates.

Multi-tasking and eating

So what about the actual mores of eating food within the home? How do eating practices vary and respond to the advent of the kitchen-diner? Again, in line with the discussion in the previous section, I suggest informality gets the upper hand. It is not only that weekday meals can be plated up away from the dinner table, as noted by Benedetta Cappellini (2010) in her recent study of food in the home. If the ubiquity of pizza, hamburgers and toasted sandwiches negates much of the difference between meals eaten at home and meals taken elsewhere, these forms of repast also allow for meals to be scoffed quickly as minimal interruptions to other forms of entertainment.[2]

This propensity to eat literally from hand to mouth does more than banish the 'civilizing' instruments of cutlery (Elias, 1969, 1982) to more formal occasions, such as Sunday lunch. The finger food on display at parties, for instance, also affords a sense of ease and informality. Forks may be lying in a self-service heap but they are no longer compulsory, just available for the more fastidious. Eating the canapés or thinly sliced quiche with one's fingers shows off a nice sense of ease and radiates confidence about who or what one is.

With all the choice of food on view, one can also pick and mix to suit. Indeed, with the whole range of meats, fish, vegetables and salads on display, fads are invisibly catered for: in serving yourself no one is dictating either what to eat, or indeed how much you should eat. Vegans mingle almost invisibly and few need be embarrassed by an aversion to certain kinds of meals, or by their allergy to specific types of food.

Informality, though, does not just happen. It has to be staged as well as performed. Those who stand as the 'face of the place', the mother figure or the new male, arrange beforehand how they want their place to 'look'. They bring out candles for special occasions and lower the dimmer switches. As curators of clutter, they may be careful to arrange the pebbles or shells from beach holidays in casual but pleasing arrangements. So this is still power of a sort. But perhaps one reserved perhaps more to the realms of *aesthetic* than it links up with ideas of domination?

The place of power

Surely, in all this democratizing of cooking and eating, the kitchen is seldom the powerhouse it was? Emancipated by modernity the kitchen no longer appears to determine the rhythm of the day. Set meal times are, for many, a thing of the past. Nor does the cook, as already noted, choose the food we ingest. To the contrary, in conformity to modernity's emphasis on 'outsourcing' production, the trend towards takeaways and supermarket 'dinners' has combined to make the cook potentially redundant.

Even when food is prepared at home, there is a de-skilling associated with the shift in focus away from the oven as the instrument for cooking roasts and casseroles and onto heating up pies and ready meals in the less messy, all-purpose microwave. With pizzas and curries deliverable within minutes of a phone call, preparation skills are not only eliminated, much of the clearing up is also reduced to stacking the dishwasher.

Indeed, within all this informality, might domestic power not dissipate altogether? When made less formal, the need to ingest food can be disposed of differently: meals can be taken at odd times and often serially, the young grazing from fridge to freezer in search of leftovers and the readymade. In helping catch this change of mood, Cappellini (2010) also reports an *absence* of what she calls centrepieces in the placing of meals on the table; items such as bread, water jugs and serving dishes that induce a sense of sharing and commonality are missing. When plated up at the cooker, even freshly cooked meals can as easily be taken off to the backstage regions to where the televisions now live.

For all this, it is nonetheless unlikely that such a critical space in the home is unaccompanied by the exercise of power. To return here to Mary Douglas's (1966, 1975) work on the polluting qualities of 'matter out of place', I have therefore one particular suggestion to make: that the aesthetics of the kitchen-diner dictate that 'clean is part of the dream'. If so, then in modernity what Durkheim called 'the sacred' shifts away from the cooking, from what we ingest, towards the rituals of a purification of space.

Having 'everything in its place' becomes a paean to the gods of modernity – so much so that the kitchen-diner intensifies the need 'to be rid of things'. This is because it is a sense of space being unoccupied – freed up from our (past) belongings and so open to the future – that dominates the kitchen-diner. What once brought us together – a communal breaking of bread – alters perhaps in favour of a continuous maintenance of 'the look'. To be sure, specific tasks like tidying up, scrubbing the pans, or emptying the dishwasher can still be devolved to others. But the endless scanning for disorder and the constant removal and rearranging of objects – and hourly wiping down of surfaces – involves us not only in living under a new aesthetic regime but brings with it a new ethics.

Changing places

It is hard to keep order, to preserve the new 'face' of the place. *For not everyone respects the new aesthetics that the kitchen-diner demands.* Not everyone is at one with the semiotics of modern design, and certainly not all of the time. Most likely, children find themselves alienated by the sterile formality exhibited by the kitchen-diner when out of use, or they retreat (invisibly) in sheer boredom from all the chattering informality when occupied.

Feeling displaced by modernity's clean, uninterrupted lines and its demand for empty, unoccupied space, children may move in consequence, along with dogs and other pets, back into the living room to recover a sense of place in which they can linger and 'chill'. Armed with their crisps and chocolate, they are freed up to watch yet another film or to go onto their playstations if they so wish. Commensurate with the kitchen becoming front-stage, this inversion creates possibilities for the erstwhile front room to go *backstage* and be recovered as a family room, to be used by all, children and adults alike.

Nothing of these reversals and counter-reversals should surprise: there appears to be a *backhandedness* to consumption that has us always having to go back to attend to the 'mess' one or other consumption practice occasions. This backhandedness is particularly evident in the case of food, where many unanticipated consequences of following fashion are to be found. For example, the consumption of white bread brought about dietary problems such as constipation, whose cure can include eating 'feel good' foods made from the very bran that is a waste product in the milling of fine grains of rice or wheat.[3]

As it happens children do not simply live in disorder. In a return of the repressed, they actively engage in what Michael Taussig (1999) calls *defacement*. Beginning first with their 'own' rooms, their bedrooms, they then move these consumption practices more generally onto the rest of the house. So there is still something for the undergrowth of family in all this reversal of spaces. Inasmuch as the spread-eagling of toys across the floor and other surfaces 'pollutes' the formal design of the kitchen-diner, the artefacts of virtual family life are moving into the former front room – in the form of giant flat screens housing the television and the DVD. So, too, assorted remotes, PCs, iPads, iPods, and mobile phones sit beside celebrity magazines crushed onto the four-year interest-free sofas, or lie among the half-empty mugs and plates littered indiscriminately on the coffee table and floor.

In this respect, informality as the counter-point to design is not the only thing going on in this re-disposal of space and time. Payne Knight, a late eighteenth-century protagonist for the Romantic garden in its revolt against the formalities of the classical garden, calls this process *dishevelment*, a return to the disarray that was equated with the 'natural' order of Nature. Where before it was the front room that was out of bounds for the dishevelment of daily living, now it is the kitchen-diner: the aesthetics of disposal dictate that children and fellow untidy creatures are no longer welcome in areas where they once sought refuge.

Refining waste

It is no exaggeration to suggest sociology is much preoccupied with waste, even if this orientation is seldom made explicit. This is not just to note classics of sociology, such as *Street Corner Society* (Whyte, 1943) and *The Police on Skid Row* (Bittner, 1967), engage with the materiality of everyday life that others see as the detritus of social order. It is to identify how modern programmes like medicine harbour designs that inevitably proceed by throwing out the chronically ill as 'crocks' (Becker, 1993), the homeless as 'normal rubbish' (Jeffery, 1979), and the frail as 'bedblockers' (Latimer, 2000). So too Bauman (2004) lays what he calls 'wasted lives' firmly at the door of modernity, suggesting presciently that in the future the 'outcasts' of globalization will have nowhere to go.

For all the attention within sociology paid to unanticipated consequences, it remains the case that examples of 'waste' still focus on inefficiency and thus do too little to call modernity itself into question over its own complicity and calumny. Mainstream views remain barricaded inside production perspectives, such as the state and markets, wherein 'outcasts' remain designated as deviant to these normative understandings of order. Nor has the more recent switch to consumption upset production perspectives. The latter are at best only slightly shaken by so-called qualitative methods that inevitably gravitate towards recording the 'individual's experience'. So, too, while Hetherington's (2004) deployment of the 'door' as a metaphor for disposal is more fecund than my earlier trope of the 'bin', his stress on secondhandedness nonetheless prolongs the consumption perspective. In revealing how things enjoy 'second' lives, his analysis is richly suggestive of unexpected uses, but fails to go on to theorize disposal in ways that restore it as primary, rather than secondary, to consumption.

My proposal is that it is only by restoring disposal to its proper place – as concerned first and foremost with arrangement and placing – will we move towards a sociology that goes beyond revalorizing the deviant, the devalued and discarded after the fact. We need to do more than refine waste products as recyclable, as if we could re-instate the marginalized and excluded back to their proper place in society.[4] We need to find ways, as well, to challenge how it is that systems of production 'outcast' materials and morals as useless, outdated, or even immobile. It is not enough to try to 'balance out' the cast-offs of production and consumption perspectives by pointing to human rights, or by recourse to markets offering compensation.

Conclusion

Identifying modernity to be a 'condition of addictive and compulsive designing', Zygmunt Bauman (2004: 30) goes on to note pithily: 'Where there is design, there is waste'. Consulting the OED, as I did in my early work on disposal, he points out that to order is 'to set or keep in order or proper condition; *to dispose according to rule*; to regulate, govern, manage' (emphasis added). In light of this dictum, it should not surprise to find that notions of disposal, in which everything has to be given a place for good or ill, have been subjugated by modernity's more normative ideas of order emphasizing design.

Order today has come to mean this need 'to dispose according to rule', see above. It is this definition that outcasts as redundant and inefficient anything which does not conform to rule. Hence it is no longer the case that there is a 'place for everything' and, with this, the meaning of disposal is truncated; those things that have no place in the production of the future must be eliminated and erased. What does not 'fit' becomes 'waste'.

In modernity, linking meanings of disposal solely to waste has created an effect on our outlook such that we conflate the 'ends' of production with the point to life. So it is perhaps unsurprising that attempts, like my own, to re-emphasize disposal in terms of its wider and more profound meanings of 'placing' and 'arrangement' have so far failed to depose the primacy accorded to production. It is salutary, for example, that Pierre Bourdieu's (1986) influential focus on consumption mainly ends up demonstrating how class is 'produced'. Equally, in their raising to the fore theories of practice, the lines of work by Elizabeth Shove and Alan Warde on consumption, important as they are, tend towards multiplying the 'rules' by which order gets accomplished, rather than they themselves deeply challenge modernist understandings of order.[5]

As such the potential revolution in sociology never really gets going. The focus on the everyday remains locked into consumption notions about the display of 'identity' or 'taste'; and so the production underpinnings of mainstream sociology stay intact. Indeed, pushed to its limit, too strong an appeal for the preservation of variety entertains the very kind of cosmopolitanism that undercuts any notion of social order, while requiring such a multiplicity of possibilities for identity and belonging that would condone whatever happens.[6]

Using the kitchen-diner as an icon of contemporary life, I have identified in this paper how modernity does more than widen choice and enhance mobility. Rather, it reformulates the 'passages' that appear open to us; and does so in ways that dictate what we need to be rid of in our lives. To be ready for what the future brings is to be ready to 'cut' the network (Strathern, 1996). Or, more specifically, to cut at least one notch in the labyrinth of networks that underpin our dwelling in modernity. Yet, given the paucity of our knowledge of the future, many of our detachments may also be made, as I have been suggesting in this paper, conveniently reversible. We may, for instance, turn our 'face' against somebody or something without amending altogether the 'fronts' that – left to themselves – might help to sustain relations and so permit reattachment when and where necessary.

In saying this, it seems important to grasp that it is not simply people or things that become 'outcasts' from modernity. Social institutions – such as formality and precedent – also get rebranded as 'outmoded' and 'muddle' – much like Strathern's (1993) pithy example of the tutorial when it is castigated as a 'Victorian invention'. Hence, what we are witnessing with the kitchen-diner, for instance, might be understood as less than being an 'outsourcing' of morality to individuals and more – in its instructive clean lines and demand for empty space – as an instance of modernity's transfer of 'order' onto the built environment.

Paradoxically, while retaining areas of domination and power, these rearrangements of space appear to free up opportunities for the deployment of social institutions that, contrastingly, parade themselves as 'informal'. Yet with this apparent freedom come its own constraints. This can be seen by the fact that 'informality' is only to be added back to the formality inherent in kitchen design in particular ways and not others. Unopened bottles of wine and plates of untouched food for instance are good; they anticipate the party that the dream kitchen-diner is all about. Occasional crowds of people are also possible, since no one is staying long enough to sit and be in the way. But 'leftovers' – whether they be the children's toys and schoolbags, the bread-earner's tools and household bills, or even the remnants of lunch – no!

The issue for me in all this is not that we should *individually* suspend judgement over morals, as seems to be the way cosmopolitanism is headed. Instead, I am arguing that the 'material' turn in sociology requires a profound re-theorization of disposal and is not to be satisfied, say, by only looking at how people consume objects as a display of identity or taste. Indeed, as I hope to have emphasized in the foregoing analysis, understanding modernity may require owning up, instead, to quite others matters. In closing, it is worth enumerating these.

First, there is the extent to which any movement between the moralities of our different modes of dwelling depends upon us 'attaching' only to materials that, in themselves, have become easily detachable. Mobile devices stand as the example par excellence here, since they now incorporate books as well as phones. Second, there is the sheer *excess* of places that serve as 'fronts'. Goffman (1959), in particular, has suggested how a doctor's front, once mobile in terms of their stethoscope and black bag, becomes increasingly incorporated into the fixtures of the surgery or operating room. Consequently, when broadly understood, waste is not something to be treated as simply an effect of modernity. In the form of our proliferating 'places' of leisure, work and exchange, it becomes integral to its very shape and development. As part of the same moment that design identifies 'waste' and casts it out as inefficiency, so too modernity creates the need for more and more 'places' that can act as 'fronts' for production, whether this takes place in the workplace or the home.

To avoid going too far down the postmodern road in which everything is to be made mobile – materials and morals alike – I have therefore proposed elsewhere an argument about the *motility* of 'worlds' (Latimer and Munro, 2009; Munro, 1996). In this paper, for instance, I have illustrated how the modern design of the kitchen-diner eases circulation and incites informality. Yet this is far from being a claim that such design satisfies all needs and purposes. To the contrary, to the extent the 'clean' regime of modern design comes to dominate, I have indicated how family members also refine their lines of flight and find themselves going backstage (to the erstwhile front room) in order to reattach themselves to their electronic devices within the areas they now keep dishevelled.

In conclusion, theorizing disposal involves more than revaluing 'waste'. It also entails understanding how it is that we can be in one of our worlds one moment, but then can find ourselves cast into a different world the next. This is not only to suggest it is important to understand how adults as well as children move from being 'social' in the clean dream of the kitchen-diner one moment to 'being themselves' among their dishevelment the next. Nor is it just to accept that matters like food and waste have become a moveable feast. So much is obvious. What is perhaps less clear is that modernity is not so much aimed at destroying social order, as it is the case that we are still learning how to perform its works by virtue of making our 'places for dwelling' motile as well as multiple.

Notes

1 A sense of time immemorial being conveyed by family heirlooms is precisely one of the themes on which Henry James's *The Ambassadors* revolves. For it is just this question of respectability that is on Strether's mind immediately ahead of his visit to Mme de Vionette, the friend of Chad – the young American who has holed up in Paris instead of returning to New England to take over the family business. 'Is her life beyond reproach?', Strether asks himself. And it is by bringing him to her apartment to witness this sense of rich sumptuousness that Chad answers Strether; who on arriving '. . . found himself making out, as a background of the occupant, some glory, some prosperity of the first Empire. . . .' – 'old accumulations' summoning up 'the air of supreme respectability' (1960: 148–151).

2 In considering cultural differences in the disposal of time in overeating one has only to contrast French cuisine of serial dishes served over several hours with multi-tasking practices common in the UK and US of eating a plateful while watching television. It is worth noting here that researchers at University Hospital Coventry and the University of Warwick are examining the extent to which 'speed-eating' contributes to obesity (Hughes, 2011). Their hypothesis is that slowing down the intake of meals might help weight loss. Where overlaps in timing of meals and favourite television programmes no doubt led in the past to eating in front of the television, it remains to be seen whether 'delay' and 'replay' devices can re-order a return to the table.

3 Medical research on food has greatly expanded, recasting media-endowed knowledge. For instance, recent findings indicate that older women taking multi-vitamin supplements to promote their health are more likely to have heart disease (Lloyd, 2011). So, too, the latest scaremongering headlines suggest women are now more likely to die from obesity-related illness than from smoking. This is ironic, since many women smoked to keep their weight down and only gave up in the light of government-backed anti-smoking campaigns.

4 There is much still to be said in favour of paying attention to waste in terms that focus on what is 'cast-off' rather than 'outcast'. Ecology movements, in different ways, for instance help to alter how we approach this particular facet of disposal, getting rid of things. Where once free-roaming swine were used inside towns to hoover up the rotting detritus and where farmers once spread pig muck and horse manure onto fields rather than chemicals, popular examples today include tapping into the methane given off by cows and transforming into fuel the packaging of food and other goods, instead of dumping this as garbage into landfill sites. It is not just Thompson's (1979) example of Regency housing in Islington that has come back from potential demolition as 'slums' in the 1960s; more generally all sorts of bric-a-brac is given value by being collected and circulated through conduits such as e-bay and car boot sales.

5 This is not to underplay the importance of unpicking the co-existence of different rules. It was after all Goffman's and Garfinkel's attention to the everyday that helped to overthrow the Parsonian equation of morality with norms (Munro, 2010). Yet, without reaching towards a law-like version of 'requisite variety', as proposed by the systems theorist Ross Ashby (1956), it strikes me that a stable society would do more than keep open multiple 'passages' – or ways of going on in the world as Giddens (1984) calls them – to balance out all the different and various conditions we undergo. As Goffman's (1972) seminal focus on civil inattention suggests, we have institutions that help us handle things we cannot 'place'. For example, since it is not always appropriate to apologize, we have to have the savvy on occasion to know when to remove ourselves in order not to make matters worse.

The Sociological Review, 60:S2, pp. 212–231 (2013), DOI: 10.1111/1467-954X.12046

6 For instance, while not suggesting 'anything goes', Delanty (2012) argues cosmopolitanism entails a weak universalism that is compatible with a conception of relativism, understood in Sahlins' formulation as 'the provisional suspension of one's own judgments in order to situate the practices at issue in the historical and cultural order that made them possible' (Sahlins, 2000: 21). Yet it is precisely this sense of historical and cultural order that the fashion for informality would erase, thus easing into place modernity and its replacement of the mores of the past with its own focus on the future.

References

Appadurai, A. (ed.), (1986), *The Social Life of Things: Commodities in Cultural Perspective*, Cambridge: Cambridge University Press.

Ashby, R., (1956), *An Introduction to Cybernetics*, London: Chapman and Hall.

Barnes, B., (1988), *The Nature of Power*, Cambridge: Polity Press.

Barthes, R., (1972), *Mythologies*, trans. Annette Lavers, New York: Noonday Press.

Bauman, Z., (2004), *Wasted Lives: Modernity and its Outcasts*, Cambridge: Polity Press.

Becker, H. S., (1993), 'How I learned what a crock was', *Journal of Contemporary Ethnography*, 22 (1): 28–35.

Bittner, E., (1967), 'The police on skid-row: a study of peace keeping', *American Sociological Review*, 32 (5): 699–717.

Blum, A., (2003), *The Imaginative Structure of the City*. Canada: McGill-Queen's University Press.

Bourdieu, P., (1986), *Distinction: A Social Critique of the Judgement of Taste*, trans. Richard Nice, London: Blackwell.

Cappellini, B., (2010), 'The culture of the meal: class, family and time in the everyday consumption of Italian cuisine', PhD thesis, University of Keele.

Carnegie, D., (1936), *How to Win Friends and Influence People*, New York: Simon and Schuster.

Cooper, T., (2005), 'Slower consumption: reflections on product life spans and the "throwaway society" ', *Journal of Industrial Ecology*, 9 (1–2): 51–67.

Csikzentmihalyi, M. and Rochberg-Halton, E., (1981), *The Meaning of Things*, Cambridge: Cambridge University Press.

Delanty, G., (2012), 'a cosmopolitan approach to the explanation of social change', *The Sociological Review*, 60 (4): 333–354.

Douglas, M., (1966), *Purity and Danger: An Analysis of Concepts of Pollution and Taboo*, London: Routledge.

Douglas, M., (1975), *Implicit Meanings: Essays in Anthropology*, London: Routledge.

Elias, N., (1969), *The Civilizing Process*, in Vol. I, The History of Manners, Oxford: Blackwell.

Elias, N., (1982), *The Civilizing Process*, in Vol. II, State Formation and Civilization, Oxford: Blackwell.

Garfinkel, H., (1967), *Studies in Ethnomethodology*, Engelwood Cliffs, NJ: Prentice Hall.

Giddens, A., (1984), *The Constitution of Society*, Cambridge: Polity Press.

Goffman, E., (1959), *The Presentation of Self in Everyday Life*, New York: Doubleday.

Goffman, E., (1972), *Relations in Public*, Harmondsworth: Penguin.

Gregson, N., Metcalfe, A. and Crewe, L., (2007), 'Identity, mobility, and the throwaway society', *Environment and Planning D: Society and Space*, 25 (4): 682–700.

Hawkins, G., (2000), 'Plastic bags: living with rubbish', *International Journal of Cultural Studies*, 4: 5–23.

Hawkins, G., (2006), *The Ethics of Waste: How We Relate to Rubbish*, Sydney: UNSW Press.

Heidegger, M., (1993a), 'Building, dwelling, thinking', in D. Krell (ed.), *Basic Writings*, 343–365. London: Routledge.

Heidegger, M., (1993b), 'The question concerning technology', in D. Krell (ed.), *Basic Writings*, 307–342, London: Routledge.

Hetherington, K., (2004), 'Secondhandedness: consumption, disposal, and absent presence', *Environment and Planning D: Society and Space*, 32: 157–173.

Hochschild, A., (2012), *The Outsourced Self: Intimate Life in Market Times*, New York: Metropolitan Books.

Hughes, J., (2011), BBC report on the Human Metabolic clinic, University Hospital Coventry and the University of Warwick, available at: http://www.bbc.co.uk/news/health-15447568.

James, H., (1960 [1904]), *The Ambassadors*, New York: Signet.

Jeffery, R., (1979), 'Normal rubbish: deviant patients in casualty departments', *Sociology of Health and Illness*, 1 (1): 90–107.

Latimer, J., (2000), *The Conduct of Care*, Oxford: Blackwell.

Latimer, J. and Munro, R., (2006), 'Driving the social', in S. Bohm, C. Jones, C. Land and M. Patterson (eds), *Against Automobility*, Sociological Review Monograph, Oxford: Oxford University Press.

Latimer, J. and Munro, R., (2009), 'Keeping and dwelling: relational extension, the idea of the home, and otherness', *Space and Culture*, 12: 317–331.

Leach, R., (2002), 'What happened at home with art: tracing the experience of consumers?', in C. Painter (ed.), *Contemporary Art and the Home*, 153–180, Oxford: Berg.

Lennox, C., (1989 [1752]), *The Female Quixote (or The Adventures of Arabella)*, New York: Oxford University Press.

Lloyd, J., (2011), 'Study flags risk of daily vitamin use among older women', *USA Today*, 10 October, available at: http://yourlife.usatoday.com/health/medical/womenshealth/story/2011-10-10/Study-Vitamins-may-boost-death-risk-in-older-women/50722104/1.

Marshall, D., (1990), 'A study of the behavioural variables influencing consumer acceptability of fish and fish products', PhD thesis, University of Newcastle-upon-Tyne.

Miller, D., (2008), *The Comfort of Things: The Objects of our Affection*, Cambridge: Polity Press.

Munro, R., (1995), 'Disposal of the meal', in D. Marshall (ed.), *Food Choice and the Food Consumer*, 313–325, Glasgow: Blackie.

Munro, R., (1996), 'The consumption view of self', in S. Edgell, K. Hetherington and A. Warde (eds), *Consumption Matters*, Sociological Review Monograph, Oxford: Blackwell.

Munro, R., (1998), 'Disposal of the X gap: the production and consumption of accounting research and practical accounting systems', *Advances in Public Interest Accounting*, 7: 139–159.

Munro, R., (1999), 'Power and discretion: membership work in the time of technology', *Organization*, 6 (3): 429–450.

Munro, R., (2001), 'Calling for accounts: numbers, monsters and membership, *The Sociological Review*, 46 (4): 473–493.

Munro, R., (2004), 'Punctualising identity: time and the demanding relation', *Sociology*, 38 (2): 293–311.

Munro, R. (with R. Collins), (2010), 'Exploring the sociological re-imagining of politics', *The Sociological Review*, 58 (4): 548–562.

Naipaul, V. S., (1957), *The Mystic Masseur*, London: Andre Deutsch.

O'Brien, M., (1999), 'Rubbish power: towards a sociology of the rubbish society', in J. Hearn and S. Roseneil (eds), *Consuming Cultures*, Basingstoke: Macmillan.

Sahlins, M., (2000), *Culture in Practice: Selected Essays*, New York: Zone Books.

Shaw, D. and Newholm, T., (2002), 'Voluntary simplicity and the ethics of consumption', *Psychology and Marketing*, 19 (2): 167–185.

Shields, R. (ed.), (1992), *Lifestyle Shopping: The Subject of Consumption*. London: Routledge.

Shilling, C., (2008), *Changing Bodies: Habits, Crisis and Creativity*, London: Sage.

Shilling, C. and Mellor, P. A., (2001), 'Durkheim, morality and modernity: collective effervescence, homo duplex and the sources of moral action', reprinted in W. S. F. Pickering (ed.), *Emile Durkheim III. Critical Assessments*, London: Routledge.

Simmel, G., (1972), *On Individuality and Social Forms*, edited and with an introduction by Donald Levine, Chicago: University of Chicago Press.

Strathern, M., (1991), *Partial Connections*, Savage, MD: Rowman and Littlefield.

Strathern, M., (1993), 'Society in drag', *Times Higher Educational Supplement*, 2 April.

The Sociological Review, 60:S2, pp. 212–231 (2013), DOI: 10.1111/1467-954X.12046

Strathern, M., (1996), 'Cutting the network', *The Journal of the Royal Anthropological Institute*, 2 (3): 517–535.

Strathern, M., (1999), 'The aesthetics of substance', in *Property, Substance and Effect*, 45–64, London: Athlone.

Strong, P., (2010), 'Open to suggestion: ordering, risk and invention in community mental health care', PhD thesis, Goldsmiths College, University of London.

Tampubolon, G., (2010), 'Social stratification and cultures hierarchy among the omnivores', *The Sociological Review*, 58: 1–25.

Taussig, M., (1999), *Defacement: Public Secrecy and the Labor of the Negative*, Stanford, CA: Stanford University Press.

Thompson, M., (1979), *Rubbish Theory*, Oxford: Oxford University Press.

Urry, J., (2002), *The Tourist Gaze*, 2nd edn, London: Sage.

Urry, J., (2007), *Mobilities*, Cambridge: Polity Press.

Whyte, W. F., (1943), *Street Corner Society: The Social Structure of an Italian Slum*, Chicago: University of Chicago Press.

Notes on contributors

Stewart Barr is Associate Professor in the Geography Department at the University of Exeter, where he obtained his PhD in 2001. His research interests focus on how environmental social science can lead academic discussions on social transformation in an age of accelerated environmental change.

Hugh Campbell is Professor in Sociology and heads the Department of Sociology, Gender and Social Work at the University of Otago, Dunedin, New Zealand. He was Director of CSAFE (Centre for the Study of Agriculture, Food and Environment) from 2001 to 2010. His research interests include the social dynamics involved in agricultural sustainability, the sociology of food, neoliberalism and new governance in agri-food systems, and masculinities in rural and agricultural contexts. He is one of the research leaders of the NZ$13.5 million Agricultural Research Group on Sustainability (ARGOS) programme, a joint venture between the Agribusiness Group, University of Lincoln and the University of Otago. His publications include *Country Boys: Masculinity and Rural Life* (Penn State Press, 2006) (with Mike Bell and Margaret Finney) and articles in the journals *Sociologia Ruralis, Rural Sociology, Journal of Rural Studies, International Journal for the Sociology of Agriculture and Food* and *Agriculture and Human Values*.

Benedetta Cappellini is Lecturer in Marketing at Royal Holloway University. Prior to that she held teaching posts at the University of Worcester and the University of Florence, Italy. She is an ethnographer interested in consumer culture, food consumption and media consumption. She has published her work in consumer research and media studies journals.

Benjamin Coles is Lecturer in Economic and Political Geography at the University of Leicester. His research interests centre on the 'core' units of geography (place, space and scale), with a particular interest in the relationship(s) between place-making, commodity culture and the production and consumption of food.

Ferne Edwards is a PhD student at the National Centre for Epidemiology and Population Health, Australian National University. Ferne has a background in

The Sociological Review, 60:S2, pp. 232–235 (2013), DOI: 10.1111/1467-954X.12047
Editorial organisation © 2013 The Editorial Board of the Sociological Review. Published by John Wiley & Sons Ltd, 9600 Garsington Road, Oxford OX4 2DQ, UK and 350 Main Street, Malden, MA 02148, USA

anthropology and specializes in areas of sustainable cities, urban food systems and social change. Her doctorate investigates alternative food movements in Australia and Venezuela.

David Evans is Lecturer in Sociology and Sustainable Consumption Institute Research Fellow at the University of Manchester. He is currently involved in projects that explore urban transitions, food consumption and waste. He is co-investigator on an ESRC funded project that looks at the relationships between processes of (eco)-innovation and the dynamics of everyday life with a particular focus on laundry and domestic lighting. He has published widely on theories of practice and their application to environmental politics, on thrift and frugality, on sustainable living and on food waste.

Zsuzsa Gille is Associate Professor at the University of Illinois at Urbana-Champaign. She is author of *From the Cult of Waste to the Trash Heap of History: The Politics of Waste in Socialist and Postsocialist Hungary* (2007 – recipient of honorable mention of the AAASS Davis Prize), co-editor of *Post-Communist Nostalgia* with Maria Todorova (Berghahn Press, 2010), and co-author of *Global Ethnography: Forces, Connections and Imaginations in a Postmodern World* (University of California Press, 2000). She has published on issues of qualitative methodology as it relates to globalization and new concepts of space, on environmental politics and on the sociology of food. She also serves on the editorial board of the journal *Ethnography*.

Steve Guilbert works on projects examining waste and environmental issues at the Universities of Aberystwyth, Sheffield and Kingston, UK. He obtained his PhD in Geography from the University of Nottingham.

Lucius Hallett IV is Assistant Professor at Western Michigan University in the Department of Geography. His research interests lie in the movements of commodities, primarily foods, the global/local dichotomy and in the possibilities of agri-tourism as 'value-added' production.

Gay Hawkins is a Research Professor and Director of the Centre for Critical and Cultural Studies at the University of Queensland, Brisbane, Australia. She is the author of two books on waste including *The Ethics of Waste* (Rowman and Littlefield, 2006) and numerous essays including 'More than Human Politics – the case of plastic bags', *Australian Humanities Review*, 46 (2009), 'Plastic Materialities' in *Political Matter* (edited by S. Whatmore and B. Braun; University of Minnesota Press, 2010). She has just commenced a major study into the rise and impacts of plastic packaging in the food industry titled 'The Skin of Commerce'.

Anna Krzywoszynska is a postdoctoral Research Associate at the department of Geography at Durham University. Her PhD was a materials-oriented ethnography of organic winemaking, and discussed economic, ethical, and cultural activity of wine-making 'things'. Her current work concerns participatory and trans-disciplinary research around photovoltaic technologies.

Angela Meah is a Research Fellow at the University of Sheffield, UK. Her research interests are concerned with gender and domesticity, and patterns of continuity and change in families' domestic provisioning practices over three generations, using life history and ethnographic methods to explore the intergenerational transfer of knowledge and practice.

Dave Mercer is an Associate Professor in the School of Global, Urban and Social Science at RMIT University, Melbourne. A geographer by training, he has degrees from Cambridge and Monash Universities and has authored over 140 publications on a wide range of social science issues including responses to natural hazards, urban land use planning and food studies.

Alan Metcalfe is a Senior Researcher at the University of Exeter. He has previously worked at the Universities of Nottingham, Sheffield and Portsmouth.

Richard Milne is a Research Associate on the European Research Council funded Consumer Culture in an Age of Anxiety project in the Department of Geography at the University of Sheffield. His research examines how information about food safety and quality is established and communicated. His PhD in Science and Technology Studies at University College London explored the geographies of the expectations associated with new biotechnologies.

Rolland Munro is Professor of the Philosophy of Organization at the University of Leicester and Managing Editor of *The Sociological Review*. He is best known for his ethnographic work on consumption, power and identity and published articles that range across a wide array of topics – including accountability, affect, bodies, class, ethics, knowledge, landscape, language, money, polyphony, reason, technology and time. These provide a bridge between humanist and anti-humanist perspectives and elaborate an emerging vocabulary of motility, disposal, engrossment and punctualizing.

Anne Murcott is Professorial Research Associate, SOAS, London University, Honorary Professor, University of Nottingham, and Professor Emerita (Sociology) London South Bank University. She was Director of the ESRC Research Programme ' "The Nation's Diet" the social science of food choice' in the 1990s. Her current work includes co-editing *The Handbook of Food Research* (Bloomsbury, 2013) with Peter Jackson and Warren Belasco, and *Food Consumption in Global Perspective: Essays in the Anthropology of Food in Honour of Jack Goody* with Jakob Klein (Palgrave, 2013) as well as service as an expert member of the UK Food Standards Agency's General Advisory Committee on Science. In 2009 she received an honorary doctorate from the University of Uppsala.

Martin O'Brien is currently a Reader in Criminology and Criminal Justice at the University of Central Lancashire, UK. He is the author of *A Crisis of Waste? Understanding the Rubbish Society* (Routledge, 2007).

Elizabeth Parsons is a Reader in Marketing and Consumer Research at Keele University. Her research interests include critical marketing, cultures of consumption and gender in the workplace. Her approach to research is ethnographic and interpretative. She has published in a range of journals including the *Journal of Marketing Management, Gender, Work and Organisation* and *Consumption, Markets and Culture*. Along with Professor Pauline Maclaran she is joint Editor in Chief of the journal *Marketing Theory*.

Mark Riley is Lecturer in Geography at the University of Liverpool. Prior to this he held AHRC-funded research fellowships at both the University of Exeter and University of St Andrews and a senior lectureship in geography at the University of Portsmouth. His broad research interests relate to social and cultural aspects of rural and environmental change.

Guy Robinson is Director of the Centre for Regional Engagement at the University of South Australia and an Adjunct Professor in the School of Population Health at the University of Adelaide. He was previously Professor of Geography at Kingston University London and has held positions at the Universities of Edinburgh and Oxford. His research interests are primarily in the areas of environmental management and rural development. He is currently the Editor of *Land Use Policy* and is the author of *Methods and Techniques in Human Geography* and *Conflict and Change in the Countryside*.

Terry Tudor is a Senior Lecturer in the Centre for Sustainable Wastes Management, at the University of Northampton. He is a member of the Chartered Institution of Wastes Management (MCIWM) and coordinates the UK-wide Healthcare Waste and Resources Research (HCWRR) Group.

Matt Watson is Senior Lecturer in Human Geography at the University of Sheffield, UK. His research explores themes of consumption, waste and mobility to advance understandings of the dynamics of everyday practices in relation to sustainability, and the means through which those practices are shaped and governed.

Index

The Sociological Review, 60:S2, pp. 236–240 (2013), DOI: 10.1111/1467-954X.12061
Editorial organisation © 2013 The Editorial Board of the Sociological Review

The Sociological Review, 60:S2, pp. 236–240 (2013), DOI: 10.1111/1467-954X.12061
Editorial organisation © 2013 The Editorial Board of the Sociological Review

Made in the USA
Lexington, KY
01 March 2017